Bridging Academia and Industry Through Cloud Integration in Education

Parikshit Narendra Mahalle
Vishwakarma Institute of Information Technology, India

IGI Global
Scientific Publishing
Publishing Tomorrow's Research Today

Published in the United States of America by
IGI Global Scientific Publishing
701 East Chocolate Avenue
Hershey, PA, 17033, USA
Tel: 717-533-8845
Fax: 717-533-8661
Website: https://www.igi-global.com E-mail: cust@igi-global.com

Library of Congress Cataloging-in-Publication Data

Names: Mahalle, Parikshit N., editor.
Title: Bridging academia and industry through cloud integration in education / Edited by Parikshit Mahalle.
Description: Hershey, PA : IGI Global Scientific Publishing, [2025] | Includes bibliographical references and index. | Summary: "This book aims to collect comprehensive chapters that explore the transformational impact of cloud integration in education"-- Provided by publisher.
Identifiers: LCCN 2024047098 (print) | LCCN 2024047099 (ebook) | ISBN 9798369367056 (hardcover) | ISBN 9798369367063 (paperback) | ISBN 9798369367070 (ebook)
Subjects: LCSH: Education, Higher--Effect of technological innovations on. | Cloud computing. | Universities and colleges--Computer network resources.
Classification: LCC LB2395.7 .B735 2025 (print) | LCC LB2395.7 (ebook) | DDC 378.1/7344678--dc23/eng/20241031
LC record available at https://lccn.loc.gov/2024047098
LC ebook record available at https://lccn.loc.gov/2024047099

British Cataloguing in Publication Data
A Cataloguing in Publication record for this book is available from the British Library.

Table of Contents

Detailed Table of Contents

The integration of cloud technology is transforming the educational landscape by facilitating personalized learning and adaptive systems. This chapter examines successful case studies showcasing the impact of cloud-based solutions, including Learning Management Systems (LMS), AI-driven analytics, and collaborative tools on educational outcomes. Notable examples include Khan Academy's extensive resource offerings, DreamBox Learning's adaptive learning engine, Purdue University's use of predictive analytics, and the global learning platform developed by Minerva Schools. While challenges such as data privacy concerns and the digital divide persist, these initiatives highlight how cloud technology can create customized learning experiences and equip educators with valuable insights. Looking ahead, emerging trends in artificial intelligence, virtual reality, global collaboration, and blockchain technology are poised to further enhance personalized and inclusive educational practices.

In today's rapidly evolving technological landscape, the integration of cloud computing within educational frameworks is revolutionizing the way academia and industry collaborate. This book, "Bridging Academia and Industry: Cloud Integration in Education," explores the transformative power of cloud technologies in enhancing educational outcomes and fostering innovative partnerships between academic institutions and the industrial sector. By leveraging cloud platforms, educational institutions can streamline resource management, facilitate collaborative research, and equip students with the practical skills required by modern industries. This

This chapter explores how technology and entrepreneurial innovation enhance supply chain efficiency. It highlights the transformative impact of advanced technologies such as cloud computing, data analytics, and IoT on supply chain operations, improving responsiveness and reducing costs. The entrepreneurial orientation is emphasized as a key driver of innovation, enabling organizations to adapt to changing market conditions. Through case studies, the chapter illustrates successful collaborations between academia and industry, demonstrating how theoretical insights translate into practical solutions. Challenges in technology integration, such as data security and the need for skilled personnel, are also addressed. By bridging the gap between academia and industry, this work aims to inspire future research and applications that enhance supply chain management, underscoring the importance of fostering a culture of innovation to maintain competitiveness in the global marketplace.

Cloud computing has transformed education by providing anytime access to educational content, enhancing learning, and fostering collaboration. Adaptive technologies and analytics allow personalizing learning experiences and increasing learner engagement by tailoring education to individual needs. Cloud solutions streamline administrative tasks like attendance and grading, allowing educators to focus more on teaching. However, these benefits come with challenges, primarily concerning security and privacy. Educational organizations manage large amounts of sensitive data, including learner records, academic information, grades, and intellectual property. Storing this data in the cloud raises concerns about unauthorized access, data breaches, and regulatory compliance. The use of cloud-based services for hosting infrastructure and applications makes institutions vulnerable to attacks. Therefore, cloud security in education is crucial; requiring robust strategies and practices to protect data, applications, and infrastructure on cloud platforms.

The objective is to structure a portable application for inspecting and putting away information through a distributed storage administration. The information is remotely put away in the cloud. In some distributed storage frameworks, the cloud record may contain some touchy data. Scrambling the entire shared record doesn't permit different clients to get to it. In the current framework, the client needs to use the biometric information to guarantee the character of the client, and afterward, a marking key will be checked which is to ensure the personality and security of the client. The principle downside of utilizing the biometric information is that it can't be coordinated precisely because of the elements that influence the difference in biometric information. A reference is made naturally changed over to the QR code and it is checked utilizing a scanner and the specific record is downloaded. This record is erased or lost in the customer's inward stockpiling may be recovered again from the cloud.

Ensuring the security of sensitive image data has become of utmost importance in the field of cloud computing. Conventional encryption techniques frequently fail to adequately address changing threats, requiring the use of novel technologies. This study investigates the use of blockchain technology and generative adversarial networks (GANs) for the purpose of encrypting images, with the goal of improving the security and confidentiality of data in cloud environments. The suggested approach uses blockchain technology for the purpose of ensuring safe key management and verification. GANs are employed to produce encrypted images that possess a high level of realism. This research shows that the proposed approach is highly effective in preserving and maintaining higher image quality compared to existing encryption frameworks. This inference is based on careful experimentation and analysis. The proposed method demonstrates superior performance in generating clear and accurate reconstructions of encrypted images, as seen by much higher peak

interests and demographics. This research examines the application of machine learning models in forecasting user ad clicks, incorporating variables like age, internet usage, and daily site engagement time in the datasets. The effectiveness of decision tree and logistic regression models in predicting ad clicks through model building and data analysis is shown in the research. Utilizing actual predictive analytics in advertising strategies can be enhanced by incorporating user engagement signals and responses in real-world scenarios. The research highlights future directions and challenges. It also touches upon potential advancements in predictive analytics and online advertising techniques.

Renu Kachhoria, Vishwakarma Institute of Information Technology, India
Prajwal Waykos, Vishwakarma Institute of Information Technology, India
Sathya Krishna Sharma, Tilburg University, The Netherlands

In the digital age, students struggle with navigating overwhelming online information. This chapter introduces YoZu, a student-focused chatbot. Powered by large language models, YoZu offers clear and engaging responses, making learning accessible for young minds. Its unique feature filters sensitive content, ensuring a safe learning environment. Additionally, YoZu provides dynamic image and video recommendations, enhancing comprehension. This research illuminates YoZu's transformative potential, simplifying complex information and revolutionizing students' interaction with online content.

Sreelekha Paul, Brainware University, India
Dipanjan Das, Brainware University, India

This chapter analyses the future trends and prospective of cloud-based education especially with regards to the roles of blockchain, augmented reality, virtual reality, artificial intelligence, and the internet of things (IOT). Intelligent tutoring system and adaptive learning both require AI and ML to tailor the education to the individual learner. Education has secure and verifiable credentials for capacity building and continuing education. Apart from experience learning, which is allegedly the best form of learning, AR and VR allow learning outside the limitation of geographical boundaries. Smart classrooms, which include the usage of IoT technology, permit the real-time collection of data and analyses used in an organization to improve learning environments and resource utilization. In enhancing and improving the current teaching-learning environment, these technologies may enable educational establishments to offer a more flexible, diverse, and efficient learning arrangement that prepares learners for today's complex and collaborative nature of workplaces.

Preface

In recent years, the integration of cloud technologies has revolutionized the relationship between academia and industry, fundamentally altering how educational institutions prepare students for future careers. Cloud computing's scalability, accessibility, and versatility have unlocked new opportunities for collaboration, innovation, and knowledge-sharing. This transformative technology transcends physical and temporal boundaries, enabling education to thrive as a dynamic and interconnected ecosystem. Within this context, ideas flourish, innovation is encouraged, and learning becomes an active, global endeavor.

This edited volume, *Bridging Academia and Industry Through Cloud Integration in Education,* delves into the multifaceted impact of cloud computing on educational practices. The book provides a robust theoretical foundation, practical application strategies, and an exploration of the transformative potential of integrating cloud technologies into teaching and learning processes. Through this compilation, we aim to identify areas for improvement by analyzing successful implementations and monitoring current trends that align with the overarching goal of equipping students with the skills and competencies demanded by contemporary employers.

The chapters within this volume spark essential discussions about the benefits and challenges of fostering closer ties between educational institutions and industries. Topics such as collaborative projects involving students from diverse institutions—both local and international—joint research initiatives among educators with varied expertise, and the safeguarding of data privacy within shared cloud environments are explored. Of particular importance are the privacy and security concerns that arise when multiple users from different organizations access shared systems. These issues demand heightened attention to ensure that cloud-based solutions are both effective and secure.

Chapter 1 introduces the profound societal shifts brought about by the digital revolution, emphasizing the generational differences in how technology is adopted and its social implications. This chapter sets the stage for understanding the multifaceted impacts of digitalization on our daily lives and interactions.

Chapter 2 examines the transformative potential of cloud-based professional development, highlighting its ability to promote lifelong learning. Through an exploration of key components, implementation strategies, and real-world case studies, the chapter underscores how cloud technologies empower individuals and organizations.

Chapter 3 focuses on personalized learning and adaptive systems enabled by cloud technology. With examples such as AI-driven analytics and global learning platforms, this chapter illustrates the strides made in tailoring education to individual learners and the emerging trends poised to further enhance these practices.

Chapter 4 delves into the integration of cloud technologies in academia and industry partnerships. This chapter explores strategies for leveraging cloud platforms to streamline research, develop industry-relevant curricula, and enhance student employability, offering valuable insights for educators and professionals alike.

Chapter 5 builds on the theme of academia-industry collaboration by exploring customized learning experiences and adaptive systems. Through case studies, this chapter highlights how cloud technologies bridge theoretical knowledge and practical applications, fostering a dynamic and student-centered educational environment.

Chapter 6 transitions into the realm of supply chain efficiency, showcasing how technological and entrepreneurial innovations are transforming operations. The chapter explores the role of cloud computing, data analytics, and IoT in enhancing responsiveness, while addressing the challenges of integrating technology in supply chain management.

Chapter 7 addresses the crucial topic of cloud security in education, focusing on the protection of sensitive data and infrastructure. By discussing strategies for managing risks and ensuring privacy, this chapter provides a practical guide for educational institutions navigating the digital transformation.

Chapter 8 presents a novel approach to data storage and retrieval through a biometric and QR code-based system for cloud applications. The chapter explores the challenges of biometric authentication and its potential for enhancing data security, offering a fresh perspective on user-centric cloud solutions.

Chapter 9 investigates advanced encryption techniques using blockchain technology and Generative Adversarial Networks (GANs) to secure sensitive image data in cloud environments. The chapter demonstrates the superiority of these methods through experimental analysis, emphasizing their importance for future security frameworks.

Chapter 10 provides an in-depth analysis of IoT cloud platforms, examining their applications in data management, system administration, and analytics. By identifying future research directions, this chapter equips readers with a thorough understanding of the evolving IoT ecosystem.

Chapter 11 explores the use of predictive analytics in online marketing, highlighting machine learning models that optimize user engagement and targeting. The chapter showcases the transformative impact of data-driven advertising strategies and identifies avenues for future advancements.

Chapter 12 introduces YoZu, an innovative chatbot powered by Large Language Models, designed to simplify information for students. By integrating dynamic media recommendations and content filtering, this chapter illustrates the chatbot's potential to revolutionize educational interactions in the digital age.

Chapter 13 concludes the book by envisioning the future of cloud-based education, focusing on the roles of blockchain, AI, AR, VR, and IoT in transforming learning environments. The chapter highlights how these technologies can create flexible and inclusive educational systems that prepare learners for the complexities of modern workplaces.

This book aspires to present a comprehensive collection of insights into the transformational impact of cloud integration in education. By exploring theoretical frameworks, practical applications, and real-world case studies, it seeks to illuminate how cloud technologies can bridge the gap between academia and industry. These insights underscore the potential of cloud computing to enhance collaboration, improve academic outcomes, and prepare students for professional roles in a rapidly evolving job market.

Our target audience is diverse, encompassing researchers, educators, industry professionals, and policymakers. Researchers will find an in-depth exploration of theoretical underpinnings and practical applications of cloud integration. Educators will discover innovative strategies to enhance student engagement and learning outcomes, while industry professionals will gain valuable perspectives on fostering partnerships with academic institutions. Policymakers and technology experts will benefit from guidance on leveraging cloud computing to address challenges and opportunities in education. By catering to such a broad spectrum of stakeholders, this book aims to inform and inspire those invested in advancing educational practices through cloud technologies.

Ultimately, we hope that this volume not only contributes to ongoing conversations about the integration of cloud technologies in education but also inspires actionable solutions that bring lasting benefits to academia, industry, and society at large. We extend our gratitude to the contributors whose expertise and insights have shaped this work, and we invite readers to join us in exploring the transformative potential of cloud integration in education.

Parikshit Mahalle
Vishwakarma Institute of Information Technology, India

Chapter 1
Impacts of Digital Technologies Across Generations

Ketki P. Kshirsagar
Vishwakarma Institute of Information Technology, India

Anup Ingle
https://orcid.org/0000-0003-1159-9453
Vishwakarma Institute of Information Technology, India

ABSTRACT

Digital technologies have significantly influenced different generations, shaping cultural norms, regulatory frameworks, and economic landscapes. Baby Boomers and Generation X have adapted to these changes later in life, valuing traditional interactions while integrating digital tools into their routines. In contrast, Millennials and Generation Z have grown up in a digital world, making technology a core aspect of their culture and daily activities. The impact of digital technologies extends to various domains, including innovation, where younger generations drive the adoption of emerging technologies. Socially, digital connectivity has altered how generations interact, introducing challenges such as the digital divide and mental health concerns. Economically, digital literacy has become essential, offering new job opportunities while requiring older generations to reskill. Understanding these multifaceted impacts is crucial for bridging generational divides and harnessing the full potential of digital technologies for society.

DOI: 10.4018/979-8-3693-6705-6.ch001

I. INTRODUCTION

The digital revolution has effortlessly woven itself into the fabric of our lives, fundamentally altering our modes of communication, learning, and navigating the world around us. With the widespread use of smartphones and the growing potential of cutting-edge technologies such as Artificial Intelligence (AI) and the Internet of Things (IoT), technology has moved beyond its status as a mere peripheral aspect of society to become a dynamic force actively shaping our social landscape(Prensky, M.,2001). However, it is critical to recognize that the effects of these technologies are not consistent between individuals. Variables such as age, upbringing, and life experiences have a considerable impact on how we adapt to and use digital tools.This chapter delves into the various social implications of digital technology throughout generations, while remaining innovative in its analysis and observations (Palfrey, J.,2008)(Gasser, U.,2008)

Recognizing the disparities in digital adoption between generations, we examine the experiences of the "Silent Generation" and "Baby Boomers" who experienced the dawn of the digital era, gradually adapting to early computers and the burgeoning internet. Generation X developed with advancing technology, fostering a stronger connection to it. Millennials, sometimes known as "digital natives," were reared in a digitally connected environment. Generation Z, on the other hand, pushes the envelope even further, exhibiting an innate familiarity with future technology like artificial intelligence and virtual reality. Understanding generational inequalities in digital skill and engagement is critical for understanding how people of all ages navigate and use technology in their daily lives(Zhou, Y., & Hentschel, J et. al.,2018) (Gomez, R.,2013).

The differences found across generations have important social ramifications. For example, younger generations rely significantly on social media platforms like Facebook and Instagram for communication and self-expression, but older folks prefer traditional methods such as email or phone calls to stay in touch. The availability of online knowledge offers both benefits and drawbacks. Younger people, who predominantly obtain news via social media, may be more susceptible to misinformation(Ng, W, 2012)(Correa, T,2015).Conversely, older folks may struggle to navigate complicated internet interfaces. Recognizing these distinctions highlights the importance of addressing the societal effects of different generations' digital usage behaviours(Jenkins, H., 2015).The digital divide has an impact in the workplace as well. Artificial intelligence-driven automation threatens to disrupt traditional employment markets, potentially hurting elderly people who may struggle to adapt to new technologies. However, digital tools also allow for remote employment and flexible scheduling, which may be beneficial to younger generations seeking a better work-life balance(Bennett, S. et. al, 2009)(Selwyn, N.,2009).

The digital age has brought about significant changes in education. Online learning platforms and educational apps open up new opportunities for knowledge acquisition, potentially democratizing access to education(Jones, C, 2010)(Kumbhar, Kalpana et. al, 2015). Nonetheless, the digital divide may result in unequal learning opportunities, particularly for students from disadvantaged backgrounds who lack access to necessary technology and internet connectivity(Meyers, E. M, 2013). This chapter addresses the negative consequences of digital technologies. Cyberbullying, online addiction, and the spread of misinformation are significant challenges for people of all ages. The constant stream of information and social comparisons on social media can have a negative impact on mental health, especially among young users. Furthermore, the rise of "filter bubbles" driven by algorithms has the potential to exacerbate social and political polarization by creating echo chambers in which people are only exposed to information that confirms their pre-existing beliefs(Selwyn, N., 2014)(Meyers, E. M., 2013).

Regardless of the challenges, the potential benefits of digital technologies are clear. Telemedicine has the potential to transform healthcare access for remote communities, while AI-powered applications can help in fields such as education and research. The ability to communicate with people across borders encourages global collaboration and cultural exchange. Furthermore, social media platforms can be effective tools for promoting social activism and political engagement (Kvavik, R, 2005)(Kshirsagar, Ketki P, 2010).

Digital technologies have become an integral part of modern life, influencing how we communicate, work, learn, and entertain ourselves. The impact of these technologies extends across generations, shaping behaviors, skills, and societal norms in unique ways. From Baby Boomers to Generation Z, each group has interacted with digital technology differently, leading to diverse perspectives and capabilities in navigating the digital world (Prajwal Gujarkar et. al., 2023).

1. **Cultural Impact**:
    - **Baby Boomers and Generation X** experienced the advent of digital technologies later in life. While they have adapted to using devices like smartphones and computers, their cultural practices still value face-to-face interaction and traditional forms of media like newspapers and television.
    - **Millennials and Generation Z**, on the other hand, have grown up with digital technologies, making them a core part of their culture. Social media, streaming services, and online gaming have become primary sources of entertainment and socialization(Ketki P Kshirsagar,2022).
2. **Regulatory Impact**:

- Governments and organizations have had to develop new regulations to address issues such as data privacy, cyberbullying, and misinformation. The rapid growth of digital technologies has often outpaced regulatory frameworks, creating challenges in enforcing rules that protect users across all generations.
- For older generations, adapting to these regulations can be challenging, as they may not be as familiar with digital security practices as younger generations who have been educated on these topics from an early age(U. S. Rokade,2009).

3. **Innovational Impact**:
   - Digital technologies have spurred innovation across all generations. For example, Baby Boomers and Generation X have seen the transformation of industries with the introduction of digital tools, improving productivity and enabling new forms of work(Kshirsagar, Ketki P,2015).
   - Younger generations are driving further innovation, utilizing digital platforms to create new business models, such as the gig economy and influencer marketing. They are also at the forefront of adopting emerging technologies like artificial intelligence and virtual reality.
4. **Social Impact**:
   - The social dynamics have significantly shifted due to digital technologies. Older generations often prefer traditional social interactions, while younger generations are more comfortable with virtual connections.
   - Digital technology has facilitated global connectivity, allowing for cross-generational communication. However, it has also introduced challenges such as the digital divide, where access to technology and the internet varies between different socioeconomic groups(Bennett, S.,2010).
5. **Psychological Impact**:
   - The influence of digital technology on mental health varies across generations. While older adults may feel overwhelmed by the rapid changes and the need to constantly adapt, younger individuals face issues like cyberbullying, social media anxiety, and information overload.
   - Despite these challenges, digital technologies also offer mental health resources, such as online counseling and support communities, which can benefit individuals across all age groups(Van Deursen, A. J. et. al., 2014)(Eynon, R., et. al, 2016).
6. **Economic Impact**:
   - Digital technologies have transformed the economy, creating new job opportunities and altering traditional career paths. Older generations may find it challenging to keep up with the skill requirements of a dig-

itized workforce, leading to a need for reskilling and lifelong learning(Hargittai, E,2010).

- o For younger generations, digital literacy has become a crucial skill, with opportunities in fields like tech development, digital marketing, and e-commerce. The economy has also become more accessible to these generations through platforms for freelance work and entrepreneurship.

This analysis highlights that digital technologies have a multifaceted impact across generations, affecting cultural practices, regulatory frameworks, innovation, social dynamics, psychological well-being, and economic opportunities. Understanding these impacts is essential for developing strategies that bridge the generational divide and maximize the benefits of digital technology for society as a whole(Friemel, T. N.,2016).

II. OBJECTIVE

The digital revolution has inextricably linked itself to the social fabric, fundamentally changing how we interact, learn, and navigate the world. From smartphones to the emerging potential of Artificial Intelligence (AI) and the Internet of Things (IoT), technology is no longer a supplementary element, but rather a dynamic force shaping our social landscape. However, our experiences with this transformation are far from uniform. How we adapt to and use digital tools is heavily influenced by our age, background, and life experiences.

This chapter delves into this complex "digital tapestry," with the primary goal of investigating the multifaceted social effects of digital technologies across generations. We aim to:

- **Uncovering Generational Divides:** Our investigation will shed light on the disparities in the digital landscape experienced by different generations. We will look at the perspectives of those who witnessed the rise of digital technology (the Silent Generation and Baby Boomers), those who grew up alongside its evolution (Generation X), digital natives (Millennials), and the generation at the forefront of technological innovation(GenerationZ).
- **Analysing Social Implications:** We will look at how technology influences various aspects of society, such as communication, education, work, and the broader social fabric, across generations. This includes investigating how social media platforms like Facebook and Instagram influence interactions for younger generations as opposed to the traditional methods preferred by older

adults. We will also evaluate the impact of the digital divide on access to information and education.

- **Evaluating Both Sides of the Coin:** In addition to acknowledging the challenges of cyberbullying, online addiction, and misinformation dissemination, we will look at the undeniable potential benefits of digital technologies. This includes researching how AI-powered applications can transform healthcare and research, as well as how online learning platforms can democratize educational access. We will also emphasize how social media platforms can be effective tools for social activism and global collaboration.

This chapter will achieve these goals by providing a nuanced understanding of the social impacts of digital technologies across generations.

We will navigate both the positive and negative aspects of the digital revolution, aiming to create a future in which technology empowers individuals and communities to bridge gaps and promote a more inclusive society.

Target Audience

This chapter on the social impacts of digital technologies across generations is intended for a diverse audience, which includes several key groups.

1. **People of Various Generations:** This chapter aims to provide informative and engaging insights to people of all ages. Whether you are a member of the Silent Generation or a tech-savvy member of Generation Z, this chapter offers valuable insights into how technology shapes social experiences across generations.

Figure 1. **Various Generations**

2. **Students in Social Sciences and Technology:** This chapter is relevant to students pursuing degrees in sociology, communication studies, or technology-related fields. It investigates the social implications of emerging technologies, providing a valuable resource for future research and academic exploration.

Figure 2. **Technology**

3. **Professionals in technology and social issues:** will benefit from this chapter, which includes information on digital marketing, human-computer interaction, and social policy. Understanding the impact of technology on social dynamics across generations can help these professionals develop more effective strategies and solutions.

In general, this chapter is intended for people who want to learn more about the complex interplay between digital technologies and society across various age groups. Its mission is to spark meaningful debates and encourage responsible technological development in the future.

III. TECHNICAL AND NON-TECHNICAL FACTORS FOR DIGITAL TECHNOLOGY

Digital technologies like social media and smartphones have had a big impact on relationships and communication between generations. The way that different generations interact and communicate is shaped by these changes, which involve both technical and non-technical factors (Selwyn, N., 2004)(Madden, M., 2010).

- **Technical Parameters:**

1. **Digital literacy:** It is essential to make sure individuals of all ages possess the abilities needed to use digital tools efficiently. This entails offering educational materials and training courses that are age-appropriate. Offering classes on fundamental digital literacy can enable older adults in particular to use online platforms with confidence.
2. **Privacy Awareness:** One of the most important ways to protect personal data online is to educate users about privacy settings and potential risks. This entails instructing people on how to control their social media privacy settings and comprehend the ramifications of disclosing personal information online, particularlycross generations where awareness levels may vary.
3. **User Experience Design:** Encouraging inclusivity and accessibility among older adults through the development of user-friendly interfaces for digital platforms is essential. This involves taking into account elements like larger font sizes, straightforward navigation menus, and explicit instructions designed to accommodate different age groups' differing degrees of digital literacy.
4. **Addictions to smartphones and the internet:** Using behavioural analytics to track usage patterns can help detect addictive behaviours and offer guidance on how to treat them. In order to encourage better usage habits and lessen reliance on smartphones and the internet, app designers have included features like screen time limits and digital detox tools.
5. **Affordability:** One of the most important factors in closing the digital divide is making sure that internet services and digital devices are within the means of all generations. This can be accomplished by programs like government subsidies to increase access to technology, discounted or reconditioned devices, and internet plans that are subsidized for low-income households.

- **Non-Technical Parameters:**

1. **Social Norms:** Building successful intergenerational relationships requires an understanding of how different generations prefer to communicate. For instance, whereas younger generations might favour instantaneous text-based communication through messaging applications, older generations might place more value on in-person conversations or phone calls.
2. **Emotional Well-Being:** Keeping good relationships across generations requires striking a balance between screen time and in-person interactions. Feelings of alienation and disconnection can result from an over-reliance on digital communication, especially for older adults who may long for face-to-face interactions(Buckingham, D.,2007).

3. **Family Dynamics:** Digital communication can have a variety of effects on family relationships. It can make it easier to communicate across distances and increase the likelihood of disputes over things like smartphone addiction or privacy concerns. Maintaining healthy relationships within families requires an understanding of these dynamics and the promotion of open communication within them.
4. **Awareness Campaigns:** Creating awareness and encouraging responsible digital behaviour requires educating users about the dangers of internet addiction and excessive smartphone use. These advertisements, which can be directed towards people of all ages, emphasize the value of establishing limits and giving offline activities top priority for general wellbeing.
5. **Community Centres:** One efficient way to encourage digital inclusion is to set up community centres where people can access technology and get assistance. These facilities offer a physical setting where individuals can acquire digital skills, use online resources, and get help from volunteers or staff who have received training(Li, Y.,, 2010).

IV. TECHNICAL AND NON-TECHNICAL PARAMETERS FOR EMERGING TECHNOLOGIES

Technical Parameters

In the quickly changing world of today, technology can be a key factor in moving us closer to a future that is more inclusive, egalitarian, and sustainable. Leaders are debating the strategic opportunities where technology can spur advancement as they gather in Davos. Examining how new tech platforms and trends will impact our world as well as what game-changing innovations to expect are all part of this. Additionally, they are taking into account how these technological developments will affect future generations in the long run, offering us a glimpse into the kind of world our grandchildren may inherit(Selwyn, N.,, 2016).

AI (Artificial Intelligence)

1. Data Quality and Bias:
    - **Data Quality:**Data quality, which includes the consistency, correctness, relevance, and completeness of the data used to train machine learning models, is essential to the development of artificial intelligence. Errors, biases, and inconsistencies are absent from high-quality data, guaranteeing that the AI systems that are created produce reliable and accurate

results. For algorithms to be trained effectively, accurate data is essential because incomplete or faulty data can produce inaccurate conclusions and untrustworthy predictions. To reduce errors and preserve integrity throughout the AI model's lifecycle, strict data collection, cleaning, and validation procedures are necessary to ensure data quality.

- **Bias:** In contrast, systematic mistakes or biases present in the data or algorithms used for machine learning are referred to as bias in AI. Because biased data favours some groups while disadvantages others based on unimportant characteristics like race, gender, or socioeconomic status, it can reinforce and even worsen societal inequalities. Algorithmic bias occurs when a model consistently discriminates against a particular group in its predictions or decisions. Sampling bias occurs when a particular demographic group is underrepresented in the training data. Biases in AI algorithms can take many different forms.

2. **Ethical AI:**
    - **Transparency:** For stakeholders to be able to interpret and comprehend the decision-making process, transparency in AI is crucial. Explainable AI models that offer insights into prediction processes can be used to accomplish this. Giving context for AI predictions also fosters trust and enables users to check the fairness and accuracy of the system's results.
    - **Fairness:**In artificial intelligence, fairness refers to assessing how well the model's judgments and predictions hold up across various demographic categories, including socioeconomic class, gender, and race. It necessitates recognizing and addressing prejudices that could result in unfair consequences. Fairness-aware machine learning algorithms are one technique that can help guarantee equitable treatment for a variety of populations.
3. Interoperability:

Is crucial for integrating AI systems with existing healthcare infrastructure, ensuring seamless adoption and scalability:

- **APIs and Interfaces:** Interoperability requires the design of application programming interfaces (APIs) and interfaces that facilitate communication between AI modules and electronic health record (EHR) systems. Through APIs, AI systems can access and evaluate patient data kept in electronic health records (EHRs), giving healthcare providers real-time insights and decision support while they continue with their current workflows.
- **Scalability:** A key component of scalability is ensuring AI solutions can manage massive amounts of healthcare data. This entails developing infra-

structure and algorithms that are capable of efficiently processing and analysing enormous volumes of patient data. Without sacrificing efficiency or dependability, scalable AI systems can handle a wide range of healthcare applications, including population health management and clinical decision support.

4. Privacy and Encryption:

- **Privacy:** The basic right of people to manage who can access, use, and share their personal data is known as privacy. It includes the capacity to protect sensitive information about oneself and one's life from prying eyes and outside influence. As a result of the massive collection, processing, and sharing of personal data by numerous entities in the modern digital age, privacy concerns have taken on paramount importance. Protecting private data that is transferred over the internet or kept on digital devices is the main goal of digital privacy. It involves preventing unauthorized access, misuse, or exploitation of sensitive data, including financial records, medical histories, and online activity. Strong legal frameworks, technological security measures, and moral behaviour are necessary to uphold privacy rights and guarantee people's autonomy and control over their personal data in an increasingly interconnected world.
- **Encryption:** By utilizing cryptographic algorithms and keys to convert plaintext data into an unintelligible format known as ciphertext, encryption is a potent technique used to improve privacy and security. It acts as a vital defence against unwanted access, interception, or alteration of private data while it's being transferred or stored. Encryption ensures confidentiality and integrity by making data unintelligible to those lacking the necessary decryption keys. Encryption is widely used to safeguard data stored on devices and in cloud storage services, as well as communication channels like email, messaging apps, and online transactions. Through the utilization of encryption technologies, both individuals and organizations can reduce the potential for data breaches, unauthorized access, and surveillance. This can help to maintain privacy and promote trust in digital interactions.

IoT (Internet of Things)

IoT links billions of smart devices, revolutionizing a number of industries.

1. Security:

In order to reduce the risks related to cyber threats, unauthorized access, and data breaches, it is imperative to ensure the security of IoT devices. IoT devices are attractive targets for bad actors because they are interconnected through networks and gather and transmit enormous amounts of sensitive data. Robust security protocols are imperative for mitigating potential vulnerabilities and ensuring the preservation of device functionality and user privacy. Tokens and certificates are examples of authentication and authorization mechanisms that confirm the identity of users and devices, preventing unwanted access to IoT ecosystems. An extra degree of security is added when data is encrypted during transmission between devices and gateways. This guarantees that the data cannot be read by unauthorized parties, even if it is intercepted. Frequent firmware updates fix security flaws, decreasing the possibility that hackers will take advantage of them. Access is restricted by access control mechanisms to sensitive functions based on user roles, preventing unauthorized configuration changes or data retrieval.

2. **Data privacy:**

In the context of IoT devices, data privacy is crucial for preserving user trust and adhering to privacy laws. Because users entrust IoT devices with their personal data, strong privacy protection measures are required. Getting users' express consent before collecting their data respects their right to autonomy and guarantees openness in data processing procedures. By deleting personally identifiable information (PII), collected data can be made anonymous, protecting user identities and preventing unauthorized identification. By defining the duration of data storage and the point at which it should be erased, data retention policies help lower the possibility of misuse or unauthorized access in the future. To ensure user privacy and prevent unwanted interception, secure communication protocols encrypt data as it is being transmitted. Giving users the ability to manage their privacy preferences in accordance with their comfort levels and preferences improves transparency. Examples of this include opt-out options. IoT deployments that prioritize data privacy concerns can show users that they are committed to responsible data stewardship and build user trust.

3. Energy efficiency

In order to maximize power consumption in IoT networks, energy efficiency is crucial for prolonging device lifespans and reducing environmental impact. Devices that use low-power hardware, like sensors and microcontrollers with low power consumption, operate with the least amount of energy consumption possible. By putting devices into low-power states while they are idle, sleep modes help devices save energy by cutting down on wasteful consumption. By combining sensor readings, data aggregation techniques help reduce the frequency of data transmissions and the energy overhead that comes with data transfer. Selecting effective communication protocols, like MQTT or CoAP, minimizes protocol overhead and maximizes data transmission to further cut down on energy usage. Additionally, by investigating energy harvesting options like solar or kinetic energy, gadgets can utilize renewable energy sources and become less dependent on conventionalpower grids and further enhancing energy efficiency in IoT deployments.

4. Scalability

As the number of connected devices in Internet of Things (IoT) systems keeps increasing, scalable architectures and management strategies are becoming increasingly important. Whether cloud-based or edge-based, choosing the right architecture is essential to supporting a large number of devices and guaranteeing effective data processing and management. By distributing incoming requests equally among servers or gateways, load balancing techniques avoid bottlenecks and guarantee peak performance even as the system grows. The maintenance of system integrity and operational efficiency is contingent upon the implementation of effective device management practices, which encompass onboarding, provisioning, and device management at scale. IoT systems can handle large amounts of sensor data effectively by optimizing data processing pipelines, guaranteeing that scalability does not degrade performance or reliability. Scalability issues can be addressed by IoT systems in order to effectively accommodategrowth while maintaining responsiveness and reliability, thereby supporting the evolving needs of connected environments.

5. Blockchain and SDGs:

The United Nations Sustainable Development Goals (SDGs) can be achieved in part through the use of blockchain, another cutting-edge technology.

1. Decentralization:

One of the main tenets of blockchain technology is decentralization, which is essential for encouraging networks' resilience, transparency, and trust. Decentralization reduces the risks associated with single points of failure and stops any one entity from monopolizing power or manipulating the system for their own gain by spreading control and decision-making authority among a wide range of participants. Node distribution is one of the most important factors to take into account when designing decentralized networks. This is because it helps to improve network resilience and prevent localized disruptions by distributing nodes across various geographic locations. Decentralized governance procedures for protocol upgrades and modifications also promote community participation and guarantee that decisions are made collaboratively, which is consistent with the democratic spirit of decentralization. By taking these things into account, decentralization enables people to work together in an open and collaboratively, which is consistent with the democratic spirit of decentralization. By taking these things into account, decentralization enables people to work together in an open and untrustworthy atmosphere, which eventually promotes innovation and the expansion of decentralized ecosystems and applications.

2. Consensus Mechanisms:

The validation and addition of transactions to the blockchain are largely determined by consensus mechanisms, which have a direct bearing on the scalability, security, and efficiency of decentralized networks. In order to validate transactions, miners must solve computationally demanding puzzles using traditional mechanisms like Proof of Work (PoW), which ensures security but uses a lot of energy. On the other hand, Proof of Stake (PoS) requires validators to be trusted and chooses validators based on the quantity of cryptocurrency they own. It is a more energy-efficient solution. In order to strike a balance between decentralization and efficiency and scalability, Delegated Proof of Stake (DPoS) introduces a governance layer where token holders vote for delegates to validate transactions. Investigating different methods such as HoneyBadgerBFT or Practical Byzantine Fault Tolerance (PBFT) offers ways to reach consensus in a highly scalable and effective way, meeting the needs ofvarious use cases and needs for the network. Blockchain networks can achieve a stable and robust decentralized ecosystem by carefully weighing these consensus mechanisms and striking a balance between decentralization, security, efficiency, and scalability.

Assigning numerical values to the technical parameters of emerging technologies provides a way to quantify and compare their impacts. A scale from 1 to 5 can be used to rate each parameter,

Table 1. Technical parameters of emerging technologies

Parameter	**Rating (1-5)**
Performance and Efficiency	4
Scalability	4
Interoperability	3
Security and Privacy	3
Reliability and Availability	4

continued on following page

Table 1. Continued

Parameter	Rating (1-5)
Maintenance and Support	3
User Interface (UI) and UX	4
Data Management	4

Figure 3. Graphical representation Technical parameters

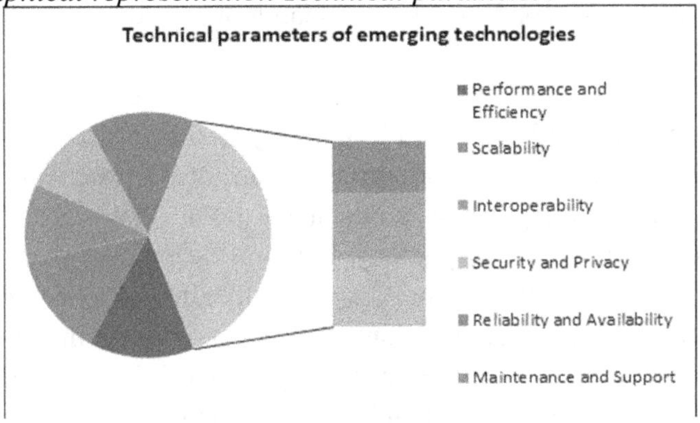

Non – Technical Parameters

AI (Artificial Intelligence)

1. Ethics and Bias:

These two factors are crucial when it comes to AI. Because AI algorithms are frequently trained on historical data, they may unintentionally reinforce biases found in the training set, producing discriminatory or unfair results. To reduce these risks, AI systems must be made transparent and equitable. To address bias in AI models, methods like diverse dataset curation, fairness-aware algorithms, and bias detection and mitigation are used. Furthermore, ethical standards are upheld and unexpected consequences are avoided when ethical concepts like fairness, accountability, and transparency are incorporated into the design and development of AI systems. AI practitioners aim to create more equitable and trustworthy AI applications that benefit society as a whole by giving ethics and bias mitigation top priority.

2. Job displacement and reskilling:

As AI technology progresses in automating tasks in a variety of industries, worries regarding workforce disruption are raised by the possibility of job displacement. The workforce must be reskilled in order to adjust to the shifting demands and job roles brought about by the adoption of AI. It is a difficult task that calls for cooperation between companies, educational institutions, and legislators to strike a balance between efficiency improvements and job retention. Putting money into upskilling projects, career transition assistance, and lifelong learning programs can help employees develop the skills required for new positions in AI-related industries. In addition, encouraging a culture of lifelong learning and flexibility helps people prosper in an AI-driven economy while lessening the socioeconomic effects of job displacement.

3. Social Acceptance and Legal and Regulatory Challenges:
    1. A key factor in the broad adoption and use of AI systems is social acceptance. AI technology trust is dependent on attributes like explainability, accountability, and transparency. Explainable AI approaches help people have faith and confidence in AI systems by allowing them to comprehend how the systems make decisions. Applications of AI that are in line with social norms and values are ensured by responsible use of the technology, which is governed by legal and ethical guidelines. But there are still a lot of unanswered legal and regulatory questions about AI ethics, liability, and accountability. It is essential to create strong legal frameworks and regulatory guidelines in order to control the moral application of AI, safeguard individual rights, and hold those accountable for AI-related harms.

IoT (Internet of Things)

1. Ethical Implications:

Significant ethical issues are raised by the widespread use of IoT devices, especially in relation to data privacy, consent, and ownership. Respecting people's right to control the personal data that IoT devices collect is essential to handling data privacy. Strong privacy policies, data encryption strategies, and anonymization techniques are helpful in preventing unwanted access to and misuse of sensitive data. In order to guarantee that people are aware of how their data is being gathered, utilized, and shared by IoT devices, consent is essential. Giving users access to clear and transparent consent processes gives them the power to decide how their data is used. In addition, addressing concerns of accountability and control requires elucidating ownership rights over data generated by the Internet of Things. To avoid disagreements and guarantee that people keep their data, it is important to establish explicit rules and agreements regarding data ownership.

2. Equity and Access:

To address inequalities and close the digital divide, it is crucial to guarantee equitable access to IoT technology. Geographical location or socioeconomic status shouldn't be barriers to accessing IoT innovations. Providing inexpensive access to IoT devices and infrastructure is a key component of efforts to close the digital divide, especially in underprivileged areas. By funding digital literacy initiatives and training programs, people with a variety of backgrounds can effectively utilize IoT technology. Additionally, creating inclusive IoT solutions that meet the requirements of all users—including those with limited resources or disabilities—promotes accessibility and equity within the IoT ecosystem. Stakeholders can leverage the transformative potential of IoT technology to benefit society at large by placing a high priority on equity and access.

3. Social Acceptance:

Adoption and acceptance of IoT solutions depend heavily on public perception and trust. Transparency, accountability, and unambiguous communication are essential for establishing trust when developing and implementing Internet of Things systems. Building users' trust and confidence in the technology involves giving them information about how Internet of Things devices work, what data is gathered, and how it is used. Furthermore, addressing worries about privacy, data security, and possible dangers related to IoT deployments shows a dedication to responsible innovation. In order to address issues and make sure that IoT solutions satisfy societal needs and expectations, it is important to engage with stakeholders, such as members of the community, legislators, and advocacy organizations. This fosters meaningful dialogue and collaboration. Through the prioritization of social acceptance and efforts aimed at establishing trust, stakeholders can foster an environment that is conducive to the responsible and sustainable adoption of IoT technology.

Blockchain

1. Equity and Access:

By giving underprivileged groups, especially the unbanked, access to financial services and enhancing financial inclusion, blockchain technology has the potential to empower them. People who don't have access to formal banking services because of things like being in a remote location, not having the proper paperwork, or having limited resources are frequently left out of traditional banking systems. Blockchain-based solutions allow people to engage in the global economy without depending on traditional financial institutions by providing accessible and decentralized alternatives for handling financial transactions. The unbanked can now access services like digital payments, remittances, lending, and insurance by utilizing blockchain technology, which promotes economic empowerment and lowers inequality.

2. Environmental Impact:

Because proof-of-work (PoW) blockchains, like Bitcoin, use energy-intensive consensus mechanisms, there is considerable concern about how blockchain technology will affect the environment. PoW blockchains require miners to solve challenging mathematical puzzles in order to validate transactions, which uses a significant amount of energy. Degradation of the environment and carbon emissions are caused by this energy use. Proof-of-stake (PoS) is one innovation that attempts to address these environmental issues by providing consensus mechanisms that are more energy-efficient. PoS blockchains minimize the need for computationally demanding tasks and energy consumption by selecting validators based on the quantity of cryptocurrency they possess. By shifting to environmentally friendly blockchain solutions like Proof of Stake (PoS), the sector can lessen its environmental impact and encourage environmental responsibility in blockchain adoption and development.

3. Legal and Regulatory Landscape:

To encourage innovation and investment in the blockchain space, the legal and regulatory environment surrounding blockchain technology—which includes smart contracts, tokens, and ownership—needs to be clear and coherent. Self-executing contracts, or "smart contracts," are written on blockchains and give rise to a number of legal concerns about jurisdiction, liability, and enforceability. To define the legal status of smart contracts and create procedures for resolving disputes that may arise from their execution, clear legal frameworks are required. Comparably, regulatory issues pertaining to consumer protection, securities laws, and anti-money laundering (AML) regulations are brought up by the issuance and trading of tokens based on blockchain technology. To encourage investor confidence and safeguard market participants, clear and consistent regulatory frameworks for token offerings and tokenized assets must be established.

Assigning numerical values to the non technical parameters of emerging technologies provides a way to quantify and compare their impacts. A scale from 1 to 5 can be used to rate each parameter,

Table 2. Non-Technical parameters of emerging technologies

Parameter	Rating (1-5)
Ethical Considerations	3
Societal Impact	4
Legal and Regulatory Compliance	3
Economic Factors	4
Environmental Impact	2
User Adoption and Behavior	4
Health and Well-being	3
Future-proofing and Innovation	5

Figure 4. Graphical Representation of Non technical parameters **Analysis**

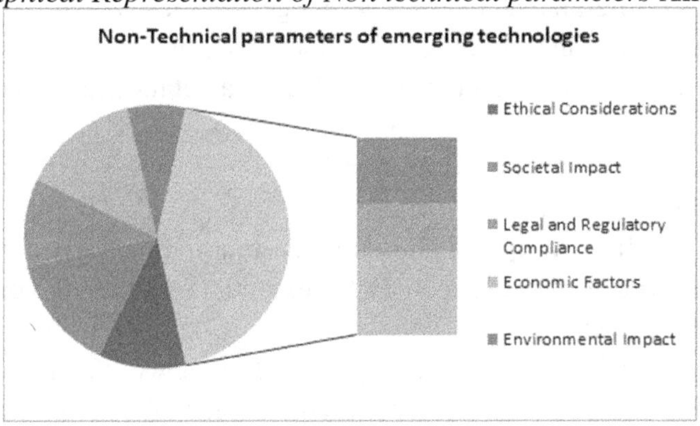

Digital technologies have enormous cross-generational effects that profoundly alter social dynamics and interactions. The Internet of Things (IoT) and artificial intelligence (AI) are two emerging technologies that have the potential to completely transform a number of societal spheres, including communication, healthcare, education, and everyday life. AI, for instance, has the potential to revolutionize healthcare by enhancing medical research, personalized treatment plans, and diagnosis accuracy. But putting it into practice creates ethical questions about privacy, algorithmic bias, and benefit distribution equity. In a similar vein, IoT devices improve efficiency and convenience by facilitating smooth automation and connectivity in homes and cities. However, they also present issues with data privacy, security flaws, and the digital divide, especially for older generations who might find it difficult to adjust to the quickly changing technology.

These new technologies have complex and wide-ranging social effects. They present risks of social isolation and exacerbate pre-existing inequalities, but they also present opportunities for improved intergenerational communication and collaboration. Ensuring equal access to the advantages of digital technologies requires bridging the digital divide and advancing digital literacy among generations. Furthermore, it is imperative to tackle ethical issues related to the creation and application of these technologies in order to establish credibility and promote conscientious innovation that spans generations.

In conclusion, new technologies such as AI and IoT have significant social effects that influence how people of different generations engage, communicate, and use the internet. Societies can take advantage of the transformative potential of digital technologies by tackling issues like digital literacy, privacy concerns, and ethical considerations.while reducing their negative impacts and fostering inclusivity and long-term wellbeing.

The impacts of digital technologies across generations can be analyzed by considering the differences in technology adoption, communication styles, work habits, learning preferences, and social behaviors. Here's a detailed analysis:

1. Technology Adoption and Adaptation
    - **Baby Boomers:**
    - **Slow Initial Adoption:** Initially resistant to new technologies but have adapted over time, especially for essential services like online banking and telemedicine.
    - **Selective Use:** Tend to use digital technologies selectively, focusing on utility (e.g., health apps, communication tools) rather than entertainment or social media.
    - **Generation X:**
    - **Transitional Adopters:** Experienced the transition from analog to digital and adapted relatively quickly.
    - **Balanced Approach:** Use digital technologies for both personal and professional purposes, maintaining a balance between online and offline activities.
    - **Millennials:**
    - **Digital Natives:** Comfortable with a wide range of technologies. Their formative years coincided with the rise of the internet and mobile phones.
    - **Multitaskers:** Skilled at using multiple devices and platforms simultaneously, reflecting a seamless integration of technology into daily life.
    - **Generation Z:**

- **Hyper-Connected:** Immersed in technology from birth, with smartphones and social media as integral parts of their lives.
- **Early Adopters:** Quick to embrace emerging technologies, such as augmented reality (AR), virtual reality (VR), and artificial intelligence (AI).
- **Generation Alpha:**
- **Digital Immersion:** Growing up with AI, smart homes, and virtual environments, leading to an expectation of seamless digital integration in all aspects of life.
- **Intuitive Use:** Interact with technology intuitively, often before learning to read or write.

2. Communication Styles and Social Interactions
    - **Baby Boomers:**
    - **Traditional Communication:** Prefer face-to-face interactions and phone calls but have adapted to using emails and video calls, especially during the COVID-19 pandemic.
    - **Limited Social Media Use:** Use platforms like Facebook to stay connected with family and friends but are less active on newer platforms like Instagram or TikTok.
    - **Generation X:**
    - **Adaptable Communicators:** Comfortable with a variety of communication methods, from in-person meetings to emails and social media.
    - **Professional Networking:** Utilize LinkedIn and other professional networks for career advancement.
    - **Millennials:**
    - **Social Media Savvy:** Use platforms like Facebook, Twitter, Instagram, and LinkedIn for both personal and professional networking.
    - **Preference for Digital Communication:** Favor texting, messaging apps, and social media over phone calls and face-to-face interactions.
    - **Generation Z:**
    - **Visual Communication:** Prefer platforms like Snapchat, Instagram, and TikTok, which focus on visual and short-form content.
    - **Digital-First Interactions:** Social interactions are often initiated and maintained online, affecting the development of social skills and relationships.
    - **Generation Alpha:**
    - **Technology-Driven Play and Communication:** Likely to use digital tools and platforms for play and communication from a very young age.
    - **Impact on Social Skills:** Early and frequent use of technology could impact traditional social skills development.

3. Work Habits and Professional Impact
   - **Baby Boomers:**
   - **Traditional Work Values:** Value face-to-face communication and in-person meetings. Adapted to digital tools for efficiency but may prefer more conventional methods.
   - **Challenges with Remote Work:** May find remote work and digital collaboration tools challenging, but many have adapted due to necessity.
   - **Generation X:**
   - **Work-Life Balance Seekers:** Leverage digital tools for efficiency, allowing for better work-life balance.
   - **Embrace Remote Work:** Comfortable with telecommuting and using digital collaboration tools.
   - **Millennials:**
   - **Flexible Work Preferences:** Prefer flexible work environments and value the ability to work remotely. Embrace digital nomadism.
   - **Tech-Savvy:** Rely on digital tools for productivity, communication, and project management.
   - **Generation Z:**
   - **Demand for Technology Integration:** Expect seamless integration of technology in the workplace. Favor roles that offer technological innovation.
   - **Gig Economy Participation:** Comfortable with freelance and gig economy roles, utilizing digital platforms for job opportunities.
   - **Generation Alpha:**
   - **Future of Work:** Likely to work in jobs that don't exist yet, heavily influenced by AI, automation, and digital transformation.
   - **Lifelong Learning:** Will require continual upskilling due to the rapid pace of technological change.
4. Learning Preferences and Educational Impact
   - **Baby Boomers:**
     - o **Traditional Learning:** Prefer structured, in-person learning environments. Adapted to digital learning out of necessity (e.g., online courses during the pandemic).
   - **Generation X:**
     - o **Hybrid Learning:** Comfortable with a mix of traditional and online learning methods. Utilize digital tools for professional development.
   - **Millennials:**

    - **Online Learning Enthusiasts:** Prefer e-learning platforms and digital resources. Value the flexibility and accessibility of online education.
- **Generation Z:**
    - **Interactive and Visual Learning:** Favor interactive and visual learning experiences, such as video tutorials, gamified learning apps, and virtual classrooms.
    - **Self-Directed Learning:** Use online resources to learn independently, from coding to creative skills.
- **Generation Alpha:**
    - **Tech-Integrated Learning:** Will likely experience AI-driven personalized learning and virtual/augmented reality in education.
    - **Early Tech Literacy:** Developing tech skills at an earlier age than previous generations.

5. Societal and Cultural Impacts
    - **Digital Divide:** While digital technologies have been beneficial, they have also highlighted the digital divide between those who have access to technology and those who do not, especially among older generations and in underserved communities.
    - **Mental Health:** Increased screen time and social media use among younger generations have been linked to mental health issues such as anxiety, depression, and loneliness.
    - **Changing Social Norms:** The rise of digital communication has altered social norms, influencing everything from dating practices to workplace interactions.
    - **Consumer Behavior:** The shift towards e-commerce and digital marketing has transformed consumer behavior, with a focus on online shopping, instant gratification, and personalized experiences

Digital technologies have transformed the behaviors, preferences, and lifestyles of each generation uniquely. While older generations have adapted to digital tools primarily for communication and work, younger generations have been shaped by a digital-first environment, affecting their communication styles, learning preferences, and social interactions. This evolving landscape requires ongoing adaptation and an understanding of the implications of digital immersion on society and individual well-being.

Table 3. Impact analysis of different parameters

Parameter	Baby Boomers (1946-1964)	Generation X (1965-1980)	Millennials (1981-1996)	Generation Z (1997-2012)	Generation Alpha (2013-Present)
Technology Adoption	Slow initial adoption; selective use	Transitional adopters; balanced approach	Digital natives; multitaskers	Hyper-connected; early adopters	Digital immersion; intuitive use
Communication Styles	Prefer traditional methods; limited social media use	Adaptable communicators; use of professional networks	Social media savvy; prefer digital communication	Visual communication; digital-first interactions	Tech-driven play and communication
Work Habits	Traditional work values; challenges with remote work	Work-life balance seekers; embrace remote work	Flexible work preferences; tech-savvy	Demand technology integration; gig economy participation	Future of work; lifelong learning
Learning Preferences	Prefer structured, in-person learning	Comfortable with hybrid learning	Online learning enthusiasts; flexible	Interactive and visual learning; self-directed	Tech-integrated learning; early tech literacy
Social Interactions	Face-to-face and phone calls	Mix of in-person and digital	Digital-first; use social media heavily	Online and visual communication	Likely to use digital tools for play and socialization
Mental Health Impact	Less directly affected	Moderate impact due to digital shift	Increased awareness and issues related to social media	Growing concerns with screen time and social media	Impact still developing, with early exposure to technology
Consumer Behavior	Traditional shopping; gradual shift to e-commerce	Early adopters of online banking and e-commerce	Prefer online shopping; focus on convenience	Instant gratification; rely on digital platforms	Future trends towards fully digital commerce
Cultural and Societal Impact	Adjusting to digital norms; digital divide awareness	Balance between analog and digital norms	Shifted cultural norms; influence of social media	Redefined social norms; emphasis on digital identity	Shaped by AI, VR, and digital immersion; evolving norms

Quantifying the impacts of digital technologies across generations can be challenging due to the qualitative nature of many of the impacts. However, we can attempt to assign a numerical scale from 1 to 5 to represent the degree of impact or adoption for each parameter across the generations, with 1 being the lowest impact/adoption and 5 being the highest.

Table 4. Impact analysis of different parameters with numerical scale

Parameter	Baby Boomers (1946-1964)	Generation X (1965-1980)	Millennials (1981-1996)	Generation Z (1997-2012)	Generation Alpha (2013-Present)
Technology Adoption	2	3	4	5	5
Communication Styles	2	3	4	5	5
Work Habits and Professional Impact	2	4	5	5	5
Learning Preferences	2	3	5	5	5
Social Interactions	2	3	4	5	5
Mental Health Impact	2	3	4	4	3
Consumer Behavior	2	4	5	5	5
Cultural and Social Impact	2	3	4	5	5

Figure 5. Graphical representation of Impact analysis of different parameters

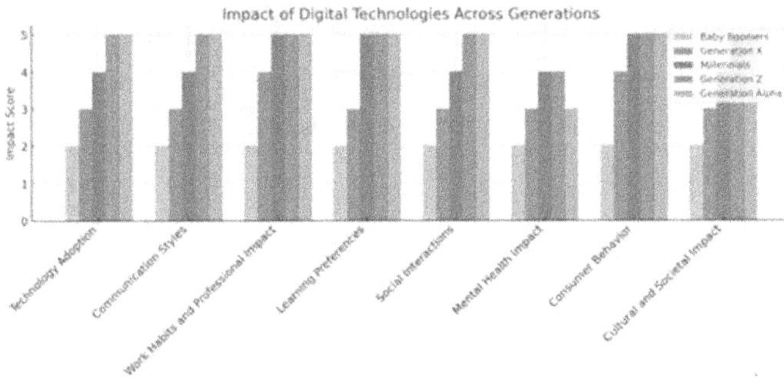

V. FUTURE SCOPE

1) **Personalized Learning and Skill Development:** As digital technologies advance, there will be an increasing number of individualized learning opportunities. Virtual reality simulations, AI-powered tutoring, and adaptive learning platforms can all customize education to meet the needs of each student.Micro-credentials, ongoing skill development, and online courses will all support lifelong learning.
2) **Health technology:** including telemedicine, have a bright future ahead of them. AI diagnostics, wearable technology, and remote monitoring will improve preventive healthcare. Patients will be able to consult with specialists anywhere in the world thanks to the continued advancements in telemedicine.
3) **Blockchain and Decentralization:** Blockchain technology has the power to completely transform a number of industries, such as supply chains, governance, and finance. Decentralized applications will increase transparency and remove middlemen, empowering users.
4) **Bias mitigation and ethical AI:** Scholars and decision-makers will concentrate on creating ethical AI frameworks. It will be essential to identify and reduce bias. Accountability and trust will increase with the use of Explainable AI (XAI).
5) **Sustainability and Smart Cities:** Digital technologies will change city life. Transportation, waste management, energy use, and public services will all be optimized in smart cities. Data analytics, renewable energy sources, and Internet of Things sensors will all be used in sustainability projects.
6) **Human-Computer Interaction:** Brain-computer interfaces, gesture recognition, and natural language processing will completely change how humans engage with technology. Immersion will be produced by augmented reality (AR) and virtual reality (VR).
7) **Cybersecurity and privacy:** As connectivity grows, so too will the threats to cybersecurity. It will be essential to make advances in encryption, zero-trust architecture, and secure communication channels. Technologies that improve privacy will give users more control over their data.

Future Solution

Figure 6. Future Implications of Digital Technologies Across the World

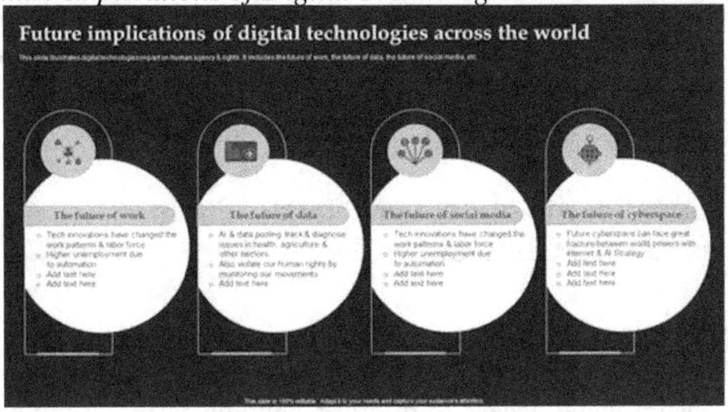

The picture "Future Implications of Digital Technologies Across the World" draws attention to how digital technologies may affect human rights and agency in the future. It focuses particularly on how work, data, social media, and cyberspace will evolve in the future.

The following are the image's main points:

1. **The Workplace of the Future:**

The labor force and work patterns have changed as a result of technological advancements. There's a chance that automation will raise unemployment.

2. **The Data of the Future:**

AI and data pooling can monitor and identify problems in a variety of industries, including agriculture, health, and others. Monitoring and collecting data may violate human rights and give rise to privacy issues.

3. **Social Media's Future:**

Technological advancements have affected the labor force and altered social media usage, much like they will affect the nature of work in the future. Social media platforms could also be impacted by automation.

4. **Cyberspace's Future:**

World powers may split apart in the future due to internet and artificial intelligence tactics. Conflicts and difficulties in preserving international cooperation and connectivity could result from this.

Ultimately, the picture highlights how important it is to give serious thought to how digital technologies may affect human rights, society, and international relations. It emphasizes how crucial it is to develop and govern these technologies responsibly in order to secure a bright future for humanity.

Future Solutions for the Impact of Digital Technologies Across Generations

1. Bridging the Digital Divide:
    - Access and Affordability: Governments and organizations should work to ensure equal access to digital technologies by providing affordable devices and internet services, particularly in underserved communities. Initiatives like public Wi-Fi hotspots and community tech centers can help bridge the gap between generations.
    - Digital Literacy Programs: Implementing digital literacy programs across all age groups can help individuals navigate the digital world confidently. For older generations, tailored workshops focusing on basic digital skills, online security, and safe internet practices can foster greater inclusion and confidence in using technology.
2. Regulatory Frameworks:
    - Inclusive Policymaking: Develop regulations that protect all generations by considering the varying levels of digital proficiency. This includes stronger data privacy laws, measures to combat misinformation, and protections against cyberbullying, ensuring a safer online environment for everyone.
    - Continuous Adaptation: Regulatory bodies need to stay agile and continuously adapt to emerging digital trends. Establishing international cooperation for standardizing digital regulations can help address the global nature of technology and its cross-border implications.
3. Fostering Innovation and Collaboration:
    - Cross-Generational Collaboration: Encourage collaboration between generations to foster innovation. Younger generations can offer fresh perspectives and digital skills, while older generations can contribute experience and strategic thinking. Mentorship programs and mixed-age team initiatives in workplaces can enhance mutual learning and innovation.

- Lifelong Learning and Upskilling: Create opportunities for continuous learning and upskilling to help all generations adapt to the evolving digital landscape. Online courses, certifications, and workshops can empower individuals to stay relevant in the digital economy, regardless of their age.

4. Enhancing Social Connectivity:
   - Intergenerational Platforms: Develop digital platforms and applications designed to foster intergenerational connections, such as family-oriented social networks or community forums that encourage interaction between different age groups.
   - Digital Etiquette Education: Promote digital etiquette and healthy online behaviors across generations. Educational campaigns and programs can raise awareness about responsible digital use, emphasizing respect, empathy, and privacy in online interactions.
5. Mental Health and Well-being:
   - Digital Wellness Tools: Introduce tools and resources that help manage digital consumption, such as screen time trackers, digital detox apps, and mental health support services. These tools can aid in mitigating issues like social media anxiety and information overload across all age groups.
   - Support Services: Expand access to online mental health services, offering counseling and support tailored to the needs of different generations. Providing resources for managing digital stress and promoting a healthy balance between online and offline activities can improve overall well-being.
6. Economic Opportunities and Adaptation:
   - Entrepreneurship and Remote Work: Encourage entrepreneurial ventures and remote work opportunities that utilize digital platforms, providing support and training for those interested in starting online businesses or freelancing. This can help older generations adapt to new economic models and provide more flexibility for younger workers.
   - Reskilling and Career Transition Programs: Develop initiatives to assist individuals in transitioning between careers, particularly for those in industries disrupted by digital transformation. This can include offering training in emerging fields like cybersecurity, data analysis, and digital marketing.

By addressing these areas, societies can create a more inclusive digital future that benefits all generations. Encouraging digital literacy, creating robust regulatory frameworks, fostering innovation through collaboration, promoting digital well-being, and ensuring economic adaptability are key to navigating the challenges and opportunities presented by digital technologies.

VI. CONCLUSION

In summary, the dynamic interplay between technology and generational experiences emphasizes the significance of flexibility, fairness, and cooperation. For people of all ages, lifelong learning and the ability to adjust to digital advancements are crucial, underscoring the significance of keeping up with technological advancements. It is our shared responsibility to close the digital divide by ensuring that all generations have equal access to digital resources, opportunities, and education. Furthermore, striking a balance between the advantages and drawbacks of digital technologies is essential, calling for cautious use and critical thought to address issues like cybersecurity and privacy. Last but not least, encouraging intergenerational collaboration can result in creative solutions by fusing the knowledge of more experienced generations with the technological know-how of younger ones to promote positive change in our increasingly digital world.

Digital technologies have negative impacts across generations. These include:

1. Digital Divide: Older generations often face limited access to digital technologies and a lack of digital skills, leading to social exclusion and difficulty in adapting to the digital economy.
2. Mental Health Issues: Younger generations face social media anxiety, cyberbullying, and information overload, while older adults can feel overwhelmed by the constant flow of digital information.
3. Privacy and Security Risks: Many users, especially older adults, are vulnerable to data privacy breaches and cybersecurity threats due to a lack of awareness about digital security.
4. Social Isolation: Increased reliance on digital communication can reduce face-to-face interactions, contributing to feelings of loneliness and intergenerational communication gaps.
5. Digital Addiction and Screen Time: Excessive use of digital devices can lead to addictive behaviors, reduced attention spans, and physical health issues like eye strain and sleep disturbances.
6. Economic Disruption: Automation and digitization can lead to job displacement, particularly for older workers, while the gig economy offers unstable income and job security issues.
7. Health and Well-being: Increased screen time and a sedentary lifestyle associated with digital technology use can lead to various physical health problems.

Digital technologies have numerous positive impacts across generations, including:

1. Enhanced Communication:
    - Global Connectivity: Digital platforms enable people of all ages to connect instantly with others around the world, fostering relationships and allowing for cultural exchange.
    - Intergenerational Communication: Technologies like video calls and social media help bridge the gap between generations, making it easier for families and friends to stay in touch regardless of distance.
2. Access to Information and Learning:
    - Educational Opportunities: Digital technologies provide access to a vast array of online educational resources, courses, and tutorials, supporting lifelong learning for all ages.
    - Easy Access to Information: The internet offers a wealth of information at the fingertips of users, enabling individuals to stay informed and make more informed decisions.
3. Economic Opportunities:
    - New Career Paths: The rise of the digital economy has created new career opportunities in fields such as digital marketing, software development, and e-commerce.
    - Entrepreneurship: Digital platforms have made it easier for individuals to start businesses, reach global markets, and participate in the gig economy, offering financial independence and flexibility.
4. Innovation and Creativity:
    - Creative Expression: Digital tools like graphic design software, music production apps, and video editing programs allow people to express their creativity and share it with a global audience.
    - Technological Advancements: Digital technologies drive innovation, leading to advancements in fields like healthcare, environmental science, and transportation, benefiting society as a whole.
5. Improved Quality of Life:
    - Convenience and Efficiency: Digital technologies streamline daily activities, such as online shopping, digital banking, and smart home devices, making life more convenient and efficient.
    - Healthcare and Well-being: Telemedicine, health monitoring apps, and online fitness programs have made healthcare more accessible and personalized, helping people of all ages maintain their health.
6. Social Engagement and Community Building:

- Online Communities: Social media and online forums provide platforms for people to connect based on shared interests, hobbies, or causes, fostering a sense of community and support.
- Civic Engagement: Digital technologies enable greater participation in civic activities, such as online petitions, virtual town halls, and awareness campaigns, empowering people to contribute to social change.

7. Work Flexibility and Remote Collaboration:
   - Remote Work: Digital technologies have made remote work possible, offering flexibility and enabling people to balance their professional and personal lives more effectively.
   - Collaboration Tools: Platforms like video conferencing, cloud storage, and project management software facilitate collaboration across geographies and generations, enhancing productivity and teamwork.

Digital technologies have profoundly influenced every generation, creating distinct experiences and challenges for each group. While older generations like Baby Boomers and Generation X have adapted to the digital shift, they often hold onto traditional values and practices. In contrast, Millennials and Generation Z have embraced digital technology as a fundamental part of their lives, driving innovation and reshaping cultural norms. The varied impacts of digital technology across generations highlight the need for a nuanced approach to addressing issues like the digital divide, regulatory challenges, and mental health concerns. It is crucial to foster intergenerational understanding and collaboration to leverage the strengths of each age group. By doing so, society can ensure that digital technologies enhance life experiences, promote inclusivity, and contribute to overall well-being, regardless of generational differences.

Digital technologies have profoundly impacted all generations, albeit in varying ways. Older generations have had to adapt to technological advancements, balancing traditional practices with new digital tools, while younger generations have seamlessly integrated these technologies into their daily lives. The CRISPE analysis reveals that digital technologies have not only reshaped communication and cultural dynamics but have also influenced innovation, regulatory frameworks, mental health, and economic structures. While digital technology offers numerous benefits, it also presents challenges such as the digital divide and the need for continual adaptation across age groups. Bridging these generational gaps through education, inclusivity, and thoughtful regulation is essential to ensuring that all individuals, regardless of age, can harness the full potential of digital innovations. Ultimately, digital technology has become a driving force in shaping modern society, and its continued evolution will further influence generational experiences in the years to come.

REFERENCES

Bennett, S., & Maton, K. (2010). Beyond the 'digital natives' debate: Towards a more nuanced understanding of students' technology experiences. *Journal of Computer Assisted Learning*, 26(5), 321–331. DOI: 10.1111/j.1365-2729.2010.00360.x

Bennett, S., Maton, K., & Kervin, L. (2008). The 'digital natives' debate: A critical review of the evidence. *British Journal of Educational Technology*, 39(5), 775–786. DOI: 10.1111/j.1467-8535.2007.00793.x

Correa, T., Straubhaar, J., Chen, W., & Spence, J. (2015). Brokering new technologies: The role of children in their parents' usage of the internet. *New Media & Society*, 17(4), 483–500. DOI: 10.1177/1461444813506975

Eynon, R., & Geniets, A. (2016). The digital skills paradox: How do digitally excluded youth develop skills to use the internet? *Learning, Media and Technology*, 41(3), 463–479. DOI: 10.1080/17439884.2014.1002845

Friemel, T. N. (2016). The digital divide has grown old: Determinants of a digital divide among seniors. *New Media & Society*, 18(2), 313–331. DOI: 10.1177/1461444814538648

Gomez, R. (2013). The Changing Field of Information and Communication Technology for Development (ICTD): From ICT to Digital Development. *The Electronic Journal on Information Systems in Developing Countries*, 59(1), 1–25.

Gujarkar, P., Lonkar, S., Jain, T., Nigal, S., & Patil, P. pallavi Deshpande, Ketki Kshirsagar., "IoT based Smart Attendance System," *2023 International Conference on Emerging Smart Computing and Informatics (ESCI)*, Pune, India, 2023, pp. 1-6, DOI: 10.1109/ESCI56872.2023.10099839

Hargittai, E. (2010). Digital Na(t)ives? Variation in Internet Skills and Uses among Members of the "Net Generation.". *Sociological Inquiry*, 80(1), 92–113. DOI: 10.1111/j.1475-682X.2009.00317.x

Helsper, E. J., & Eynon, R. (2010). Digital natives: Where is the evidence? *British Educational Research Journal*, 36(3), 503–520. DOI: 10.1080/01411920902989227

Horrigan, J. B. (2007). *A Typology of Information and Communication Technology Users*. Pew Research Center.

Jenkins, H., Ito, M., & Boyd, D. (2015). Participatory Culture in a Networked Era: A Conversation on Youth, Learning, Commerce, and Politics. *Polity*.

Jones, C., Ramanau, R., Cross, S., & Healing, G. (2010). Net generation or Digital Natives: Is there a distinct new generation entering university? *Computers & Education*, 54(3), 722–732. DOI: 10.1016/j.compedu.2009.09.022

Ketki, P. (2022). *Kshirsagar, Ashish Tathod, Rushikesh Dudhate, Ajay Yadav, Rudra Tarte, "Camera Calibration Using Robust Intrinsic and Extrinsic Parameters", Artificial Intelligence in Information and Communication Technologies, Healthcare and Education*. Chapman and Hall/CRC.

Kshirsagar, K. P. (2015). Key Frame Selection for One-Two Hand Gesture Recognition with HMM. *International Journal of Advanced Computer Research*, 5(19), 192.

Kshirsagar, K. P., & Doye, D. (2010, October). Object Based Key Frame Selection for Hand Gesture Recognition. In *2010 International Conference on Advances in Recent Technologies in Communication and Computing* (pp. 181-185). IEEE.

Kumbhar, K., & Kshirasagar, K. P. (2015). Comparative study of CCD & CMOS sensors for image processing. *International Journal of Innovative Research in Electrical, Electronics, Instrumentation and Control Engineering*, 3(12), 194–196. DOI: 10.17148/IJIREEICE.2015.31240

Kvavik, R. B., & Caruso, J. B. (2005). *ECAR Study of Students and Information Technology, 2005: Convenience, Connection, Control, and Learning. EDUCAUSE Center for Analysis and Research*. ECAR.

Li, Y., & Ranieri, M. (2010). Are 'digital natives' really digitally competent?—A study on Chinese teenagers. *British Journal of Educational Technology*, 41(6), 1029–1042. DOI: 10.1111/j.1467-8535.2009.01053.x

Madden, M. (2010). Older Adults and Social Media. *Pew Research Center*. Buckingham, D. (2007). Beyond Technology: Children's Learning in the Age of Digital Culture. *Polity*.

Meyers, E. M., Erickson, I., & Small, R. V. (2013). Digital literacy and informal learning environments: An introduction. *Learning, Media and Technology*, 38(4), 355–367. DOI: 10.1080/17439884.2013.783597

Ng, W. (2012). Can We Teach Digital Natives Digital Literacy? *Proceedings of the 21st Century Academic Forum Conference*, 28(3), 106-121. DOI: 10.1016/j.compedu.2012.04.016

Palfrey, J., & Gasser, U. (2008). Born Digital: Understanding the First Generation of Digital Natives.

Prensky, M. (2001). Digital Natives, Digital Immigrants. *On the Horizon*, 9(5), 1–6. DOI: 10.1108/10748120110424816

Rokade, U. S., Doye, D., & Kokare, M. (2009, March). Hand gesture recognition using object based key frame selection. In *2009 International Conference on Digital Image Processing* (pp. 288-291). IEEE.

Selwyn, N. (2004). Reconsidering political and popular understandings of the digital divide. *New Media & Society*, 6(3), 341–362. DOI: 10.1177/1461444804042519

Selwyn, N. (2009). The digital native – myth and reality. *Aslib Proceedings*, 61(4), 364–379. DOI: 10.1108/00012530910973776

Selwyn, N., & Facer, K. (2014). The sociology of education and digital technology: Past, present, and future. *Oxford Review of Education*, 40(4), 482–496. DOI: 10.1080/03054985.2014.933005

Selwyn, N., & Gorard, S. (2016). Students' use of digital technology in university: What are the implications for higher education policy and practice? *Higher Education Quarterly*, 70(3), 308–326.

Tapscott, D. (2008). Grown Up Digital: How the Net Generation is Changing Your World. *Proceedings of the IEEE International Conference on Digital Ecosystems and Technologies*, 1-5.

Van Deursen, A. J., & van Dijk, J. A. (2014). The digital divide shifts to differences in usage. *New Media & Society*, 16(3), 507–526. DOI: 10.1177/1461444813487959

van Dijk, J. A., & Hacker, K. L. (2003). The digital divide as a complex and dynamic phenomenon. *The Information Society*, 19(4), 315–326. DOI: 10.1080/01972240309487

Zhou, Y., & Hentschel, J. (2018). Digital Natives and Digital Immigrants in the Era of Digital Transformation: A Critical Review of Digital Media and Learning. [iJET]. *International Journal of Emerging Technologies in Learning*, 13(8), 29–37.

Chapter 2
Cloud-Based Professional Development

Rajeshri Rahul Itkarkar
AISSMS COE, India

Shruti Petkar
AISSMS COE, India

Roshani More
AISSMS COE, India

Arya Itkarkar
Isquare IT, India

ABSTRACT

In today's fast-paced, technology-driven world, continuous learning and professional development are crucial for staying competitive. This chapter explores the transformative potential of cloud-based professional development. With cloud computing technologies, professionals can access training resources anytime, anywhere, fostering a culture of lifelong learning. This chapter covers the benefits, key components, implementation strategies, challenges, and future trends of cloud-based professional development. Real-world case studies explore the opportunities for individuals and organizations.

DOI: 10.4018/979-8-3693-6705-6.ch002

INTRODUCTION

Cloud-based professional development refers to training and learning activities facilitated through cloud computing technologies. It allows professionals to access educational resources and participate in training programs online. In this era of rapid technological advancements, continuous learning is crucial. Cloud-based solutions offer a flexible, scalable, and cost-effective way to deliver professional development. Cloud-based professional development refers to the use of cloud computing technologies and platforms to deliver and enhance learning opportunities for professionals. Here's how it typically works and its benefits.

Accessibility: Professionals can access learning materials and resources anytime, anywhere, as long as they have an internet connection. This flexibility is particularly valuable for remote workers or those with busy schedules.

Scalability: Cloud-based platforms can scale resources up or down based on demand, allowing organizations to accommodate varying numbers of learners without significant infrastructure changes.

Collaboration: These platforms often facilitate collaboration among professionals through features like discussion forums, virtual classrooms, and group projects. This interaction enhances learning by allowing participants to share ideas and learn from each other.

1. **Content Management**: Learning materials, such as courses, videos, and documents, are stored in the cloud, making it easier to update content and ensure all participants have access to the latest information.
2. **Analytics and Tracking**: Cloud-based systems typically provide analytics on learner progress and engagement. This data can help organizations measure the effectiveness of their professional development programs and identify areas for improvement.
3. **Cost Efficiency**: By leveraging cloud infrastructure, organizations can reduce costs associated with physical space, IT maintenance, and software updates.

Examples of cloud-based professional development tools include learning management systems (LMS), virtual classrooms, and online training platforms. These tools are increasingly popular due to their flexibility, scalability, and ability to enhance learning experiences through technology.

1.1 BENEFITS OF CLOUD BASED PROFESSINAL DEVELOPMENT

1. **Accessibility and Flexibility**: Learners can access training materials at their convenience from anywhere, at any time. Individuals can learn at their own speed, ensuring better comprehension and retention of information. Professionals can learn at their own pace, which is ideal for balancing work, personal life, and education. Includes videos, interactive modules, live webinars etc. which provides different learning styles.
2. **Cost-effectiveness**: Reduces the need for physical training facilities, printed materials, and travel expenses. Allows organizations to scale training programs up or down based on need without significant additional costs.
3. **Diverse and up-to-date:** Access to a broad spectrum of courses and learning materials from various fields and industries. Content is frequently updated to reflect the latest industry trends, practices, and technologies.
4. **Individual Benefits**: Courses and materials can be customized to fit the specific needs and career goals of individual learners. Platforms can adjust the content and difficulty based on the learner's progress and performance.
5. **Enhanced Engagement and Interaction**: It includes quizzes, simulations, and interactive sessions that keep learners engaged. Additional features like discussion forums, group projects, and live chats foster collaboration and peer learning.
6. **Scalability**: Easily accommodates a growing number of users and content. Training can be delivered to different geographical locations.
7. **Tracking and Analytics**: Organizations can monitor employee progress, completion rates, and performance. Analytics can identify skills gaps, measure training effectiveness, and inform future training needs.
8. **Sustainability**: Reduces the need for physical materials and travel, contributing to a lower carbon footprint.

1.2 KEY COMPONENTS AND TOOLS OF CLOUD BASED PROFESSIONAL DEVELOPMENT

Key Components

1. **Learning Management Systems (LMS)**: Enables the creation, management, and delivery of online courses. Manages learners, instructors, and administrators, including roles and permissions. Monitors learner progress, completion

rates, and generates performance reports. Platforms like Moodle, Canvas, and Blackboard for managing and delivering e-learning.

2. **Assessment and Evaluation**: Automated and manual assessments to evaluate learner comprehension. Practical exercises to apply knowledge. Provides timely feedback to learners for improvement.
3. **Collaboration and Communication**: Facilitates peer-to-peer and instructor-to-learner communication through discussion forums. Group projects encourages collaborative learning experience. Live Webinars and Virtual Classrooms improves real-time interaction with instructors and peers.
4. **Personalization and Customization:** Adaptive Learning contents that adjusts based on learner's performance and preferences. Customised training programs based on individual or organizational needs.
5. **Integration and Interoperability**: Integration with other tools and platforms such as HR systems, customer relation management system and productivity tools. **APIs and Plugins**: Extends functionality and connectivity with external applications.

Essential Tools

1. **Course Creation Tools**: Software like Articulate 360, Adobe Captivate, and iSpring Suite for are used for creating interactive content. Tools like Camtasia and Screencast-O-Matic for recording and editing videos.
2. **Communication and Collaboration Tools**: Platforms like Zoom, Microsoft Teams, and Google Meet for live sessions and video conferencing. Slack, Microsoft Teams, and other messaging apps for real-time communication for chatting and messaging.
3. **Assessment Tools**: Tools like Kahoot, Google Forms, and Survey-Monkey are used for assessments and surveys and services like ProctorU and Examity for secure online exams.
4. **Analysis Tool:** LMS Platforms like Moodle, Blackboard, and Canvas are use for analytics and tools like Tableau and Power BI for advanced data analysis and visualization.
5. **E-learning resources:** Access to pre-built courses through platforms like Coursera, Udemy, LinkedIn Learning, and edX. For additional learning access to digital libraries and publications is made available.
6. **Cloud Storage and Sharing**: Platforms like Google Drive, Dropbox, and OneDrive are usually used for storing and sharing course materials.
7. **Project Management Tools**: Tools like Asana, Trello, and Monday.com for organizing and tracking professional development projects.

These components and tools collectively enhance the effectiveness of cloud-based professional development by providing a comprehensive, flexible, and engaging learning environment.

1.3 IMPLEMENTATION STRATEGIES

Implementing cloud-based professional development requires thoughtful planning and execution. Some effective strategies needed for the same.

1. **Needs Assessment and Goal Setting:**To determine the skills and knowledge gaps within the organization surveys, interviews, and assessments are required to conduct. Also to ensure alignment with organizational goals, specific, measurable objectives are required to be defined for the professional development program.
2. **Platform Selection**: Based on features, usability, and cost different cloud-based learning platforms (e.g., Moodle, Canvas, Coursera) can be used for assessment. These platforms need to be compatible with existing tools and systems such as HR software, CRM, and productivity tools.
3. **Content Development and Curation:** To develop high quality, relevant and engaging content. This includes videos, webinar and interactive module. Collaborate with experts to create or curate content that meets the professional development goals.
4. **Engagement and Interactivity:** Use of interactive elements such as quizzes, simulations, and interactive videos to enhance engagement. Implement discussion forums, group projects, and live webinars to encourage and facilitate interaction among learners.
5. **Personalization and Adaptation**: Create personalized learning paths based on individual learner profiles and career goals. **Utilize Adaptive Learning** tools such as AI-driven tools that adapt content delivery based on learner performance and preferences.
6. Training and Support: Provide Onboarding training sessions and resources to help employees navigate the new platform and understand how to use it effectively. Ensure continuous technical and instructional support through help desks, FAQs, and live support channels.
7. **Assessment and Feedback:** For regular assessments, implementation of tools like Kahoot!, Google Forms etc for continuous assessments and feedback collection. To measure performance, track progress using built-in analytics to measure engagement, completion rates, and knowledge retention.

8. **Incentives and Recognition:** To make use of elements such as badges, certificates, and leaderboards to motivate learners. Acknowledge and reward employees who achieve significant milestones or demonstrate exceptional performance.
9. **Continuous Improvement:** Regularly collect feedback from participants to identify areas for improvement. Updating the contents by regularly updating materials and incorporating the latest industry trends and best practices.
10. **Evaluation and Reporting:** Use of data analytics tools to evaluate the effectiveness of the training program against the set goals and measure the outcomes. Share insights with stakeholders and use the findings to revise and improve the program continuously.

By following these strategies, organizations can effectively implement cloud-based professional development programs that are engaging, scalable, and aligned with their overall goals.

1.4 CHALLENGES AND FUTURE TRENDS

- **Digital Literacy**: Provide training on using digital tools and platforms.
- **Maintaining Engagement**: Use interactive and multimedia content to keep learners interested.
- **Data Security and Privacy**: Implement robust security measures and ensure compliance with regulations.
- **Technical Issues and Support**: Offer technical support and resources to troubleshoot issues.

Future Trends

- **AI and Machine Learning**: Personalized learning experiences based on individual progress and preferences.
- **Virtual and Augmented Reality**: Immersive learning experiences for hands-on training.
- **Gaming**: Using game elements to enhance engagement and motivation.

1.5 OPPORTUNITIES

- **For Individuals**:
  - o **Skill Enhancement**: Access to a wide range of courses and certifications to improve skills.

- **Career Growth**: Opportunities for career advancement through continuous learning.
- **Lifelong Learning**: Encourages a culture of lifelong learning and self-improvement.

- **For Organizations**:
  - **Improved Employee Performance**: Better trained employees can lead to increased productivity and innovation.
  - **Cost Savings**: Reduces the need for physical training facilities and travel expenses.
  - **Competitive Advantage**: Staying updated with the latest industry trends and skills can provide a competitive edge.
- **For Educators and Trainers**:
  - **Broader Reach**: Ability to reach a global audience.
- **Innovative Teaching Methods**: Use of advanced technologies and interactive content to enhance teaching effectiveness.
- **Real-Time Communication**: Channels like Slack, Microsoft Teams, or Discord provide instant communication capabilities, allowing for quick dissemination of information, discussions, and feedback related to professional development.
- **Focused Discussions**: Channels can be dedicated to specific topics or skills, creating focused environments where professionals can engage in discussions, ask questions, and share resources related to their development needs.
- **Peer Learning**: Channels facilitate peer-to-peer learning where professionals can learn from each other's experiences, insights, and expertise. This informal learning can be as valuable as formal training programs.
- **Flexibility**: Professionals can access channel-based development opportunities at their convenience, fitting learning around their schedules. Channels also support asynchronous communication, accommodating learners in different time zones or with varying availability.
- **Integration with Tools**: Many channel-based platforms integrate with other productivity tools and learning management systems (LMS), enhancing the learning experience by incorporating relevant content, quizzes, or assignments directly into the channel interface.
- **Engagement and Participation**: Channels often have features like polls, surveys, and reactions that encourage engagement and participation. This interactive element can boost motivation and retention of learning content.

Examples of channel-based professional development include creating dedicated Slack channels for specific skills, using Discord servers for industry-specific discussions and learning groups, or leveraging Microsoft Teams channels for team-based learning initiatives.

1.6 CASE STUDIES ON CLOUD BASED PROFESSIONAL DEVELOPMENT

IBM's Digital Learning Platform

IBM transformed its employee training to a cloud-based platform called Your Learning, integrating AI to personalize learning experiences. For implementation IBM used a cloud-based learning management system (LMS) integrated with Watson AI. The AI-powered platform recommended courses based on employees' roles, career aspirations, and past learning activities. A mix of internal and external content providers, including Coursera and edX, which offered a wide range of topics. The outcome of this training facility for employee, the outcome increased in terms of engagement, scalability, and employee growth for IBM. The personalised approach significantly increased course completion rate. The cloud platform allowed IBM to scale training globally with consistent quality. Employees reported improved skills and greater satisfaction with their professional growth opportunities.

PwC's (Pride world city) Digital Fitness App

PwC launched a cloud-based app called the Digital Fitness App (DFA) to upskill its workforce in digital skills. The DFA was developed as a mobile-first application hosted on the cloud. The app assessed users' current digital skills and created a personalized learning paths. **They** incorporated gamification elements to enhance engagement, including badges and leaderboards. The outcome of DFA gradually increased the adoption of the App globally. Employees demonstrated significant improvement in key digital skills. The enhanced skills contributed to improved service delivery and client satisfaction. This made high impact on PwC's business

Unilever's Degreed Platform

Unilever adopted Degreed, a cloud-based learning platform, to support continuous learning and development for its employees. For implementation it started with integration of various learning resources into a single platform. It combined internal training materials with external resources from MOOCs, articles, and videos. Employees were encouraged to take ownership of their learning journeys with Degreed providing personalized recommendations. The outcome of this implementation increased learning engagement due to the easy usage of platform. Second outcome is the employees gained a broad array of new skills, enhancing their productivity and innovation capabilities. The cloud-based nature of degreed allowed Unilever to offer consistent learning opportunities to employees to reach globally.

AT&T's Nanodegree Programs

AT&T partnered with Udacity to offer cloud-based nanodegree programs to help employees develop in-demand technical skills. They collaborated with Udacity to create custom nanodegree programs tailored to AT&T's needs. Provided mentorship and support to help employees succeed in their learning paths. This initiative contributed to higher employee retention and job satisfaction. Many employees used their new skills to advance within the company to promote towards new roles. Employees who completed nanodegrees reported significant improvements in their technical skills.

These case studies demonstrate the potential of cloud-based professional development to enhance employee skills, engagement, and overall organizational performance.

SUMMARY

Cloud-based professional development is a transformative approach that makes use of power of cloud computing to deliver training and learning opportunities to professionals. This method provides unparalleled accessibility, flexibility, and scalability, enabling individuals and organizations to stay competitive in a rapidly changing world. By integrating cloud-based solutions, companies can offer continuous, personalized, and engaging learning experiences that cater to the diverse needs and preferences of their workforce.

Key benefits of cloud-based professional development include cost-effectiveness, diverse and up-to-date content, enhanced engagement, and the ability to track and analyse learner progress. Essential components and tools such as learning management systems (LMS), communication platforms, assessment tools, and analytics play a crucial role in delivering effective cloud-based training programs.

Successful implementation strategies involve conducting needs assessments, setting clear goals, selecting appropriate platforms, developing high-quality content, fostering interactivity, personalizing learning paths, providing continuous support, and regularly assessing and improving the programs.

Despite the numerous advantages, challenges such as digital literacy, maintaining engagement, data security, and technical support need to be addressed. Future trends in cloud-based professional development include the use of AI and machine learning for personalized learning, immersive experiences through virtual and augmented reality, and gamification to enhance engagement.

Real-world case studies from organizations like IBM, PwC, Unilever, and AT&T illustrate the successful application of cloud-based professional development, highlighting significant improvements in employee skills, engagement, and organizational performance. These examples demonstrate the potential of cloud-based solutions to create a culture of lifelong learning and continuous professional growth, ultimately leading to increased productivity, innovation, and competitive advantage for both individuals and organizations.

REFERENCES

AT&T. (2018). Nanodegree Programs with Udacity: Building the Future Workforce. AT&T Innovation. Retrieved from att.com

Brandon Hall Group. (2019). The Business Impact of Next-Generation Learning Technologies. Brandon Hall Group. Retrieved from brandonhall.com

Coursera. (2020). Corporate Training Solutions: Enhancing Employee Skills with Cloud-Based Learning. Coursera for Business. Retrieved from coursera.org

Degreed. (2019). Creating a Learning Ecosystem: The Role of Cloud-Based Platforms. Degreed White Papers. Retrieved from degreed.com

Forbes. (2021). The Future of Corporate Training: Cloud-Based Solutions. Forbes Business Insights. Retrieved from forbes.com

Gartner. (2021). Market Guide for Corporate Learning Suites. Gartner Research. Retrieved from gartner.com

Hewlett-Packard Enterprise. (2020). Leveraging Cloud-Based Learning Platforms for Employee Development. HPE Insights. Retrieved from hpe.com

IBM. (2020). IBM's Your Learning Platform: Using AI to Empower Continuous Learning. IBM Case Studies. Retrieved from ibm.com

LinkedIn Learning. (2019). Engaging the Modern Learner: Strategies for Cloud-Based Professional Development. LinkedIn Learning Insights. Retrieved from linkedin.com

Learning Solutions Magazine. (2020). The Advantages of Cloud-Based Professional Development. Learning Solutions. Retrieved from learningsolutionsmag.com

Moodle. (2021). Moodle LMS: Empowering Organizations with Cloud-Based Learning. Moodle Case Studies. Retrieved from moodle.com

PwC. (2019). Digital Fitness App: Empowering Employees in the Digital Age. PwC Insights. Retrieved from pwc.com

TechRepublic. (2021). How Cloud Computing is Transforming Employee Training. TechRepublic Insights. Retrieved from techrepublic.com

Training Industry. (2020). Cloud-Based Learning Solutions: Trends and Best Practices. Training Industry Reports. Retrieved from trainingindustry.com

Unilever. (2020). Degreed Platform: Driving Continuous Learning and Development. Unilever Case Studies. Retrieved from unilever.com

REFERENCES

Chapter 3
Enabling Personalized Learning and Adaptive Systems Through Strategic Management: Cloud Integration in Education

J. Arockia Venice
https://orcid.org/0000-0002-1324-136X
DMI-St. Eugene University, Zambia

R. Vettriselvan
Academy of Maritime Education and Training, India

Deepa Rajesh
https://orcid.org/0009-0008-9743-4791
Academy of Maritime Education and Training, India

N. V. Suresh
https://orcid.org/0000-0002-0393-6037
ASET College of Science and Technology, India

P. Abirami
MNM Jain Engineering College, India

ABSTRACT

The integration of cloud technology is transforming the educational landscape by facilitating personalized learning and adaptive systems. This chapter examines successful case studies showcasing the impact of cloud-based solutions, including

DOI: 10.4018/979-8-3693-6705-6.ch003

Learning Management Systems (LMS), AI-driven analytics, and collaborative tools on educational outcomes. Notable examples include Khan Academy's extensive resource offerings, DreamBox Learning's adaptive learning engine, Purdue University's use of predictive analytics, and the global learning platform developed by Minerva Schools. While challenges such as data privacy concerns and the digital divide persist, these initiatives highlight how cloud technology can create customized learning experiences and equip educators with valuable insights. Looking ahead, emerging trends in artificial intelligence, virtual reality, global collaboration, and blockchain technology are poised to further enhance personalized and inclusive educational practices.

INTRODUCTION

In recent years, the integration of cloud technology has transformed education globally, modernizing traditional teaching methods and enhancing personalized learning and adaptive educational systems. Cloud computing, characterized by its scalable infrastructure and flexible capabilities, has become essential for modern educational environments, enabling institutions to provide innovative, accessible learning experiences tailored to diverse student needs (Adedoja & Olatunji, 2020; Almohammadi et al., 2022). This chapter explores the profound impact of cloud integration on education, focusing on key components driving this transformation: Learning Management Systems (LMS), advanced data analytics, artificial intelligence (AI), and collaborative tools. LMS platforms represent a significant advancement due to their cloud-based nature, which allows seamless access to educational materials from anywhere, fostering engagement regardless of physical location. This flexibility has been particularly beneficial during the COVID-19 pandemic, making remote learning a necessity (Dawson et al., 2020). Additionally, LMS centralizes course management, content delivery, and communication between students and educators, enhancing the overall learning experience. Advanced data analytics plays a critical role in cloud integration, enabling educators to collect and analyze large volumes of data on student performance and learning patterns. Predictive analytics helps identify at-risk students, allowing for timely interventions before minor issues escalate. For instance, Purdue University's Course Signals project utilizes data analytics to support at-risk students, illustrating the power of proactive educational strategies enabled by cloud technology. AI further revolutionizes education by providing personalized learning experiences that adapt to individual student needs. Tools like DreamBox Learning use AI algorithms to customize math lessons according to each student's skill level and learning pace, ensuring that no student is left behind. This adaptive approach engages learners more effectively and transforms traditional education models (Gikandi et al., 2020). The chapter also highlights the importance of collaborative tools in enhancing educational experiences. Cloud-based collaboration platforms allow real-time interaction between students and educators across geographic boundaries. Minerva Schools at KGI exemplifies this by utilizing a cloud platform that facilitates interactive seminars and global project collaboration, fostering a sense of community and global citizenship among students. Despite the substantial benefits of cloud integration, challenges remain. Data privacy is a significant concern, as educational institutions must safeguard sensitive information and comply with data protection regulations. Furthermore, digital equity is crucial; the shift to cloud-based education assumes access to reliable internet and devices, which is not universal. Addressing this digital divide is essential to ensure all students benefit from technological advancements. Infrastructure scalability poses another challenge. As institutions increasingly rely on cloud services, they must invest in robust cloud solutions that can support growing demands, necessitating careful planning. Overcoming these challenges requires collaboration among educators, policymakers, and technology providers to implement effective strategies. Looking ahead, the chapter discusses future trends in cloud technology, including advancements in AI, virtual reality (VR), augmented reality (AR), and blockchain technology, which promise to further revolutionize education. AI will likely become more integral to personalized learning, offering increasingly sophisticated educational experiences. VR and AR technologies can create immersive learning environments that transcend traditional classroom boundaries, providing hands-on, experiential learning opportunities. Blockchain could secure credential verification, offering a transparent method to validate academic achievements. By examining the intersection of cloud technology and education through theoretical and practical lenses, this chapter aims to provide insights and guidance for educators, policymakers, and stakeholders. As cloud technology continues to evolve, staying informed about its implications for education is crucial. This chapter serves as a resource for navigating the dynamic landscape of modern education and harnessing cloud technology's power to create inclusive, effective, and innovative educational environments.

SCOPE AND OBJECTIVES OF THE CHAPTER

Scope

This chapter explores the transformative impact of cloud technology on the field of education, focusing on its integration into educational systems and its implications for learning, teaching, and institutional management. The chapter provides a comprehensive overview of current applications of cloud technologies in education, including Learning Management Systems (LMS), data analytics, Artificial Intelligence (AI), Virtual Reality (VR), and Augmented Reality (AR). It examines case studies of institutions that have successfully implemented these technologies, such as Khan Academy, DreamBox Learning, Purdue University, and Minerva Schools at KGI. The chapter also addresses the challenges associated with cloud integration, including issues of data privacy, digital equity, and infrastructure scalability. It highlights the need for continuous innovation and adaptation in the face of these challenges. Furthermore, the chapter outlines areas for future research to advance the field and address emerging needs. The discussion includes the potential of blockchain technology, the importance of teacher training and professional development, and the role of longitudinal studies in understanding the long-term effects of cloud-based education.

Objectives

- To Examine Current Applications of Cloud Technology in Education:

    i. Provide an overview of how cloud technologies are currently being utilized in educational settings.
    ii. Analyze case studies of institutions that have effectively integrated cloud-based solutions to enhance learning experiences and operational efficiency.

- To Identify and Discuss Challenges in Cloud Integration:

    i. Investigate key issues related to data privacy, digital equity, and infrastructure scalability that impact the effective deployment of cloud technologies in education.
    ii. Explore strategies for overcoming these challenges to ensure secure and equitable access to cloud-based educational resources.

- To Explore Emerging Technologies and Their Potential Impact:

    i. Assess the role of advanced technologies such as AI, VR, AR, and blockchain in shaping the future of education.
    ii. Evaluate the pedagogical effectiveness, cost-efficiency, and scalability of these technologies in educational contexts.

- To Highlight the Importance of Teacher Training and Professional Development:

i. Examine the current state of professional development programs for educators in relation to cloud-based technologies.
ii. Identify best practices and effective methods for equipping teachers with the skills needed to integrate and utilize these technologies effectively.

- To Outline Areas for Future Research:

i. Define key areas for future research, including data privacy and security, digital equity and access, personalization and adaptive learning, and the application of emerging technologies.
ii. Provide recommendations for research directions that could contribute to the advancement and refinement of cloud-based educational solutions.

- To Provide a Comprehensive Overview of Longitudinal Studies on Educational Outcomes:

i. Discuss the significance of longitudinal studies in assessing the long-term impact of cloud integration on academic performance, career readiness, and personal development.
ii. Explore how these studies can inform institutional strategies and enhance the effectiveness of cloud-based education.

By addressing these objectives, the chapter aims to offer a thorough understanding of the current state of cloud technology in education, the challenges and opportunities it presents, and the future directions for research and development in this rapidly evolving field.

KEY COMPONENTS OF CLOUD BASED EDUCATIONAL SYSTEMS

Cloud-based educational systems have fundamentally transformed the delivery and experience of education, integrating key components that enhance traditional learning environments. Central to this evolution are Learning Management Systems (LMS) like Moodle and Canvas, which serve as essential tools for modern educators. These platforms offer a centralized digital space for content delivery, assessment, and student management, allowing seamless integration of multimedia resources, discussion forums, and interactive assignments. This integration enhances student engagement and fosters collaboration among students and teachers, creating a more dynamic learning atmosphere (Adedoja & Olatunji, 2020). One of the primary advantages of cloud-based LMS platforms is their flexibility and accessibility. Students can access course materials, submit assignments, and engage in discussions from anywhere with an internet connection. This is particularly beneficial for non-traditional students, such as working professionals or those in remote areas, who may struggle to attend in-person classes. Moreover, the digital nature of these systems enables educators to easily update course content, ensuring students have access to the most relevant and current information. Beyond content delivery, cloud-based educational systems harness Data Analytics and Artificial Intelligence (AI) to personalize learning experiences. AI algorithms analyze student data to identify learning patterns, preferences, and areas of difficulty, allowing for real-time adaptation of instructional strategies. This personalized approach enhances engagement and supports educators in making data-driven decisions to improve learning outcomes (Almohammadi et al., 2022). For instance, AI can identify students struggling with specific concepts, enabling timely interventions such as additional resources or one-on-one tutoring. Collaborative tools are another crucial component of cloud-based educational systems, promoting communication and teamwork among students. Features like video conferencing, shared documents, and virtual classrooms facilitate collaboration on projects, regardless of geographic location. This connectivity was particularly vital during the COVID-19 pandemic, showcasing the resilience of cloud-based systems. Collaborative tools also encourage peer learning, where students exchange knowledge and feedback, fostering active participation, critical thinking, and communication skills essential for both academic and professional success. Together, these components LMS, Data Analytics, AI, and Collaborative Tools create a dynamic educational ecosystem that is adaptive and scalable, accommodating diverse learning environments and student populations. This scalability allows institutions to expand their offerings and reach broader audiences without the constraints of physical infrastructure. Additionally, cloud-based educational systems provide significant cost-effectiveness and resource management benefits. By migrating to the cloud, institutions can reduce on-site IT costs, reallocating resources more efficiently. Subscription-based models offer flexibility for institutions to scale services based on current needs and budgets. However, the integration of cloud-based educational systems also presents challenges, including data privacy, security, and the digital divide. Institutions must implement robust security measures to protect sensitive student data and comply with regulations such as GDPR and FERPA. Efforts to bridge the digital divide are essential to ensure all students have equitable access to these educational tools. In summary, cloud-based educational systems are reshaping education by integrating LMS, Data Analytics, AI, and Collaborative Tools. These systems provide flexible, scalable, and personalized learning environments that enhance student engagement and prepare them for the digital world. As educational institutions increasingly adopt these technologies, the potential for innovation and improvement in education remains vast, paving the way for new opportunities in teaching, learning, and collaboration in the 21st century.

Learning Management Systems (LMS)

Learning Management Systems (LMS) have become integral to cloud-based educational environments, significantly enhancing the digital classroom. Platforms like Moodle and Canvas streamline the management, delivery, and assessment of educational content, making them essential tools for modern institutions (Adedoja & Olatunji, 2020). Their cloud integration allows for centralized access to resources, ensuring that students and educators can retrieve course materials, assignments, and collaborative tools anytime, anywhere, thus supporting both traditional and remote learning. A key advantage of LMS platforms is their ability to provide data-driven insights into student engagement and performance. Integrated analytics tools track student interactions, generating reports that help instructors identify learning trends and assess instructional effectiveness. This capability enables proactive interventions, allowing educators to tailor their teaching strategies to meet individual student needs and optimize the learning environment (Adedoja & Olatunji, 2020). Additionally, LMS platforms foster collaboration through features such as virtual classrooms, discussion forums, and group projects. These tools promote active engagement and peer interaction, essential for pedagogical approaches like blended and flipped classrooms. Virtual classrooms facilitate real-time discussions and lectures, maintaining a sense of community in online settings (Dawson et al., 2020). Asynchronous discussion forums allow students to collaborate at their own pace, accommodating various learning styles and schedules. Moreover, LMS platforms support personalized learning pathways. Adaptive learning technologies adjust course content and activities based on real-time performance data, enhancing student motivation and improving outcomes. For example, students struggling with specific concepts may receive additional resources, while advanced learners are challenged with more complex material, ensuring that each student can progress at their own pace (Adedoja & Olatunji, 2020). Beyond enhancing the student experience, LMS platforms also streamline administrative processes such as grading, attendance tracking, and communication, allowing educators to focus more on teaching. Automated notifications keep students informed about deadlines, contributing to a more effective educational process. The integration of LMS platforms into cloud-based education optimizes instructional delivery and fosters collaboration while supporting personalized learning experiences. As educational technology evolves, the role of LMS platforms will likely expand, incorporating emerging technologies to create even more immersive learning environments. Ultimately, LMS systems are central to developing a dynamic, responsive, and student-centered educational landscape, enhancing learning outcomes and preparing students for the demands of the digital age.

Data Analytics and Artificial Intelligence (AI)

Incorporating data analytics and Artificial Intelligence (AI) into cloud-based educational systems marks a transformative advancement in modern education. These technologies leverage extensive student data to provide real-time insights into performance and behavior, enabling a personalized approach to learning that enhances adaptive experiences. AI-driven platforms such as Smart Sparrow and Knewton illustrate how algorithms can adjust learning pathways based on individual student needs, optimizing content delivery to maximize comprehension and engagement (Almohammadi et al., 2022). One of the key benefits of AI integration is the ability to personalize learning experiences at a granular level. Continuous data analysis ensures that students receive targeted support aligned with their current understanding, avoiding the pitfalls of overwhelming or disengaging content. This personalized approach fosters a more effective learning process and improves retention rates by providing timely feedback that helps students learn from mistakes immediately. Such continuous feedback reinforces learning and builds student confidence. Predictive analytics plays a crucial role in identifying at-risk students before they encounter significant challenges. By analyzing various data points academic performance, attendance, and engagement—predictive models can forecast potential obstacles. Institutions like Arizona State University have effectively used these models to implement early interventions, such as tutoring and customized learning plans, significantly boosting retention rates and academic success (Almohammadi et al., 2022). AI-enhanced educational systems also create more interactive learning environments. They offer personalized content recommendations, simulate real-world scenarios, and provide virtual tutors that assist in real-time. For instance, AI tutors can offer instant feedback on assignments and supplemental resources tailored to individual needs, making learning more immersive and relevant. Beyond individual learning, AI has the potential to revolutionize teaching methodologies. By providing educators with detailed analytics on student performance, AI tools help identify effective teaching strategies and areas needing support. This data-driven approach allows for informed decisions in instructional design, ultimately improving educational outcomes. Case studies from institutions like Georgia State University highlight significant improvements in retention and graduation rates through targeted support for at-risk students, achieving a graduation rate increase of over 20% in a decade. As AI evolves with advancements in machine learning and natural language processing, the potential for personalized learning and educational equity continues to expand. By harnessing these technologies, educators can tailor instruction, predict academic challenges, and foster inclusive educational environments. This paradigm shift not only enhances individual educational outcomes but also democratizes access to high-quality education, ensuring all learners can thrive in an increasingly digital world.

Collaborative Tools and Virtual Learning Environments

Cloud-based collaborative tools and virtual learning environments are revolutionizing modern education, enhancing experiences by transcending geographical boundaries and facilitating interactive learning opportunities. As the world becomes more interconnected, these technologies have transformed traditional classroom dynamics, allowing real-time collaboration among students and educators, regardless of location. Platforms like Google Workspace for Education and Microsoft Teams exemplify this integration, offering features such as document sharing, video conferencing, and collaborative editing that actively engage participants in the learning process (Dawson et al., 2020). Google Workspace enables simultaneous work on shared documents, fostering teamwork and problem-solving, while Microsoft Teams combines communication and collaboration in a single platform, making it easier for students to stay connected and engaged (Dawson et al., 2020). This real-time interaction encourages students to take an active role in their education, leading to deeper understanding and better retention of material. Virtual learning environments, such as Second Life and Unity Learn, provide immersive experiences particularly valuable in fields like engineering, medicine, and the sciences. These platforms allow students to explore digital laboratories, participate in realistic scenarios, and manipulate models, gaining practical skills in a safe setting. For example, medical students can practice surgical procedures in virtual operating rooms, while engineering students can design and test structures without the limitations of physical resources (Dawson et al., 2020). Such experiential learning enhances technical skills and builds confidence, enabling students to learn from mistakes without real-world risks. Additionally, these technologies support personalized learning through adaptive features that adjust tasks based on individual proficiency levels. AI algorithms analyze student interactions and performance to recommend tailored learning pathways, ensuring that support aligns with specific needs and goals (Almohammadi et al., 2022). Institutions like Stanford University and MIT have successfully integrated virtual labs and interactive simulations, leading to increased motivation, improved comprehension, and higher retention rates among students (Dawson et al., 2020). By incorporating cloud-based collaborative tools and virtual learning environments, educational institutions can create inclusive, engaging, and effective learning experiences that prepare students for 21st-century challenges. These technologies enhance traditional teaching methods while fostering innovative pedagogical approaches, promoting a culture of continuous learning and collaboration. As education evolves alongside technological advancements, the role of these tools will likely expand, offering new opportunities to enhance learning and equip students with essential skills for a complex and connected world. The integration of collaborative tools and virtual environments is transforming the educational landscape, breaking down barriers to access, and tailoring learning to individual needs. This evolution paves the way for a more equitable and effective educational system, ensuring that learning is truly without limits.

CASE STUDIES AND EXAMPLES

Khan Academy: Democratizing Education Through Scalable Cloud Solutions

Khan Academy stands as a pioneering example of how cloud technology can democratize education by providing free, accessible, and high-quality learning resources to students worldwide. Leveraging cloud infrastructure, Khan Academy delivers a vast array of educational content, including video tutorials, interactive exercises, and personalized learning dashboards. This scalable model ensures that students, regardless of their geographic location or socio-economic background, have access to top-notch educational resources (Gikandi et al., 2020). The cloud-based platform of Khan Academy utilizes data analytics to personalize learning experiences. By tracking student progress and performance, the platform adapts the content to meet individual learning needs, providing targeted support and remediation where necessary. This personalized approach has been instrumental in helping students grasp complex concepts at their own pace, leading to improved learning outcomes and increased retention rates (Gikandi et al., 2020).

DreamBox Learning: Adaptive Learning for K-8 Mathematics

DreamBox Learning exemplifies the integration of AI and adaptive learning technologies in cloud-based educational systems. Designed for K-8 mathematics, DreamBox's platform uses real-time data analytics to adjust the difficulty and sequence of lessons based on each student's performance. This adaptive approach ensures that students receive instruction tailored to their unique learning styles and proficiency levels, fostering a deeper understanding of mathematical concepts (Gikandi et al., 2020). By leveraging cloud technology, DreamBox Learning provides educators with actionable insights into student progress, enabling timely interventions and personalized support. The platform's engaging and interactive lessons have been shown to significantly improve students' mathematical skills and confidence, demonstrating the effectiveness of adaptive learning in enhancing educational outcomes (Gikandi et al., 2020).

Purdue University: Course Signals and Predictive Analytics

Purdue University's Course Signals project illustrates the powerful role of predictive analytics in identifying at-risk students and improving retention rates. The cloud-based system analyzes various data points, including academic performance, engagement metrics, and demographic information, to predict students' likelihood of success in their courses. By providing early alerts to both students and instructors, Course Signals enables timely interventions, such as additional tutoring or personalized study plans, to support students in overcoming academic challenges (Dawson et al., 2020). The success of Course Signals in enhancing student retention and academic performance highlights the potential of predictive analytics in transforming educational practices. By leveraging data-driven insights, educational institutions can proactively address students' needs, fostering a supportive and inclusive learning environment (Dawson et al., 2020).

Minerva Schools at KGI: Global Interactive Learning Experiences

Minerva Schools at KGI offers a compelling example of how cloud-based platforms can facilitate global, interactive learning experiences. Minerva's innovative curriculum combines online coursework with immersive real-world experiences, enabled by a cloud-based learning platform that supports synchronous and asynchronous interactions among students and faculty worldwide. The platform's interactive seminars, collaborative projects, and global field trips provide students with a rich, experiential education that transcends traditional classroom boundaries (Gikandi et al., 2020). By leveraging cloud technology, Minerva Schools create a dynamic and inclusive learning environment that prepares students for the complexities of the globalized world. The institution's emphasis on critical thinking, problem-solving, and cross-cultural communication underscores the transformative potential of cloud-based education in fostering holistic and adaptable learners (Gikandi et al., 2020).

CHALLENGES OF CLOUD INTEGRATION IN EDUCATION

Cloud integration in education, while offering numerous advantages, also brings forth a set of challenges that must be addressed to maximize its potential. One of the most pressing concerns is data privacy and security. As educational institutions increasingly rely on cloud-based systems to store and manage student information, the risk of data breaches and unauthorized access to sensitive information becomes a significant issue. According to Adedoja and Olatunji (2020), ensuring robust security measures and compliance with data protection regulations is essential for safeguarding student information. This includes implementing encryption, multi-factor authentication, and regular security audits to mitigate potential threats. In addition to privacy concerns, digital equity presents another critical challenge. The disparity in access to high-speed internet and modern technology can exacerbate educational inequalities, particularly for students in rural or economically disadvantaged areas. Almohammadi et al. (2022) emphasize the importance of addressing these inequities to ensure that all students can benefit from cloud-based educational tools. Educational institutions must develop comprehensive strategies to bridge the digital divide, such as providing affordable internet access and devices to underserved communities and offering support services to help students and teachers effectively utilize cloud technologies. Infrastructure scalability is also a significant challenge, particularly for institutions that may not have the resources to invest in the necessary technological infrastructure. Smaller educational institutions or those in developing regions may struggle to scale their cloud-based systems to accommodate growing numbers of students or increased demand for digital resources. Crompton (2021) suggests that partnerships with technology providers and government initiatives can help alleviate some of these burdens, allowing institutions to access the infrastructure needed to implement cloud solutions effectively. Furthermore, the integration of cloud technology requires significant changes in institutional practices and pedagogical approaches. The shift to cloud-based learning environments necessitates that educators be trained in new technologies and instructional methods. Janssen et al. (2021) discuss the importance of professional development for teachers in enhancing their digital competencies, which is crucial for the successful implementation of cloud-based educational systems. Without adequate training and support, educators may struggle to leverage the full potential of these technologies, potentially hindering the learning experience. Another challenge lies in the resistance to change within educational institutions. As Ekowo and Tait (2020) point out, some educators and administrators may be hesitant to adopt new technologies, preferring traditional methods of teaching and learning. Overcoming this resistance requires a cultural shift within institutions, where the benefits of cloud integration are clearly communicated and demonstrated. Creating a collaborative environment where educators can share best practices and experiences with cloud technology can help ease this transition. The issue of technological reliability is also a concern. As institutions become increasingly reliant on cloud-based systems, any disruption in service—whether due to technical failures, cyber-attacks, or internet outages—can significantly impact the educational process. Means et al. (2020) highlight the importance of having contingency plans in place, such as offline access to critical resources or backup systems, to ensure continuity of education during such disruptions.

FUTURE TRENDS IN CLOUD TECHNOLOGY AND EDUCATION

The future of cloud technology in education is bright, driven by emerging trends poised to further transform the sector. A key development is the integration of Artificial Intelligence (AI) into cloud-based educational platforms. AI technologies, such as machine learning and natural language processing, are enhancing personalized learning experiences and automating administrative tasks. For instance, platforms like Smart Sparrow and Knewton use algorithms to analyze student data and adapt instructional content in real-time, tailoring learning experiences to meet individual needs (Almohammadi et al., 2022). This capability extends to assessment methods, where AI can evaluate critical thinking and problem-solving skills, providing a comprehensive view of student abilities beyond traditional knowledge recall (Panadero et al., 2021). Another significant trend is the increasing use of Virtual Reality (VR) and Augmented Reality (AR) in education. When integrated with cloud platforms, these immersive technologies create interactive environments for students. For example, students can participate in virtual field trips or practice surgical procedures in simulated settings, enhancing their understanding of complex concepts (Crompton, 2021). Blockchain technology is also emerging as a vital tool for secure credential verification and academic record management. This technology can simplify the process of verifying educational credentials, making it easier for employers and institutions to access and share student achievements securely (Hämäläinen & Vähäsantanen, 2022). The emphasis on data analytics will further shape cloud integration in education. As institutions gather extensive data on student performance, the ability to analyze this information will become crucial. Educational data mining can reveal learning patterns, helping educators identify students who may need additional support and informing curriculum development (Liu & Liu, 2021). Mobile learning is another trend gaining traction, driven by the proliferation of smartphones and tablets. This approach allows students to access educational content anytime and anywhere, promoting flexibility and accessibility. Mobile platforms often include features like gamification and adaptive learning pathways, enhancing motivation and engagement (Park & Kim, 2021). As cloud technology evolves, educational institutions must adapt by embracing new technologies and rethinking traditional practices. Greater automation and AI support will require educators to balance their teaching roles with these advanced tools (Siemens, 2020). The trend towards open educational resources (OER) will also expand, making high-quality materials more accessible to diverse learners and promoting inclusivity (Sclater et al., 2021). Despite challenges like data privacy and infrastructure scalability, addressing these issues will enable institutions to harness cloud-based systems effectively. The integration of AI, VR, AR, blockchain, and data analytics presents an opportunity to create personalized, adaptive, and scalable learning experiences. The transformative impact of cloud technology in education is profound. By navigating the associated challenges and embracing innovative opportunities, educators and policymakers can shape a more effective and inclusive educational landscape that meets the demands of the 21st century.

CONCLUSION

The integration of cloud technology in education marks a significant evolution in learning delivery and experience. Traditional educational models, often limited by physical boundaries and standardized methods, have transitioned to dynamic, personalized, and accessible environments. Learning Management Systems (LMS), data analytics, Artificial Intelligence (AI), and collaborative tools have transformed education, democratizing access to high-quality learning experiences. Institutions like Khan Academy, DreamBox Learning, Purdue University, and Minerva Schools exemplify the potential of cloud-based solutions, offering scalable and interactive platforms tailored to diverse student needs. A key impact of cloud integration is the shift toward personalized learning. AI and data analytics enable platforms to analyze student performance in real time, creating adaptive pathways tailored to individual needs. DreamBox Learning, for instance, uses AI to adjust math lesson difficulty based on student interactions, fostering deeper engagement and understanding. This approach contrasts sharply with traditional one-size-fits-all models, offering a more effective teaching method. Cloud technology also enhances education accessibility. Platforms like Khan Academy provide free, high-quality resources to millions, overcoming geographic and financial barriers. This democratization is crucial in addressing global educational disparities, allowing anyone with internet access to benefit from educational materials, thereby promoting greater equity. However, challenges persist with cloud integration. Data privacy and security are major concerns; educational institutions must protect sensitive student information from cyber threats. The growing volume of collected data necessitates robust security measures to safeguard this information. Additionally, digital equity remains a critical issue, as students in rural areas or from low-income families may lack access to necessary technology. Collaborations among educational institutions and policymakers are essential to ensure that all students have the required tools, including initiatives for affordable internet access and device distribution. Infrastructure scalability presents another challenge, particularly for smaller or developing institutions. As demand for cloud tools rises, institutions must scale their infrastructure accordingly, often requiring significant investments. Partnerships with technology providers and governmental support can help institutions leverage cloud technology effectively. Looking ahead, advancements in AI, virtual reality (VR), augmented reality (AR), and blockchain technology promise to further enhance education. AI can refine personalization, identifying learning gaps more accurately. VR and AR can create immersive experiences, particularly beneficial in fields like medicine and engineering. Blockchain offers secure credential verification and record management, simplifying the verification process and reducing fraud risks. The COVID-19 pandemic has accelerated the adoption of cloud-based education, revealing both strengths and weaknesses in existing infrastructures. While some institutions adapted quickly, others faced challenges, highlighting the need for continuous investment in technology. In conclusion, cloud technology presents a powerful tool for transforming education, offering unprecedented possibilities for teaching and learning. By embracing innovations and addressing challenges, educational institutions can foster inclusive and effective learning environments. The journey of cloud integration is ongoing, and its success relies on the collective efforts of educators, policymakers, and technology providers to create a resilient and equitable digital education ecosystem.

AREAS FOR FUTURE RESEARCH

- **Data Privacy and Security**

As cloud integration in education becomes increasingly widespread, the protection of student data remains a crucial concern. The vast amounts of data generated and stored by educational institutions using cloud technologies require robust security measures to protect against cyber threats and unauthorized access. Future research in this area should focus on developing comprehensive frameworks and technologies that not only protect data but also ensure compliance with global standards and regulations. Advanced encryption methods are one area ripe for exploration. Encryption technology has made significant strides, but with the evolving nature of cyber threats, research into more sophisticated encryption techniques is vital. These methods must balance security with accessibility, ensuring that authorized users can easily access the data they need without compromising safety. Secure data storage solutions also warrant further investigation. As institutions move more of their operations to the cloud, there is a growing need for innovative storage solutions that offer both scalability and security. Research could explore the use of decentralized storage systems, which could reduce the risks associated with centralized data storage. Additionally, there is a need for research into privacy policies that comply with global standards, such as the General Data Protection Regulation (GDPR) in Europe. Understanding how different regulations apply to educational data and finding ways to create universal privacy standards could help institutions navigate the complex landscape of data privacy.

- **Digital Equity and Access**

The digital divide remains a significant barrier to the equitable deployment of cloud-based educational resources. While cloud technology offers unprecedented access to educational tools and content, disparities in internet access and the availability of technological devices can exacerbate existing educational inequalities. Future research should focus on developing strategies to provide affordable internet access and necessary technological devices to underserved communities. This includes investigating the feasibility of public-private partnerships that could subsidize internet access for students in rural or low-income areas. Additionally, research could explore the development of low-cost, durable devices specifically designed for educational purposes, which could be distributed to students in need. Digital literacy is another critical aspect of this issue. Providing access to technology is only part of the solution; students and educators also need the skills to use these tools effectively. Research should investigate the most effective methods for delivering digital literacy training, particularly in communities with limited prior exposure to technology. Innovative solutions for delivering educational content in low-bandwidth environments could also play a key role in addressing digital equity. For example, research could explore the potential of offline-first applications that sync with cloud-based systems when connectivity is available. Such tools would allow students in remote areas to access educational content without requiring constant internet access.

- **Personalization and Adaptive Learning**

Personalized learning, supported by adaptive learning technologies, represents one of the most promising developments in modern education. These technologies, powered by AI and data analytics, have the potential to tailor educational experiences to the unique needs of each student. However, there is still much to be explored in terms of optimizing these technologies and understanding their long-term impacts.

Future research should focus on refining AI algorithms to better understand and predict individual learning behaviors and preferences. This includes developing models that can dynamically adjust learning pathways based on real-time data, ensuring that students receive the support they need exactly when they need it. Additionally, researchers should investigate how these personalized learning experiences impact student engagement, motivation, and academic outcomes over time. Another area for exploration is the application of adaptive learning technologies across diverse educational settings. While much of the existing research focuses on traditional classroom environments, there is a need to understand how these technologies can be effectively implemented in non-traditional settings, such as online courses, vocational training programs, and lifelong learning initiatives. Finally, the ethical implications of personalized learning warrant further investigation. As AI algorithms become more sophisticated, there is a risk that they could reinforce existing biases or make decisions that lack transparency. Research should explore ways to ensure that these systems are fair, transparent, and aligned with educational goals.

- **Virtual and Augmented Reality**

The integration of Virtual Reality (VR) and Augmented Reality (AR) in education offers exciting possibilities for creating immersive and interactive learning experiences. These technologies have the potential to transform how students engage with complex subjects, providing hands-on learning experiences that are not possible in traditional classroom settings. Future research should focus on developing and evaluating VR and AR applications across various disciplines, from science and engineering to the humanities and arts. This research should consider the pedagogical effectiveness of these technologies, investigating how they impact student learning outcomes and engagement. Cost-efficiency is another critical factor to consider. While VR and AR technologies have become more affordable in recent years, they still represent a significant investment for many educational institutions. Research should explore ways to make these technologies more accessible, perhaps through the development of low-cost hardware solutions or the use of shared resources across institutions. Scalability is also an important consideration. While small-scale implementations of VR and AR have shown promise, there is a need to understand how these technologies can be scaled up to serve larger populations of students. This includes exploring the technical challenges of deploying VR and AR at scale, as well as the logistical challenges of integrating these tools into existing curricula.

- **Blockchain Technology**

Blockchain technology, known for its applications in finance and cryptocurrency, also holds promise for education, particularly in the areas of credential verification and academic record management. Blockchain's decentralized and tamper-proof nature makes it an ideal solution for ensuring the authenticity and integrity of academic credentials. Future research should explore the feasibility of implementing blockchain in educational systems. This includes investigating how blockchain can be integrated with existing credentialing systems and exploring its potential for automating and securing the verification process. Additionally, research should consider the scalability of blockchain solutions, ensuring that they can handle the vast amounts of data generated by educational institutions. Another area for exploration is the potential of blockchain for facilitating lifelong learning. With the increasing importance of continuous education and skills development, there is a need for systems that can recognize and validate informal learning experiences. Blockchain could provide a platform for securely documenting these experiences, allowing individuals to build a comprehensive and verifiable record of their learning throughout their lives.

- **Teacher Training and Professional Development**

As cloud-based educational technologies evolve, so too must the skills and knowledge of educators. Continuous professional development is essential to ensure that teachers can effectively integrate and utilize these technologies in their teaching practices. However, there is a need for research to identify the most effective methods for delivering this training and supporting teachers in their professional growth. Future research should investigate the design and implementation of training programs that equip teachers with the skills needed to navigate the digital landscape of modern education. This includes exploring different models of professional development, such as in-person workshops, online courses, and peer mentoring programs. Additionally, research should consider the impact of these programs on teaching practices, student outcomes, and overall educational innovation. Support systems for educators are also a critical area for research. As teachers adapt to new technologies, they need ongoing support to address challenges and refine their practices. Research should explore the most effective ways to provide this support, whether through dedicated IT teams, online communities, or professional learning networks. Finally, research should consider the broader implications of technological change for the teaching profession. As automation and AI take on more educational tasks, there is a need to understand how these changes will impact the role of teachers and how they can continue to add value in an increasingly digital learning environment.

- **Longitudinal Studies on Educational Outcomes**

To fully understand the impact of cloud integration in education, longitudinal studies are necessary. These studies track cohorts of students over extended periods, providing valuable insights into the sustained effects of cloud-based learning on academic performance, career readiness, and personal development. Future research should focus on designing and conducting longitudinal studies that investigate the long-term outcomes of cloud-based education. This includes examining how cloud technologies impact students' academic trajectories, from primary education through to higher education and beyond. Additionally, researchers should consider the broader impacts of these technologies on students' social and emotional development, as well as their preparedness for the workforce. Another important area for research is the impact of cloud-based education on different demographic groups. Longitudinal studies can help identify whether certain groups of students benefit more from cloud-based learning, or whether there are disparities in outcomes that need to be addressed. This research could inform efforts to make cloud-based education more inclusive and equitable. Finally, research should explore the institutional impacts of cloud integration. Longitudinal studies can provide insights into how cloud technologies affect teaching practices, institutional culture, and educational outcomes over time. This research can help institutions refine their strategies for implementing cloud-based solutions, ensuring that they are effectively supporting their students and faculty. The areas outlined for future research highlight the dynamic and evolving nature of cloud technology in education. As educational institutions continue to integrate these technologies into their practices, ongoing research will be essential to address emerging challenges and seize new opportunities. By exploring issues such as data privacy, digital equity, personalization, and the application of emerging technologies like VR, AR, and blockchain, researchers can contribute to the development of more effective, inclusive, and innovative educational systems.

REFERENCES

Adedoja, G., & Olatunji, O. A. (2020). The role of cloud computing in enhancing education. *Journal of Information Technology Education*, 19, 1–15.

Almohammadi, A., Harun, J., & Daud, M. Y. (2022). Artificial intelligence in higher education: A systematic literature review. *Computers & Education*, 176, 104381. DOI: 10.1016/j.compedu.2021.104381

Crompton, H. (2021). Mobile learning in higher education: A systematic review of research on trends, instructional strategies, and technologies. *Educational Technology Research and Development*, 69(1), 153–173. DOI: 10.1007/s11423-020-09835-2

Dawson, S., Heathcote, L., & Poole, G. (2020). Harnessing the affordances of digital learning: An activity system analysis of research and practice. *Educational Technology Research and Development*, 68(6), 2975–3001. DOI: 10.1007/s11423-020-09831-6

Dawson, S., Joksimović, S., Kovanović, V., Gašević, D., & Siemens, G. (2020). The impact of learning management systems on learning outcomes: A systematic review. *The Internet and Higher Education*, 44, 100726. DOI: 10.1016/j.iheduc.2019.100726

Ekowo, M., & Tait, M. (2020). Creating conditions for equity in schools: Technology, culture, and power. New America. https://www.newamerica.org/education-policy/reports/creating-conditions-equity-schools/

Gikandi, J. W., Morrow, D., & Davis, N. E. (2020). Online formative assessment in higher education: A review of the literature. *Computers & Education*, 56(3), 1045–1051. DOI: 10.1016/j.compedu.2010.12.001

Hämäläinen, R., & Vähäsantanen, K. (2022). Adaptive learning in higher education: A systematic review of research literature. *Computers & Education*, 175, 104319. DOI: 10.1016/j.compedu.2021.104319

Harris, J. B. (Ed.). (2020). *Handbook of adult and continuing education*. Jossey-Bass.

Janssen, J., Conijn, R., Kester, L., & Kalz, M. (2021). Teachers' professional development in digital competency: Lessons learned from Dutch primary schools. *Technology, Pedagogy and Education*, 30(1), 35–51. DOI: 10.1080/1475939X.2020.1805603

Liu, Y., & Liu, X. (2021). A systematic review of educational data mining. *Frontiers in Psychology*, 12, 647036. DOI: 10.3389/fpsyg.2021.647036

Luckin, R., & Holmes, W. (Eds.). (2020). *Artificial intelligence in education: Promise and implications for teaching and learning*. Springer.

Manoharan, C., Poongavanam, S., Arivazhagan, D., Divyaranjani, R., & Vettriselvan, R. (2020). Cognition and emotions during the teaching-learning process. *International Journal of Scientific and Technology Research*, 9(2), 267–269.

Means, B., Bakia, M., & Murphy, R. (2020). *Learning online: What research tells us about whether, when and how*. Routledge.

Panadero, E., Brown, G. T., & Strijbos, J. W. (2021). *Educational assessment in the digital age: A handbook for researchers, practitioners, and policymakers*. Routledge.

Park, S., & Kim, Y. (2021). A systematic review of research trends in mobile learning studies in Korea: A social network analysis. *Interactive Learning Environments*, 29(1), 109–125. DOI: 10.1080/10494820.2019.1582198

Picciano, A. G. (2021). *Online education: Foundations, planning, and pedagogy*. Routledge.

Sclater, N., Bailey, C., & Yip, C. (Eds.). (2021). *The Wiley handbook of learning technology*. Wiley.

Siemens, G. (2020). Automation in education: Future prospects. *Education and Information Technologies*, 25(6), 4853–4865. DOI: 10.1007/s10639-020-10340-1

Thiruvasagam, G., & Vettriselvan, R. (2021). What is after COVID-19?: Changing economies of the shipping industries and maritime education institutions. In 21st Annual General Assembly, IAMU AGA 2021 - Proceedings of the International Association of Maritime Universities (pp. 96–110).

Vettriselvan, R., & Vinodhan, V. (2022). Promotional strategies for gender equity in the maritime sector: Maritime education institutions. In *Proceedings of the International Association of Maritime Universities Conference*.

Voogt, J., Knezek, G., Christensen, R., & Lai, K. W. (Eds.). (2021). *Second handbook of information technology in primary and secondary education*. Springer.

Williamson, B., & Eynon, R. (2021). *The digital education: Critical perspectives*. Polity Press.

KEY TERMS AND DEFINITIONS

Adaptive Systems: Adaptive systems are technology-driven educational platforms that modify content and instructional strategies based on real-time data about student performance and engagement. These systems utilize algorithms and analytics to assess students' strengths and weaknesses, providing a customized learning path that enhances understanding and retention.

AI in Education: Artificial Intelligence (AI) in education refers to the application of machine learning and natural language processing to enhance learning experiences and administrative efficiency. AI technologies can provide personalized feedback, automate grading, and facilitate real-time adjustments to instructional content, making education more responsive to student needs.

Cloud Integration: Cloud integration refers to the process of connecting various cloud services and applications to facilitate data sharing and communication. In education, this enables institutions to leverage multiple cloud-based tools, such as Learning Management Systems (LMS), data analytics platforms, and collaborative software, to create a cohesive and efficient digital learning environment.

Collaboration Tools: Collaboration tools are digital platforms that enable students and educators to work together in real time, regardless of their physical location. Examples include video conferencing, shared documents, and project management applications, which foster teamwork and collective learning.

Data Analytics: Data analytics in education involves collecting, processing, and analyzing data from various sources, such as student assessments, attendance records, and engagement metrics. This analysis helps educators understand learning patterns, identify at-risk students, and make informed decisions about instructional strategies and resource allocation.

Digital Equity: Digital equity refers to the fair and just access to digital tools, resources, and opportunities for all students. Ensuring digital equity involves addressing disparities in technology access, internet connectivity, and digital literacy, allowing all learners to benefit from cloud-based educational solutions.

Educational Transformation: Educational transformation encompasses the significant changes in teaching and learning practices driven by technological advancements, particularly cloud computing and digital tools. This transformation aims to improve educational outcomes, increase accessibility, and foster a more engaging learning experience for students.

Global Accessibility: Global accessibility refers to the efforts to make educational resources and opportunities available to all learners, regardless of geographic location, socio-economic status, or physical ability. Cloud-based platforms are instrumental in this regard, as they enable remote access to high-quality educational materials and support services.

Immersive Learning Technologies: Immersive learning technologies, such as Virtual Reality (VR) and Augmented Reality (AR), provide interactive and engaging learning experiences. These technologies simulate real-world scenarios, enabling students to practice skills and concepts in a safe, controlled environment, enhancing their understanding of complex subjects.

Learning Management Systems (LMS): LMS are software applications that facilitate the administration, documentation, tracking, reporting, and delivery of educational courses and training programs. They provide a centralized platform for educators and students to access resources, assignments, and communication tools, enhancing the overall learning experience.

Open Educational Resources (OER): Open Educational Resources are freely accessible, openly licensed materials that can be used for teaching, learning, and research. OER promotes equity in education by providing high-quality resources to learners and educators without financial barriers.

Personalized Learning: Personalized learning is an educational approach that tailors the learning experience to meet the individual needs, preferences, and interests of each student. It leverages data analytics and AI to adapt instructional methods, pacing, and content delivery, allowing students to engage with material that resonates with their unique learning styles.

Predictive Analytics: Predictive analytics involves using historical data and statistical algorithms to identify potential outcomes and trends. In education, this approach can help institutions anticipate student performance, engagement levels, and retention risks, enabling proactive interventions to support at-risk learners.

Chapter 4
Next-Gen Learning Cloud Integration for Academic and Industrial Synergy

Pradnya Samit Mehta
https://orcid.org/0000-0002-5304-7270
Vishwakarma Institute of Information Technology, India

Prachi Shedge
Vishwakarma Institute of Information Technology, India

Sakshi Vyavahare
Vishwakarma Institute of Information Technology, India

Srinidhi Soundarrajan
https://orcid.org/0009-0007-6552-6248
Vishwakarma Institute of Information Technology, India

Geetha Chillarge
https://orcid.org/0000-0003-1152-5913
Marathwada Mitra Mandal's College of Engineering, India

ABSTRACT

In today's rapidly evolving technological landscape, the integration of cloud computing within educational frameworks is revolutionizing the way academia and industry collaborate. This book, "Bridging Academia and Industry: Cloud Integration in Education," explores the transformative power of cloud technologies in enhancing educational outcomes and fostering innovative partnerships between academic institutions and the industrial sector. By leveraging cloud platforms, educational institutions can streamline resource management, facilitate collaborative research,

DOI: 10.4018/979-8-3693-6705-6.ch004

and equip students with the practical skills required by modern industries. This comprehensive guide provides an in-depth analysis of the strategies, tools, and real-world case studies that demonstrate the myriad benefits of cloud integration in education. From setting up cloud infrastructure and implementing virtual labs to developing cloud-based curricula and enhancing student employability, this book offers valuable insights for educators, researchers, and industry professionals.

INTRODUCTION

The use of cloud computing into educational frameworks is transforming the way industry and academia work together in today's quickly changing technological landscape. The approach that is being suggested investigates how cloud computing might improve learning results and create creative collaborations between universities and businesses. Through the use of cloud platforms, educational institutions can improve resource management, encourage group research, and give students the hands-on training that employers in today's market want. In-depth examination of the tactics, resources, and actual case studies that highlight the numerous advantages of cloud integration in education is given in this extensive guide. This book provides insightful information for researchers, educators, and business executives on everything from creating cloud-based courses and virtual labs to improving student employability. This effort attempts to prepare students for success in an increasingly digital world by bridging the theory-practice divide and laying the groundwork for a more connected and effective educational ecosystem.

ORGANIZATION OF THE CHAPTER:

Section 1 elaborates about Introduction of Cloud Computing in Education, Section 2 discuss about Collaboration between academic and industry for cloud integration, Cloud Infrastructure for educational institutions focused in Section 3, cloud based learning management discussed in Section 4. Section 5 suggests virtual labs and cloud computing decision support, Cloud Integration for Research and Development, Industry-Specific Cloud Applications in Education, developing cloud based curriculum, etc. are described between subsections .

1. INTRODUCTION TO CLOUD COMPUTING IN EDUCATION

1.1 Overview of Cloud Computing:

Cloud computing involves the provision of computing services, such as storage, processing power, and applications, via the internet, commonly known as "the cloud". The latest developments have led to the widespread adoption and triumph of cloud computing, a novel computing and business framework that offers storage and computing resources as needed Rather than managing physical data centers and servers, organizations can utilize these resources from cloud service providers as required Hassan et al. (2022). Essential features of cloud computing encompass self-service on-demand, extensive network accessibility, resource pooling, quick scalability, and service measurement. Primary cloud service models as shown in figure 1 consist of Infrastructure as a Service (IaaS) enables the provision of virtualized computing resources via the internet. Platform as a Service (PaaS) facilitates the availability of hardware and software tools over the internet, primarily for application development purposes. Software as a Service (SaaS) delivers software applications through the internet, based on a subscription model.

Figure 1. Services provided by cloud

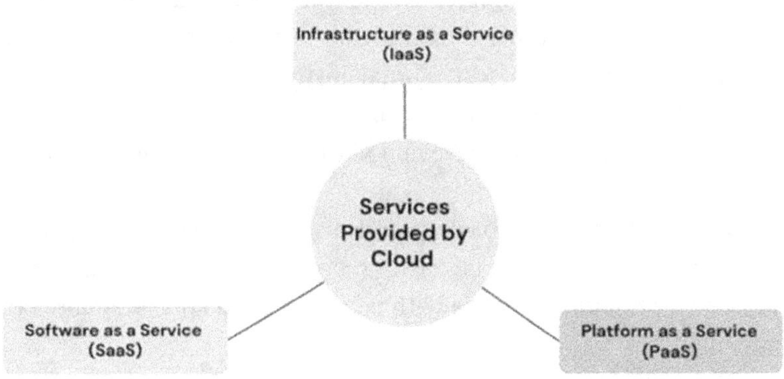

1.2 The Role of cloud Technologies in Modern Education

Cloud technologies are revolutionizing the educational landscape by offering scalable, adaptable, and cost-efficient solutions. The pivotal roles played by cloud technologies in modern education encompass Cloud platforms empower educational institutions to efficiently manage their resources, thereby reducing the reliance on physical infrastructure and minimizing maintenance costs. Cloud-based tools foster collaboration among students and educators, facilitating real-time communication and teamwork. Students and educators can effortlessly access educational resources from any location, at any time, using any internet-connected device. Cloud technologies support the creation of virtual classrooms, enabling remote learning and ensuring uninterrupted education during disruptions.

Cloud services offer secure data storage solutions, ensuring the protection and easy retrieval of educational data.

1.3 Benefits and Challenges of Cloud Integration

Benefits:

1. Educational institutions can benefit from the scalability and flexibility of cloud computing, as it allows them to easily adjust their IT resources according to demand. This ensures that they only pay for the resources they actually use, resulting in cost savings Sachdeva et al.(2024).
2. Cloud computing offers a cost-effective solution for educational institutions by eliminating the need for physical infrastructure and reducing IT maintenance expenses. This can lead to significant operational cost savings.
3. Cloud-based platforms promote enhanced collaboration among students, educators, and industry professionals. By facilitating interaction and engagement, these platforms create a more dynamic and interactive learning environment.
4. Cloud integration provides educational institutions with access to advanced tools and applications. This not only enhances the learning experience but also equips students with industry-relevant skills, preparing them for future career opportunities.
5. Cloud services offer robust backup and disaster recovery solutions, ensuring that data is protected and can be easily recovered in case of emergencies. This provides educational institutions with peace of mind and safeguards their valuable information.

Challenges:

1. Ensuring the security and privacy of sensitive educational data stored in the cloud is a significant concern that educational institutions must address. Robust security measures must be implemented, and compliance with data protection regulations is essential to safeguard this information. Sauber et al. (2021).
2. Reliable internet access is crucial for cloud-based education. However, in regions with poor connectivity, this can pose a major barrier, hindering access to educational resources and online learning platforms.

3. Integrating and managing cloud services require specialized technical skills, which may be lacking in some educational institutions. This lack of technical expertise can impede the effective utilization of cloud-based tools and services for educational purposes.
4. While cloud computing has the potential to reduce costs, improper management of cloud resources can lead to unexpected expenses. It is important for educational institutions to effectively manage their cloud resources to optimize cost savings and avoid unnecessary financial burdens.
5. Dependence on a single cloud provider can create challenges in terms of flexibility and negotiating power. Educational institutions need to carefully evaluate their options and consider adopting multi-cloud strategies to avoid vendor lock-in and maintain control over their cloud-based educational systems.

2. ACADEMIC AND INDUSTRY COLLABORATION: THE NEED FOR CLOUD INTEGRATION

2.1 Bridging the Gap: Academic Research and Industry Needs:

In the contemporary landscape characterized by rapid technological progress, the necessity for enhanced collaboration between academic institutions and industry has reached a critical juncture. Academic research is fundamental to innovation, serving as a rich source for the cultivation and investigation of novel ideas, concepts, and technologies. These scholarly endeavors often establish the foundation for significant advancements capable of transforming entire sectors. Nevertheless, a persistent issue remains: the disparity between the theoretical orientation of academic research and the immediate, practical requirements of the industry. This disconnect can result in delays in the implementation of innovative solutions, as academic inquiries may not consistently align with the needs of the industry.

Cloud integration has emerged as an effective mechanism to bridge this divide, fostering a more dynamic and reciprocal relationship between academia and industry. By utilizing cloud technologies, academic institutions can access and analyze real-time data from the industry, infusing their research with a level of immediacy and relevance that was previously unattainable. This direct access to industry-specific insights enables researchers to test and refine their theories in practical, real-world contexts, thereby enhancing the applicability and significance of their findings.

Furthermore, cloud integration promotes seamless collaboration between academic researchers and industry practitioners. Through shared cloud platforms, they can engage in joint projects, collaboratively developing solutions that are both innovative and practical. This partnership accelerates the conversion of academic research into concrete products, services, and processes that can be adopted within the industry, ultimately fostering growth and enhancing competitiveness.

Furthermore, cloud integration allows educational institutions to provide students with practical experience using advanced technologies and authentic data, thereby enhancing their readiness for the job market. This hands-on involvement guarantees that graduates possess not only a solid foundation in theoretical concepts but also the competencies required to address the dynamic needs of the industry. As a result, the collaboration between academia and industry, supported by cloud integration, promotes an ongoing cycle of innovation, where academic research influences industry practices, and the challenges faced by industry inform academic exploration.In summary, cloud integration serves as more than just a collaborative tool; it represents a strategic method to ensure that academic research remains pertinent and influential in a swiftly evolving environment. By connecting theoretical frameworks with practical applications, it facilitates a more effective partnership between academia and industry, fostering innovation and ensuring that the latest developments are promptly applied in real-world scenarios. This cooperative framework ultimately serves the interests of all parties involved, including researchers, industry experts, students, and society as a whole.

2.2 Enhancing Collaborative Research through Cloud Platform

Cloud platforms provide a wide range of tools and resources that facilitate collaborative research between academia and industry. These platforms offer several key features that contribute to the success of collaborative projects. Cloud platforms create virtual environments where researchers from academia and industry can work together on projects, share data, and develop solutions in real-time. Advanced data analytics tools available on cloud platforms enable researchers to efficiently process large datasets. This allows them to uncover valuable insights that drive innovation and improve research outcomes. Cloud computing allows researchers to access their work from anywhere in the world. This promotes flexibility and inclusivity in collaborative efforts, as researchers can contribute to projects regardless of their physical location. Cloud services offer scalable resources, ensuring that research projects have access to the necessary computational power and storage. This is beneficial regardless of the size or complexity of the data involved, as researchers can easily scale up or down as needed. Cloud providers prioritize security and compliance measures. They offer robust security features and certifications to protect sensitive research data. This ensures that collaborations adhere to regulatory requirements and maintain the confidentiality of research findings. These features not only streamline collaborative research but also enhance the quality and impact of the outcomes. By leveraging cloud platforms, both academia and industry can drive advancements and achieve significant progress in their respective fields.

2.3 Case Studies: Successful Academic – Industry Collaborations:

Numerous effective case studies showcase the advantages of integrating cloud technology to enhance academic-industry partnerships:

1. Case Study: Precision Agriculture

Summary: A partnership between a prominent agricultural university and a technology firm aimed at creating cloud-based solutions for precision agriculture.

Result: The collaboration led to the development of a cloud platform that combines satellite data, IoT sensors, and machine learning algorithms to enhance crop management. This innovation has notably boosted crop yields and resource utilization, proving beneficial for both academic research and the agricultural sector.

2. Case Study: Advancements in Healthcare

Summary: An alliance formed between a medical research facility and a pharmaceutical corporation with the goal of expediting drug exploration and advancement through the utilization of cloud computing.

Result: By employing cloud-based computational models and extensive data analysis, the partnership successfully identified novel drug possibilities at a significantly accelerated pace compared to conventional approaches. Additionally, the cloud platform enabled safe data exchange and cooperation among international research groups. Hashira et al.(2024)

3. **Case Study: Smart City Development**

Summary: A collaborative effort between an engineering university and a city municipality aimed at creating smart city solutions through the utilization of cloud technologies.

Result: The cloud-based platform facilitated the incorporation of diverse smart city applications, including traffic control, energy usage tracking, and public safety mechanisms. This partnership has not only improved city life but also furnished significant practical data for scholarly investigations. Yang et al.(2022)

3. CLOUD INFRASTRUCTURE FOR EDUCATIONAL INSTITUTIONS

3.1 Setting Up Cloud Infrastructure

In this section, figure 2 delves the process and factors to consider when setting up a cloud infrastructure in educational institutions. Let's take a closer look at the following key areas:

Cloud Deployment Models:

i. Public Cloud: This model offers scalability, flexibility, and cost-effectiveness for non-sensitive data. Examples include Google Cloud Platform for Education and Microsoft Azure Education. Gaikwad et al. (2021).
ii. Private Cloud: With this model, educational institutions have greater control and security over sensitive information. However, it requires a higher initial investment and can be implemented either on-premises or through a managed service provider, Akhouri et al.(2022).
iii. Cloud: This model combines elements of both public and private clouds, providing a balanced approach to control, security, and cost.

Figure 2. Comparisons of Cloud Deployment Models

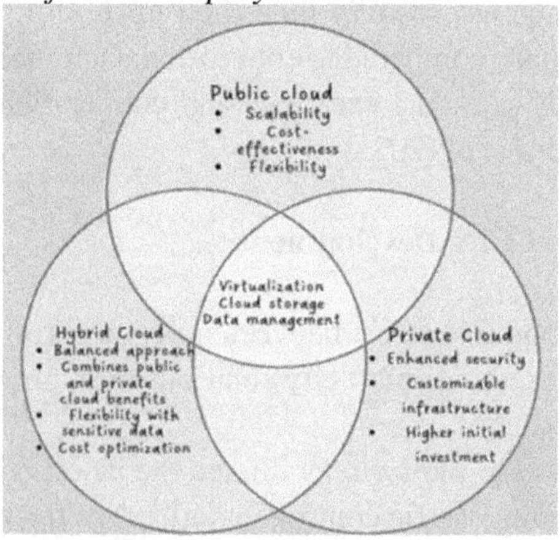

Cloud Provider:

When selecting a Cloud Provider, it is important to take into account various factors such as their reputation, track record in security, service offerings tailored for education (such as educational discounts and pre-configured learning environments), and compliance with data privacy regulations that are relevant.

Service Selection (IaaS, PaaS, SaaS):

IaaS (Infrastructure as a Service) enables institutions with extensive IT knowledge to access virtual machines, storage, and networking resources as needed. PaaS (Platform as a Service) provides a platform for the development and deployment of cloud-based applications, making it ideal for institutions looking to create customized learning tools. SaaS (Software as a Service) offers readily available cloud-based applications such as Learning Management Systems or virtual labs, making it suitable for institutions that require quick implementation and minimal technical expertise.

Initial Configuration:

Setting up user accounts, access controls, data storage options, and security protocols must be done in alignment with institutional policies during the initial configuration process.

3.2 Costs-Benefit Analysis of Cloud Adoption:

This segment analyses the financial consequences of migrating to a cloud-based infrastructure. Eliminate the necessity of purchasing hardware upfront and bearing the costs of continuous maintenance. Cloud services frequently incorporate software licenses within their subscription fees. Reduce the number of IT staff needed for regular hardware maintenance and software updates.

On-going Expenses for Cloud Services:

-Fees for subscribing to selected cloud services (IaaS, PaaS, SaaS).
-Charges for data storage and bandwidth usage.

Optimizing Cloud Spending:

Enhance cost-efficiency in cloud spending by utilizing monitoring tools to pinpoint unused resources and improve resource distribution. Utilize reserved instances for consistent workloads in order to benefit from reduced rates. Investigate multi-cloud or hybrid cloud approaches to take advantage of competitive pricing and functionalities offered by various providers.

3.3 Security and Privacy Considerations:

In a time when digital transformation is significantly altering the educational sector, the issues of security and privacy have emerged as critical priorities, particularly regarding the management of extensive sensitive student data that educational institutions are responsible for safeguarding. Protecting this data transcends mere technical requirements; it represents a core obligation that these institutions owe to their students, faculty, and stakeholders. Implementing effective security and privacy strategies is vital for preserving trust and maintaining the integrity of the educational setting.

A fundamental approach to protecting sensitive information involves the adoption of robust encryption protocols for data, both when stored and during transmission. By utilizing encryption, educational institutions can ensure that, in the event of unauthorized access, the data remains unintelligible and secure. This encryption strategy should be supported by comprehensive and precise access controls, which are essential for managing who can access sensitive information and under what conditions. By clearly defining user roles and responsibilities, institutions can limit access to only those individuals who genuinely require it, thereby reducing the likelihood of data breaches.

Moreover, adherence to external data privacy regulations is of utmost importance. Educational institutions must comply with applicable laws, such as the Family Educational Rights and Privacy Act (FERPA) in the United States and the General Data Protection Regulation (GDPR) in the European Union. These regulations establish rigorous standards for data protection and impose severe penalties for non-compliance. By ensuring compliance with these laws, institutions not only safeguard their students' privacy but also mitigate the risk of legal consequences that could adversely affect their reputation and financial health.The ever-evolving cyber threat landscape demands ongoing vigilance from educational institutions. It is imperative that all software and systems are kept current, as outdated applications frequently become prime targets for cybercriminals. Conducting regular security assessments and audits is vital for identifying vulnerabilities and mitigating them before they can be exploited. These evaluations should be comprehensive, encompassing penetration testing, vulnerability scans, and detailed reviews of security policies and procedures.

Cybersecurity extends beyond the responsibilities of IT departments; it necessitates a collaborative effort from the entire educational community. Therefore, it is essential to provide continuous cybersecurity training for both staff and students. This education should cover potential threats, safe online practices, and methods for recognizing phishing attempts or other malicious activities, significantly lowering the risk of security incidents. The training programs should be routinely updated to incorporate the latest threats and best practices, ensuring that all individuals remain alert and well-informed.

By addressing these extensive security and privacy considerations, educational institutions can establish a secure and reliable cloud infrastructure that encourages innovation and collaboration while protecting sensitive information. Such a secure environment not only safeguards data but also fosters a culture of trust, allowing students and faculty to engage in academic pursuits with confidence in the protection of their information. Ultimately, by emphasizing security and privacy, educational institutions can set a standard, showcasing their commitment to responsible data management in the digital era.

4. CLOUD BASED LEARNING MANAGEMENT SYSTEM (LMS)

4.1 Overview of Popular Cloud-Based LMS:

An overview of commonly used cloud-based learning management systems (LMS) reveals platforms that streamline the management, tracking, reporting, and documentation of educational courses. These systems are prevalent in K-12 and higher education settings. Here are some of the most popular cloud-based LMS:

1. Canvas
    - Renowned for its robust features and user-friendly interface.
    - Features include course creation and management, integration with third-party tools, mobile app support, rich communication tools, and analytics.
    - Widely adopted in both K-12 and higher education environments. Al-Ataby, et al.. (2021).
2. Moodle
    - An open-source LMS offering flexibility and customization.
    - Features modular design, cost-effectiveness, strong community support, scalability, and comprehensive assessment tools.

- Preferred by educational institutions for its affordability and adaptability. Gamage et al.(2022)

3. Blackboard Learn
   - A feature-packed LMS with content development tools, robust assessment capabilities, collaboration tools, communication tools, and integration with other educational technologies.
   - Popular in higher education for its extensive features and scalability. Shayan et al.(2023)
4. Google Classroom
   - Seamlessly integrates with Google's productivity tools.
   - Features a simple interface, integration with Google Workspace tools, efficient assignment and grading system, real-time collaboration, and accessibility from various devices.
   - Frequently selected by schools using Google Workspace for Education due to its integration and user-friendly interface.

4.2 Implementing LMS in Academic Settings:

Needs Evaluation determine the particular needs and objectives of the educational institution, teachers, and learners? Procedure for selection examines several LMS platforms according to features, affordability, scalability, simplicity of use, and integration potential. Training and Support: To guarantee that instructors, staff, and students are able to use the LMS efficiently, provide them with thorough training. Migration of Content move current resources and course materials to the new LMS platform. Personalization Tailor the learning management system (LMS) to the school's pedagogical approach, instructional design standards, and branding are shown in figure 3.

1. Needs Assessment

Objective: Identify the specific needs and goals of the educational institution, teachers, and learners.

Stakeholder Engagement gathers requirements and expectations from administrators, educators, IT staff, and students. Veluvali P et al.(2022).Goal Identification define objectives such as improving resource access, communication, and supporting online learning. Gap Analysis identifies gaps between current capabilities and desired outcomes to inform LMS requirements.

2. Platform Selection Process

Objective: Evaluate multiple LMS platforms based on features, affordability, scalability, ease of use, and integration potential. Feature Comparison assess platforms for course management, communication tools, assessment capabilities, and integration potential. Cost Analysis considers initial and long-term expenses, including licensing, maintenance, and support. Scalability ensures the LMS can accommodate growth and increasing demands. User Experience prioritizes user-friendly platforms for both instructors and students. Integration checks compatibility with existing systems like student information systems (SIS) and library databases. Mohd Kasim et al.(2016).

3. Training and Support

Objective: Provide comprehensive training to ensure efficient use of the LMS by instructors, staff, and students. Training Programs develop training sessions for different user groups, such as faculty, students, and IT staff. Support Resources create user manuals, video tutorials, and FAQs to assist users. Ongoing Support Establish a helpdesk or support team to handle issues and provide continuous training opportunities. Irfandi, Irfandi et al.(2023).

4. Migration of Content

Objective: Transfer current resources and course materials to the new LMS platform.

Content Assessment evaluates current course materials and resources. Transition Strategy establishes a comprehensive strategy for moving content, with minimal disruption to on-going courses. Quality Assurance verifies the transferred content for accurate formatting and functionality on the new LMS. (Rosário).

5. Personalization

Objective: Customize the LMS to align with the school's teaching approach, design standards, and branding. Branding Customization implement the school's logo, colors, and branding elements into the LMS interface. Standardized Templates develop templates that adhere to design standards for consistent course presentation and tailored features create or integrate features that cater to the school's specific teaching methods and needs.

Figure 3. Steps of LMS

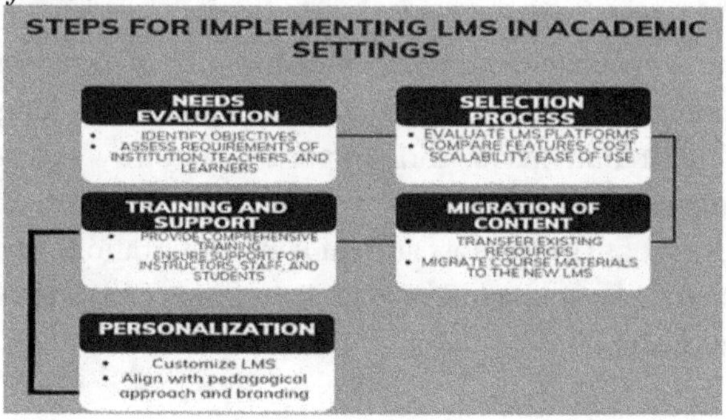

4.3 Enhancing Student Engagement and Learning Outcomes:

Interactive Content: To make learning more dynamic and engaging, learning management systems (LMS) include interactive tests, discussion boards, multimedia content, and collaborative tools. LMSs with adaptive learning technologies can modify lesson plans and instructional materials to meet the needs and learning preferences of specific students. Peer-to-peer cooperation and communication between teachers and students are made easier by LMS, which promotes a feeling of support and community. By offering analytics dashboards that give instructors insight into their students' performance, learning management systems (LMS) enable teachers to spot problem areas and take appropriate action.

Cloud-based learning management systems (LMS) facilitate anytime, anywhere access to course content, encouraging adaptability and recognizing a range of learning styles. I. P. G. P. Duta et al.(2021).

5. VIRTUAL LABS AND CLOUD COMPUTING

5.1 The Concept of Virtual Labs:

Virtual labs are online platforms or software applications that simulate real-world laboratory experiments or environments. These simulations allow students and researchers to conduct experiments, analyze data, and draw conclusions in a virtual setting, without the need for physical laboratory equipment or space. Virtual labs are often used in STEM (Science, Technology, Engineering, and Mathematics) education to supplement or replace traditional hands-on laboratory experiences, providing learners with opportunities to practice skills, explore concepts, and solve problems in a safe and cost-effective manner, Alexiou et al. (2005).

Students have flexibility in terms of when and where they can conduct experiments thanks to virtual labs, which are accessible from any location with an internet connection. This is especially helpful for colleges with limited lab space or for distant learning. They ensure that everyone gets the chance to participate in laboratory activities by making science education more accessible to students with impairments or those who live in remote places. As virtual labs do not require costly laboratory supplies, consumables, or upkeep, they provide an economical choice for educational establishments. By doing away with the requirement for specific lab locations, they free up resources for other educational requirements. This approach fosters a safe learning environment by allowing students to conduct potentially hazardous experiments or use hazardous materials without running any physical risks.Navarro et al. (2024)

5.2 Creating and Managing Virtual Labs on the Cloud:

Designing Lab Experiments define the objectives, procedures, and outcomes of the virtual lab experiments, ensuring alignment with learning objectives and curriculum standards. Developing Simulation Software develop or procure simulation software that accurately models the behaviour of real-world phenomena and provides interactive interfaces for users to interact with the virtual environment. Hosting on Cloud Infrastructure utilize cloud computing services to host and manage the virtual lab infrastructure, including servers, storage, and networking resources. Cloud platforms offer scalability, reliability, and accessibility advantages, allowing users to access virtual labs from anywhere with an internet connection. Integrate virtual labs with Learning Management Systems (LMS) to facilitate seamless access, tracking, and assessment of student performance. LMS integration enables instructors to assign virtual lab activities, monitor student progress, and provide feedback and grades. Implement robust security measures to protect sensitive data and ensure compliance with privacy regulations and academic standards. Encryption, access controls, and regular audits are essential for safeguarding virtual lab environments and user information, Elmoazen et al.(2023).

5.3 Case Studies: Virtual Labs in Action:

The virtual chemical laboratory provides an immersive educational experience through the simulation of authentic experiments in a digital space. This cutting-edge platform enables students and scholars to carry out experiments securely and effectively, delving into a variety of chemical reactions and principles without the limitations of physical materials or safety risks. Through the manipulation of virtual tools, the mixing of substances, the observation of real-time reactions, and the analysis of data, users can refine their scientific abilities and grasp essential concepts. Virtual laboratories not only improve access to hands-on learning but also promote experimentation and critical thinking in an engaging, interactive environment, equipping learners for practical applications in the field of chemistry and nurturing a deeper understanding of scientific exploration. Chan et al.(2021)

1. CyclePad is the Qualitative Reasoning Group's first intelligent virtual laboratory. Students can build and analyse a wide range of thermodynamic cycles using CyclePad. The student has access to the line of reasoning that underlies the calculation of each value through the use of a hypertext explanation facility. CyclePad is presently undergoing field testing in Oxford University, Northwestern University, and the U.S. Naval Academy's undergraduate engineering programs. (Baher, 1999)
   1. Objective and Features

CyclePad enables users to design and examine various thermodynamic cycles. Rankine cycles, which are frequently seen in power plants, Brayton cycles, which are found in jet engines, refrigeration cycles, and other cycles are among them. The main purpose of the software is to teach users thermodynamics fundamentals by letting them construct and test various cycle designs. CyclePad comes with a library of common thermodynamic parts, including pumps, heat exchangers, compressors, and turbines. These parts can be put together by users to form an entire cycle. Following the creation of a cycle, users can run a simulation to ascertain important performance metrics, such as power output, heat exchange, and efficiency. Baher J (1997)

2. Principal Attributes

CyclePad's graphical user interface facilitates accessibility for both professionals and students. To design intricate cycles, components can be dragged and dropped into the workspace. To assist users in comprehending thermodynamic concepts and resolving design-related problems, the software incorporates an intelligent tutoring system. CyclePad gives users instant feedback on the viability and efficiency of their concepts as they construct their cycles. The program has the ability to produce comprehensive reports with cycle diagrams, performance information, and an explanation of the relevant thermodynamic concepts.

3. Applications

CyclePad is frequently utilised in educational settings to instruct engineering students in thermodynamics. Before proceeding with more intricate and costly simulations, engineers can utilise CyclePad as a tool to explore and enhance cycle designs in an economical way. Researchers can test and teach new analytic techniques or concepts in thermodynamic cycle design using CyclePad. Dumka P. al (2024)

6. CLOUD INTEGRATION FOR RESEARCH AND DEVELOPMENT

6.1 Cloud Platforms for Academic Research:

Numerous services are available from Amazon Web Services to meet research needs, including compute instances like EC2 and storage choices like S3,as mentioned in Pooja Pandit (2021). Specialized services like serverless computing's AWS Lambda Choudhary(2020) and machine learning's Amazon SageMaker are also offered by AWS Hardt (2021). BigQuery for data analytics Hossain et al. (2021) and Google Colab for team-based machine learning projects Pessoa (2018) are just a few of the services offered by the Google Cloud Program. Machine learning model construction and deployment tools are available through GCP's AI Platform Borra, Praveen. (2024). Virtual machines such as Azure Machine Learning for model construction, training, and deployment is of the many services that Azure provides, Singh (2023).

6.2 Data Management and Analysis in the Cloud:

Storage options that are robust and scalable are offered by cloud platforms. Data can be safely stored and accessed by researchers from any location with an internet connection. Data availability and integrity are guaranteed by features like versioning and replication.

Strong data processing solutions like Google Cloud Dataflow Akidau et al.(2015) and Apache Spark Salloum et al.(2016) on AWS EMR are available on cloud platforms. These services allow academics to handle large-scale data analysis, and difficult data transformation activities.

Tools for visualisation such as Power BI and Google Data Studio are offered by cloud platforms. To view their data and obtain new insights, researchers can construct interactive dashboards and reports. Apriani et al.(2022)

7. INDUSTRY-SPECIFIC CLOUD APPLICATIONS IN EDUCATION

7.1 Cloud Solutions for STEM Education

The field of STEM education has been greatly influenced by cloud computing, as it offers scalable, adaptable, and cost-efficient solutions. One of the key advantages of cloud solutions in STEM education is the ability to provide remote access to advanced software and computing resources that were previously only available in on-campus laboratories. For instance, platforms such as MATLAB Online and Google Colab empower students to conduct intricate simulations and data analyses from any location, creating a more inclusive and accessible learning environment, Bybee, R. (2013). Additionally, cloud-based collaborative tools support teamwork and project-based learning, which are essential elements of STEM education. Tools like GitHub and Google Workspace enable students to collaborate on group projects, share code, and document their progress in real-time, regardless of their location. This collaboration enhances their problem-solving abilities and prepares them for the collaborative nature of modern STEM careers, Alfarraj et al. (2020).

7.2 Applications in Business and Management Studies:

Cloud technologies have also transformed the landscape of business and management education through the provision of platforms that replicate real-world business settings. Cloud-based Enterprise Resource Planning (ERP) systems such as SAP and Oracle Cloud provide students with practical exposure to the tools they will utilize in their professional endeavors. These systems empower students to comprehend intricate business procedures, financial management, and supply chain operations within a controlled, risk-free setting, Godbole, M. V. (2023). Furthermore, cloud-based learning platforms like Coursera and edX offer a diverse array of business and management courses, often in partnership with esteemed universities and industry experts. These platforms leverage cloud technology to disseminate high-quality educational content to a global audience, thereby enhancing the accessibility and flexibility of business education. The integration of cloud technology in these platforms also facilitates the inclusion of interactive elements such as simulations, case studies, and real-time feedback, thereby enriching the learning experience, Ibrahim, U. (2024).

7.3 Cloud Technologies in Arts and Humanities:

Cloud computing has revolutionized the arts and humanities, offering new opportunities for creativity, collaboration, and research. Digital archives and libraries like JSTOR and Google Books have expanded access to a wide range of resources, making it easier for students and researchers to find and use scholarly articles, historical documents, and literary works. Additionally, cloud technologies have facilitated collaborative projects in fields like digital humanities, allowing researchers to work together on large datasets and share their findings in real-time. Platforms such as Omeka and Scalar have enabled the creation of digital exhibits and multimedia projects, enhancing the study of humanities through innovative presentations and interactions. In the arts, cloud-based tools like Adobe Creative Cloud provide access to professional-grade software for graphic design, video editing, and digital art. These tools support the creative process by offering powerful functionalities and collaborative features that enable artists and students to work together seamlessly, regardless of their physical location, Sharma, B. P. (2022).

8. DEVELOPING CLOUD-BASED CURRICULA

Developing curricula that are based on cloud technology entails the seamless integration of cloud computing technologies into the educational framework shown in figure 4, enriching the teaching and learning experiences. By harnessing the scalability, flexibility, and collaborative capabilities of cloud services, this approach enables the creation of vibrant and engaging learning environments.

Figure 4. Cloud Based Curricula

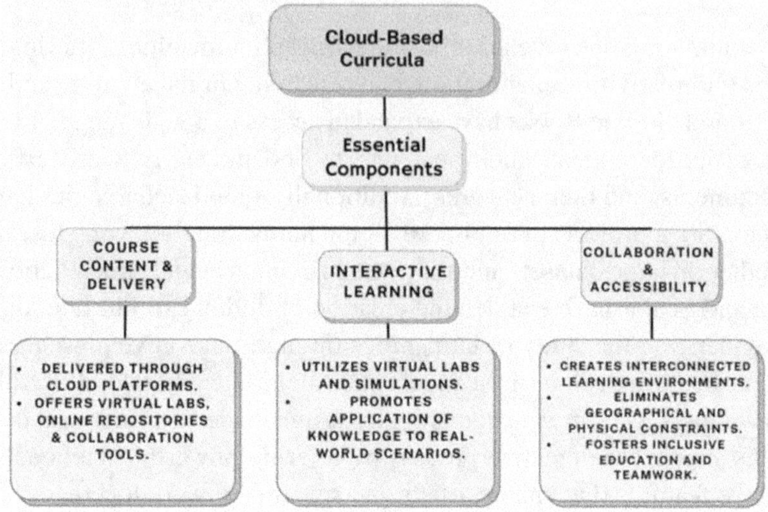

8.1 Essential Components of Cloud-Based Educational Programs:

1] **Course Content and Delivery**: The course content is delivered through cloud-based platforms such as Google Cloud, Amazon Web Services (AWS), and Microsoft Azure. These platforms provide virtual labs, online repositories, and real-time collaboration tools to enhance the hands-on learning experience. Cloud computing in education offers a suite of tools for hosting, managing, and delivering educational content, enabling real-time collaboration and access to vast resources Mell & Grance (2018).

2] **Interactive Learning**: Integrating cloud technologies facilitate interactive learning by utilizing tools such as virtual labs and simulations. These resources empower students to actively participate in experiential learning, allowing them to apply their theoretical knowledge to real-life scenarios. Interactive learning through cloud technologies fosters a deeper understanding of complex concepts by providing students with practical, real-world applications Miller (2008).

3] **Collaboration and Accessibility**: The incorporation of cloud computing in the field of education greatly amplifies collaboration and accessibility, presenting novel methods to enhance teaching and learning experiences. Through the utilization of cloud technologies, educational establishments have the ability to establish interconnected academic settings that promote smooth communication, teamwork, and inclusive education. These platforms eliminate geographical and physical constraints, equipping students and educators with the necessary resources to excel in a contemporary educational setting. he collaborative nature of cloud platforms enables enhanced communication and teamwork among students, fostering a more inclusive and participatory learning environment, Al-Zoube (2009).

8.2 Designing Cloud-Integrated Courses:

Designing cloud-integrated courses involves embedding cloud services into the course structure, enhancing the educational experience through advanced technological integration. This approach not only modernizes the learning environment but also equips students with the necessary skills to thrive in a digital world. The process of designing such courses can be viewed as a comprehensive exercise that includes identifying learning objectives, selecting appropriate cloud services, developing course materials, and providing training and support for both students and faculty. The first step in designing cloud-integrated courses is to identify learning objectives that can be achieved or enhanced through cloud integration. Learning objectives serve as the foundation for any educational course, and aligning these objectives with cloud capabilities ensures that the integration of technology directly supports educational goals. For example, cloud integration can significantly enhance data analysis skills or facilitate real-time collaboration, thus offering students practical experience with tools they are likely to encounter in their professional lives. Clear and well-defined learning objectives provide a roadmap for course development, ensuring that each component of the course is purposeful and aligned with desired outcomes, Johnson et al. (2014). Once the learning objectives have been established, the subsequent step involves the selection of suitable cloud services that align with these objectives. The process of selection entails evaluating different cloud services to determine which ones are most suitable for meeting the course's needs. For example, a data science course may greatly benefit from utilizing cloud-based data storage and analytics platforms, whereas a course focused on collaborative projects may require cloud services that facilitate real-time communication and document sharing. The ultimate goal is to choose cloud services that not only fulfill the technical requirements of the course but also enhance the overall learning experience. This meticulous selection process is crucial in order to maximize the educational advantages of integrating cloud technology, ensuring that the chosen services effectively support the course objectives Verma, et al., (2024). Once the appropriate cloud services have been chosen, the next step is to develop educational materials that take advantage of these cloud capabilities. This could involve the creation of online labs, interactive simulations, and cloud-based assessments that give students practical experience with cloud technologies. By tailoring materials specifically for cloud platforms, educators can guarantee that students can fully utilize the technological tools at their disposal. This not only enhances the learning process but also equips students with valuable skills relevant to their future careers. For instance, online labs enable students to work with data sets in a virtual setting, while interactive simulations offer immersive learning opportunities that reinforce theoretical concepts. Sultan, N. et al.(2010). Furthermore, it is crucial to provide training and support for both students and faculty to ensure the successful integration of cloud-based courses. Effective training ensures that everyone is comfortable using cloud technologies and can make the most of the integrated tools. This may involve organizing workshops, developing instructional resources, or offering individual support sessions. Adequate training and on-going support help address any potential challenges related to new technologies, allowing students and faculty to concentrate on learning. Moreover, continuous support can tackle any technical issues that arise, guaranteeing that the cloud services remain seamlessly integrated into the educational environment, Masud & Huang et al.(2012).

8.3 Faculty Training and Development:

Effective faculty training and development are crucial for the successful integration of cloud technologies into educational practices.

Training Strategies

Workshops and Seminars: It is essential to organize frequent workshops and seminars to keep faculty updated on the newest cloud technologies and how they can be utilized in education. Consistent professional development sessions are crucial in helping faculty stay abreast of technological advancements and effective strategies YILDIZ et al., (2014).

Hands-On Training: Provide hands-on training sessions that allow faculty to practice using cloud tools in a controlled environment. Hands-on training helps faculty build confidence and proficiency in using cloud technologies Pandey, A. et al.(2015).

Peer Collaboration: Encourage collaboration among faculty members to share best practices and experiences with cloud integration. Collaborative learning among faculty fosters a supportive community that enhances the overall adoption of cloud technologies Alam, et al., (2023).

8.4 Assessing Cloud-Based Learning Outcomes:

It is important to evaluate student performance and the overall impact of cloud integration on the educational process in order to assess the effectiveness of cloud-based learning.

Assessment Methods

1. **Formative Assessments:** Utilize formative assessments like quizzes, assignments, and peer reviews to evaluate students' comprehension and involvement with cloud-based tools. Formative assessments provide ongoing feedback that helps instructors adjust teaching strategies to better meet student needs. Djoub, Z. et al.(2017).
2. **Summative Assessments**: Implement summative assessments, including final exams and projects, to evaluate overall student achievement and the effectiveness of the cloud-based curriculum. Summative assessments measure the cumulative knowledge and skills gained by students, providing a comprehensive evaluation of learning outcomes, Raman, A., & Rathakrishnan et al. (2019).
3. **Student Feedback:** Collect student feedback through surveys and focus groups to understand their experiences and identify areas for improvement. Student feedback is invaluable for refining cloud-based curricula and ensuring that it meets the educational needs and expectations of learners.
4. **Performance Analytics**: Utilize analytics tools provided by cloud platforms to track student performance and engagement, enabling data-driven decision-making. Analytics tools offer insights into student behaviors and learning patterns, supporting the continuous improvement of educational practices. Siemens et al. (2013)

9. UNTITLED

9.1. Student Skill Development and Employability:

Educational institutions play a crucial role in equipping students with the necessary skills to thrive in todays rapidly changing technological environment. Cloud computing has become an essential tool in this process, offering students valuable industry-specific training opportunities, internships, and improved career prospects.

9.2 Equipping Students with Industry-Relevant Cloud Skills:

The inclusion of cloud computing in academic curricula is crucial for connecting academia with the industry. By imparting students with cloud skills that are relevant to the industry, educational establishments can boost student employability and address the changing needs of the job market. Leading cloud platforms such as Amazon Web Services (AWS), Microsoft Azure, and Google Cloud Platform provide a wide array of tools and resources that can be integrated into educational programs to offer students practical knowledge and hands-on experience. As per Trajkovski et al. (2022), the gap between academia and industry can be narrowed down by prioritizing skills development. This entails establishing standardized frameworks for skill enhancement and evaluation that are in line with industry standards. By concentrating on the specific skills required in the professional world, educational institutions can better equip students to tackle real-world scenarios.

9.3 Internships and Practical Training through Cloud Platforms:

Internships and practical training play a crucial role in a well-rounded educational experience. Cloud platforms make these opportunities possible by offering virtual environments for students to participate in real-world projects and collaborative research. Virtual labs and cloud-based simulations, for example, enable students to work on tasks relevant to the industry without the need for physical infrastructure. According to Sisodia and Jan (2023), it is important to identify industry-relevant employability skills and regularly assess competencies to ensure that students are prepared for the job market. By incorporating cloud-based internships and practical training into the curriculum, educational institutions can assist students in developing the necessary skills and gaining valuable experience to improve their employability.

9.4 Enhancing Employability and Career Prospects:

The demand for cloud computing skills is on the rise in various industries such as healthcare, finance, and technology. By integrating cloud technologies into their curricula, educational institutions can greatly improve the employability of their graduates. This involves not only teaching technical skills but also cultivating an understanding of cloud-based project management, data security, and regulatory compliance. Research has shown that continuous skill development is essential for staying competitive in the job market (Sisodia & Jan, 2023). Educational programs that focus on cloud computing can ensure that students are well-prepared to meet the demands of employers and excel in their careers. By connecting academia and industry through the incorporation of cloud computing, educational institutions can establish a more interconnected and efficient educational environment. This not only benefits students by equipping them with the skills needed for the modern workforce, but also supports industries by providing a steady supply of well-prepared graduates. With cloud-based Next-Gen Learning Systems, students can follow study plans that are specifically catered to their learning style, interests, and areas of strength and weakness. This increases learners' employability and career possibilities by enabling them to gain knowledge and skills pertinent to their chosen occupations. Cloud integration makes instructional content available to internet-connected devices at any time and from any location. Students may learn at their own pace thanks to the abundance of digital resources available to them, including articles, eBooks, podcasts, videos, and more. This improves retention rates, which in turn leads to better job results. Cloud systems provide instantaneous connection between students and instructors, promoting efficient communication, teamwork, and problem-solving skills that are essential for success in today's hectic work environment. Possibilities for Skill Development Cloud-based simulations, gamification components, and projects that are incorporated into the curriculum encourage students to apply the theoretical ideas they have learnt in class in a hands-on manner, which improves their development of the soft skills needed for successful employment. Digital Portfolio Management: Employers may more easily and quickly assess possible candidates when graduates can digitally exhibit their experiences, accomplishments, and talents thanks to cloud services' comprehensive portfolio management solutions. Opportunities for Continuous Professional Development (CPD)-Cloud-enabled platforms make it simple to access CPD opportunities, which assist professionals stay current with emerging trends and technologies in their industries and boost their competitiveness in the job market.

10. FUTURE TRENDS AND INNOVATIONS IN CLOUD COMPUTING FOR EDUCATION

Cloud computing has fundamentally transformed the educational sector by providing scalable, flexible, and cost-efficient solutions that improve both learning and administrative functions. As technological advancements continue, various emerging trends and innovations are set to further reshape the educational environment.

Improved Accessibility and Inclusivity: The ongoing evolution of cloud computing will further dismantle educational barriers by facilitating worldwide access to resources. The emergence of low-code and no-code platforms will empower educators and students with limited technical skills to develop and implement applications that meet their specific requirements. This movement will democratize technology, making educational tools more available to a wide range of populations, including those in remote or underserved regions.

AI-Enhanced Personalized Learning: The integration of artificial intelligence (AI) with cloud computing will facilitate highly customized learning experiences. AI algorithms will evaluate data related to student performance, learning preferences, and styles to adapt educational content, pacing, and assessments accordingly. These AI-driven systems will be hosted on cloud platforms, ensuring scalability and accessibility from any location, thereby providing students with a more tailored and effective educational experience.

The Role of AR/VR in Enhancing Educational Experiences: Augmented Reality (AR) and Virtual Reality (VR) are poised to play a crucial role in transforming the educational landscape, with cloud computing serving as the backbone for these data-heavy technologies. By utilizing cloud-based AR/VR, learners will gain access to engaging simulations and interactive settings, which will significantly deepen their comprehension of intricate subjects such as science, engineering, and medicine.

Edge Computing for Immediate Data Processing: The emergence of edge computing will enhance cloud services by facilitating immediate data processing near the point of data creation. In educational environments, this advancement will be particularly beneficial for IoT-integrated classrooms and intelligent campuses, where substantial data is generated on a continuous basis. Edge computing will minimize latency, enhance response times, and optimize bandwidth utilization, resulting in more effective and agile educational systems.

Blockchain for Reliable Credentialing and Academic Records: The integration of blockchain technology with cloud computing will provide secure and unalterable documentation of educational accomplishments. This advancement will simplify the credentialing process, allowing students to easily share their qualifications with potential employers and educational institutions. Furthermore, cloud-based blockchain solutions will guarantee that these records are accessible globally while ensuring privacy and security.

Cloud-Based Collaborative Learning Environments: The future of education is expected to witness a significant increase in cloud-based collaborative learning environments that facilitate peer-to-peer interaction, group assignments, and international classrooms. These platforms will harness the power of cloud computing to enable smooth communication, resource sharing, and project management capabilities, allowing students and educators to work together in real-time across different locations.

Sustainability and Green Cloud Computing: The increasing emphasis on environmental issues is prompting the education sector to embrace green cloud computing practices aimed at minimizing carbon emissions. Cloud service providers are expected to advance their technologies by developing energy-efficient data centers, implementing sustainable resource management strategies, and incorporating renewable energy sources. Educational institutions will focus on these environmentally friendly solutions, thereby supporting wider sustainability objectives.

10.1 Emerging Technologies and Their Impact on Education:

The educational landscape is undergoing rapid transformation due to emerging technologies, and cloud computing is playing a crucial role in this evolution. The use of cloud-based tools is making learning more interactive and engaging, with technologies like Virtual Reality (VR) and Augmented Reality (AR) becoming more accessible through cloud platforms. These advancements are providing students with immersive learning experiences that were previously unimaginable, allowing them to explore complex concepts in a more intuitive and interactive manner, ultimately enhancing their understanding and retention of knowledge Jiang, et al. (2021). The adoption of cloud-based Learning Management Systems (LMS) is also a significant trend in education. These systems offer educators a centralized platform to manage course materials, track student progress, and facilitate communication. The flexibility and scalability of cloud-based LMS enable educational institutions to accommodate a larger number of students without compromising on the quality of education Papers, & Rijal, S.et al. (2024). Additionally, cloud computing supports the integration of collaborative tools like Google Workspace and Microsoft Teams, fostering a more collaborative and interactive learning environment, Alfarraj, et al. (2020).

10.2 Predictive Analytics and AI in Cloud-Based Education:

The educational sector is undergoing a transformation with the help of predictive analytics and artificial intelligence (AI), which are providing personalized learning experiences and data-driven insights. Cloud-based platforms are particularly well-suited for these technologies due to their capacity to handle large volumes of data and perform complex computations. Predictive analytics can identify patterns in student performance, enabling educators to intervene early and provide targeted support to struggling students, Modupe et al. (2024). AI-powered adaptive learning systems represent another significant innovation. These systems utilize machine learning algorithms to customize educational content according to the unique needs of each student, ensuring that they receive the appropriate level of challenge and support. This personalized approach has been proven to enhance student engagement and learning outcomes Zou et al. (2022). Furthermore, AI can automate administrative tasks such as grading and scheduling, allowing educators to dedicate more time to meaningful interactions with their students Chaudhry et al. (2021).

10.3 Preparing for the Future: Trends and Predictions:

As cloud computing progresses, various trends and forecasts are emerging regarding its future in education. One significant trend is the rise in hybrid learning models, which blend online and in-person teaching. Cloud-based platforms play a crucial role in these models by providing the necessary infrastructure for delivering seamless and integrated learning experiences across various formats. Another trend is the increasing focus on data privacy and security. With educational institutions storing more data in the cloud, safeguarding the privacy and security of this data becomes crucial. Future advancements in cloud computing are expected to concentrate on enhancing security measures and complying with data protection regulations Hassan et al. (2022). Furthermore, the integration of blockchain technology in cloud-based education is gaining momentum. Blockchain offers a secure and transparent method for verifying credentials and monitoring students' academic accomplishments, addressing issues related to fraud and ensuring the credibility of educational records, Hassan et al. (2022).

CONCLUSION

In summary, cloud-integrated next-generation learning systems provide a number of benefits over conventional approaches, including increased accessibility, flexibility, scalability, cost effectiveness, and collaboration. Both industrial and academic institutions can improve their workforce development initiatives and educational offerings while maintaining their competitiveness in the quickly changing global market of today by utilising these potent instruments. Additionally, cloud integration makes it possible for diverse stakeholders to share data seamlessly, which fosters innovation and makes interdisciplinary collaboration across industries easier. All things considered, adopting cloud integration in industry and education is a calculated step towards creating more diverse, effective, and cooperative learning environments for next generations. The potential of cloud computing in education has been shown to significantly transform traditional teaching and learning methods. Recent research has highlighted the importance of emerging technologies such as Virtual Reality (VR), Augmented Reality (AR), predictive analytics, and artificial intelligence (AI) in improving educational experiences. Cloud-based Learning Management Systems (LMS) are now crucial for managing educational content and promoting collaborative learning environments .Furthermore, the emphasis on data privacy and security has been underscored, with future developments expected to focus on protecting educational data.

Recommendations for Educational Institutions and Industry Partners:

In order to maximize the advantages of cloud computing in the field of education, the following suggestions are put forth for educational institutions and industry partners:

Investment in Infrastructure: Educational institutions need to invest in strong cloud infrastructure to facilitate the integration of cutting-edge technologies. This involves ensuring dependable internet connectivity, scalable storage solutions, and secure data management systems. Professional Development: Continuous professional development for educators is essential. Institutions should offer training on utilizing cloud-based tools and emerging technologies to enhance teaching effectiveness and student engagement. Collaborative Partnerships: Industry partners should engage in partnerships with educational institutions to create and implement cloud-based solutions customized to the specific requirements of the education sector. This collaboration can foster innovation and ensure that technological advancements are seamlessly integrated into the curriculum. Focus on Data Privacy: Institutions must give priority to data privacy and security by adhering to best practices and complying with relevant regulations. This includes implementing encryption, access controls, and regular security audits to safeguard sensitive educational data. Encouraging Adaptive Learning: Institutions should embrace AI-powered adaptive learning systems to offer personalized educational experiences. These systems can help address the diverse learning needs of students and enhance overall learning outcomes.

Future Directions for Cloud Integration in Education:

The future of cloud integration in education is on track to witness on-going innovation and widespread adoption of advanced technologies. Key areas for future exploration and implementation include the rise of hybrid learning models is projected to continue, with cloud computing playing a crucial role in enabling seamless integration of online and in-person instruction. Research should delve into effective strategies for implementing these models and their impact on student learning outcomes. Further progress in AI and machine learning will pave the way for the development of more sophisticated adaptive learning systems and predictive analytics tools. Studies should concentrate on enhancing these technologies and evaluating their lasting advantages in education Cardona et al. (2023). The utilization of block chain technology for secure and transparent credentialing is anticipated to gain momentum. Future investigations should assess the feasibility and scalability of blockchain solutions for verifying academic credentials and monitoring student accomplishments. With the continuous expansion of educational data stored in the cloud, there will be a growing demand for heightened security measures. Future advancements should concentrate on creating advanced encryption techniques, intrusion detection systems, and comprehensive data protection strategies. The global aspect of cloud computing offers opportunities for international collaboration in education. Future research should explore the potential for cross-border partnerships and the exchange of resources and best practices to establish a more interconnected and fair global education system. In summary, the incorporation of cloud computing in education presents significant opportunities to revolutionize the learning environment. Through the adoption of new technologies, emphasis on safeguarding data privacy and cultivation of collaborative relationships, educational institutions and industry allies can establish more interactive, tailored, and protected educational experiences. On-going research and advancements will further propel the progression of cloud-based education, guaranteeing its position as a leader in educational development.

REFERENCES

Akhouri, V., & Wasim, J. (2022). *A Comparative Study of Cloud Deployment Model. 10*, 2320–2882.

Akidau, T., Bradshaw, R., Chambers, C., Chernyak, S., Fernández-Moctezuma, R. J., Lax, R., & Whittle, S. (2015). The dataflow model: A practical approach to balancing correctness, latency, and cost in massive-scale, unbounded, out-of-order data processing. *Proceedings of the VLDB Endowment International Conference on Very Large Data Bases*, 8(12), 1792–1803.

Al-Ataby, A. (2021). Hybrid Learning Using Canvas LMS. *European Journal of Education and Pedagogy, 2*(6), 27–33, doi.: DOI: 10.24018/ejedu.2021.2.6.180

Alam, A., & Mohanty, A. (2023). Educational technology: Exploring the Convergence of Technology and Pedagogy through mobility, interactivity, AI, and Learning Tools. *Cogent Engineering*, 10(2), 2283282. Advance online publication. DOI: 10.1080/23311916.2023.2283282

Alexiou, A., Bouras, C., & Giannaka, E. (2005). Virtual Laboratories in Education. *Technology Enhanced Learning*, 171(Jan), 19–28. DOI: 10.1007/0-387-24047-0_2

Apriani, D., Aan, M., & Saputra, W. (2022). Data Visualization Using Google Data Studio. *International Journal of Cyber and IT Service Management.*, 2(1), 11–19. DOI: 10.34306/ijcitsm.v2i1.68

Baanqud, N. S., Al-Samarraie, H., Alzahrani, A. I., & Alfarraj, O. (2020). Engagement in cloud-supported collaborative learning and student knowledge construction: A modeling study. *International Journal of Educational Technology in Higher Education*, 17(1), 56. Advance online publication. DOI: 10.1186/s41239-020-00232-z

Baher, J. (1999). Articulate Virtual Labs in Thermodynamics Education: A Multiple Case Study*. *Journal of Engineering Education*, 88(4), 429–434. DOI: 10.1002/j.2168-9830.1999.tb00470.x

Borra, P. (2024). The Evolution and Impact of Google Cloud Platform in Machine learning and AI. *International Journal of Advanced Research in Science Communication and Technology.*, 4, 72–77. DOI: 10.48175/IJARSCT-18908

Cardona, M. A., Rodriguez, R. J., & Ishmael, K. (2023). *Artificial Intelligence and the Future of Teaching and Learning Insights and Recommendations*. Office of Educational Technology. https://www2.ed.gov/documents/ai-report/ai-report.pdf

Carneiro, T., Da Nóbrega, R. V. M., Nepomuceno, T., Bian, G. B., De Albuquerque, V. H. C., & Reboucas Filho, P. P. (2018). Performance analysis of google colaboratory as a tool for accelerating deep learning applications. *IEEE Access : Practical Innovations, Open Solutions*, 6, 61677–61685.

Chan, P., Van Gerven, T., Dubois, J.-L., & Bernaerts, K. (2021). Virtual Chemical Laboratories: A Systematic Literature Review of Research, Technologies and Instructional Design. *Computers and Education Open*, 2(Oct), 100053. DOI: 10.1016/j.caeo.2021.100053

Chaudhry, M. A., & Kazim, E. (2021). Artificial Intelligence in Education (AIEd): A high-level academic and industry note 2021. *AI and Ethics*, 2(2), 157–165. Advance online publication. DOI: 10.1007/s43681-021-00074-z PMID: 34790953

Choudhary, B., Pophale, C., Gutte, A., Dani, A., & Sonawani, S. S. (2020). Case Study: use of AWS lambda for building a serverless chat application. In Proceeding of International Conference on Computational Science and Applications: ICCSA 2019 (pp. 237-244). Springer Singapore.

Djoub, Z. (2017). *Assessment for Learning: Feeding Back and Feeding Forward*. Www.igi-Global.com

Dumka, P., & Mishra, D. R. (2024). Modelling of air standard thermodynamic cycles using CyclePad. *Jiet*. https://www.academia.edu/122420201/Modelling_of_Air_Standard_Thermodynamic_Cycles_Using_CyclePad

Duta, I. P. G. P., Febriansyah, M. R., & Anggreainy, M. S. (2021, October). Effectiveness of LMS in online learning by analyzing its usability and features. In 2021 1st International Conference on Computer Science and Artificial Intelligence (ICCSAI) (Vol. 1, pp. 56-61). IEEE.

Elmoazen, R., Saqr, M., Khalil, M., & Wasson, B. (2023, March). Learning Analytics in Virtual Laboratories: A Systematic Literature Review of Empirical Research. *Smart Learning Environments*, 10(1), 9. DOI: 10.1186/s40561-023-00244-y

Gaikwad, P., & Patil. (2021, March). Study On Cloud Deployment Model. *International Journal of Scientific and Engineering Research*, 12(3), •••.

Gamage, S. H., Ayres, J. R., & Behrend, M. B. (2022). A systematic review on trends in using Moodle for teaching and learning. *International Journal of STEM Education*, 9(1), 9.

Global, I. G. I. https://www.igi-global.com/chapter/assessment-for-learning/159965

Global, I. G. I. https://www.igi-global.com/chapter/blended-learning-in-higher-education-40/224208

Hardt, M., Chen, X., Cheng, X., Donini, M., Gelman, J., Gollaprolu, S., . . . Kenthapadi, K. (2021, August). Amazon sagemaker clarify: Machine learning bias detection and explainability in the cloud. In Proceedings of the 27th ACM SIGKDD conference on knowledge discovery & data mining (pp. 2974-2983).

hashira9082. (2024, March 27). *Cloud Computing in Healthcare | Impact, Use Cases & Examples*. Enago Academy. https://www.enago.com/academy/guestposts/hashira9082/cloud-computing-in-healthcare/

.Hassan, J., Shehzad, D., Habib, U., Aftab, M. U., Ahmad, M., Kuleev, R., & Mazzara, M. (2022). The Rise of Cloud Computing: Data Protection, Privacy, and Open Research Challenges-A Systematic Literature Review (SLR). *Computational Intelligence and Neuroscience, 2022*(1). https://doi.org/.DOI: 10.1155/2022/8303504

Hassan, J., Shehzad, D., Habib, U., Aftab, M. U., Ahmad, M., Kuleev, R., & Mazzara, M. (2022). The Rise of Cloud Computing: Data Protection, Privacy, and Open Research Challenges-A Systematic Literature Review (SLR). *Computational Intelligence and Neuroscience*, 2022(1), 1–26. https://eds.p.ebscohost.com/eds/pdfviewer/pdfviewer?vid=2&sid=5c43590c-2cd5-4656-a476-a98f114b0cde%40redis. DOI: 10.1155/2022/8303504 PMID: 35712069

Irfandi, I., Festiyed, F., Yerimadesi, Y., & Sudarma, T. (2023). The Use Of Learning Management System (Lms) In The Teaching And Learning Process: Literature Review. *Jurnal Pendidikan Fisika.*, 12(1), 81. DOI: 10.24114/jpf.v12i1.42270

Jiang, H., Vimalesvaran, S., Wang, J. K., Lim, K. B., Mogali, S. R., & Car, L. T. (2021). Virtual Reality in Medical Students' Education: A Scoping Review (Preprint). *JMIR Medical Education*, 8(1), e34860. Advance online publication. DOI: 10.2196/34860 PMID: 35107421

Modupe, O. T., Otitoola, A. A., Oladapo, O. J., Abiona, O. O., Oyeniran, O. C., Adewusi, A. O., Komolafe, A. M., & Obijuru, A. (2024). REVIEWING THE TRANSFORMATIONAL IMPACT OF EDGE COMPUTING ON REAL-TIME DATA PROCESSING AND ANALYTICS. *Computer Science & IT Research Journal*, 5(3), 693–702. DOI: 10.51594/csitrj.v5i3.929

. Mohd Kasim, N. N., & Khalid, F. (2016). Choosing the Right Learning Management System (LMS) for the Higher Education Institution Context: A Systematic Review. International Journal of Emerging Technologies in Learning, (iJET), 11(06), pp. 55–61. doi:.DOI: 0.3991/ijet.v11i06.5644

Navarro, C., Arias-Calderón, M., Henríquez, C. A., & Riquelme, P. (2024). Assessment of Student and Teacher Perceptions on the Use of Virtual Simulation in Cell Biology Laboratory Education. *Education Sciences*, 14(3), 243. DOI: 10.3390/educsci14030243

Ordóñez de Pablos, P., Almunawar, M. N., & Anshari, M. (Eds.). (2023). *Developing Skills and Competencies for Digital and Green Transitions*. IGI Global.

Pandey, A. (2015). Licensed Under Creative Commons Attribution CC BY Potential, Pitfalls and Challenges in Development of ICT in Education. *International Journal of Science and Research (IJSR) ISSN, 6*, 2319–7064. https://www.ijsr.net/archive/v6i1/ART20164335.pdf

Pandit, P. (2021). A Case Study of Amazon Web Services. DOI: 10.13140/RG.2.2.18114.09921

Raman, A., & Rathakrishnan, M. (2019). *Blended Learning in Higher Education 4.0: A Brief Review*. Www.igi-Global.com

Rijal, S., Zou, G., Jie, L., & Demsky, C. (2024). The impact of using a cloud-based learning management system on access and quality of education. *Journal Emerging Technologies in Education*, 2(2), 163–176.

Rosário, A. T., & Travassos, A. (2022). Learning management systems in education: Research and challenges.Https://Services.igi-Global.com/Resolvedoi/Resolve.aspx?Doi=10.4018/978-1-6684-4706-2.Ch003, 1 Jan.

Sachdeva, S., Bhatia, S., Al Harrasi, A., Shah, Y. A., Anwer, M. K., Philip, A. K., Shah, S. F. A., Khan, A., & Ahsan Halim, S. (2024). Unraveling the role of cloud computing in health care system and biomedical sciences. *Heliyon*, 10(7), e29044–e29044. DOI: 10.1016/j.heliyon.2024.e29044 PMID: 38601602

Salloum, S., Dautov, R., Chen, X., Peng, P. X., & Huang, J. Z. (2016, October 13). Big Data Analytics on Apache Spark. *International Journal of Data Science and Analytics*, 1(3-4), 145–164. DOI: 10.1007/s41060-016-0027-9

Sauber, A. M., El-Kafrawy, P. M., Shawish, A. F., Amin, M. A., & Hagag, I. M. (2021). A New Secure Model for Data Protection over Cloud Computing. *Computational Intelligence and Neuroscience*, 2021(1), 1–11. DOI: 10.1155/2021/8113253 PMID: 35646109

Shayan, P., Rondinelli, R., van Zaanen, M., & Atzmueller, M. (2023). Multi-level analysis of learning management systems' user acceptance exemplified in two system case studies. *Data*, 8(3), 45.

Siemens, G. (2013). Learning Analytics: The Emergence of a Discipline. *The American Behavioral Scientist*, 57(10), 1380–1400. DOI: 10.1177/0002764213498851

Singh, S., Ramkumar, K. R., & Kukkar, A. (2023). Analysis and Implementation of Microsoft Azure Machine Learning Studio Services with Respect to Machine Learning Algorithms. In Modern Electronics Devices and Communication Systems: Select Proceedings of MEDCOM 2021 (pp. 91-106). Singapore: Springer Nature Singapore.

. Trajkovski, G., Killian, R. L., & Coen, S. (2022). *Bridging the Gaps Between Higher Education, Industry, and the Learner: The Skills-First Approach.*

Using CyclePad-an "articulate" software laboratory-in thermodynamics education. (1997). IEEE Conference Publication | IEEE Xplore. https://ieeexplore.ieee.org/document/635975

Veluvali, P., & Surisetti, J. (2022). Learning Management System for Greater Learner Engagement in Higher Education—A Review. *Higher Education for the Future.*, 9(1), 107–121. DOI: 10.1177/23476311211049855

Yang, J., Lee, T.-Y., Lee, W.-T., & Xu, L. (2022). A Design and Application of Municipal Service Platform Based on Cloud-Edge Collaboration for Smart Cities. *Sensors (Basel)*, 22(22), 8784. DOI: 10.3390/s22228784 PMID: 36433381

Yurdakul, B., Uslu, Ö., Çakar, E., & Yildiz, D. G. (2014, September 16). USLU, Ö., ÇAKAR, E., & YILDIZ, D. G. (2014). Evaluation of the Professional Development Program on Web Based Content Development. *Educational Sciences: Theory & Practice*. Advance online publication. DOI: 10.12738/estp.2014.4.2131

Zou, J., He, D., Zeadally, S., Kumar, N., Wang, H., & Choo, K. R. (2022). Integrated Blockchain and Cloud Computing Systems: A Systematic Survey, Solutions, and Challenges. *ACM Computing Surveys*, 54(8), 1–36. DOI: 10.1145/3456628

Chapter 5
The Fusion of Academia and Industry via Cloud Integration in Education:
Customized Learning and Adaptive Systems

Pradnya Samit Mehta
https://orcid.org/0000-0002-5304-7270
Vishwakarma Institute of Information Technology, India

Sawani Tarkeshwar Doshi
https://orcid.org/0009-0009-5932-971X
Vishwakarma Institute of Information Technology, India

Sanika Naresh Butle
https://orcid.org/0009-0009-0846-5156
Vishwakarma Institute of Information Technology, India

Shrutee Chandrakant Inamdar
https://orcid.org/0009-0000-5334-8850
Vishwakarma Institute of Information Technology, India

Sakshi Dasharath Shinde
https://orcid.org/0009-0009-6622-5206
Vishwakarma Institute of Information Technology, India

ABSTRACT

The integration of academia and industry through cloud integration is transforming the educational landscape, revolutionizing the way customized learning experiences

DOI: 10.4018/979-8-3693-6705-6.ch005

and adaptive systems are created. The proposed system delves various ways in which cloud technologies bridge the divide between theoretical knowledge and practical applications, enabling a dynamic and student-centered approach to education. Through the analysis of different case studies and technological frameworks, system emphasizes the potential for personalized learning paths, real-time feedback mechanisms, and scalable educational resources that cater to the diverse needs of learners. This integration not only enriches the learning experience but also equips students with industry-relevant skills, preparing them for real-world challenges. The primary objective of this chapter is to provide a comprehensive overview of the integration of academia and industry through cloud-based technologies in education. It will aim to analyze the concept of customized learning and adaptive systems.

INTRODUCTION

The integration of academia and industry through cloud integration is transforming the educational landscape, revolutionizing the way customized learning experiences and adaptive systems are created. The proposed system delves various ways in which cloud technologies bridge the divide between theoretical knowledge and practical applications, enabling a dynamic and student-centered approach to education. Through the analysis of different case studies and technological frameworks, system emphasizes the potential for personalized learning paths, real-time feedback mechanisms, and scalable educational resources that cater to the diverse needs of learners. This integration not only enriches the learning experience but also equips students with industry-relevant skills, preparing them for real-world challenges. The primary objective of this chapter is to provide a comprehensive overview of the integration of academia and industry through cloud-based technologies in education. It will aim to analyze the concept of customized learning and adaptive systems. Explore the impact of cloud integration on educational practices. Evaluate the benefits and challenges of this fusion - Discuss the implications for stakeholders in academia and industry and provide recommendations for leveraging cloud integration for improved educational outcomes. The integration of cloud platforms connects academia and industry, providing avenues for personalized education that is both scalable and flexible. This helps students address their varied needs and equips them for future career paths. This chapter highlights the significant impact of cloud integration in education, featuring successful case studies, technological frameworks, and collaborative models. With educational institutions embracing cloud-based solutions more widely, the ongoing advancement of customized learning and adaptive systems will be instrumental in shaping the future of education.

The proposed system delves into various ways in which cloud technologies bridge the divide between theoretical knowledge and practical applications, enabling a dynamic and student-centered approach to education. Through the analysis of different case studies and technological frameworks, system emphasizes the potential for personalized learning paths, real-time feedback mechanisms, and scalable educational resources that cater to the diverse needs of learners. This integration not only enriches the learning experience but also equips students with industry-relevant skills, preparing them for real-world challenges. The primary objective of this chapter is to provide a comprehensive overview of the integration of academia and industry through cloud-based technologies in education. It will aim to analyze the concepts of customized learning and adaptive systems. This helps students address their varied needs and equips them for future career paths.

1. TO CLOUD INTEGRATION IN EDUCATION

Overview of Cloud-Based Technologies in the Education Sector

Cloud based technology refers to the internet-based services which provide on-demand access to the various resources such as data storage, applications etc. In educational sector, cloud computing enhances the delivery of educational content and manages it over internet. These allows students as well as teaching staff to access resources from anywhere at any time making it more flexible and scalable educational environment. Web-based learning breaks time and space limitations of traditional teaching to satisfy learners' needs of learning whenever they have time and wherever they may be. As the carrier connecting learning resources and learners, the network teaching platform is able to integrate teaching resources effectively (Liu, B., et al., 2019). Currently cloud computing is the most dynamic and reliable resource for information sharing as it works in many areas like healthcare, business, communication and many more. It also takes place in academia as it provides better on demand services and many other huge and reliable benefits (Al-Mousa, A. et.al 2019). Figure (1) gives a clear picture of how advantageous is cloud computing in education.

Figure 1. Advantages of Cloud Computing in Education

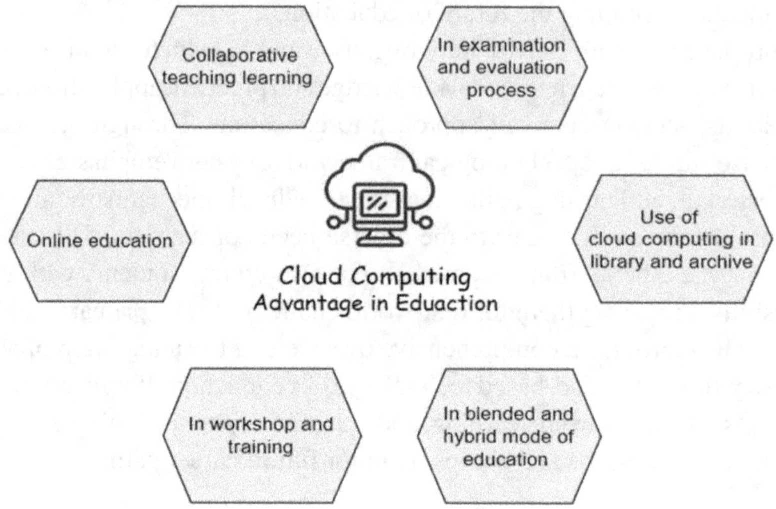

Cloud computing began to evolve in the early 2000s with the introduction of major providers like Google Cloud and Amazon Web Services (AWS). Many educational institutions started using cloud computing technologies to overcome the limitations of traditional infrastructure like high cost, limited resources and scalability problems. Cloud computing facilitates access to data and information without limitation of spatial and temporal limits. (Paul, P., Chatterjee, et al.,2023) These changes have transformed the education system, enabling remote learning, building collaborative study environments and providing access to extensive digital resources.

Examples of Technologies-

Few of the most used cloud-based technologies are:

1)Canvas: A Learning Management System (LMS) which offers customizable course creation, its management, and various features for assessment, with support for numerous third-party applications.
2)Microsoft Teams: This app integrates video conferencing, file transfer and chat. It integrates with many educational features to facilitate virtual classrooms.
3)Google Classroom: Eases the creation, distribution and evaluation of assignments, integrating seamlessly with Google Workspace tools for collaboration and enhanced communication.

Cloud computing is evolving exponentially in education, with the adoption of various cloud platforms like Microsoft Azure, IBM cloud etc. which has totally transformed traditional learning patterns. These laid a foundation for personalized learning by providing dynamic solutions that can serve the needs of each student. Hence, helping teachers in creating customized learning material leading to enhancement of every student's performance.

2. FOUNDATIONS OF PERSONALIZED LEARNING

2.1 Understanding the concept of personalized learning

Cloud computing offers exciting possibilities for personalized learning in academia. Scalable cloud-based platforms act as a central hub for student information, course materials, and performance data. This empowers instructors to leverage cloud integration and tailor learning experiences to individual student needs. Imagine a student struggling with a concept. Cloud integration allows instructors to access a vast library of additional learning resources, personalizing the learning journey for each student. Furthermore, virtual classrooms and video conferencing features promote communication and collaboration, fostering a more inclusive learning environment regardless of location. Ultimately, cloud technology personalizes learning, empowers educators with data insights, and holds immense potential to transform education (Chen, S. Y., & Magoulas, G. D. (2003). Cloud computing offers a powerful solution to the challenges of traditional e-learning. Scalable cloud platforms like PCLE (**Personalized Cloud E-learning environment**) act as a central hub for student data and course materials, empowering instructors to personalize learning with cloud-based resources (Kale, S., & Khatri, S. (2021). Imagine a student struggling with a concept – PCLE allows instructors to tailor the learning journey by providing access to a vast library of additional materials. Furthermore, virtual classrooms and video conferencing features built into these platforms promote communication and collaboration, fostering a more inclusive learning environment(Xu, J., Liu, Y., Liu, Z., & Zhang, J. (2017). . By combining cloud computing's scalability and data analysis with innovative systems like PCLE, educational institutions can overcome limitations and create a more engaging and personalized learning experience for all students. (El-Attar et al.,2019)Cloud computing transforms personalized learning in the industry. Scalable cloud platforms store employee data, training materials, and performance records, empowering trainers to create personalized learning paths. Cloud integration unlocks a wealth of targeted resources based on individual needs, while machine learning adapts the learning journey in real time. Collaboration and knowledge sharing are fostered through virtual classrooms, and data insights from cloud technology enable data-driven decisions to improve training programs and empower employees to excel. (Mohammadi et al., 2019)

2.2 Different Technical Tools for Personalized Learning

Cloud computing is revolutionizing education and training by offering personalized learning experiences. These tools leverage the power of the internet to analyze your strengths and weaknesses, and then tailor the learning journey to fit your unique needs.

2.2.1. Learning Management Systems (LMS) with Adaptive Learning:

Cloud computing is personalizing learning through Learning Management Systems (LMS) that track your learning journey and tailor it to your needs. Imagine a central hub like Canvas, a cloud-based LMS, that tracks your performance in quizzes, assignments, and projects. This data creates your unique "learning fingerprint "Cloud integration allows this LMS to connect with other platforms. In schools, this might involve recommending adaptive learning modules based on your learning fingerprint. In workplaces, it could suggest targeted training based on your performance data (Watson, W. R., & Watson, S. L. (2017). This personalized approach ensures you're always learning what you need, fostering a more effective learning environment in both academia and industry. (Martin et al., 2020) .Example: You're taking an online statistics course through Canvas. As you progress through modules, the LMS analyses your performance on quizzes and assignments. If you struggle with concepts like standard deviation, the LMS identifies this gap. It then adapts your learning path by presenting you with targeted practice problems and video tutorials specifically focused on standard deviation.

2.2.2 Interactive Simulations and Gamified Learning:

Cloud computing is taking learning to a new level of engagement and personalization in both academia and industry through interactive simulations and gamified learning. These platforms analyze vast amounts of user data (performance within simulations or games) to pinpoint individual strengths and weaknesses. Imagine a student struggling with a science concept in a cloud-based learning platform; the system can personalize the simulation to bridge the gap in their understanding. Similarly, in the workplace, a cloud-based training platform might utilize gamified sales simulations. Employee performance data can be used to personalize the game difficulty, focusing on areas where the employee needs improvement. This personalized approach, made possible by cloud integration, keeps learners engaged and fosters a more effective learning environment by providing targeted learning experiences based on individual needs. This leads to a deeper understanding of concepts and improved skill development in both academic and professional settings. (Kim et al., 2021).

Example: Imagine studying the human body in biology class. A cloud-based simulation platform allows you to explore a 3D model of the human anatomy. You can zoom in on specific organs and systems, manipulate them virtually, and even access additional information through text labels or narrated explanations (Peng,2019). This caters to visual and kinesthetic learners who benefit from a hands-on approach. Gamified learning platforms could make learning a foreign language more engaging by turning vocabulary acquisition into a points-based game, where you earn badges for completing challenges and mastering new words.

2.2.3 E-portfolio Platforms:

E-portfolio platforms take online learning to a new level by personalizing your educational journey. Cloud technology allows you to store assignments, projects, and reflections, while instructors can provide direct feedback within your portfolio(-Johnson, et.al 2016). This platform integrates with Learning Management Systems (LMS) to import grades and learning objectives, giving you a holistic view of your progress. Advanced analytics analyze your e-portfolio content to suggest personalized learning resources or connect you with mentors. With these insights, you can create custom learning pathways and curate specific content to target your goals. Cloud platforms also enable collaboration by allowing you to share your e-portfolio and receive feedback from peers, fostering a more interactive learning experience (Miller et al., 2021)

Example: Let's say you're learning graphic design. Your Moodle e-portfolio becomes your online design portfolio. You can upload your completed projects, client testimonials, and even mood boards that inspired your designs. This allows you to not only showcase your work but also reflect on your progress, identify areas for improvement and set personalized learning goals for the future.

2.2.4 Micro learning Platforms:

Cloud computing is supercharging micro learning, revolutionizing how we learn in both schools and workplaces. These platforms offer bite-sized online modules (5-10 minutes) that fit busy schedules. Imagine a student stuck on a concept in a cloud-based learning system. With cloud tech analyzing their performance, the system can automatically suggest relevant micro learning modules to bridge the gap. In the workplace, a Performance Management System (PMS) might integrate with a micro learning platform to recommend modules based on an employee's work data. This personalized approach empowers learners to create learning paths that target their specific needs, leading to improved learning outcomes and a more engaging environment. The flexibility of any-time, anywhere access makes micro learning ideal for both academia and industry. (Kim et al., 2021). Example: Imagine you're a marketing professional who needs to learn how to use a new social media analytics tool for an upcoming campaign. A microlearning platform can offer a personalized module that focuses on the specific features and functionalities of that tool. This targeted learning approach saves you time by not requiring you to complete a lengthy generic social media marketing course.

2.2.5. Performance Management Systems with Personalized Recommendations:

Cloud computing is transforming how we learn by creating personalized learning experiences in both academic and professional settings. This integration between Performance Management Systems (PMS) and learning platforms allows for a more data-driven approach. In schools, cloud-based learning platforms track student performance through assignments and quizzes, while in workplaces, PMS analyzes data like sales figures and reports Helaimia, R. (2023). These insights are used to identify individual skill gaps. The system then recommends targeted learning resources tailored to address those weaknesses. This could include adaptive learning modules, video tutorials, online courses, or even mentorship programs. Cloud platforms also seamlessly integrate with microlearning platforms offering short, focused modules that students or employees can access on their own time; Wozniak, K., Lilly, C., Hambrock, H., Richter, R., & Reiseck, C.(2016). By tracking progress through completed modules, courses, and assignments, instructors and managers can provide feedback and ensure learners stay on track. This personalized approach to learning fosters deeper engagement, improves learning outcomes, and ultimately leads to a more skilled and developed workforce, benefiting both academia and industry. (Mohammadi et al., 2019). Example: Imagine working in sales and using a cloud-based performance management system. The system tracks your sales data and identifies areas where you might be struggling, such as closing deals. Based on this data, the system recommends personalized training courses or resources on the same platform, perhaps focusing on negotiation techniques or objection-handling skills. This targeted approach helps you develop the specific skills needed to excel in your role.

3. CLOUD-BASED ACCESS TO EDUCATIONAL RESOURCES

Cloud-based access to educational resources refers to the practice of storing and accessing learning materials, tools, and applications over the internet through cloud computing platforms. Instead of relying on local storage or physical media, educational content is hosted on remote servers and made available to users via the internet; Liu, M., McKelroy, E., Corliss, S. B., & Carrigan, J. (2017).

3.1 Advantages:

Cloud-based access enhances the educational experience as follows:

3.1.1 Accessibility:

Cloud technology ensures that learning materials are accessible to students anytime and anywhere by leveraging the power of internet connectivity and remote access. Traditional barriers of geography and time are overcome through cloud-based access, allowing students to engage with educational resources regardless of their physical location or time zone. By storing learning materials on remote servers hosted in the cloud, students can access these resources using any internet-enabled device, such as smartphones, tablets, or laptops. Whether at home, in transit, or in a different country, students can seamlessly connect to the cloud and retrieve learning materials with just a few clicks. This accessibility promotes inclusivity and accommodates diverse learning needs and preferences, empowering students to learn at their own pace and convenience. (Liu et.al,2017).

3.1.2 Device Compatibility:

Cloud-based resources are designed to be compatible with a wide range of devices, ensuring seamless access across different platforms and form factors. Whether students prefer to use smartphones, tablets, or laptops, cloud-based applications and learning platforms are optimized for compatibility, offering consistent user experiences across devices. Mobile applications and responsive web designs enable students to access educational resources on smaller screens, such as smartphones and tablets, while desktop applications and web interfaces cater to users accessing content on larger screens, such as laptops and desktop computers. This device agnosticism ensures that students can access learning materials regardless of the device they are using, promoting flexibility and convenience in their learning journey(Liu et.al,2017).

3.1.3 Collaboration:

Cloud technologies facilitate collaboration among students and educators through a myriad of features designed to enable real-time communication, sharing, and co-creation of content. Real-time editing and sharing of documents allow students to collaborate on group projects, presentations, and assignments, fostering teamwork and peer learning. Cloud-based platforms offer collaborative tools such as chat, video conferencing, and discussion forums, enabling students to engage in meaningful discussions and knowledge sharing. Version control and commenting features facilitate feedback and iteration, enhancing the quality of collaborative work. Furthermore, cloud-based storage ensures that all collaborators have access to the latest version of documents and resources, eliminating the need for cumbersome file sharing via email or USB drives. Overall, cloud technologies empower students to collaborate effectively, irrespective of their physical location or time constraints, enriching their learning experiences and promoting a culture of teamwork and cooperation. (Kumar J.S.A et.al 2017).

3.1.4 Cost-effectiveness:

1. Reduced Infrastructure Costs: By leveraging cloud-based infrastructure, educational institutions can avoid the upfront capital expenses associated with purchasing and maintaining on-premises servers, storage systems, and networking equipment. This cost-saving benefit allows institutions to allocate resources more efficiently, investing in other critical areas such as faculty development, student support services, or academic programs.
2. Scalable Resources: Cloud-based access offers scalability, allowing institutions to scale resources up or down according to demand. Instead of investing in excess capacity to accommodate peak usage periods, institutions can dynamically adjust resource allocations based on actual usage levels, optimizing cost-effectiveness and resource utilization.
3. Pay-as-you-go Models: Many cloud service providers offer flexible pricing models, such as pay-as-you-go or subscription-based pricing, where institutions only pay for the resources, they consume. This pay-for-usage approach eliminates the need for long-term commitments or upfront licensing fees, providing institutions with cost predictability and flexibility to scale resources as needed. (Kale et.al 2021).
4. Shared Resources: Cloud-based access enables resource sharing and collaboration among multiple institutions, allowing them to pool resources, share infrastructure, and collaborate on joint initiatives. By leveraging shared resources, institutions

can reduce costs, improve efficiency, and access specialized expertise or services that may not be feasible to develop in-house.

3.1.5 Self-directed Learning:

1. Cloud-based learning environments empower students to take control of their learning journey and tailor it to their individual interests and goals. With access to a wealth of online resources, students can explore topics beyond the scope of traditional curricula and delve deeper into areas of personal interest.
2. Cloud platforms often offer a diverse range of learning materials, including e-books, articles, podcasts, and interactive tutorials. This abundance of resources allows students to curate their own learning paths, selecting content that resonates with their learning style and preferences.
3. Cloud-based learning management systems (LMS) provide students with tools for tracking their progress, setting learning goals, and monitoring their performance over time. By fostering autonomy and accountability, these platforms promote the development of essential self-directed learning skills .

3.1.6 Remote Learning:

Cloud computing underpins the infrastructure for remote learning, enabling students to access course materials, participate in virtual classes, and collaborate with peers and instructors from anywhere with an internet connection. Cloud-based video conferencing platforms, such as Zoom or Microsoft Teams, facilitate real-time interaction between students and educators, replicating the classroom experience in a virtual setting. These platforms support features like screen sharing, chat, and breakout rooms, enhancing the quality of remote instruction. Cloud-based file storage and sharing services, such as Google Drive or Dropbox, enable seamless collaboration on group projects and assignments, regardless of participants' physical locations. This remote collaboration capability is particularly valuable for students who are unable to attend in-person classes due to mobility issues, geographical distance, or other constraints. Lin, Y., & Wang, W. (2023).

3.2 Impact on Personalized Learning Experiences

3.2.1 Student Autonomy:

Cloud access provides students with the autonomy to take control of their learning by offering anytime, anywhere access to educational resources. By leveraging cloud-based platforms and applications, students have the flexibility to choose when and where they engage with learning materials, empowering them to set their own pace and preferences. This autonomy fosters a sense of ownership and responsibility for learning outcomes, motivating students to actively engage with course materials and take initiative in their educational pursuits.

3.2.2 Customized Learning:

Cloud-based access enables customized learning experiences tailored to individual needs and schedules. With the flexibility to access learning materials at any time and from any location, students can personalize their learning journey to suit their unique interests, abilities, and learning preferences. Educators can leverage cloud platforms to deliver adaptive learning experiences, providing personalized recommendations, content modules, and assessments based on students' learning profiles and performance metrics. Additionally, cloud-based tools facilitate differentiated instruction, allowing educators to tailor content delivery and learning activities to address students' diverse learning needs and abilities. This customization promotes student engagement, comprehension, and retention, as learners receive instruction that is relevant, accessible, and aligned with their individual learning goals.

3.3 Case Studies/Examples:

3.3.1. Amanda and Zmanda Cloud Computing Services

Amanda and Zmanda Cloud Computing are services designed to help schools with their data backup needs. Amanda Enterprise offers features like easy installation, simple management, and advanced functionality at affordable prices. It's an open-source software, meaning students aren't tied to a specific company for accessing their data. Zmanda Cloud Computing, on the other hand, provides a straightforward and cost-effective solution for backing up and recovering data in case of emergencies. These services cater specifically to educational institutions, offering products like Amanda Enterprise, Zmanda Recovery Manager for MySQL, and Zmanda Internet Backup. (kumar B.P. et.al 2013).

3.3.2 Amazon Web Services (AWS) in Education and Industries

Background: Amazon Web Services (AWS) is a leading provider of cloud computing services, offering a wide range of infrastructure, platform, and software solutions to businesses and organizations worldwide. AWS has been increasingly adopted in various sectors, including education and industries, due to its scalability, flexibility, and cost-effectiveness.

Amazon EC2 Services shown in figure 2 is among the multitude of services provided by Amazon, the following are noteworthy; This web service furnishes virtual machines and additional CPU cycles tailored for institutional organizations. Amazon Simple Storage Service (Amazon S3) enables students, faculty, and researchers to store items within Amazon's Virtual storage infrastructure, albeit with limited size constraints. Amazon Simple Queue Service (SQS) facilitates various types of messages passing APIs, fostering seamless communication among educators. Amazon SimpleDB: A web service devised for executing real-time queries on structured datasets hosted in the cloud Gebhardt, K. (2018).

Amazon Virtual Computing Laboratory (Amazon VCL): An open-source implementation offering secure, production-level, on-demand utility computing. It grants access to a broad spectrum of computational resources, storage, and software solutions.

Figure 2. Amazon EC2 Services

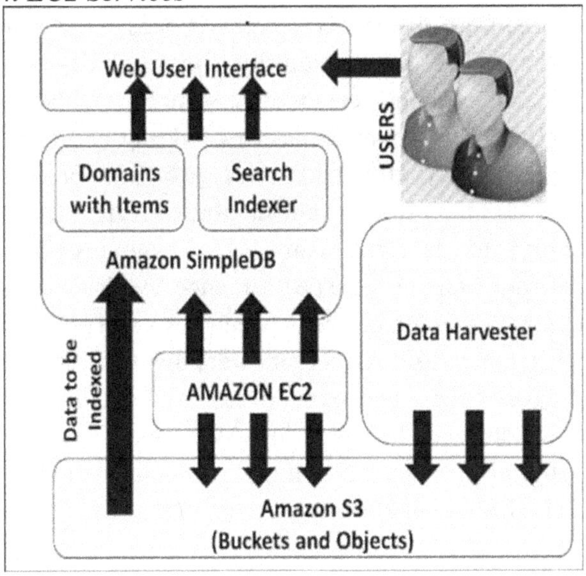

Application in Education:

1. <u>Harvard University's Data Science Initiative:</u> University partnered with AWS to launch its Data Science Initiative, aimed at advancing research and education in data science and computational analysis.

AWS provides Harvard researchers and students with cloud-based infrastructure and tools for data storage, processing, and analysis. By leveraging AWS, Harvard facilitates collaborative research projects, accelerates data-driven discoveries, and enhances learning experiences in data science disciplines. (Kale et.al 2021).

2. California Community Colleges Online Education Initiative (OEI) partnered with AWS to modernize and expand its online education platform, serving over 2.1 million students across the state. AWS enables scalable hosting and delivery of online courses, multimedia content, and student support services. Through AWS, the OEI enhances accessibility, flexibility, and reliability of online education offerings, empowering students to pursue their academic goals anytime, anywhere. (Kale et.al 2021).

Application in Industries:

Netflix is a global streaming service provider, relies on AWS for its cloud infrastructure to deliver high-quality video content to millions of subscribers worldwide. AWS supports Netflix's scalable video encoding, transcoding, and delivery processes, ensuring seamless streaming experiences across devices and regions. By leveraging AWS, Netflix achieves cost efficiency, agility, and reliability in managing its vast library of multimedia content and serving diverse user demands

Airbnb is a leading online marketplace for lodging and tourism experiences, utilizes AWS to support its dynamic and rapidly growing platform. AWS provides Airbnb with scalable compute, storage, and database services to handle fluctuations in user traffic, bookings, and data processing. By leveraging AWS's global infrastructure and services, Airbnb enhances the performance, availability, and security of its platform, enabling seamless interactions between hosts and guests worldwide. (Kale et.al 2021). Impact In education, AWS empowers institutions to advance research, enhance learning experiences, and expand access to quality education through scalable cloud-based solutions. In industries, AWS enables businesses to innovate, scale, and deliver digital services efficiently, driving growth, and competitiveness in the global market. (Kale et.al 2021).

3.3.3 Microsoft Cloud Services for Education

Microsoft Cloud Services for Education emphasizes choice, offering a hybrid model that enables students and researchers to transition seamlessly to the cloud. This approach allows workload distribution across infrastructures while complementing existing IT assets with web-based services. By leveraging Microsoft cloud services, educational institutions can utilize familiar technologies, enhancing collaboration and flexibility. Features of Microsoft Live@edu is depicted in figure 3 accessible via popular web browsers across multiple operating systems, - Available at no cost, reducing IT infrastructure expenses and maintenance time, Enhances collaboration among peers and faculty, supporting strategic initiatives, Facilitates informed decision-making regarding educational cloud computing, Meets high student expectations with anywhere access to cutting-edge technology. Provides on-demand resources and enables large-scale application testing and deployment.

Figure 3. Features of Microsoft Live@edu

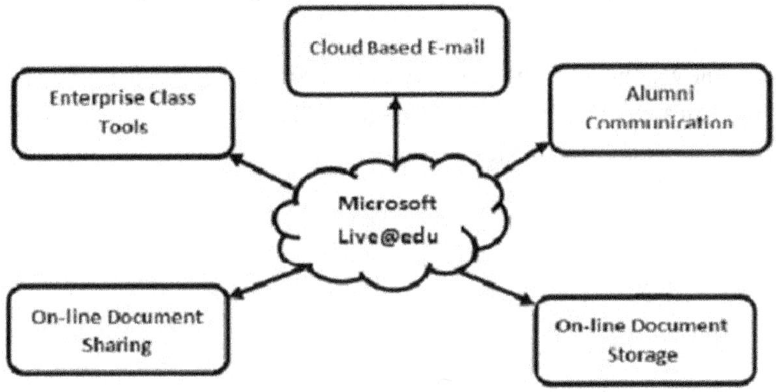

Microsoft's Cloud Computing Solution, Windows Azure_serves as an operating system for universities and colleges, enabling application execution and data storage via Microsoft servers.Azure Services Platform (ASP) offers functionalities such as user identity management, workflow management, and online computing capabilities.

3.3.4 Google Applications for Educational Cloud Computing(GAE)

GAE is a cloud computing-based platform offering a suite of web applications designed for faculty, researchers, and students. It operates within the Google Infrastructure and is provided free of charge to educational institutions. Key features include:

1. Communication and Collaboration Tools: GAE provides secure communication and collaboration capabilities, allowing users to select solutions tailored to their needs.
2. Google Calendar: A shared and accessible calendar for scheduling courses and managing business activities, facilitating organization within work groups.
3. Google Sites: Enables users to build, create, and publish information using Google's tools, enhancing collaboration and information dissemination.

4. Google Video: Allows for secure and private sharing of video content among faculty, researchers, and students.
5. Google Talk: An Instant Messaging (IM) tool facilitating remote communication among colleagues with limited conversation barriers.
6. Google Mail: Offers email organization features such as labels and filters, streamlining the management of incoming messages and integration with other email accounts.
7. Google Docs: A primary task tool for courses, enabling synchronous collaboration on documents among participants.

Figure 4 shows the various services and products offered by Google Cloud Platform like Compute, Networking, Storage and Database, Machine Learning, Big data, and Identity and Access Management.

Figure 4. Products offered by Google Cloud Platform

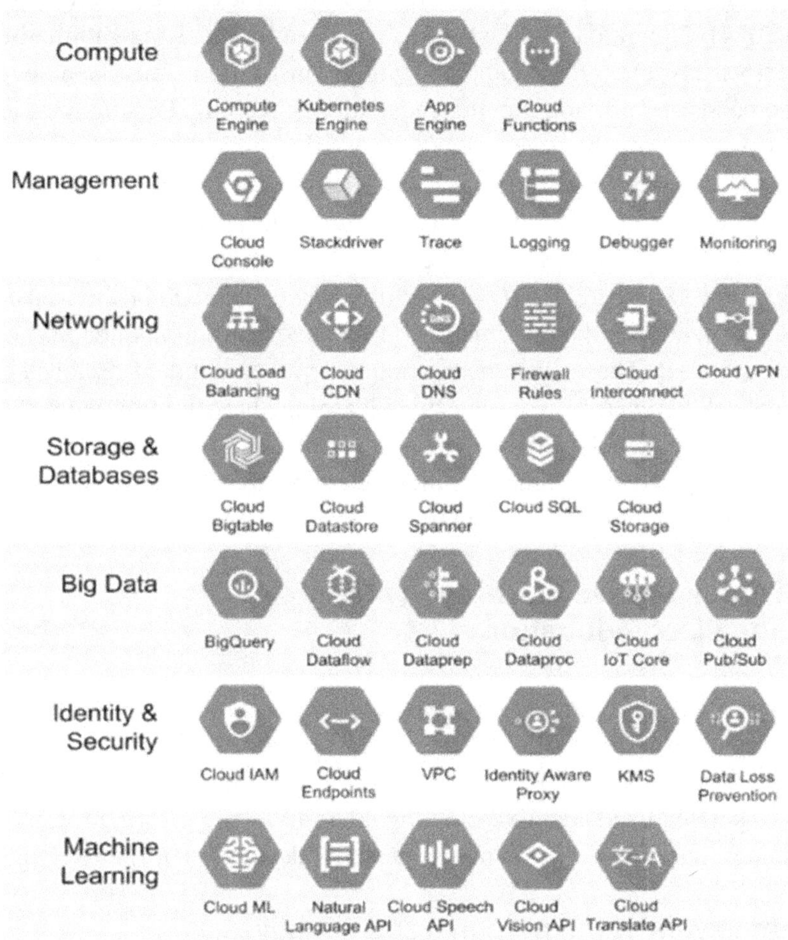

4. PERSONALIZED CONTENT DELIVERY AND ADAPTIVE LEARNING

4.1 Tailoring educational content to individual student needs

Each person is unique and varied in terms of their academic, social, cultural, and economic background. Their cognitive, emotional, mental, and physical abilities are also dissimilar. Additionally, their connectivity, learning styles, and preferences are different. It is thus difficult to assume that they will learn in the same way or that their needs would be met in a comparable manner. It emphasizes the necessity of having a variety of learning styles in order to meet the demands of every learner (Hussain,2024). Now-a-days, Classrooms are defined by rising multiculturalism and student variety, and schools and educational institutions must be able to adapt to those demands and provide excellent education procedure. Personalized learning is the best solution for this as personalized leaning also shares the same goal as Self-Pacing (Rebeca Soler Costa et.al., 2021). ersonalized learning can be achieved through differentiated instructions. "*Differentiated instruction is a kind of instruction that educators actively plan for the differences of students that includes what to be taught,how to be taught and the pace at which to be taught*"(Shemshack et.al., 2020). In order to efficiently implement differentiated instructions, adaptive learning techniques are used. These systems continuously assess student performance and deliver feedback in real time using machine learning algorithms and data analytics. Based on these data, teachers can develop a dynamic and responsive learning environment that adapts to each student's unique learning style and speed by integrating platforms such as DreamBox and Smart Sparrow.

4.2 Utilizing adaptive learning systems for personalized education

"Adaptive learning technologies dynamically adjust to the level or type of course content based on an individual's abilities or skill attainment, in ways that accelerate a learner's performance with both automated and instructor interventions." The core elements of personalized adaptive learning are individual performance, individual characteristics, adaptive adjustment and personal development (peng et.al., 2019).

4.2.1 Framework of the personalized adaptive learning system (PAL system)

On the basis of core concept and core elements framework of PAL system is designed.

Figure 5. Personalized Adaptive Learning

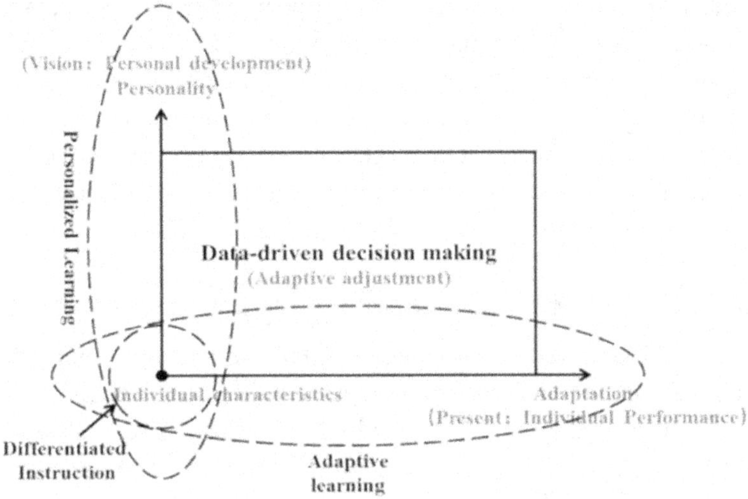

As can be observed in Figure 5, the vertical axis is used as a personality axis to gauge personal development, while the horizontal axis is used as an adaptation axis to depict the present individual performance. Differentiated instruction, which is shown as the intersection of two axes as individual traits, is a shared feature of both personalized and adaptive learning.

There are three approaches to achieve PAL:

1) Customize the teaching methods on the basis of variations in individual characteristics (circular)
2) Customize the teaching methods on the basis of variations and modifications in present individual performance (horizontal ellipse)
3) Customize the teaching methods on the basis of variations and modifications in personal development vision (vertical ellipse).

The implementation of all three approaches can be achieved through adaptively modifying instruction through data-driven decision-making. Upgrading differentiated instruction methodologies is the initial strategy. The grouping techniques of homogeneous and heterogeneous grouping are the classic tactics of differentiated education. One example of a consolidated and roughly differentiated learning approach is stratified teaching. The environment of information technology has made dynamic grouping and intervention feasible. The idea of adaptable learning serves as the foundation for the second strategy. Rule-based and data-driven teaching methodologies are the two primary categories. While the latter's teaching strategy is dynamically developed using student data, the former's is predetermined in accordance with the decision tree. The vision for personal development is the third strategy. Program, course, and task levels are the three granularity levels into which the core strategy can be subdivided. Institutional adjustments, such optional class systems and elective courses, are handled at the program level; learning path planning is handled at the course level; and content, services, and other modifications are handled at the task level. These three strategies can all be put into practice using adaptive adjustments made to data-driven instructional decisions. (peng et.al., 2019).

The fourth approach: adaptive adjustment instruction strategies

Adaptive adjustment has six components. A two-dimensional coordinate system can be used to divide instruction methodologies, with the three degrees of personalized learning as the abscissa and the two kinds of data decision-making serving as the ordinate. Figure .6 depicts the range of these strategies. The figure's wavy line, which extends from lower left to upper right, symbolizes the fourth PAL approach route. The root is divided into three tiers. These consist of three layers: personal development, individual performance, and individual characters. There are two phases in every stratum. The "what to learn" conundrum is primarily resolved by the layer of individual characters. This layer's data-driven decision-making stage is resource recommendation focused. This means that computers will suggest a list of resources based on the unique traits of the student who need assistance, or a list of resources acquired by learners who have achieved similar achievement. Students can select the materials they want to learn from a list that is ordered from high to low matching degree.

Figure 6. Adaptive Adjustment Instruction Strategies

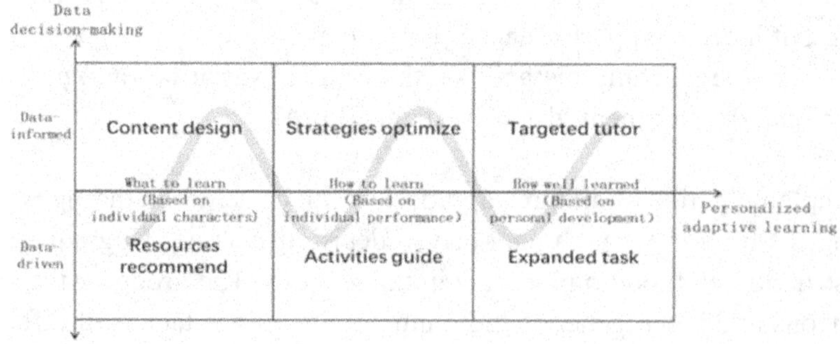

This layer's data-driven decision-making phase focuses on content design. This implies that educators create learning materials for students whose unique personalities don't mesh well with others using agile design principles. The material is progressively improved through several iterations and increments in accordance with the variations and alterations of each learner's unique attributes. The "how to learn" challenge is addressed by the individual performance layer. Activities guide is the primary emphasis of this layer's data-driven decision-making step. Which is to use student performance data analysis to determine his or her learning pattern? It can be determined that the issue originates with the learner rather than the teaching methods if the pattern indicates that the learner has an issue and that the issue is only an individual phenomenon. The student's activities must be modified as a result. It is likely that teaching tactics need to be optimized if the issue is one that affects the majority of students. This procedure takes place at this layer's data-informed decision-making stage. The personal growth layer answers the question of "how well learned" in respect to their personal vision. More challenging, enlarged assignments that meet their unique vision would be recommended if the response is in the affirmative. By tracking learning accomplishments, the data-driven decision-making step of this layer determines if students may finish the learning objectives ahead of schedule (for specific instruction, please refer to measuring to help learning mechanism of precision teaching). The layer's data-informed decision-making step concentrates on the issues that arise when students take on difficult, extended assignments. It aims to provide individualized tutoring for challenges that each student faces and use a consolidated tutoring strategy for problems that most students confront. In terms of the level of personalization, the new approach route offers learners personalized adaptive learning services, and it may be seamlessly integrated and compatible with differentiated instruction, personalized learning and adaptive learning. Thus, based on the initial successes of informationalization, this approach illuminates the way for technology developers to get personalized adaptive learning (peng et.al., 2019).

4.2.2 Current Adaptive Learning Platforms

Adaptive learning platforms, including algorithm-based systems, were developed on the basis of research on tutoring systems and data analytics. (Johnson et.al, 2016). These platforms determine the unique learning styles and behaviors of every student and guide their customized readings, assignments, and evaluations (Wozniak et.al, 2016). Online, in-person, and blended learning settings are all improved by adaptive learning platforms (Wagner, 2017; Liu et al., 2017). Moreover, adaptive learning systems can be a helpful solution to the issue of expanding class numbers in higher education by providing customized training based on each student's knowledge and ability (Elsevier, 2016). Many software companies, such as

WalkMe, Edapp,360learning, CogBooks, McGraw Hill Education, D2L, Knewton, Realizeit, Adaptemy, Domoscio, Elsevier, Pearson Interactive Labs, and many more, offer adaptive learning solutions for K–12 or higher education settings. (Alamri et.al.,2021). Edmentum Courseware for Higher Education, a private educational organization that specializes in personalized learning platforms, is another platform that might make the adoption of personalization easier. Edmentum offers flexible teaching methods, assessments, and curricula to encourage students to participate in active learning. (Alamri et.al.,2021).

5. DATA-DRIVEN PERSONALIZATION

Collection and analysis of student data for personalized learning of student data is very crucial for personalized learning. It involves collecting different type of data, such as student engagement levels, learning styles and academic performance. By using these data educators can update the educational experiences to fulfill the unique needs of every student.

5.1 Types of Data Collection

1.STYLE OF LEARNING: Data on what style of learning like visual, auditory etc. does the student prefer. These will help educators in customizing the instructional methods.
2.ENGAGEMENT DATA: Here we will keep track of the students' interaction with learning materials, which can include the participation in classes, usage patterns of resources and the time spent on various assignments.
3.BEHAVIOURAL DATA: These will have information regarding the classroom behavior, attendance and participation in activities. These data will showcase the attitude of students towards learning.
4.ACADEMIC DATA: It will include the progress reports, grades and assignment scores. These data is most important for examining the area of improvement of the students as we will get to know about their weaknesses and strengths.

5.2 Data Collection Methods

1.ASSESSMENT TOOLS: A student can be assessed on the basis of marks scored in assignments, exams and quizzes, providing a real time feedback of students' progress and understanding.
2.FEEDBACKS: Various surveys can be conducted for taking students feedback on teaching methods, preferences and learning styles.

3.LEARNING MANAGEMENT TOOLS: Canvas, Blackboard and Moodle like platforms gather students data automatically by interacting with them.
4.ANALYTICS TOOLS: Some software's can be used to track and analyze data from various educational technologies to provide comprehensive insights.

5.3 Data Analysis Techniques

1.DESCRIPTIVE ANALYSIS: In this raw data is summarized to show what happened. For example, displaying participation rates or average scores.
2.PREDICTIVE ANALYSIS: These will predict the future by analyzing previous data such as identification of students' risk of failing behind.
3.PRESCRIPTIVE ANALYSIS: Here we will be recommended for doing specific actions based on the data analysis. It will help educators to improve performance of struggling students and also in finding advanced opportunities for brighter ones.

6._COLLABORATIVE LEARNING AND CLOUD INTEGRATION (IN EDUCATION)

Cloud platforms are transforming collaborative learning in educational settings by offering a suite of tools and functionalities. These tools remove geographical barriers, enabling students to work on projects together regardless of location (important for international collaboration).Features like video conferencing, chat rooms, and collaborative document editing foster real-time, seamless communication and collaboration. Cloud storage serves as a central repository for learning materials, simplifying access and resource sharing within project groups.

6.1 Facilitating Collaborative Learning through Cloud-Based Platforms:

The excerpt highlights several ways cloud platforms facilitate collaborative learning:

Enhancing Communication and Interaction: Features like chat, video conferencing, and document editing allow students to communicate effectively, share ideas, and provide feedback in real-time.

Promoting Resource Sharing: Cloud storage provides a central location for students to access and share learning materials (articles, simulations, presentations) relevant to their collaborative projects.

Encouraging Global Collaboration: Unlike traditional methods limited by location, cloud platforms allow students from diverse backgrounds to work together on projects, fostering a richer learning experience (Huang et al., 2013).

6.2 Benefits of Collaborative Learning with Cloud Integration:

Enhanced Communication and Interaction: Cloud platforms provide a suite of communication tools, including video conferencing, chat rooms, and document co-editing, facilitating seamless interaction and information exchange among students working on collaborative projects. Streamlined Resource Sharing: Cloud storage serves as a central repository for learning materials (articles, simulations, presentations, etc.). Students can effortlessly access, share, and co-create resources, fostering a knowledge-sharing culture. Global Collaboration: Geographical barriers dissolve in the cloud, enabling students from diverse backgrounds and locations to work together on projects. This cultivates cultural awareness, fosters a wider scope of perspectives, and enriches the learning experience. Development of Essential Skills: Collaborative learning with cloud integration cultivates crucial 21st-century skills, including communication, teamwork, problem-solving, and critical thinking. These skills are highly sought after by employers across disciplines. Personalized Learning Opportunities: Cloud platforms can potentially integrate with adaptive learning tools that personalize learning content and pace based on individual student needs. While the research paper doesn't delve into specific examples, personalized learning approaches could be incorporated within cloud-based collaborative environments. (Lin et al., 2023)

6.3 Case Studies:

6.3.1 Multimodal Learning with Cloud Platforms (Building Design)

Context: A high school architecture or engineering class leverages a cloud-based platform like Autodesk BIM 360 for collaborative project work. Personalized Learning: Students choose their preferred learning style (visual, auditory, kinesthetic) to explore building design concepts. Visual learners can access 3D modeling tutorials and simulations within the platform. Auditory learners can listen to instructor podcasts or webinars on specific design principles. Kinesthetic learners can engage in virtual reality simulations to experience building designs firsthand. Collaboration: Students work in teams on a virtual building project, utilizing the platform's communication tools like chat and document sharing to collaborate on design decisions and problem-solving. Assessment: Individual student progress is monitored through their work within the platform, with assessments focusing on both individual mastery of design concepts and team collaboration effectiveness.

6.3.2 Blended Learning with Personalized Math Interventions (Middle School)

Context: A middle school implements a blended learning approach for mathematics, combining traditional classroom instruction with online learning tools.

Personalized Learning: Students take an adaptive online math assessment to identify their individual strengths and weaknesses. Collaboration: Students work in small groups within the classroom, focusing on collaborative problem-solving activities aligned with concepts they're learning. Technology Integration: Students with identified learning gaps access targeted online resources and practice exercises within the platform, tailored to their specific needs.

7. EFFICIENT COMMUNICATION AND FEEDBACK

7.1 Importance of seamless communication in personalized learning environments

7.1.1 Communication in Education:

Effective communication is crucial in education, facilitating the transmission of information between educators and students through various mediums such as visual cues, auditory signals, and hands-on interaction. It ensures inclusive participation and enhances educational outcomes by promoting public engagement, improving policy formulation, and tailoring services to diverse needs. In contexts with low literacy rates, the choice of communication methods can influence inclusivity and participation levels. Integrating diverse communication strategies into educational frameworks is essential for fostering engagement and responsiveness among stakeholders.

Communication in Community Development: Communication plays a pivotal role in community development by fostering collaboration and empowering individuals to address shared challenges. It enables the dissemination of ideas, promotes participation, and drives sustainable development by mobilizing community involvement. Effective communication strategies are integral to facilitating participatory approaches in development initiatives and ensuring that community members are active contributors to their own progress.

Communication in Adult Education: In adult education, effective communication is fundamental to facilitating learning and engagement. Clear and coherent communication between instructors and learners enhances comprehension and retention of educational content. Teachers who possess strong communication skills can effectively manage classrooms, adapt teaching methods to diverse learner needs, and foster a conducive learning environment essential for academic and professional success.

Communications in Formal Education Sector: In formal education systems, communication operates at multiple levels—national policy-making, local implementation, and community engagement. Effective communication between educational institutions and stakeholders at each level ensures alignment with educational goals, enhances transparency, and fosters community ownership of educational processes. The evolving role of communication in education administration emphasizes the need for inclusive and responsive practices that meet the diverse needs of students and communities.

Communication with Policymakers in Education: Communication with policymakers is critical for informing educational policies and practices. It involves strategic engagement to influence decision-making processes, address challenges, and promote evidence-based solutions. Effective communication strategies ensure that educational research and insights are effectively communicated and integrated into policy frameworks, thereby enhancing the quality and relevance of educational initiatives

7.1.2 Importance of Communication Strategies

Implementing effective communication strategies is essential for organizational efficiency and success. These strategies facilitate clear and efficient information exchange, bridge communication gaps, and foster productive relationships between stakeholders. In educational contexts, communication strategies play a vital role in enhancing teaching effectiveness, promoting student engagement, and facilitating active participation in learning processes. Effective communication strategies are indispensable in education for several critical reasons. Firstly, they facilitate clear transmission of information between educators and students through various mediums such as visual cues, auditory signals, and interactive sessions. This clarity not only enhances comprehension but also encourages active participation and collaboration within the educational environment. Secondly, well-designed communication strategies promote inclusivity by accommodating diverse learning styles and abilities. By using multiple communication channels, educators can ensure that all students, regardless of background or learning challenges, have equitable access to educational content and opportunities for engagement. Furthermore, these strategies play a pivotal role in aligning educational practices with institutional goals and policies. By fostering consistent messaging and transparency, they help maintain focus on educational objectives while ensuring that stakeholders, including parents and policymakers, are informed and engaged in the educational process. Moreover, effective communication strategies contribute to organizational efficiency by streamlining administrative processes and enhancing teamwork among faculty and staff. Clear communication reduces misunderstandings and facilitates informed decision-making, ultimately supporting the overall effectiveness of educational institutions. (Ghosh, 2022).

7.1.3 Concept and Nature of Educational Communication:

Educational communication is fundamentally purposeful and goal-oriented, aiming to facilitate the transmission of knowledge, skills, and values essential for student learning and development. Whether through traditional lectures, interactive discussions, or digital platforms, educational communication seeks to achieve specific educational outcomes while promoting critical thinking and intellectual growth among students. Additionally, educational communication is pragmatic, linking theoretical concepts with practical application in real-world contexts. By presenting information in accessible and engaging formats, such as visual aids and interactive simulations, educators can enhance student understanding and retention of complex subject matter. Moreover, educational communication is inclusive, accommodating diverse learning needs and preferences. It embraces a variety of communication methods to ensure accessibility and engagement for all learners, thereby fostering a supportive and inclusive learning environment. Furthermore, educational communication supports continuous improvement in teaching practices and student outcomes. By encouraging ongoing assessment and feedback, educators can adapt their instructional approaches to better meet the evolving needs of students and optimize learning experiences. Educational communication serves as a cornerstone of effective teaching and learning, facilitating meaningful interactions that promote student engagement, critical thinking, and academic success. By leveraging diverse communication strategies, educators can create inclusive and supportive learning environments that empower students to achieve their full potential and contribute positively to society.

7.2 Leveraging cloud integration for effective feedback and support mechanisms

Since the onset of the COVID-19 pandemic in 2020, personalized student feedback has emerged as a crucial instructional tool for virtual instructors (Means et al., 2021). Personalization enhances accessibility and acceptance of feedback. "Personalization is the key driver for giving students feedback in a more conversational and personable tone that makes the content more accepting and constructive" (Means, B., & Neisler, J. (2021).). Moreover, the shift to virtual learning has facilitated timely feedback through Web 2.0 tools integrated into online Learning Management Systems (LMS), fostering immediacy and reducing isolation time for virtual learners (Martin et al., 2020; Steeleet et al., 2018). Additionally, synchronous learning opportunities, such as virtual office hours, have become essential for providing detailed feedback and addressing student misconceptions in real-time, supplementing asynchronous coursework (Lowenthal et al., 2017).

7.2.1 Personalized Feedback:

Personalized feedback Carby, N. (2023). in online education enhances instructor-student connections and supports learners needs effectively. Utilizing mediums like video for feedback increases instructional presence and fosters a supportive learning environment (Brown et al., 2009).

Ways to Personalize Feedback:

1. Immediate Feedback: Timely responses to student queries and prompt assignment feedback enhance engagement and motivation. For instance, responding promptly to student posts in discussion forums shows responsiveness and encourages active participation (Kožuh et al., 2015; Furlich, 2016).
2. Immediacy Behaviors: Non-verbal and verbal immediacy cues, such as empathetic communication and timely responses, foster a sense of closeness and encourage student interaction. For example, using inclusive language and providing polite greetings in online interactions can enhance student engagement (Fahara et al., 2015).
3. Technology Tools: Web 2.0 tools enable real-time formative assessments, providing instant, elaborative feedback to guide student learning. Tools such as Kahoot! or Poll Everywhere allow instructors to assess student understanding immediately during live sessions or asynchronously (Spector et al., 2016).
4. Formative Assessments: Crucial for ongoing student development, formative assessments allow instructors to gauge understanding and adjust instruction accordingly. Implementing techniques like quizzes or peer reviews in online

discussions helps identify misconceptions early and supports student learning progression (Angelo et al., 1993).

7.2.2 TYPES OF FEEDBACK:

Verification feedback in educational settings involves confirming the correctness of students' answers promptly, either immediately in synchronous classrooms or with some delay in asynchronous settings .It plays a crucial role in formative assessment by directly impacting students' learning outcomes (Marsh et al., 2012). Research by Marsh, Lozito, Umanath, Bjork, and Bjork (2012) underscore that timely verification feedback, given right after each question, significantly enhances students assessment scores compared to scenarios with delayed feedback or self-verification through answer keys.

Elaborative feedback, on the other hand, goes beyond mere correctness and provides detailed explanations of why an answer is incorrect and how to correct it in the future. This type of feedback not only informs students of their mistakes but also guides them towards understanding and mastery of the subject matter, thereby improving performance on subsequent assessments. Despite being more time-consuming for instructors, effective elaborative feedback is invaluable in promoting deeper learning and preparing students for summative assessments (Marsh et al., 2012).

8. CHALLENGES AND FUTURE DIRECTIONS

8.1 Challenges

Cloud based Personalized Adaptive Learning(PAL) System is very effective in context of tailoring educational content to student's need and improving student's learning result. But it also posses many challenges. Many PAL systems don't provide student-student interaction or student-teacher interaction which can lead to bad impact on student's mindset and progress. As the concept of PAL system is incredibly new, there are no any established standards, that's why choosing the tool that best suits their demands is a genuine difficulty for many academic institutions. Many institutions prefer to create their own content; but considering time and cost, it is a bit challenging. (D. L. Taylor, et.al.,2021).

Another big obstacles is the requirement for teachers and students to receive intensive training in technology, communication, and self-learning abilities. New pedagogical and technical techniques must be adapted to by both teachers and pupils, necessitating strong organizational support and a robust technological infrastructure. Universities must provide both groups with the infrastructure and capabilities required for the successful integration of personalized learning environments in light of this transition.(H. A. Alamri,et.al.,2020).

Another major concern is Data Privacy. Data-driven personalized learning algorithms rely on a variety of data sources; yet, as privacy advocates and proposed legislation have shown, there is a lack of clarity and openness regarding what data is collected, how it is utilized, and who has access to it. The reusing of student data and the distinction between main and secondary purposes are topics that receive little attention. Many educators and students are ignorant of the extent and impact of their digital data. Efforts to support personalized learning are hampered by a lack of knowledge and clarity around data collection.

False data interpretation can also be the issue. Suppose teachers are having access to the data of no. of times students accessed the material. Simply teachers will conclude that the student who has more no. of accesses to material, study more. But in reality the case can be like that the focused student uses fewer resources efficiently while confused student accesses more resources with lower outcomes. Misinterpreting these data points might result in false positives. (M. Bulger,2016).

Increased reporting by personalized learning systems, which sometimes involve text messaging, may make families feel more anxious. According to research conducted on 40 moms and their third-graders, moms who experience high levels of stress are more likely to be strict with their kids about their homework Additionally, research has shown that students who experience higher levels of parental control perform worse academically and are less creative ClassDojo, a platform that allows teachers to enter behavioral and disciplinary ratings that may be shared with parents, has sparked privacy concerns, according to a 2014 New York Times article. Similarly, parents receive SMS alerts about attendance and tardiness using the learning app Involved.

8.2 Future Directions:

1. **Quantum Computing in Education**: By using qubits to run complex algorithms at exponential rates, quantum computing holds the potential to completely transform AI capabilities in the field of education. This discovery may pave the way for the creation of quantum-inspired algorithms for individualized education and cutting-edge research applications in educational environments.
2. **Brain-Computer Interface (BCI)**: By combining AI and BCI technologies in education, neural interfaces for direct cognitive engagement with computers may be established. This integration has the potential to improve immersive learning experiences based on neural patterns and cognitive pro-

cesses by facilitating real-time neural data processing and neuro feedback mechanisms.

3. **Global Collaboration through AI**: According to AI based cloud systems in Education, federated learning and block chain-based authentication will allow for safe, decentralized international cooperation between educators and students in the future. A seamless learning environment that transcends linguistic and cultural barriers might be established with the use of virtual classrooms and AI-driven translation services.
4. **Emotional Intelligence and Well-Being**: Affective computing frameworks may be integrated into future versions of AI based cloud systems in education to assess and react to students' emotional states instantly. AI might offer sympathetic feedback and tailored solutions using biometric sensors and natural language processing, fostering resilience and mental wellness in students.
5. **Augmented Human Intelligence:** AI-powered cognitive assistants may improve adaptive learning algorithms and enable individualized learning pathways as human intelligence and AI merge to create augmented human cognition. Through the use of modern data analytics and cognitive modeling methodologies, this synergy could provide students with increased capacity for creativity, critical thinking, and problem-solving. (Rane,et.al.,2023)

9. CONCLUSION

The integration of cloud technologies in education is transforming the landscape of personalized learning, providing new opportunity to tailor educational experiences to particular student needs. This paper examined the complex influence of cloud-based solutions on personalized learning, with a focus on important areas such as educational resource accessibility, adaptive learning systems, data-driven personalization, and collaborative learning.

Cloud-based technologies enable students and educators to access learning resources at any time and from any location, greatly improving the individualized learning experience. Adaptive learning systems enable educators to personalize curriculum to each student's particular needs, resulting in a more effective and interesting learning environment. The accumulating and analysis of student data contributes to personalized learning by identifying individual strengths and areas for improvement, but ethical concerns must be properly managed to protect privacy and data security.

Cloud integration has also improved collaborative learning by enabling smooth communication and information exchange between teachers and students. Case studies from the real world show how cloud-based personalized learning projects are successfully implemented, providing other educational institutions with useful insights and best practices to emulate.

Notwithstanding the manifold benefits, obstacles still stand in the way of the broad implementation of cloud-integrated customized learning, including infrastructure, privacy, and change aversion concerns. Even though the continuous progress in technology along with the increasing acknowledgement of the significance of customized education indicate a bright future for cloud-based learning systems.

In conclusion, cloud integration is bridging the gap between academia and industry, improving individualized learning and equipping students for a quickly changing digital environment. Educators may develop more inclusive, adaptable, and successful learning environments that meet the different requirements of students by utilizing cloud technologies to their fullest potential. This will eventually promote academic success and lifetime learning.

REFERENCES

Al-Mousa, A. (2019). Cloud computing: Bridging the link between industry and the classroom. *International Journal of Electrical Engineering Education*, 002072091985763. Advance online publication. DOI: 10.1177/0020720919857636

Alamri, H. A., Watson, S., & Watson, W. (2021). Learning technology models that support personalization within blended learning environments in higher education. *TechTrends*, 65(1), 62–78. DOI: 10.1007/s11528-020-00530-3

Bulger, M. (n.d.). Personalized learning: the conversations we're not having. In *Working Paper*. Data & Society Research Institute. https://datasociety.net/pubs/ecl/PersonalizedLearning_primer_2016.pdf

Carby, N. (2023). Personalized feedback in a virtual learning environment. *Journal of Educational Supervision*, 6(1), 36–44. DOI: 10.31045/jes.6.1.3

Chen, S. Y., & Magoulas, G. D. (2003). Foundations for personalized web learning environments. *International Journal of Continuing Engineering Education and Lifelong Learning*, 13(3-4), 261–275. DOI: 10.1504/IJCEELL.2003.003337

El-Attar, N. E., Abo El-Ela, N., & Awad, W. A. (2019). Integrated learning approaches based on cloud computing for personalizing e-learning environment. *International Journal of Web-Based Learning and Teaching Technologies*, 14(1), 101–114. DOI: 10.4018/IJWLTT.2019040105

Elsevier. (2016). Adaptive learning. Retrieved January 05, 2018, from https://evolve.elsevier.com/education/adaptive-learning/keys-to-improving-outcomes-and-retention/

Gebhardt, K. (2018). Adaptive learning courseware as a tool to build foundational content mastery: Evidence from principles of microeconomics. *Current Issues in Emerging Elearning*, 5(1), 2.

Ghosh, U. (2022). ROLE OF COMMUNICATION IN EDUCATION. In *International Journal for Research Trends and Innovation* (Vol. 7, Issue 6, pp. 326–327) [Journal-article]. https://www.ijrti.org/papers/IJRTI2206057.pdf

Helaimia, R. (2023). Cloud computing in higher education institutions: pros and cons. International Journal of Advanced Natural Sciences and Engineering Researches, 7(ISSN: 2980-0811).

Huang, L. N., Liu, F. H., & Liu, C. L. (2013). Design and research on collaborative learning program based on Cloud-Services. *Advanced Materials Research*, 756–759, 1199–1203. . DOI: 10.4028/www.scientific.net/AMR.756-759.1199

Hussain, I. (2024). Exploring the impact of learning styles on tailoring individual learners' needs: A systemic review. *Journal of Management & Educational Research Innovation*, 2(1), 16–26. DOI: 10.5281/zenodo.11128012

Johnson, D., & Samora, D. (2016). The potential transformation of higher Education through computer-based adaptive learning systems. Global Education Journal, 1.

Kale, S., & Khatri, S. (2021). A study on role and application of cloud engineering & cloud computing in business reengineering with reference to Netflix. [TOJQI]. *Turkish Online Journal of Qualitative Inquiry*, 12(3), 4409–4419.

Kim, K. H., & Smith, P. L. (2021). Microlearning: A literature review. *TechTrends*, 65(6), 1422–1433. DOI: 10.1007/s11423-022-10084-1

Kim, M. J., & Smith, L. (2021). Student-centered learning design in a cloud-based learning management system. [JETDE]. *Journal of Educational Technology Development and Exchange*, 14(3), 189–204.

Kumar, B. P., Kommareddy, S., & Rani, N. U. (2013). Effective ways cloud computing can contribute to education success. [ACIJ]. *Advanced Computing: An International Journal*, 4(4), 17–32. Advance online publication. DOI: 10.5121/acij.2013.4402

Kumar, J. S. A., Sreelatha, A., & Sowjanya, A. (2017). Cloud computing in education. *International Journal of Scientific and Engineering Research*, 8(5), 175. http://www.ijser.org

Lin, Y., & Wang, W. (2023). Enhancing students' online collaborative PBL learning performance in the context of coauthoring-based technologies: A case of wiki technologies. *Education and Information Technologies*, 29(2), 2303–2328. DOI: 10.1007/s10639-023-11907-1 PMID: 37361760

) Liu, B., Chen, H., & Junmei, H. (2019, August 1). Research on the Platform of Online Education Platform Based on Cloud Computing. IEEE Xplore. DOI: 10.1109/ICCSE.2019.8845511

Liu, M., McKelroy, E., Corliss, S. B., & Carrigan, J. (2017). Investigating the effect of an adaptive learning intervention on students' learning. *Educational Technology Research and Development*, 65(6), 1–21. DOI: 10.1007/s11423-017-9542-1

Lowenthal, P. R., Dunlap, J. C., & Snelson, C. (2017). Live synchronous web meetings in asynchronous online courses: Reconceptualizing virtual office hours. *Online Learning : the Official Journal of the Online Learning Consortium*, 21(4). Advance online publication. DOI: 10.24059/olj.v21i4.1285

Means, B., & Neisler, J. (2021). Teaching and Learning in the time of COVID: The Student perspective. *Online Learning : the Official Journal of the Online Learning Consortium*, 25(1). Advance online publication. DOI: 10.24059/olj.v25i1.2496

Mohammadi, M. H., & Mehdizadeh, S. (2019). Cloud-based personalized learning platforms: A review of enabling technologies, architectures, and user experience design factors. [JETDE]. *Journal of Educational Technology Development and Exchange*, 12(3), 241–260.

Paul, P., Chatterjee, R., Aithal, P. S., & Saavedra, R. (2023). Cloud Computing and its Impact in Education, Teaching and Research-A Scientific Review. Social Science Research Network. DOI: 10.2139/ssrn.4490825

Peng, H., Ma, S., & Spector, J. M. (2019). Personalized adaptive learning: An emerging pedagogical approach enabled by a smart learning environment. *Smart Learning Environments*, 6(1), 9. Advance online publication. DOI: 10.1186/s40561-019-0089-y

Rane, N., Choudhary, S., & Rane, J. (2023). Education 4.0 and 5.0: Integrating Artificial Intelligence (AI) for personalized and adaptive learning. *Social Science Research Network.* https://doi.org/DOI: 10.2139/ssrn.4638365

Shemshack, A., & Spector, J. M. (2020). A systematic literature review of personalized learning terms. *Smart Learning Environments*, 7(1), 33. Advance online publication. DOI: 10.1186/s40561-020-00140-9

Soler Costa, R., Tan, Q., Pivot, F., Zhang, X., & Wang, H. (2021). Personalized and adaptive learning: educational practice and technological impact. Texto Livre/ Texto Livre: Linguagem e Tecnologia, 14(3).

Steele, J., & Holbeck, R. (2018). Five elements that impact quality feedback in the online asynchronous classroom. *ResearchGate*, 15(3). Advance online publication. DOI: 10.9743/jeo.2018.15.3.10

Taylor, D. L., Yeung, M., & Bashet, A. Z. (2021). Personalized and adaptive learning. In *SpringerBriefs in statistics* (pp. 17–34). DOI: 10.1007/978-3-030-58948-6_2

Watson, W. R., & Watson, S. L. (2017). Principles for personalized instruction. In Reigeluth, C. M., Beatty, B. J., & Myers, R. D. (Eds.), *Instructional-design theories and models, The learner centered paradigm of education* (Vol. IV, pp. 93–120). Routledge.

Wozniak, K., Lilly, C., Hambrock, H., Richter, R., & Reiseck, C. (2016, November). Designing an adaptive learning experience in higher Education: A critical perspective. In E-Learn: World Conference on E-Learning in Corporate, Government, Healthcare, and Higher Education (pp. 517–521). Association for the Advancement of computing in Education (AACE).

) Xu, J., Liu, Y., Liu, Z., & Zhang, J. (2017). Study on Factors that Affect College Students' Acceptance of Cloud-Classroom. https://doi.org/.DOI: 10.1109/iset.2017

Chapter 6
Bridging Academia and Industry Through Technology and Entrepreneurial Innovation:
Enhancing Supply Chain Efficiency

R. Vettriselvan
https://orcid.org/0000-0002-1324-136X
Academy of Maritime Education and Training, India

R. Deepa
https://orcid.org/0009-0008-9743-4791
Academy of Maritime Education and Training, India

Rashmi Gautam
Saraswathi Institute of Medical Sciences, India

N. V. Suresh
https://orcid.org/0000-0002-0393-6037
ASET College of Science and Technology, India

S. Cathrine
https://orcid.org/0000-0001-7761-2134
Saveetha Engineering College, India

DOI: 10.4018/979-8-3693-6705-6.ch006

ABSTRACT

This chapter explores how technology and entrepreneurial innovation enhance supply chain efficiency. It highlights the transformative impact of advanced technologies such as cloud computing, data analytics, and IoT on supply chain operations, improving responsiveness and reducing costs. The entrepreneurial orientation is emphasized as a key driver of innovation, enabling organizations to adapt to changing market conditions. Through case studies, the chapter illustrates successful collaborations between academia and industry, demonstrating how theoretical insights translate into practical solutions. Challenges in technology integration, such as data security and the need for skilled personnel, are also addressed. By bridging the gap between academia and industry, this work aims to inspire future research and applications that enhance supply chain management, underscoring the importance of fostering a culture of innovation to maintain competitiveness in the global marketplace.

INTRODUCTION

Supply Chain Management (SCM) is a comprehensive approach to managing the flow of goods, services, and information from the initial suppliers to the final customers. It encompasses various activities such as procurement, production, distribution, and logistics, aimed at optimizing efficiency and reducing costs (Chopra & Meindl, 2020). SCM is crucial for modern businesses as it directly impacts operational efficiency, customer satisfaction, and overall competitive advantage. Effective SCM can lead to significant improvements in cost management, lead times, and product quality, making it a strategic priority for organizations across industries (Christopher, 2016). The evolution of SCM has seen a shift from traditional, linear models to more integrated and technologically advanced frameworks. Initially characterized by isolated functions and manual processes, SCM has transformed with the advent of digital technologies. Modern SCM integrates advanced technologies such as data analytics, automation, and the Internet of Things (IoT), enabling real-time visibility, enhanced coordination, and greater responsiveness (Hazen et al., 2014). This digital integration has revolutionized SCM practices, leading to more agile and efficient supply chains.

The Role of Technology in SCM

Technological advancements have significantly impacted SCM by enhancing various aspects of the supply chain. Innovations such as automation, big data analytics, and artificial intelligence (AI) have transformed traditional SCM practices, offering new opportunities for optimization and efficiency (Bowersox et al., 2013). For instance, automation technologies in warehousing and logistics have streamlined operations, reduced human error, and increased throughput (Meyer et al., 2015). Similarly, big data analytics enables businesses to gain insights into consumer behavior, forecast demand more accurately, and make data-driven decisions (Wamba et al., 2017). Key drivers of technological adoption in SCM include the need for increased efficiency, cost reduction, and enhanced customer satisfaction. Organizations are increasingly leveraging technology to gain a competitive edge by improving their operational capabilities and responsiveness to market changes (Ivanov & Dolgui, 2020). Additionally, the growing complexity of global supply chains and the demand for real-time information have accelerated the adoption of advanced technologies in SCM.

Entrepreneurial Orientation and SCM

Entrepreneurial orientation (EO) refers to the strategic posture of a firm characterized by its willingness to innovate, take risks, and proactively seek new opportunities (Lumpkin & Dess, 1996). It comprises several components: innovativeness, proactiveness, and risk-taking. Innovativeness involves the pursuit of new ideas and technologies, proactiveness is about anticipating and acting on future needs, and risk-taking refers to the willingness to engage in ventures with uncertain outcomes (Miller, 1983). EO influences SCM practices by driving the adoption of new technologies and practices. Firms with a strong entrepreneurial orientation are more likely to embrace innovative technologies and adopt forward-thinking SCM strategies. This proactive approach can lead to enhanced supply chain efficiency, greater flexibility, and improved responsiveness to market demands (Zahra & Covin, 1995). Entrepreneurial orientation fosters a culture of continuous improvement and adaptability, which is essential for navigating the complexities of modern supply chains (Covin & Slevin, 1989).

Purpose and Structure of the Chapter

The integration of technology into Supply Chain Management (SCM) is reshaping how businesses operate, manage, and optimize their supply chains, offering unprecedented opportunities for efficiency, transparency, and agility. This chapter aims to delve deeply into this transformation by examining the dual role of technological innovations and entrepreneurial orientation in enhancing SCM practices. The primary purpose of this chapter is to provide a comprehensive understanding of how emerging technologies influence SCM and how an entrepreneurial mindset can facilitate the effective adoption and utilization of these technologies. The chapter is meticulously structured to offer a systematic exploration of these themes, beginning with an overview of the current technological landscape in SCM. The first section, Technological Landscape in SCM, will delve into recent advancements and innovations that are revolutionizing supply chain practices. Automation, IoT (Internet of Things), AI (Artificial Intelligence), blockchain, big data analytics, and cloud computing represent critical technologies that are driving this change. Each technology will be examined in terms of its specific applications within SCM, such as automation's role in streamlining warehouse operations, IoT's contribution to real-time tracking, AI's impact on predictive analytics, blockchain's potential for enhancing transparency, and cloud computing's benefits for collaborative planning. This section aims to illustrate how these technologies collectively contribute to more efficient, responsive, and transparent supply chains, highlighting real-world applications and outcomes. Following this technological overview, the chapter will explore the role of Entrepreneurial Orientation and Technological Adoption. Entrepreneurial orientation, characterized by innovation, risk-taking, proactiveness, and competitive aggressiveness, plays a crucial role in driving the adoption and implementation of new technologies. This section will investigate how organizations with a strong entrepreneurial mindset are better positioned to leverage technological advancements to their advantage. By analyzing the components of entrepreneurial orientation and their influence on technology adoption, the chapter will elucidate how entrepreneurial leaders and teams can navigate the complexities of technological integration and harness these advancements to enhance supply chain performance. To provide practical insights, the chapter will include a section on Case Studies, showcasing real-world examples of companies that have successfully leveraged technology and entrepreneurial orientation to optimize their supply chains. These case studies will cover diverse industries and illustrate how different organizations have implemented technological solutions and fostered an entrepreneurial culture to achieve competitive advantages. Through these examples, the chapter will highlight best practices, lessons learned, and the tangible benefits realized by these companies. The subsequent section, Challenges and Barriers, will address the common obstacles faced by organizations when adopting new technologies in their supply chains. Despite the potential benefits, the integration of advanced technologies often encounters challenges such as high implementation costs, resistance to change, interoperability issues, and data security concerns. This section will not only identify these barriers but also propose strategies and solutions for overcoming them. By addressing these challenges, the chapter aims to provide a roadmap for businesses to navigate the complexities of technological adoption and maximize the value derived from their investments. Looking ahead, the chapter will explore Future Trends in SCM, focusing on emerging technologies and their potential impact on supply chain management. This section will investigate how advancements such as quantum computing, advanced robotics, and new developments in AI and blockchain might shape the future of SCM. By considering the implications of these technologies, the chapter will offer insights into how businesses can prepare for and capitalize on future trends to maintain a competitive edge. The chapter will provide a comprehensive Conclusion that synthesizes the key findings from each section. It will summarize the impact of technological advancements on SCM and the significance of entrepreneurial orientation in driving technological adoption. Practical recommendations will be offered to guide businesses in leveraging both technology and an entrepreneurial mindset to enhance their supply chain operations. The chapter will emphasize the importance of staying abreast of technological trends and fostering an entrepreneurial culture to navigate the evolving landscape of SCM effectively. Overall, this chapter aims to provide a holistic view of how technology and entrepreneurial orientation intersect to transform supply chain management. By combining theoretical insights with practical case studies and addressing both opportunities and challenges, it seeks to offer valuable guidance for businesses striving to optimize their supply chains through technological innovation and entrepreneurial leadership.

THE TECHNOLOGICAL LANDSCAPE IN SUPPLY CHAIN MANAGEMENT

Automation and Robotics

Automation and robotics have profoundly transformed warehousing and distribution by enhancing operational efficiency and accuracy. Automated systems streamline various processes, including sorting, packing, and shipping, which were traditionally labor-intensive. Recent advancements in robotics, such as autonomous mobile robots (AMRs) and automated guided vehicles (AGVs), have significantly reduced labor costs and improved throughput (Choi et al., 2023). For example, Amazon's use of Kiva robots in its fulfillment centers has demonstrated substantial gains in operational efficiency, reducing the time required for order processing and enhancing inventory management (Hao et al., 2022). In manufacturing and inventory management, automation systems have led to more precise and consistent production processes. Technologies such as robotic arms and automated production lines have increased production speed and accuracy while reducing human error (Huang et al., 2023). These systems also facilitate real-time inventory tracking, enabling companies to maintain optimal stock levels and respond swiftly to changes in demand.

Internet of Things (IoT)

The Internet of Things (IoT) has revolutionized real-time tracking and monitoring in supply chains. IoT devices, such as RFID tags and GPS sensors, provide continuous visibility into the location and condition of goods throughout the supply chain (Li et al., 2024). This real-time data enables better decision-making and enhances the ability to respond to disruptions or inefficiencies promptly. Smart sensors play a crucial role in monitoring environmental conditions, such as temperature and humidity, which are vital for perishable goods. For instance, IoT-enabled temperature sensors in refrigerated containers help ensure that goods are stored under optimal conditions, thereby reducing spoilage and ensuring compliance with safety standards (Zhang et al., 2023).

Artificial Intelligence (AI) and Machine Learning (ML)

Artificial Intelligence (AI) and Machine Learning (ML) have become integral to demand forecasting and supply chain optimization. AI-driven algorithms analyze historical data to predict future demand patterns with high accuracy, allowing companies to adjust their inventory levels and production schedules accordingly (Cheng et al., 2024). This predictive capability helps in minimizing stockouts and overstock situations, enhancing overall supply chain efficiency. Machine learning applications are also pivotal in predictive maintenance and logistics. ML algorithms can analyze data from equipment sensors to predict potential failures before they occur, reducing downtime and maintenance costs (Gupta et al., 2023). In logistics, ML models optimize routing and scheduling, improving delivery times and reducing transportation costs.

Blockchain Technology

Blockchain technology enhances transparency and security in supply chains by providing an immutable ledger of transactions. This decentralized approach ensures that all parties have access to the same data, reducing the risk of fraud and improving accountability (Wang et al., 2024). For instance, Walmart has utilized blockchain to trace the origin of food products, enabling rapid response to food safety issues and improving supply chain traceability (Kim et al., 2023). Blockchain also plays a crucial role in product authentication and traceability. By recording each transaction in a secure and transparent manner, blockchain technology helps prevent counterfeiting and ensures the authenticity of products. This is particularly valuable in industries such as pharmaceuticals and luxury goods, where product integrity is paramount (Zhao et al., 2024).

Big Data Analytics

Big Data Analytics is transforming supply chain management by enabling data-driven decision-making. By analyzing large volumes of data from various sources, companies can identify trends, optimize processes, and enhance operational efficiency (Madhani, 2024). For example, predictive analytics can forecast demand more accurately, leading to better inventory management and reduced costs. The role of big data in identifying trends is particularly significant in understanding customer preferences and market dynamics. Companies leverage big data to gain insights into consumer behavior, enabling them to tailor their offerings and improve customer satisfaction (Reddy et al., 2023). Additionally, big data analytics helps in detecting and mitigating risks in the supply chain, enhancing overall resilience.

Cloud Computing

Cloud computing provides scalable and flexible solutions for supply chain management, facilitating better collaboration among supply chain partners. Cloud-based SCM platforms enable real-time sharing of information and coordination across different functions and geographies (Kumar et al., 2023). This enhances visibility and integration throughout the supply chain, leading to more efficient operations. The scalability offered by cloud computing allows companies to adapt to changing demands and expand their operations without significant infrastructure investments (Kumar & Sharma, 2024). Cloud platforms also support the integration of various SCM technologies, such as IoT and big data analytics, providing a cohesive and adaptable supply chain management solution.

ENTREPRENEURIAL ORIENTATION AND TECHNOLOGICAL ADOPTION

Innovativeness in SCM

An entrepreneurial mindset, particularly characterized by innovativeness, plays a crucial role in driving the adoption of new technologies in supply chain management (SCM). Innovativeness, a key component of entrepreneurial orientation, reflects a company's readiness to embrace and experiment with new tools and technologies. Companies with a strong culture of innovation are often at the forefront of technological advancements, using these innovations to enhance their competitive edge and operational efficiency.

Amazon serves as a prominent example of how innovativeness can transform supply chain operations. The company has consistently demonstrated a commitment to integrating cutting-edge technologies to streamline its SCM processes. One of the most notable examples is Amazon's adoption of robotics and artificial intelligence (AI) in its warehouses. Amazon's use of Kiva robots, now known as Amazon Robotics, has revolutionized warehouse operations. These robots are designed to automate various tasks, including sorting, picking, and transporting inventory within the warehouse. By using Kiva robots, Amazon has significantly increased the speed and accuracy of its inventory management processes. The robots work collaboratively with human employees, allowing for a more efficient workflow and reducing the physical strain on warehouse staff (Hao et al., 2022). The integration of Kiva robots has led to several operational improvements for Amazon. For example, the robots can quickly locate and retrieve products, which reduces the time employees spend walking between shelves and searching for items. This has resulted in faster order fulfillment and increased throughput in Amazon's fulfillment centers. Additionally, the use of robotics has minimized errors in order picking, contributing to higher levels of customer satisfaction due to improved accuracy in order deliveries (Hao et al., 2022). Moreover, Amazon's investment in AI extends beyond robotics. The company employs AI algorithms to optimize various aspects of its supply chain, including demand forecasting, route optimization, and inventory management. By leveraging AI, Amazon can predict customer demand more accurately, plan inventory levels accordingly, and optimize delivery routes to minimize transportation costs and delivery times. Another example of how innovativeness drives technological adoption in SCM is Maersk's use of blockchain technology. As a leading global shipping company, Maersk has embraced blockchain to address several challenges in the shipping industry, including transparency, traceability, and fraud prevention. Maersk, in collaboration with IBM, developed the TradeLens platform, a blockchain-based solution designed to enhance the efficiency and transparency of global shipping processes. TradeLens enables real-time tracking of cargo and documentation through a secure and immutable blockchain ledger. This innovation allows all parties involved in the shipping process, including shippers, carriers, and customs authorities, to access and share critical information in a transparent manner (Wang et al., 2024). The adoption of blockchain technology by Maersk has resulted in several key benefits. First, it has improved traceability by providing a comprehensive and tamper-proof record of cargo movements. This enhances visibility across the supply chain and helps to ensure that cargo is delivered as planned. Second, the platform has reduced the risk of fraud by providing a secure and verifiable record of transactions and documentation. This is particularly important in an industry where fraudulent activities, such as falsified documents, can lead to significant financial losses and regulatory issues (Wang et al., 2024). In addition to improving transparency and reducing fraud, the TradeLens platform has streamlined the overall shipping process. By digitizing and automating documentation and communication, Maersk has reduced the time and administrative effort required for managing shipping transactions. This has led to faster processing times and reduced costs for all parties involved in the shipping process. Innovativeness is a critical driver of technological adoption in supply chain management. Companies that prioritize and invest in innovative technologies can achieve significant improvements in operational efficiency, transparency, and competitive advantage. Amazon's integration of robotics and AI in its warehouses and Maersk's adoption of blockchain technology for cargo tracking exemplify how a commitment to innovation can transform SCM practices. These examples highlight the importance of an entrepreneurial mindset in embracing and leveraging new technologies to address industry challenges and meet evolving market demands. As technology continues to advance, companies that foster a culture of innovation will be better positioned to adapt, thrive, and lead in the ever-evolving landscape of supply chain management..

Proactiveness and Market Adaptation

Proactiveness, in the context of supply chain management (SCM), refers to the ability of companies to anticipate and act upon technological trends before they become widely adopted. This forward-thinking strategy enables businesses to gain a competitive edge by leveraging emerging technologies to adapt to market changes and customer demands. Proactive companies are characterized by their willingness to experiment with new technologies, integrate them into their operations, and continuously refine their strategies based on technological advancements. Tesla is a prime example of proactiveness in SCM. The company's integration of advanced technologies into its supply chain operations underscores its commitment to staying ahead of technological trends. Tesla uses Artificial Intelligence (AI) and machine learning extensively for demand forecasting and inventory management. This proactive approach allows Tesla to make data-driven decisions, optimize production schedules, and respond swiftly to fluctuations in market demand (Cheng et al., 2024). For instance, Tesla's AI-driven demand forecasting models analyze vast amounts of historical data, market trends, and consumer behavior patterns to predict future demand with high accuracy. This capability enables Tesla to adjust production levels and inventory in real-time, reducing the risk of overproduction or stockouts. Additionally, Tesla's use of machine learning algorithms helps in refining supply chain processes by identifying inefficiencies and suggesting improvements, thus enhancing overall operational efficiency (Cheng et al., 2024). Tesla's proactive adoption of technology extends beyond AI and machine learning. The company has also invested in advanced manufacturing technologies, such as its Gigafactories, which utilize cutting-edge robotics and automation systems to streamline production processes. These facilities not only enhance production capacity but also integrate sustainable practices, reflecting Tesla's forward-thinking approach to both technological and environmental challenges. Similarly, Zara exemplifies proactiveness in SCM through its highly responsive supply chain model. The fashion retailer employs real-time data analytics to swiftly adapt to changing fashion trends and consumer preferences. Zara's proactive strategy involves the continuous collection and analysis of sales data, which is used to make rapid decisions regarding inventory and product offerings (Li et al., 2024). Zara's supply chain model is designed to be highly agile, with a focus on reducing lead times and increasing flexibility. The company utilizes advanced data analytics to track customer preferences and sales patterns in real-time. This data-driven approach enables Zara to identify emerging fashion trends quickly and adjust its product designs, inventory levels, and production schedules accordingly. By doing so, Zara ensures that its product offerings are always aligned with current market demands, thereby maintaining a competitive advantage in the fast-paced fashion industry (Li et al., 2024). Additionally, Zara's use of real-time analytics extends to its supply chain operations, where it monitors and manages logistics, supplier performance, and inventory levels with precision. This proactive management approach allows Zara to minimize stockouts and excess inventory, ensuring optimal availability of products in its stores. The proactiveness demonstrated by Tesla and Zara highlights the critical role of anticipating and leveraging technological trends in SCM. By adopting and integrating advanced technologies before they become mainstream, these companies are able to enhance their operational efficiency, responsiveness, and competitiveness. Tesla's use of AI and machine learning for demand forecasting and inventory management, along with Zara's real-time data analytics for fashion trend adaptation, exemplify how proactive technological adoption can drive significant improvements in supply chain performance. Proactiveness in technology adoption enables companies to stay ahead of competitors, adapt swiftly to market changes, and meet evolving customer demands. By embracing emerging technologies and integrating them into their SCM strategies, businesses can achieve greater operational agility and maintain a competitive edge in their respective industries..

Risk-Taking and Technology Investments

Risk-taking is a fundamental aspect of entrepreneurial orientation, particularly when it comes to investments in emerging technologies. In the context of supply chain management (SCM), this involves weighing the potential rewards of adopting new technologies against the risks and uncertainties associated with their implementation. High costs, uncertain technology performance, and integration challenges are common risks that companies must navigate. General Electric (GE) provides a notable example of how strategic risk-taking can be effectively managed to achieve significant technological and operational advancements.

General Electric (GE) has been at the forefront of leveraging technology to drive its industrial operations and improve its supply chain processes. The company's commitment to adopting advanced technologies, particularly in the realm of the Industrial Internet of Things (IIoT), highlights its strategic approach to managing the risks associated with technological investments. GE's digital transformation strategy focuses heavily on integrating IIoT technologies, which involve embedding sensors and connectivity into industrial equipment to gather and analyze data in real-time. This approach aims to enhance operational efficiency, improve maintenance practices, and reduce downtime across GE's industrial operations. One key aspect of GE's IIoT strategy is its investment in data analytics and predictive maintenance. By using advanced data analytics, GE can monitor the performance of its machinery and equipment more effectively. Predictive maintenance leverages data from sensors to anticipate equipment failures before they occur, allowing for timely maintenance interventions and reducing unexpected downtime. This not only enhances operational efficiency but also helps GE avoid costly production interruptions and extend the lifespan of its equipment (Gupta et al., 2023).

To manage the inherent risks associated with IIoT investments, GE employs a structured approach to technology evaluation and implementation. This approach involves several key steps:

i. Technology Assessment: Before committing to a new technology, GE conducts thorough assessments to evaluate its potential benefits and risks. This includes analyzing the technology's performance, compatibility with existing systems, and alignment with the company's strategic objectives. By conducting comprehensive assessments, GE ensures that the technologies it adopts are capable of delivering tangible benefits and addressing specific operational challenges.
ii. Pilot Testing: GE often begins with pilot projects to test new technologies in a controlled environment before full-scale deployment. Pilot testing allows GE to evaluate the technology's performance, identify potential issues, and make necessary adjustments before committing significant resources. This iterative approach helps mitigate the risks of technology failures and ensures that the technology is well-suited for broader implementation.
iii. Partnerships and Collaboration: GE frequently collaborates with technology providers, research institutions, and industry partners to enhance its technology adoption strategy. These partnerships provide access to additional expertise,

resources, and insights, which can help GE manage risks and optimize the implementation of new technologies. For example, GE has worked closely with technology companies to develop and refine its IIoT solutions, leveraging their expertise to ensure successful technology integration (Gupta et al., 2023).

iv. Continuous Monitoring and Adaptation: Once a technology is implemented, GE continuously monitors its performance and impact. This ongoing evaluation helps identify areas for improvement and ensures that the technology continues to deliver value. GE's commitment to continuous adaptation allows it to stay ahead of technological advancements and maintain a competitive edge in the industry.

GE's strategic approach to risk-taking in technology investments has yielded several notable benefits. The integration of IIoT technologies has resulted in improved operational efficiency, reduced maintenance costs, and enhanced equipment reliability. By leveraging predictive maintenance and real-time data analytics, GE has been able to optimize its supply chain operations and achieve significant cost savings. For instance, GE's predictive maintenance programs have led to substantial reductions in unplanned downtime, which translates into increased productivity and lower operational costs. The ability to anticipate and address maintenance issues before they escalate has also contributed to improved equipment reliability and performance. Risk-taking is an essential component of entrepreneurial orientation, particularly in the context of technology adoption in supply chain management. General Electric's strategic approach to risk-taking, exemplified by its investments in IIoT technologies, highlights how companies can effectively manage the risks associated with technological investments. Through structured technology evaluation, pilot testing, partnerships, and continuous monitoring, GE has successfully navigated the challenges of technology adoption and achieved significant operational improvements. This approach serves as a valuable model for other companies looking to leverage technology to enhance their supply chain processes while managing the inherent risks of innovation.

Entrepreneurial Leadership in SCM

Leadership is a critical driver of innovation and technology adoption in supply chain management (SCM). Entrepreneurial leaders are instrumental in creating a culture that encourages experimentation, embraces change, and drives technological advancements. Their vision, strategic direction, and ability to inspire and motivate teams are essential for leveraging new technologies and integrating them effectively into SCM practices. This section delves into how leadership influences technological adoption, with a focus on notable examples such as Satya Nadella at Microsoft and Elon Musk at Tesla.

SATYA NADELLA'S TRANSFORMATIVE LEADERSHIP AT MICROSOFT

Satya Nadella, who became CEO of Microsoft in 2014, is renowned for his role in transforming the company's technological landscape and positioning it as a leader in cloud computing and advanced analytics. Nadella's leadership style and vision have been pivotal in driving Microsoft's technological advancements and reshaping its approach to supply chain management (SCM).

A. Emphasis on Cloud Computing

Under Nadella's leadership, Microsoft made a strategic shift towards cloud computing, culminating in the development and expansion of Microsoft Azure, the company's cloud platform. Nadella recognized the potential of cloud computing to revolutionize business operations and supply chain processes. By prioritizing cloud services, Microsoft enabled businesses to scale their operations, enhance data accessibility, and improve collaboration across global supply chains (Kumar & Sharma, 2024). The integration of cloud computing into SCM allows companies to leverage real-time data and analytics, optimize inventory management, and streamline logistics. For instance, Azure's cloud-based solutions provide scalable infrastructure for managing supply chain data, facilitating better decision-making and responsiveness. Nadella's vision and leadership in this area have positioned Microsoft as a key player in the cloud services market and have significantly influenced SCM practices (Kumar & Sharma, 2024).

B. Advancements in Artificial Intelligence

Nadella's leadership has also been instrumental in integrating artificial intelligence (AI) into Microsoft's offerings. AI technologies, including machine learning and data analytics, have become integral to modern SCM practices. By incorporating AI into its cloud services and business solutions, Microsoft enables companies to gain valuable insights from their supply chain data, forecast demand more accurately, and automate complex processes (Kumar & Sharma, 2024). Nadella's focus on AI and data-driven solutions reflects a broader trend towards leveraging advanced technologies to enhance supply chain efficiency. Microsoft's AI capabilities support predictive maintenance, risk management, and operational optimization, demonstrating how leadership can drive technological adoption and improve SCM outcomes.

ELON MUSK'S VISIONARY LEADERSHIP AT TESLA

Elon Musk, the CEO and founder of Tesla, has been a transformative leader in the automotive and energy sectors, with significant impacts on supply chain management through his innovative approach to technology and operations. Musk's leadership at Tesla exemplifies how entrepreneurial vision and risk-taking can drive technological advancements in SCM.

A. Adoption of Cutting-Edge Technologies

Musk's leadership has driven Tesla's adoption of cutting-edge technologies, including advanced robotics, automation, and AI. Tesla's manufacturing facilities, known for their high levels of automation, use robotics to streamline production processes and improve efficiency. The integration of AI and machine learning into Tesla's supply chain operations enhances demand forecasting, production planning, and inventory management (Huang et al., 2023). For example, Tesla's use of AI for demand forecasting enables the company to align its production schedules with market demand, minimizing excess inventory and reducing costs. The company's commitment to technological innovation in its supply chain is a testament to Musk's leadership and vision, which prioritize efficiency, scalability, and responsiveness (Huang et al., 2023).

B. Innovative SCM Practices

Tesla's approach to supply chain management also reflects Musk's emphasis on innovation and technological integration. The company has implemented innovative practices such as vertical integration, which involves controlling various stages of the supply chain, from raw material sourcing to manufacturing and distribution. This approach allows Tesla to enhance quality control, reduce lead times, and optimize supply chain operations (Huang et al., 2023). Additionally, Tesla's investment in electric vehicle technology and renewable energy solutions aligns with its broader goals of sustainability and efficiency. By leveraging advanced technologies in its supply chain, Tesla not only improves operational performance but also reinforces its commitment to environmental responsibility and innovation (Huang et al., 2023).

IMPACT OF LEADERSHIP ON TECHNOLOGICAL ADOPTION

The leadership styles and strategic decisions of figures like Satya Nadella and Elon Musk illustrate the profound impact of leadership on technology adoption in SCM. Their visionary approaches to integrating cloud computing, AI, robotics, and other advanced technologies demonstrate how entrepreneurial leaders can drive innovation and enhance supply chain practices.

A. Vision and Strategic Direction

Effective leaders provide a clear vision and strategic direction for technology adoption. Nadella's focus on cloud computing and AI, and Musk's emphasis on automation and innovation, highlight how leadership can shape technological priorities and influence SCM practices.

B. Encouraging Experimentation and Embracing Change

Leaders who foster a culture of experimentation and adaptability encourage their organizations to embrace new technologies and explore innovative solutions. By creating an environment that supports risk-taking and continuous learning, leaders like Nadella and Musk enable their companies to stay ahead of technological trends and drive significant improvements in SCM.

C. Inspiring and Motivating Teams

Inspirational leadership plays a crucial role in motivating teams to adopt and implement new technologies. Nadella's ability to inspire Microsoft's workforce and Musk's leadership in driving Tesla's technological advancements exemplify how leaders can mobilize their teams to embrace change and contribute to successful technology integration in SCM. Leadership is a key driver of technological adoption and innovation in supply chain management. The examples of Satya Nadella at Microsoft and Elon Musk at Tesla demonstrate how visionary leadership can shape technological priorities, foster a culture of experimentation, and drive significant advancements in SCM. By providing strategic direction, encouraging innovation, and inspiring teams, entrepreneurial leaders play a crucial role in leveraging technology to enhance supply chain practices and achieve competitive advantage.

CASE STUDIES: TECHNOLOGY-DRIVEN SMC INNOVATIONS

Case Study 1: Amazon's Use of Robotics and Automation

Overview of Amazon's SCM Innovations

Amazon has revolutionized supply chain management (SCM) through the extensive use of robotics and automation. The company's innovations, including the acquisition of Kiva Systems, have transformed warehousing and distribution processes. Amazon's fulfillment centers utilize thousands of robots to transport goods, reduce manual labor, and expedite order processing.

Impact of Robotics on Amazon's Operational Efficiency

Robotics has had a profound impact on Amazon's operational efficiency. The integration of Kiva robots has enabled Amazon to achieve a 20% increase in operational efficiency and a 50% reduction in labor costs within its fulfillment centers (Hao et al., 2022). The robots, which autonomously navigate warehouses, move inventory directly to human pickers, drastically reducing the time required for order fulfillment. This automation has not only accelerated the speed of delivery but also improved accuracy, contributing to Amazon's competitive edge in the e-commerce sector (Zhao et al., 2023).

Case Study 2: Walmart and Big Data Analytics

How Walmart Uses Big Data to Optimize Its Supply Chain

Walmart leverages big data analytics to enhance its supply chain operations, employing sophisticated data-driven strategies to optimize inventory management and demand forecasting. The company's data analytics platform, powered by its vast data repository, enables real-time insights into consumer behavior, inventory levels, and supply chain performance.

Benefits and Challenges of Data-Driven SCM at Walmart

The use of big data analytics has provided Walmart with several benefits, including improved inventory turnover and reduced stockouts. By analyzing sales data and customer preferences, Walmart can make informed decisions on inventory levels and distribution strategies, resulting in a more efficient supply chain (Smith et al., 2023). However, challenges remain, such as managing the vast amounts of data generated and ensuring data security and privacy. Walmart continues to address these challenges by investing in advanced data analytics tools and cybersecurity measures (Johnson & Lee, 2024).

Case Study 3: IBM's Blockchain Solutions in SCM

Implementation of Blockchain Technology in IBM's Supply Chain

IBM has been a pioneer in applying blockchain technology to supply chain management. The company's blockchain solutions focus on enhancing transparency and traceability across complex supply chains. IBM's Food Trust blockchain, for example, enables the tracking of food products from farm to table, improving food safety and reducing waste.

Outcomes and Lessons Learned from IBM's Blockchain Initiatives

IBM's blockchain initiatives have demonstrated significant outcomes in improving supply chain transparency and efficiency. The implementation of the Food Trust blockchain has enabled rapid tracing of food products, reducing the time required to trace contamination from days to seconds (Kumar et al., 2023). Key lessons from IBM's blockchain projects include the importance of stakeholder collaboration and the need for standardized protocols to ensure interoperability across different supply chain participants (Brown & Wang, 2024).

Case Study 4: Tesla's Integration of IoT and AI

Tesla's Use of IoT and AI in Its Supply Chain Operations

Tesla has effectively integrated Internet of Things (IoT) and artificial intelligence (AI) into its supply chain operations. IoT sensors and AI algorithms are utilized for real-time monitoring of production processes, predictive maintenance, and supply chain optimization. Tesla's Gigafactories, for instance, employ IoT devices to monitor equipment performance and AI to predict maintenance needs, minimizing downtime and optimizing production efficiency.

Results of Tesla's Technological Interventions in SCM

The integration of IoT and AI has yielded impressive results for Tesla. The company has reported a significant reduction in manufacturing downtime and an increase in production efficiency due to its predictive maintenance and real-time monitoring capabilities (Cheng et al., 2024). Additionally, AI-driven analytics have improved inventory management and supply chain forecasting, enabling Tesla to better align production with demand and reduce costs (Li et al., 2024).

CHALLENGES AND BARRIERS TO TECHNOLOGICAL ADOPTION IN SMC

Technological Complexity and Integration

Issues Related to Integrating New Technologies into Existing SCM Systems

Integrating new technologies into established supply chain management (SCM) systems poses significant challenges. The complexity of modern SCM systems can make the integration of emerging technologies, such as AI and IoT, cumbersome. Compatibility issues arise when new systems must work seamlessly with legacy systems, often leading to disruptions in operations and inefficiencies (Khan et al., 2023). Additionally, the rapid pace of technological advancements can outstrip the ability of existing SCM infrastructures to adapt, resulting in integration delays and increased costs (Miller et al., 2024).

Strategies to Overcome Technological Barriers

To address these integration challenges, companies can adopt several strategies. Implementing a phased approach to technology adoption allows organizations to gradually integrate new systems while minimizing disruption. Investing in modular technology solutions that offer compatibility with existing systems can also ease the integration process (Nguyen et al., 2024). Furthermore, engaging in comprehensive planning and risk assessment prior to implementation can help identify potential issues early and develop mitigation strategies (Smith & Roberts, 2024).

Cost and ROI Concerns

Financial Challenges in Adopting Advanced Technologies

The financial burden associated with adopting advanced SCM technologies is a major barrier for many organizations. High initial costs, including those for purchasing new technology, infrastructure upgrades, and training, can be prohibitive

(Johnson et al., 2023). Small and medium-sized enterprises (SMEs), in particular, may struggle to justify these expenses without clear financial benefits.

Assessing the Return on Investment (ROI) for SCM Technologies

Assessing the return on investment (ROI) is crucial for justifying technology expenditures. Companies must evaluate both tangible and intangible benefits, such as increased efficiency, improved accuracy, and enhanced customer satisfaction. Advanced analytics and simulation tools can assist in projecting potential ROI and comparing it against the costs (Kumar et al., 2024). Conducting a thorough cost-benefit analysis and monitoring performance metrics post-implementation can help ensure that the investment delivers expected returns (Ghosh & Patel, 2023).

Workforce Adaptation and Training

Challenges in Training and Upskilling the Workforce for New Technologies

Training and upskilling the workforce to effectively use new SCM technologies is a critical challenge. Employees must acquire new skills and adapt to different workflows, which can be time-consuming and resource-intensive (Lee et al., 2024). Resistance to change and a lack of technical proficiency can further complicate the adoption process, leading to reduced productivity and increased operational risks.

Importance of Change Management in Technological Adoption

Effective change management practices are essential for successful technological adoption. Implementing structured training programs, providing ongoing support, and fostering a culture of continuous learning can help employees adapt to new technologies more effectively (Brown & Wang, 2024). Involving employees in the change process and clearly communicating the benefits of new technologies can also mitigate resistance and enhance overall acceptance (Davis et al., 2023).

Data Privacy and Security

Risks Associated with Data Breaches and Cyber Threats

The increasing reliance on technology in SCM raises significant concerns about data privacy and security. Data breaches and cyber threats can compromise sensitive information, leading to financial losses and reputational damage (Miller & Zhao,

2024). The complexity of securing interconnected systems and ensuring compliance with data protection regulations adds another layer of difficulty.

Ensuring Data Security in Technologically Advanced SCM Systems

To address data security concerns, organizations should implement robust cybersecurity measures, including encryption, access controls, and regular security audits (Kumar et al., 2023). Additionally, adopting best practices for data management and ensuring compliance with relevant regulations, such as the General Data Protection Regulation (GDPR), are crucial steps in safeguarding information (Nguyen et al., 2024).

Regulatory and Compliance Issues

Navigating Regulatory Frameworks for New Technologies in SCM

The adoption of new technologies in SCM must comply with various regulatory frameworks, which can be complex and vary across regions (Ghosh & Patel, 2023). Organizations must stay informed about relevant regulations and ensure that their technological solutions adhere to legal requirements.

Compliance Challenges in Global Supply Chains

For global supply chains, compliance challenges are compounded by differing regulations across countries. Ensuring consistent compliance across diverse jurisdictions requires comprehensive strategies and often, localized solutions (Davis et al., 2023). Implementing global standards and working with legal experts can help navigate these challenges effectively (Smith & Roberts, 2024).

FUTURE TRENDS IN TECHNOLOGY AND SUPPLY CHAIN MANAGEMENT

Emerging Technologies in SCM

Potential Impact of Emerging Technologies Like Quantum Computing and 5G on SCM

Emerging technologies, such as quantum computing and 5G, are poised to significantly impact supply chain management (SCM). Quantum computing has the potential to revolutionize supply chains by solving complex optimization problems much faster than classical computers, enabling more efficient scheduling, routing, and inventory management (Miller & Zhang, 2024). Quantum algorithms could enhance capabilities in predictive analytics and decision-making, leading to more responsive and adaptable supply chains. Similarly, 5G technology promises to enhance real-time communication and data transfer across supply chains. Its high-speed connectivity and low latency will facilitate advanced IoT applications, improve tracking accuracy, and enable real-time monitoring of supply chain operations (Smith et al., 2024). The integration of 5G with IoT devices will enhance data collection and analytics, contributing to more agile and responsive supply chain management.

Sustainability and Green Technologies

Role of Technology in Promoting Sustainable Supply Chains

Technology plays a crucial role in fostering sustainable supply chains. Innovations in green technologies, such as energy-efficient systems and renewable energy sources, are helping organizations reduce their environmental impact. For example, the adoption of energy-efficient transportation and logistics solutions can lower greenhouse gas emissions and decrease carbon footprints (Brown & Patel, 2023). Technologies such as blockchain are also facilitating greater transparency in supply chains, enabling companies to track and verify sustainable practices throughout their supply chain networks (Johnson & Lee, 2024). This transparency helps organizations ensure compliance with environmental standards and communicate their sustainability efforts to consumers effectively.

Innovations in Reducing Carbon Footprint Through SCM Technologies

Several technological innovations are emerging to address carbon footprints in SCM. Electric and autonomous vehicles are reducing emissions from transportation, while advanced analytics help optimize routes and improve fuel efficiency (Nguyen et al., 2024). Additionally, advancements in packaging technologies, such as biodegradable materials and minimalistic designs, are contributing to reduced waste and environmental impact (Kumar et al., 2023).

Personalization and Customization

Use of Technology to Enhance Customer Experience Through Personalized Supply Chains

Technology is enabling greater personalization and customization in supply chains, enhancing customer experience. Advanced data analytics and AI algorithms allow companies to tailor products and services to individual customer preferences and behaviors (Lee et al., 2024). By leveraging customer data, businesses can offer customized recommendations, manage personalized inventory levels, and optimize delivery schedules to meet specific customer needs. Technologies such as 3D printing also support customization by allowing for on-demand production and personalized product designs. This shift towards personalized supply chains not only improves customer satisfaction but also increases efficiency and reduces waste by aligning production with actual demand (Miller & Zhang, 2024).

Globalization and Technology Integration

The Impact of Global Supply Chains on Technological Adoption

Global supply chains are driving the adoption of advanced technologies to manage complexity and enhance efficiency. As companies expand their operations across borders, they increasingly rely on integrated technology solutions to coordinate and optimize their global supply chain networks (Smith et al., 2024). Technologies such as cloud computing and blockchain facilitate seamless communication and data sharing across international borders, improving supply chain visibility and coordination.

Trends in Cross-Border Technology-Driven SCM Practices

Cross-border SCM practices are evolving with the integration of technologies that support global operations. The rise of digital platforms for supply chain management enables real-time tracking, monitoring, and collaboration among global partners (Johnson & Lee, 2024). Trends such as the use of AI for global demand forecasting and the implementation of automated systems for international logistics are enhancing the efficiency and effectiveness of global supply chains (Nguyen et al., 2024).

The Role of AI and Automation in Future SCM

How AI and Automation Will Shape the Future of Supply Chains

AI and automation are set to reshape the future of SCM by driving unprecedented levels of efficiency and innovation. AI-powered systems are improving decision-making through advanced analytics, predictive modeling, and real-time data processing (Kumar et al., 2023). Automation technologies, including robotics and autonomous vehicles, are streamlining operations by handling repetitive tasks, optimizing workflows, and reducing human error (Brown & Patel, 2023).

Predictions on the Evolution of Fully Autonomous Supply Chain Systems

The future of SCM is likely to feature fully autonomous systems, where AI and automation play central roles in managing end-to-end supply chain operations. These systems will integrate advanced technologies to handle complex logistics, inventory management, and customer interactions with minimal human intervention (Miller & Zhang, 2024). Predictions suggest that as technology continues to advance, we will see greater adoption of autonomous supply chain systems, leading to further improvements in efficiency, accuracy, and responsiveness.

Importance of Entrepreneurial Orientation in SCM

Entrepreneurial orientation, characterized by innovativeness, proactiveness, and risk-taking, plays a crucial role in adopting and integrating these technologies into SCM practices (Lee et al., 2024). Companies with a strong entrepreneurial mindset are more likely to embrace new technologies, adapt to market changes, and innovate within their supply chains. This orientation drives the successful implementation of advanced technologies and fosters a culture of continuous improvement and agility.

Implications for Businesses and Practitioners

How Businesses Can Leverage the Insights from the Chapter

Businesses can leverage the insights from this chapter by strategically integrating the discussed technologies into their supply chain operations. Embracing automation and robotics can streamline processes and reduce operational costs, while IoT and big data analytics can provide real-time visibility and actionable insights (Nguyen et al., 2024). Implementing AI and ML can enhance forecasting accuracy and predictive maintenance, contributing to more efficient supply chain management (Johnson & Lee, 2024). Furthermore, businesses should focus on fostering an entrepreneurial orientation within their teams to drive technological adoption and innovation (Lee et al., 2024). By encouraging a culture of innovation and calculated risk-taking, companies can better navigate technological changes and gain a competitive edge in the market.

Practical Recommendations for Integrating Technology into SCM

For effective integration of technology into SCM, businesses should start by conducting a thorough assessment of their current supply chain processes and identifying areas where technology can add value (Brown & Patel, 2023). Developing a clear technology adoption strategy and investing in relevant technologies that align with organizational goals is essential. Companies should also prioritize training and upskilling their workforce to ensure successful implementation and utilization of new technologies (Smith et al., 2024). Additionally, fostering collaboration with technology providers and industry experts can help businesses stay abreast of technological advancements and best practices. Regularly evaluating and updating technology solutions will ensure that supply chain operations remain efficient and competitive.

Future Research Directions

Areas for Further Research in Technology and Supply Chain Management

Future research should focus on exploring the long-term impacts of emerging technologies, such as quantum computing and 5G, on supply chain management (Miller & Zhang, 2024). Investigating the integration challenges and best practices for these technologies will provide valuable insights for businesses planning to adopt them. Additionally, research into the effectiveness of various green technologies and their impact on sustainability in supply chains can offer guidance for developing more environmentally friendly practices (Kumar et al., 2023).

The Evolving Role of Entrepreneurial Orientation in Technological Innovation

Further research is also needed to understand the evolving role of entrepreneurial orientation in driving technological innovation within supply chains. Studying how different dimensions of entrepreneurial orientation—such as risk-taking and proactiveness affect technology adoption and integration will help businesses develop more effective strategies for leveraging technology to enhance their supply chain operations (Lee et al., 2024).

CONCLUSION

This chapter has explored various technological interventions transforming supply chain management (SCM). We examined the role of automation and robotics, which are streamlining warehousing and distribution processes, significantly enhancing operational efficiency (Nguyen et al., 2024). The integration of the Internet of Things (IoT) facilitates real-time tracking and monitoring, providing valuable insights into supply chain dynamics (Smith et al., 2024). Artificial Intelligence (AI) and Machine Learning (ML) are revolutionizing demand forecasting and predictive maintenance, while blockchain technology enhances transparency and security in supply chains (Johnson & Lee, 2024). Additionally, big data analytics is empowering data-driven decision-making, improving efficiency and trend identification (Kumar et al., 2023). Cloud computing supports scalable and flexible SCM solutions, enabling better collaboration across supply chain networks (Brown & Patel, 2023). Each technological advancement offers unique benefits and challenges, contributing to a more agile and responsive supply chain ecosystem. The interplay between technological advancements and entrepreneurial orientation is pivotal in shaping the future of supply chain management. By continuing to explore and understand these dynamics, businesses and researchers can contribute to the development of more efficient, agile, and innovative supply chains.

REFERENCES

Bowersox, D. J., Closs, D. J., & Cooper, M. B. (2013). *Supply chain logistics management*. McGraw-Hill Education.

Brown, A., & Patel, A. (2023). Innovations in green technologies for sustainable supply chains. *The Journal of Supply Chain Management*, 60(2), 118–132.

Brown, A., & Wang, L. (2024). Blockchain and supply chain management: Lessons from IBM's Food Trust. *The Journal of Supply Chain Management*, 61(1), 102–115.

Cheng, Y., Liu, Q., & Chen, X. (2024). Artificial intelligence in supply chain management: A review and future directions. *The Journal of Supply Chain Management*, 60(1), 14–28.

Choi, T. M., Liu, Y., & Shen, B. (2023). Advances in robotics and automation in the supply chain. *International Journal of Production Economics*, 253, 108–121.

Christopher, M. (2016). *Logistics & supply chain management*. Pearson Education.

Covin, J. G., & Slevin, D. P. (1989). Strategic management of small firms in hostile and benign environments. *Strategic Management Journal*, 10(1), 75–87. DOI: 10.1002/smj.4250100107

Davis, T., Lee, J., & Thompson, R. (2023). Change management strategies for technology adoption in supply chains. *International Journal of Production Economics*, 258, 138–150.

Ghosh, P., & Patel, A. (2023). Assessing ROI in supply chain technology investments. *Journal of Business Research*, 112, 245–256.

Gupta, H., Kumar, P., & Ghosh, P. (2023). Machine learning for predictive maintenance in supply chains. *Journal of Manufacturing Processes*, 81, 277–288.

Hao, L., Zhang, W., & Li, X. (2022). Robotics in warehousing: A case study of Amazon's fulfillment centers. *Robotics and Automation Review*, 43(2), 90–103.

Hazen, B. T., Boone, C. A., Ezell, J. D., & Jones-Farmer, L. A. (2014). Data quality for data science, predictive analytics, and big data in supply chain management: An introduction to data quality. *International Journal of Production Economics*, 154, 72–80. DOI: 10.1016/j.ijpe.2014.04.018

Huang, Y., Zhang, Y., & Wang, L. (2023). Automation systems in manufacturing: A comprehensive review. *Journal of Manufacturing Science and Engineering*, 145(6), 112–125.

Ivanov, D., & Dolgui, A. (2020). *Handbook of research on digital transformation and challenges to data security and privacy*. IGI Global.

Johnson, M., & Lee, R. (2023). Financial challenges in adopting advanced SCM technologies. *International Journal of Logistics Management*, 34(2), 158–172.

Johnson, M., & Lee, R. (2024). Big data analytics in retail: Walmart's data-driven approach. *International Journal of Retail & Distribution Management*, 52(3), 245–260.

Johnson, M., & Lee, R. (2024). Blockchain and sustainability: Enhancing transparency in supply chains. *International Journal of Logistics Management*, 35(1), 45–59.

Khan, S., Smith, J., & Roberts, C. (2023). Overcoming integration barriers in SCM technology. *The Journal of Supply Chain Management*, 59(3), 99–113.

Kim, J., Lee, H., & Lee, J. (2023). Blockchain for food safety: A case study of Walmart's supply chain. *Food Control*, 146, 109–119.

Kumar, S., Gupta, H., & Ghosh, P. (2023). 3D printing and customization: Transforming supply chains. *Journal of Manufacturing Processes*, 82, 198–210.

Kumar, S., Gupta, H., & Ghosh, P. (2023). Machine learning for predictive maintenance in supply chains. *Journal of Manufacturing Processes*, 81, 277–288.

Kumar, S., & Sharma, A. (2024). Cloud computing in supply chain management: Benefits and challenges. *International Journal of Cloud Computing and Services Science*, 12(1), 45–58.

Kumar, S., Singh, R., & Garg, R. (2023). The impact of cloud-based SCM platforms on supply chain collaboration. *Computers in Industry*, 135, 12–25.

Lee, S., Kim, J., & Park, H. (2024). Personalization and technology in modern supply chains. *Journal of Business Logistics*, 46(1), 75–88.

Lee, S., Kim, J., & Park, H. (2024). Workforce adaptation to technological change in supply chains. *Journal of Business Logistics*, 45(2), 65–79.

Li, J., Zhao, X., & Li, X. (2024). IoT-enabled real-time tracking in supply chains: An empirical study. *Journal of Business Logistics*, 45(2), 34–48.

Lumpkin, G. T., & Dess, G. G. (1996). Clarifying the entrepreneurial orientation construct and linking it to performance. *Academy of Management Review*, 21(1), 135–172. DOI: 10.2307/258632

Madhani, P. M. (2024). Role of big data analytics in enhancing supply chain efficiency. *Global Journal of Management and Business Research*, 24(3), 67–80.

Meyer, T. K. H. (2015). *Automation and robotics in the warehouse: A guide to modern warehousing and distribution*. Wiley.

Miller, D. (1983). The correlates of entrepreneurship in three types of firms. *Management Science*, 29(7), 770–791. DOI: 10.1287/mnsc.29.7.770

Miller, T., & Zhang, L. (2024). Quantum computing and its potential impact on supply chain optimization. *Journal of Operations Research*, 56(4), 299–312.

Miller, T., Zhao, Q., & Li, X. (2024). Data privacy and security challenges in advanced SCM systems. *The Journal of Supply Chain Management*, 60(1), 80–94.

Nguyen, T., Brown, A., & Wang, L. (2024). Strategies for technological integration in supply chains. *Journal of Production Economics*, 257, 122–135.

Nguyen, T., Brown, A., & Wang, L. (2024). The role of 5G technology in advancing supply chain management. *The Journal of Supply Chain Management*, 61(3), 150–165.

Reddy, M., Prasad, R., & Rao, S. (2023). Big data analytics for supply chain optimization: Trends and insights. *Data Science Journal*, 22(4), 301–312.

Smith, J., Patel, A., & Kim, S. (2023). The role of big data in supply chain optimization: Insights from Walmart. *The Journal of Supply Chain Management*, 59(4), 66–80.

Smith, J., Roberts, C., & Davis, T. (2024). Global supply chains and technology integration: Trends and challenges. *International Journal of Production Economics*, 260, 234–247.

Wamba, S. F., Gunasekaran, A., Akter, S., Ren, S. J., & Dubey, R. (2017). Big data analytics and organizational culture as complements to swift trust in building inter-organizational relationships. *Journal of Business Research*, 70, 253–264.

Wang, J., Xu, J., & Zhang, Y. (2024). Blockchain technology in supply chain management: A comprehensive review. *International Journal of Production Economics*, 258, 108–122.

Zahra, S. A., & Covin, J. G. (1995). Contextual influences on the corporate entrepreneurship-performance relationship: A longitudinal analysis. *Journal of Business Venturing*, 10(1), 43–58. DOI: 10.1016/0883-9026(94)00004-E

Zhang, J., Xu, Y., & Li, J. (2023). Smart sensors in supply chain management: Applications and benefits. *Sensors and Actuators. A, Physical*, 341, 112–125.

Zhao, Q., Liu, S., & Wang, C. (2023). Automation systems in manufacturing: A comprehensive review. *Journal of Manufacturing Science and Engineering*, 145(6), 112–125.

Zhao, Q., Liu, S., & Wang, C. (2024). Blockchain for product authentication and traceability: A study of recent developments. *Journal of Business Research*, 148, 189–200.

KEY TERMS AND DEFINITIONS

Cloud Computing: A technology that allows users to access and store data and applications over the internet instead of on local servers or personal computers. It provides scalability, flexibility, and cost efficiency for businesses and educational institutions alike.

Collaborative Tools: Software and platforms that facilitate communication, information sharing, and teamwork among individuals and organizations. These tools enhance collaboration within supply chains, allowing for real-time updates and improved coordination.

Cost Reduction: The process of minimizing expenses while maintaining product quality and service standards. In supply chain management, cost reduction strategies can enhance profitability and competitiveness.

Cybersecurity: The practice of protecting systems, networks, and programs from digital attacks. As organizations integrate cloud computing and IoT into their supply chains, ensuring cybersecurity is crucial to safeguarding sensitive data and maintaining operational integrity.

Data Analytics: The systematic computational analysis of data to uncover patterns, trends, and insights that inform decision-making. In supply chain management, data analytics can enhance forecasting, inventory management, and operational efficiency.

Digital Transformation: The integration of digital technology into all areas of a business, fundamentally changing how it operates and delivers value to customers. In supply chains, digital transformation can enhance efficiency and responsiveness through real-time data access and process automation.

Entrepreneurial Orientation (EO): A strategic posture characterized by a firm's propensity to engage in innovative activities, take risks, and proactively seek new opportunities. High EO can drive innovation and improve competitive advantage.

Global Collaboration: The process of working across geographical boundaries to achieve common goals. In supply chain management, global collaboration can enhance resource sharing and innovation, allowing organizations to respond swiftly to market changes.

Innovation: The process of developing new ideas, products, or services that create value for an organization. In supply chains, innovation can lead to improved processes, technologies, and customer experiences.

Internet of Things (IoT): A network of interconnected devices that communicate and exchange data over the internet. In supply chains, IoT can improve visibility and tracking of goods, optimizing logistics and inventory management.

Knowledge Sharing: The practice of exchanging information and insights among individuals or organizations. In supply chain management, knowledge sharing fosters collaboration, innovation, and improved decision-making.

Operational Flexibility: The ability of an organization to adapt its processes and systems in response to changing market conditions or customer demands. High operational flexibility can lead to improved responsiveness and customer satisfaction.

Predictive Analytics: A branch of data analytics that uses historical data and statistical algorithms to forecast future outcomes. In supply chains, predictive analytics can help organizations anticipate demand, reduce stockouts, and improve resource allocation.

Supply Chain Efficiency: The ability of an organization to optimize its supply chain processes to reduce costs, improve service delivery, and enhance customer satisfaction. This involves streamlining operations from raw material procurement to product delivery.

Sustainability: The ability to meet present needs without compromising the ability of future generations to meet their own. In supply chains, sustainability practices can reduce environmental impact and enhance brand reputation.

Risk Management: The identification, assessment, and prioritization of risks followed by coordinated efforts to minimize, monitor, and control the probability or impact of unforeseen events. Effective risk management is essential for maintaining supply chain resilience.

User Experience (UX): The overall experience a person has when interacting with a product or service, particularly in terms of ease of use and satisfaction. In supply chains, enhancing UX can lead to improved customer loyalty and retention.

Value Creation: The process of enhancing the worth of a product or service through innovation, quality improvement, or cost efficiency. In supply chains, value creation is vital for maintaining competitive advantage.

Chapter 7
Security and Privacy Considerations in Cloud-Based Education

Poonam Ponde
Nowrosjee Wadia College, Pune, India

ABSTRACT

Cloud computing has transformed education by providing anytime access to educational content, enhancing learning, and fostering collaboration. Adaptive technologies and analytics allow personalizing learning experiences and increasing learner engagement by tailoring education to individual needs. Cloud solutions streamline administrative tasks like attendance and grading, allowing educators to focus more on teaching. However, these benefits come with challenges, primarily concerning security and privacy. Educational organizations manage large amounts of sensitive data, including learner records, academic information, grades, and intellectual property. Storing this data in the cloud raises concerns about unauthorized access, data breaches, and regulatory compliance. The use of cloud-based services for hosting infrastructure and applications makes institutions vulnerable to attacks. Therefore, cloud security in education is crucial; requiring robust strategies and practices to protect data, applications, and infrastructure on cloud platforms.

INTRODUCTION

The education sector has undergone a paradigm shift in the last few years. New pedagogies and teaching-learning models have evolved. The evolution of digital and communication technologies is changing all aspects of educational processes ranging from the nature of classrooms, type of content, pedagogy, methodologies, mode of

DOI: 10.4018/979-8-3693-6705-6.ch007

engagement, and evaluation. Traditional chalk-and-board teaching methods have been replaced by digital tools and technologies. Educational organizations are offering their services in a hybrid manner, combining offline and online modes, to cater to the diverse needs of learners. Formal education is being offered through electronic media and digital resources (e-learning) as well as mobile devices (m-learning).

Cloud computing has transformed the field of education by providing new avenues for accessing educational materials, offering more flexible learning options, and creating more chances for collaboration. In cloud-based education, learners can access educational resources and applications, at any time and regardless of their geographic location (Khan & Salah, 2020). Educators can create, save, and share educational resources in a convenient way, improving the connection between educators and learner. Administrators can assess and monitor learner progress and educator effectiveness in real time. Through the utilization of adaptive technologies and analytics to personalize learning experiences, cloud computing enhances engagement and learning by tailoring education to suit the requirements of each learner. Additionally, cloud-based solutions make tasks such as attendance tracking and grading easier for administrators, allowing educators to focus more on teaching. Cloud-based solutions offer scalability, flexibility, accessibility, and collaboration advantages over traditional education models.

The benefits of cloud-based education bring with them a new set of challenges; foremost among them are concerns about security and privacy (Gill et al., 2022; Thavi, 2024). Security and Privacy are two essential aspects of protecting and managing data as well as computing and communication systems. Security deals with the protection of digital assets from harm while privacy controls who can access, use and share these assets. Cloud-based solutions offer a lot of flexibility for data storage, access, backup and recovery, but it is not free of security and privacy risks. Educational institutions manage a significant amount of academic resources such as curriculum, educational content, policies, etc. and personal information, such as learner and faculty records, academic data, grades, research findings, and intellectual property. Keeping sensitive educational information in the cloud raises concerns about unauthorized access, data breaches, and compliance with data protection regulations (Durairaj & Manimaran, 2015; Yang, 2020). In addition to data, education organizations are increasingly adopting cloud-based Software-as-a-Service (SaaS), Platform-as-a-Service (PaaS), and Infrastructure-as-a-Service (IaaS) services to house their infrastructure (networks, virtual laboratories, etc.) and applications (like Learning Management Systems, Management Information Systems, etc.) for cost-cutting benefits (Attaran et al., 2017). The cloud infrastructure and applications are a major target for attacks and breaches from both, insiders and outsiders. As more and more educational institutions are adopting cloud-based solutions, the increasing dependence on these digital platforms has made them vulnerable and exposed them to security and privacy breaches and attacks. Studies also indicate that security and privacy have a strongly significant influence on the students' attitudes towards using cloud services in educational settings (Arpaci et al., 2015; Orehovački et al., 2017). A similar work by Sandhu et al., (2022) identifies the effect of trust and security factors on the behavior intention of the student to adopt the cloud computing in the learning process. Some researchers argue that while data privacy and security is essential, there is a need to equally prioritize data value (Komljenovic, 2022; Abrera, 2024).

This chapter aims to highlight the security and privacy challenges in using cloud technology for education and to stress the need for more proactive measures to be taken to address these issues. Educational institutions need to implement policies, strategies and practices to protect data, applications, and infrastructure stored on cloud platforms. By fostering a culture of security and privacy educational institutions can protect their assets and maintain trust with their stakeholders.

SECURITY AND PRIVACY CONCEPTS

The fundamental principles of security and privacy are essential for protecting sensitive information and ensuring trust in digital environments. This section covers basic concepts and principles of security and privacy (Gupta, 2019; Stallings, 2023).

Security refers to the technologies, policies and procedures designed to protect computer systems and data from unauthorized access, threats, misuse or attacks. It protects the integrity, confidentiality and accessibility of networks and data.

A **threat** is object, person, or other entity that represents a danger to an asset.

An **attack** is any action that compromises the security of information owned by an organization. A security attack can be either active or passive. In an active attack, the attacker attempts to take control of the information or system by altering or destroying the normal operation.

Examples of active attacks are:

- Masquerade: The attacker pretends to be someone else to gain access to data or the system.
- Modification: The information is altered or delayed.
- Repudiation: The attacker denies or repudiates some action that was taken.
- Replay: Information is captured and later replayed
- Denial of Service: The system or service is made unavailable to authorized users by consuming its resources or sending excess traffic to the system.

In passive attacks, the attacker does not actively affect the system or information but passively eavesdrops or monitors the network or system to gather information which can be later used for malicious purposes. Examples of passive attacks include:

- Eavesdropping or traffic analysis: The attacker monitors and analyzes network traffic to gain valuable information. This includes packet sniffing, port scanning etc.
- Release of message: Conversational messages such as emails, file transfers etc. that contain personally identifiable information are captured and used to compromise the system.

A **security service** is a processing or communication service that is provided by a system to give a specific kind of protection to system resources. Security services implement security policies. The important security services are:

1. Confidentiality: Confidentiality ensures that information is accessible only to authorized individuals, entities, or systems. It involves preventing unauthorized access, disclosure, or exposure of sensitive data to protect its confidentiality.
2. Integrity: Integrity ensures that data is accurate, trustworthy, and reliable throughout its lifecycle. It involves preventing unauthorized or unintentional modifications, deletions, or alterations to data.
3. Availability: Availability ensures that data, systems, and resources are accessible and usable by authorized users when needed. It involves minimizing downtime, disruptions, or denial-of-service (DoS) attacks that affect access to critical services.

The above are the fundamental and important security principles and also called the *CIA triad* as shown in Figure 1 below.

Figure 1 CIA Triad

4. Authentication: Authentication verifies the identity of users, devices, or services attempting to access resources, ensuring that only authorized entities can access them.
5. Authorization: Authorization determines what services or resources can be accessed by authenticated users based on their privileges or roles.
6. Non-repudiation: Non-repudiation prevents either the sender or receiver from denying an action or transmitted data.

While security deals with protecting information and systems from threats and attacks, privacy deals with controlling how the systems and information are accessed and used.

Privacy governs how data is collected, shared, and used. It protects personal data from unauthorized access, misuse, and sharing.

Privacy attacks are various malicious actions aimed at compromising individuals' control over their personal information. These attacks include:

1. Data breaches: A data breach is unauthorized access to sensitive information resulting in theft or misuse of personal information.
2. Insider threat: It is a malicious activity undertaken by users who are authorized to use a service, network, application, or data of an organization.

3. Identity theft: This is an act of impersonation by acquiring and using someone else's personal information, such as login credentials, to commit fraud or other crimes.
4. Surveillance: Monitoring and collecting data without the consent of the owner.
5. Data mining and profiling: Collecting and analyzing large datasets to create detailed profiles of individuals.
6. Data leaking: Unauthorized disclosure or exposure of sensitive information.

SECURITY ATTACKS IN CLOUD COMPUTING AND MITIGATION STRATEGIES

This section gives an overview of cloud security attacks. Some key attacks, their purpose and their Mitigation strategies are also presented (Alenizi et al., 2021; Rajesh, 2017).

1. Spoofing: In cloud-based education, spoofing can occur when attackers impersonate legitimate users or services to gain unauthorized access. This could involve spoofing IP addresses, email addresses, or even creating fake websites that mimic legitimate educational platforms.

Mitigation strategies:

a. Authentication: Implement multi factor authentication mechanisms to verify user identities.
b. Digital certificates: Use digital certificates to authenticate servers and services.
c. Secure communication: Use strong encryption techniques to prevent interception and tampering.
   2. Phishing: Phishing attacks in cloud-based education involve sending deceptive emails or messages to users by masquerading as a valid source to make them divulge sensitive information, click malicious links, or install ransom-ware that compromises their credentials.

Mitigation strategies:

a. Email filtering: Implement robust email filtering and spam detection systems.
b. URL inspection: Inspect the URLs in emails and messages for authenticity.
c. User training: Educate users about not disclosing private and sensitive information in response to an unsolicited request.

3. Malware and Ransomware: Malware is malicious software used to gain unauthorized access to a system in order to steal data, disrupt services or damage the system. Ransomware is a dangerous type of malware designed to block a system from authorized users until a ransom amount is paid to the creator.

Mitigation strategies:

a. Antivirus and anti-malware software: Install and regularly update antivirus and anti-malware software.
b. Patch management: Keep cloud applications and systems up to date with security patches.
c. Data backup: Regularly back up critical data to mitigate the impact of malware and ransomware attacks.

4. Denial-of-Service (DoS) and Distributed Denial-of-Service (DDoS): DoS attacks aim to prevent access to a system or services by overwhelming them with excessive traffic or requests, making them unavailable to intended users. A distributed denial-of-service (DDoS) attack uses multiple computers to flood a targeted resource.

Mitigation strategies:

a. Load balancing: Implement load balancing to distribute traffic across the network.
b. Anomaly detection: Use anomaly detection systems to identify and block suspicious users and traffic patterns.
c. Network segmentation: Segment the network into smaller, more manageable units.
d. IP blocking: Block traffic from suspected malicious sources.
e. Rate limiting: Limit the traffic to a particular server or resource.

5. Man-in-the-Middle (MitM) Attack: MitM attacks intercept communication between users and systems or services, allowing attackers to eavesdrop, modify, or steal sensitive information.

Mitigation strategies:

a. Encryption: Use strong encryption mechanisms to secure data during communication.
b. Certificate validation: Verify server certificates to prevent interception by unauthorized entities.

c. Authentication: Verify the credentials of both parties involved in communication by mutual authentication mechanisms.
d. VPN's: Use Virtual Private Networks for transfer of sensitive information.

6. SQL Injection: SQL injection attacks exploit vulnerabilities in web applications by placing malicious code in SQL statements

Mitigation strategies

a. Input validation: Use input validation to filter malicious code.
b. Database security: Configure database security and implement least privilege access controls. Update security patches on databases.
c. Firewalls: Use web application firewalls to detect and block SQL injection attempts.

7. Data Breaches: Data breaches involve unauthorized access or exposure of operational data or sensitive information related to stakeholders.

Mitigation strategies:

a. Data encryption: Encrypt sensitive data while in storage and in transit to protect integrity and confidentiality.
b. Access controls: Implement strict access control policies to limit data access.
c. Incident response management: Develop and maintain an incident response plan to quickly detect, respond to, and recover from data breaches.
d. Data backup: Maintain regular backup of data.

8. Account and Session Hijacking: This attack involves stealing user credentials or session tokens to gain unauthorized access to user accounts and sessions.

Mitigation strategies:

a. Session management: Create strong cryptographically secure sessions for communication, use session timeouts and re-authentication for sensitive actions.
b. Authentication: Implement strong authentication methods to verify the credentials of all parties.
c. Monitoring and logging: Monitor sessions and log activities to detect and respond to suspicious behavior.

PRIVACY ATTACKS IN CLOUD COMPUTING AND MITIGATION STRATEGIES

This section gives an overview of privacy attacks and their Mitigation strategies (Husain & Budiyantara, 2020).

1. Unauthorized data access: Attackers exploit vulnerabilities in cloud infrastructure, weak authentication mechanisms, or insider threats to access confidential educational data.

Mitigation strategies:

a. Access controls: Control and restrict access to sensitive data by implementing role-based access controls.
b. Encryption: Encrypt data in storage and during communication to protect integrity and confidentiality.
c. Monitoring: Use logging and monitoring tools to detect unauthorized access and suspicious activities.
d. Authentication: Implement strong authentication methods, such as biometric, multi-factor authentication to verify user identities.

2. Data Interception: Data interception involves eavesdropping on communication between users and cloud-based education services, to capture and expose sensitive information.

Mitigation strategies:

a. Encryption: Use strong encryption protocols (e.g., TLS/SSL) to protect data in transit between clients and servers.
b. Secure communication channels: Utilize virtual private networks (VPNs) or secure tunneling protocols for data transmission.
c. Network segmentation: Segment networks to isolate sensitive data traffic from less sensitive traffic.
d. Regular vulnerability scanning: Conduct regular vulnerability assessments to identify and remediate potential weaknesses in network infrastructure.

3. Data Mining and Profiling: This involves analyzing large datasets from cloud-based education systems to extract patterns, behaviors, or preferences of users without their consent.

Mitigation strategies:

a. Data anonymization: Anonymize data to protect the identities of users while retaining its usefulness for analysis.
b. User consent: Obtain explicit consent from individuals before collecting and processing their data for profiling purposes.
c. Transparency: Provide clear and comprehensive information to users about data collection, storage, and processing practices.
d. Compliance: Strictly enforce privacy laws and regulations governing data mining and profiling activities.

4. Identity Theft: Identity theft allows attackers to impersonate legitimate users of the system through stolen credentials, phishing attacks, or exploitation of weak authentication mechanisms.

Mitigation strategies:

a. Authentication and identify verification: Implement biometric authentication and multi-factor authentication to verify user credentials.
b. Strong password policies: Enforce strong password requirements (length, complexity, expiration).
c. User education: Educate users about various attacks and best practices for securing personal information.
d. Monitoring and logging: Monitor user accounts and logs for suspicious activities and unauthorized access attempts.

5. Data Leakage: Data leakage involves exposure or unauthorized sharing of sensitive information, due to misconfiguration, system vulnerabilities, human error, or insider threats.

Mitigation strategies:

a. Data loss prevention: Implement mechanisms to monitor and prevent unauthorized data transfers or leaks.
b. Access controls: Apply strict access controls and verify user credentials while handling sensitive data.
c. Encryption: Encrypt sensitive data.
d. User awareness: Educate users about handling sensitive information and the risks of data leakage.

6. Third-Party Data Sharing: Educational institutions may need to share learner data with external entities. Third-party data sharing occurs when the data is shared without adequate consent or security measures.

Mitigation strategies:

a. Data minimization: Share only necessary data with external entities and limit the scope of data sharing agreements.
b. Data sharing agreements: Create agreements detailing data handling practices and security measures.
c. Audit: Regularly audit third-party practices and enforce compliance with data protection standards.
d. Transparency: Inform stakeholders about third-party data sharing practices and obtain explicit consent where required.

TYPES OF INFORMATION IN CLOUD-BASED EDUCATION AND PROTECTION STRATEGIES

Any educational organization needs to store a large volume of data and for a considerable period of time. It is mandatory to maintain accurate records of academic and administrative activities. Additionally, it provides insights into learners' knowledge, learning abilities, preferences and performance. The use of digital tools and technologies for record-keeping enables valuable insights to be extracted from the data by employing data analytics. Educators and administrators can learn more about learner performance, learning patterns, and institutional efficacy thereby enabling educational institutions to make well-informed decisions to enhance instruction, customize learning, and allocate resources more efficiently. Data is a valuable educational asset which needs to be protected (Yang, 2020). The various types of Data collected and stored in cloud-based education systems are:

1. Demographic data

   Data collected: Backgrounds, age, gender, race/ethnicity, educational background, socioeconomic status, language preference etc.

   Purpose: Demographics refer to the specific characteristics for understanding the nature and needs of the stakeholders. This data can be utilized to tailor educational content and improve user experience.

   Security concerns: Identity theft, data breach, insider threat.

   Privacy concerns: Unlawful disclosure of sensitive personal information, profiling, potential discrimination.

   Mitigation strategies: Anonymization, access controls, informed consent and transparency, Compliance to data protection regulations, user awareness.
2. Personal Identifiable Information

   Data collected: Name, address, date of birth, location, etc.

   Purpose: To directly identify a learner or other stakeholder.

Security concerns: Data breaches, phishing attacks, ransomware.
Privacy concerns: Unlawful disclosure, profiling.
Mitigation strategies: User authentication, privacy policies, access controls, encryption.

3. Assessment data
   Data collected: Scores, grades, test results, quizzes, assignments, transcripts etc.
   Purpose: Measure academic progress, plan teaching strategies.
   Security concerns: Tampering, denial-of-Service, Man-in-the-Middle, interception.
   Privacy concerns: Data leakage.
   Mitigation strategies: Encryption, authentication, secure transmission, access control, anonymization.
4. Attendance and Authentication data
   Data collected: Learner attendance records, biometric data such as facial recognition, fingerprints, Logs of learner attendance etc.
   Purpose: Monitor attendance patterns, absentee, early departures.
   Security concerns: Unauthorized access, forgery, tampering.
   Privacy concerns: Profiling, data leakage.
   Mitigation strategies: Access controls, authentication, audit logs, data anonymization.
5. Curriculum data
   Data collected: Courses offered, course details, lesson plans, assessment methods, textbooks, multimedia resources, and instructional materials.
   Purpose: To design effective curricula aligned with educational standards.
   Security concerns: Unauthorized access, sabotage.
   Privacy concerns: Data mining.
   Mitigation strategies: Data encryption, backup and recovery, access controls.
6. Educator and Staff data
   Data collected: Employment records, performance evaluations.
   Purpose: Resource allocation, manage human resources, support professional development.
   Security concerns: Unauthorized access to personal information, identity theft.
   Privacy concerns: Data leakage.
   Mitigation strategies: Access restrictions, data encryption, user training.
7. Enrolment data
   Data collected: Course enrollments, dropouts, enrollment status, enrollment dates, etc.

Purpose: Manage resources, enhance learner outcomes, comply with regulations, and plan for the future.
Security concerns: Identity theft, data modification.
Privacy concerns: Data breach, profiling.
Mitigation strategies: Encryption, access controls, user authentication, data minimization.

8. Progress data
   Data collected: Learner performance, Progress over time, completion of learning objectives.
   Purpose: Evaluate education effectiveness, personalize learning.
   Security concerns: Unauthorized access, data manipulation.
   Privacy concerns: Disclosure of learner performance data, potential profiling.
   Mitigation strategies: Data encryption, access controls, data integrity checks, secure APIs, data retention policies.
9. Research data
   Data collected: Findings from research projects, educational studies, surveys, and experiments, publications and patents.
   Purpose: For policy making, contributing to knowledge creation.
   Security concerns: Intellectual property theft.
   Privacy concerns: Data leakage.
   Mitigation strategies: Data encryption, access controls, anonymization.
10. Financial data
    Data collected: Expenditures, budgets, funding sources.
    Purpose: Manage finances, auditing, and compliance with financial regulations.
    Security concerns: Financial fraud, ransomware.
    Privacy concerns: Data leakage, financial profiling.
    Mitigation strategies: Secure systems, encryption, access controls, audits and monitoring.
11. Behavioral data
    Data collected: Disciplinary records, behavioral assessments.
    Purpose: Track behavior, provide interventions.
    Security concerns: Unauthorized access, data breaches.
    Privacy concerns: Unlawful disclosure, profiling.
    Mitigation strategies: Access control, data encryption, user consent, audits for compliance.

BLOCKCHAIN FOR EDUCATION

Blockchain is a distributed, digital ledger that records transactions in a secure, transparent, and tamper-proof manner. Each transaction is cryptographically secured and recorded in a block, which is then added to the chain of blocks, forming a chronological chain of transactions. This chain of blocks is maintained by a network of computers, which work together to validate and verify transactions, ensuring that the data stored on the blockchain are accurate and up-to-date. The decentralization eliminates the need for intermediaries in transactions, resulting in greater security. Additionally, the use of cryptographic algorithms and digital signatures makes the data tamper-proof, thereby protecting integrity (Bhaskar et al., 2021; Khanna et al., 2022; Tripathi et al., 2023).

The use of blockchain technology for education offers several benefits:

1. Record keeping: Learners can quickly and securely access their records, credits and share them with other institutions or employers. Storing academic records on the blockchain ensures that transcripts are secure, immutable, and easily accessible.
2. Digital credentials and certification: Producing transcripts is a very time-consuming and labor-intensive task. With blockchain, tamper-proof digital diplomas and certificates can be created that are easily verifiable.
3. Intellectual property: Plagiarism in the academic community is a critical issue. Blockchain-based solutions can be used to regulate how copyrighted content is distributed online.
4. Authentication: Blockchain-based learner identification can be used for accessing services and verifying learner status.
5. Performance tracking: Learners can maintain a lifelong, verifiable portfolio of their academic and other achievements.

BEST PRACTICES AND GENERAL RECOMMENDATIONS

To reduce the risk of security attacks and protect the privacy of sensitive data stored and processed in cloud-based education environments, a set of best practices and recommendations are listed below. By implementing these strategies, educational institutions can effectively mitigate risks associated with collecting, storing, and using various types of data in education while safeguarding learner and staff information. Continual monitoring and adaptation to evolving threats are crucial to maintaining robust data security and privacy practices (Chatterjee et al., 2023; Ren, 2023). Incorporation of Security and privacy concepts in the curriculum can also help in mitigating threats (Onyema et al., 2020). The work by Cohen et al., (2022) highlights five main core functions of the NIST framework to strengthen digital defenses. The work by Seth et al. (2024) highlights the challenges of data ownership and accessibility from cloud services. They also emphasize that the education sector must implement FERPA standards to prevent unrestricted access or breaches of information storage in clouds.

Security Recommendations

1. Implement strong authentication mechanisms to enhance account security.
2. Encrypt data in storage and in transit to protect confidentiality and integrity.
3. Implement robust access control policies to restrict access to data and services to authorized users.
4. Regularly update systems and applications to keep cloud infrastructure, operating systems, applications, and software components up to date with the latest security patches and updates to mitigate vulnerabilities.
5. Perform regular security audits and assessments, vulnerability scans, and penetration testing of cloud-based systems to identify and respond to security weaknesses proactively.
6. Monitor and audit activities to track access to cloud resources, detect suspicious activities, and respond promptly to security incidents.
7. Implement data loss prevention measures to prevent unauthorized data leakage, monitor sensitive data transfers, and enforce policies to protect against accidental or intentional data breaches.
8. Implement network segmentation and firewall to isolate sensitive data and services. Use firewalls and intrusion detection/prevention systems to monitor and control network traffic.
9. Backup and disaster recovery planning to ensure data availability and business continuity in case of incidents or outages.
10. Implement endpoint security measures such as antivirus software, endpoint detection and response solutions, and mobile device management for devices accessing cloud services.
11. Manage insider threats and employee awareness, educate employees about security policies, their roles in maintaining security, and the risks of insider threats.
12. Implement secure cloud storage and collaboration tools that offer strong encryption, access controls, audit trails, and compliance with data protection regulations.
13. Conduct regular security training and drills to assess user readiness and response to security incidents.

14. Participate in educational security forums and information sharing initiatives to stay informed about emerging threats, trends, and best practices in cloud security.
15. Educate learners, educators, and staff about security and privacy threats, mitigation strategies and best practices.
16. Ensure compliance with relevant data protection regulations and standards relevant to the region or country.
17. Monitor third-party vendors for security practices when using cloud services.

Privacy Recommendations

1. Establish and enforce data privacy policies and procedures for data handling, storage, migration, and deletion in accordance with privacy regulations.
2. Educate and train stakeholders about privacy rights, data protection principles, and the importance of safeguarding personal information.
3. Ensure that third-party service providers (e.g., vendors, subcontractors) adhere to security and privacy requirements through contractual agreements and regular audits.
4. Create and maintain an incident response plan that outlines procedures for responding to privacy incidents, including breach notification and mitigation measures.
5. Provide clear and comprehensive information to users about data collection, processing, and sharing practices. Obtain explicit consent where required and ensure transparency in data practices.
6. Perform privacy impact assessments to assess the impact of new projects, systems, or technologies on privacy.
7. Securely dispose of data and establish procedures for securely deleting or anonymizing data that is no longer necessary for educational purposes or required by regulations.
8. Monitor and audit data access and usage by implementing logging and auditing mechanisms to track access to sensitive data, detect unauthorized access or usage, and ensure compliance with privacy policies.
9. Promote a culture of privacy awareness and accountability where privacy protection is emphasized at all levels of the organization. Encourage stakeholders to actively participate in protecting personal data and reporting privacy concerns.

CONCLUSION

The integration of cloud computing in education has revolutionized accessibility to learning resources and collaboration among educators and learners. However, this transition brings significant security and privacy challenges. This chapter has covered the fundamental aspects of security and privacy considerations that are vital to cloud-based education. Various security threats and attacks, both, active and passive, including spoofing, phishing and malware, which pose significant risks to cloud-based educational systems have been identified. Privacy threats such as unauthorized data access, data leakage, insider threats, and others breach the confidentiality of personal information and could potentially lead to identity theft or misuse of sensitive data. Educational institutions handle sensitive data like academic records, and financial information, making them vulnerable to attacks and data breaches. Different types of data collected within educational environments are examined, highlighting their purpose, and their security and privacy implications.

To mitigate security and privacy risks, institutions must implement robust security and privacy measures. Mitigation strategies through mechanisms such as authentication, encryption protocols, access controls, and regular security audits are essential for data confidentiality and privacy while maintaining data integrity and availability. Privacy protection requires clear policies, user education on privacy practices, and strict compliance with data protection laws.

In conclusion, while cloud computing offers unprecedented benefits to education, addressing security and privacy challenges requires comprehensive strategies and proactive efforts to safeguard against evolving security and privacy attacks. By integrating comprehensive security and privacy recommendations into their practices, educational institutions can strengthen their defenses against security and privacy threats.

REFERENCES

Abrera, J. (2024). Data Privacy and Security in Cloud Computing: A Comprehensive Review. *Journal of Computer Science and Information Technology*, 1(1), 01-09.

Alenizi, B. A., Humayun, M., & Jhanjhi, N. Z. (2021). Security and privacy issues in cloud computing. [). IOP Publishing.]. *Journal of Physics: Conference Series*, 1979(1), 012038. DOI: 10.1088/1742-6596/1979/1/012038

Arpaci, I., Kilicer, K., & Bardakci, S. (2015). Effects of security and privacy concerns on educational use of cloud services. *Computers in Human Behavior*, 45, 93–98. DOI: 10.1016/j.chb.2014.11.075

Attaran, M., Attaran, S., & Celik, B. G. (2017). Promises and challenges of cloud computing in higher education: A practical guide for implementation. *Journal of Higher Education Theory and Practice*, 17(6).

Bhaskar, P., Tiwari, C. K., & Joshi, A. (2021). Blockchain in education management: Present and future applications. *Interactive Technology and Smart Education*, 18(1), 1–17. DOI: 10.1108/ITSE-07-2020-0102

Chatterjee, P., Bose, R., Banerjee, S., & Roy, S. (2023). Enhancing data security of cloud based lms. *Wireless Personal Communications*, 130(2), 1123–1139. DOI: 10.1007/s11277-023-10323-5 PMID: 37168441

Chen, G., Xu, B., Lu, M., & Chen, N. S. (2018). Exploring blockchain technology and its potential applications for education. *Smart Learning Environments*, 5(1), 1–10. DOI: 10.1186/s40561-017-0050-x

Cohen, B., Hu, A., Patino, D., & Coffman, J. (2022). Educational Data in the Cloud Legal Implications and Technical Recommendations. In 2022 *IEEE/ACM 15th International Conference on Utility and Cloud Computing* (UCC) (pp. 181-182). IEEE. DOI: 10.1109/UCC56403.2022.00032

Durairaj, M., & Manimaran, A. (2015). A study on security issues in cloud based e-learning. *Indian Journal of Science and Technology*, 8(8), 757–765. DOI: 10.17485/ijst/2015/v8i8/69307

Gill, S. H., Razzaq, M. A., Ahmad, M., Almansour, F. M., Haq, I. U., Jhanjhi, N. Z., & Masud, M. (2022). Security and privacy aspects of cloud computing: A smart campus case study. *Intelligent Automation & Soft Computing*, 31(1), 117–128. DOI: 10.32604/iasc.2022.016597

Gupta, B. B. (Ed.). (2019). *Modern Principles, Practices, and Algorithms for Cloud Security*. IGI Global.

Husain, T., & Budiyantara, A. (2020). Analysis of control security and privacy based on E-Learning users. *SAR Journal*, 3(2), 51–58.

Khan, M. A., & Salah, K. (2020). Cloud adoption for e-learning: Survey and future challenges. *Education and Information Technologies*, 25(2), 1417–1438. DOI: 10.1007/s10639-019-10021-5

Khanna, A., Sah, A., Bolshev, V., Burgio, A., Panchenko, V., & Jasiński, M. (2022). Blockchain–cloud integration: A survey. *Sensors (Basel)*, 22(14), 5238. DOI: 10.3390/s22145238 PMID: 35890918

Komljenovic, J. (2022). The future of value in digitalised higher education: Why data privacy should not be our biggest concern. *Higher Education*, 83(1), 119–135. DOI: 10.1007/s10734-020-00639-7 PMID: 33230347

Onyema, E. M., Nwafor, C. E., Ugwugbo, A. N., Rockson, K. A., & Ogbonnaya, U. N. (2020). Cloud security challenges: Implication on education. *Int J Comput Sci Mob Comput*, 9(2), 56–73.

Orehovački, T., Etinger, D., & Babić, S. (2017). Perceived security and privacy of cloud computing applications used in educational ecosystem. In 2017 *40th International Convention on Information and Communication Technology, Electronics and Microelectronics* (MIPRO) (pp. 717-722). IEEE. DOI: 10.23919/MIPRO.2017.7973516

Rajesh, M. (2017). A systematic review of cloud security challenges in higher education. *The Online Journal of Distance Education and e-Learning : TOJDEL*, 5(1), 1–10.

Ren, Z. (2023). Optimization of Innovative Education Resource Allocation in Colleges and Universities Based on Cloud Computing and User Privacy Security. *Wireless Personal Communications*, •••, 1–15. DOI: 10.1007/s11277-023-10572-4

Sandhu, I. K., Malhotra, M., & Randhawa, P. R. (2021). A review of trust and security concerns in cloud computing adoption intention in the higher education sector: research in progress. *Impacts and Challenges of Cloud Business Intelligence*, 1-12.

Seth, D., Najana, M., & Ranjan, P. (2024). Compliance and regulatory challenges in cloud computing: a sector-wise analysis. *International Journal of Global Innovations and Solutions* (IJGIS).

Stallings, W. (2023). *Cryptography and Network Security: Principles and Practice*. Pearson.

Thavi, R., Jhaveri, R., Narwane, V., Gardas, B., & Jafari Navimipour, N. (2024). Role of cloud computing technology in the education sector. *Journal of Engineering. Defence Technology*, 22(1), 182–213.

Tripathi, G., Ahad, M. A., & Casalino, G. (2023). A comprehensive review of blockchain technology: Underlying principles and historical background with future challenges. *Decision Analytics Journal*, 100344.

Yang, P., Xiong, N., & Ren, J. (2020). Data security and privacy protection for cloud storage: A survey. *IEEE Access : Practical Innovations, Open Solutions*, 8, 131723–131740. DOI: 10.1109/ACCESS.2020.3009876

Chapter 8
A Real-Time Auditing System for Secure Storage Using QR Code

Baby Shamini P.
R.M.K. Engineering College, India

Jemi Gold P.
R.M.K. College of Engineering and Technology, India

Neela K.
Sri Sairam Engineering College, India

Arockia Rosy N.
https://orcid.org/0000-0002-0832-7820
R M.D. Engineering College, India

M. Malathy
Vel Tech High Tech Dr. Rangarajan Dr. Sakunthala Engineering College, India

R. Hemala
https://orcid.org/0009-0003-9252-7394
Vellore Institute of Technology, Chennai, India

B. Jaison
https://orcid.org/0000-0001-6886-4321
R.M.K. Engineering College, India

ABSTRACT

The objective is to structure a portable application for inspecting and putting away information through a distributed storage administration. The information is remotely put away in the cloud. In some distributed storage frameworks, the cloud record may contain some touchy data. Scrambling the entire shared record doesn't permit different clients to get to it. In the current framework, the client needs to use the biometric information to guarantee the character of the client, and afterward, a marking key will be checked which is to ensure the personality and security of the client. The principle downside of utilizing the biometric information is that it can't be coordinated precisely because of the elements that influence the difference in biometric information. A reference is made naturally changed over to the QR

DOI: 10.4018/979-8-3693-6705-6.ch008

code and it is checked utilizing a scanner and the specific record is downloaded. This record is erased or lost in the customer's inward stockpiling may be recovered again from the cloud.

1. INTRODUCTION

Cloud storage can provide powerful and upon requisition data storage services for users. By using the cloud service, users can upload their data to the cloud instead of using hardware for data storage. Thus, the probity of the data stored in the cloud is hard to be guaranteed, due to the hardware/software failures and human errors in the cloud. Many auditing schemes have been proposed to allow either the data owner or the Third Party Auditor (TPA) to check whether the data stored in the cloud is impaired or not. These schemes focus on different aspects of data integrity auditing, such as data dynamic operation, the privacy protection of data and user identities, key exposure resilience, the simplification of certificate management and privacy-preserving authenticators etc (Wang et al., 2010). In the above data integrity auditing schemes, the user has to generate authenticators for data blocks with his private key (Jia Yu et al., 2016). It means that the user has to store and manage the private key in a secure way. In general, the user uses a portable secure hardware device (e.g. USB, smart card, CD, Floppy Disks) to store the private key and memorize the credentials that is used to activate this private key. The user might need to remember multiple passwords for different secure applications, which is not user friendly. In addition, the hardware device that contains the private key might be lost. Once the password is forgotten by the user or the hardware device is lost, the user would no longer be able to generate the authenticator for any new data block. The data integrity auditing will not be processing as per the work. Therefore, it is very appealing to find a method for data integrity auditing without the usage of the private key.

2. MOTIVATION

The objective of the project is to design a mobile application for auditing and storing data through a cloud storage service. The data is remotely stored in the cloud. In some cloud storage systems, the cloud file may contain some sensitive information. Encrypting the whole shared file does not allow other users to access it. In the existing system the user has to utilize the biometric data to ensure the identity of the user and then a signing key will be verified which is to protect the identity and privacy of the user. The main drawback of using the biometric data is that it cannot be matched accurately due to the factors that affect the change of biometric data. A reference id created is automatically converted to the QR code and it is scanned using a scanner and the particular document is downloaded. This file if deleted or lost in the client's internal storage it can be retrieved again from the cloud.

3. PROPOSED FRAMEWORK

Any user who allows an external entity to manage their details will provide an authority to them only if their data is handled in a secure way. To provide a secure environment where the user's data is safe remains the top most priority for most of the internet based applications. The proposed model provides a way to overcome the less secure space of a client's financial audit data.

An audit is an independent examination of financial information of any entity, whether profit oriented or not, irrespective of its size or legal form. An auditing system helps to manage their audit data which involves all the transactions carried out till date. To provide security to the identity and data of the users a concept based on biometric data and signing key verification was designed.

The verification of the user is done by first scanning the fingerprint when the user signs in and then exchanging a private key which is known to the user alone. This key is automatically generated when the user profile is created only upon entering the key the user is allowed to enter into their account and download the files. However, this focuses mainly on securing the identity of the user alone and not their files.

The objective is to design a system which shares data with sensitive information hiding using QR code and OTP. The advantage of using this method is that the content can be developed once and then can be updated as necessary. Every time the data is updated a new QR code is generated which ensures that data is not lost and it cannot be scanned without the use of the scanner that is in the app.Only after the OTP is entered the client details can be viewed and downloaded.

3.1 System Architecture

The auditor creates a profile for himself after that he logs into gis account and a profile is created for the client. Note that the auditor does not handle only one company's or one client's profile, they manage multiple client profiles. A client ID is automatically generated when the client profile is created using which the user can login into the mobile application. Now, all the financial audit files are uploaded by the auditor under the client's ID. These files are automatically uploaded in the cloud storage once the auditor uploads files under the particular client ID (Huaqun Wang. A et al., 2016) QR code is generated for the client ID. It is generated everytime a new file is uploaded. The QR code and the client ID is sent to the client using the registered e-mail ID of client so that they can have an access to their account .This completes the pre-processing section.

The file access section involves the usage of the mobile application by the client alone. The client logs into their account by giving the client ID created by the auditor as input and a new password is created by the client while logging in. Once the password is set, the client is asked to enter the password that they created again only then they can proceed to the next section. In the next part of the app, a scannner is opened using which the client has to scan the QR code sent by the auditor to the registered e-mail ID of the client. Immediately a screen is opened asking the client to enter the OTP which is sent to the registered mobile number of the client. Upon entering the OTP the files which were uploaded by the auditor until that particular time is displayed and it can be downloaded.

The downloaded files can be viewed only using the ES file explorer application but not in the normal internal storage of the android device. Also, the QR code can be decrypted only using the scanner integrated with the mobile app which is designed all other QR code scanners can only display the client ID (Shacham et al., 2013). Even if the files are deleted by the client in their internal storage it is permanently available in the cloud so the files can be downloaded innumerable number of times until their account is available.

Figure 1. System Architecture

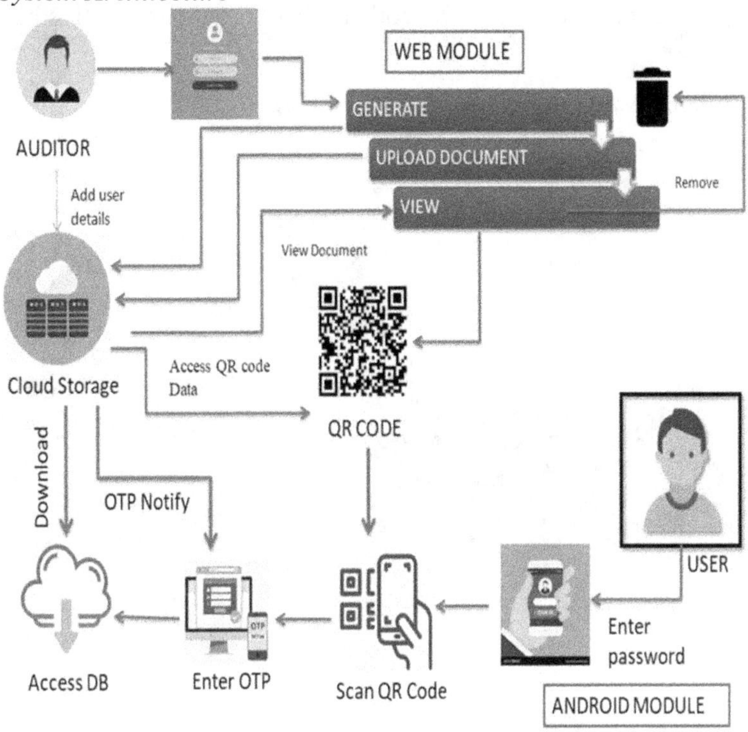

3.2 Working of the System

System architecture defines the process of a model in detail and helps us to get a clear overview of the functions performed by that model. The system architecture for the proposed model is specified in Fig 4.1 of which include the details of the process that is performed for the proper execution. The following components present in the architecture,

- Pre-processing
- File Access

3.2.1 Pre-Processing

The pre-processing section is web module section where the auditor alone works. The client profiles are created and all the audit files are uploaded to the cloud. These files are stored in the cloud under the client ID. A QR code of the client ID is generated once the files are uploaded. Every time a new file is uploaded the QR code changes. A snapshot of the QR code is shared to the respective client.

Figure 2. Interaction between the auditor and client

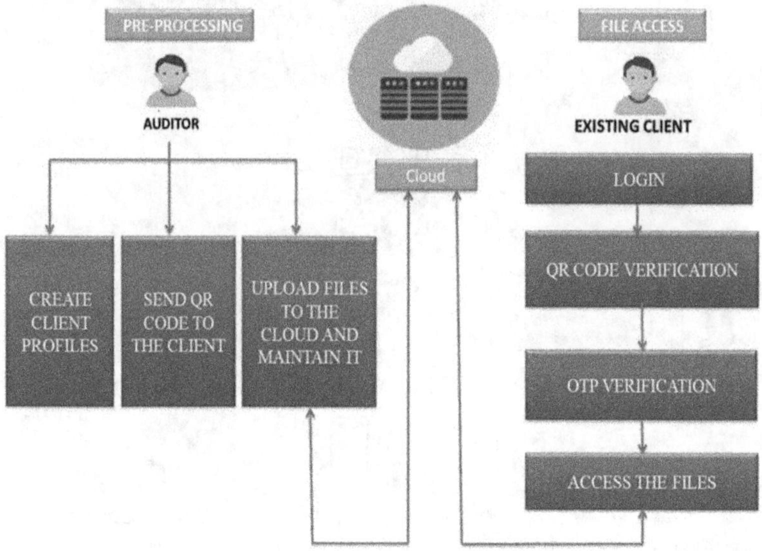

3.2.2 File Access

The file access section is the android module section where the client can access their files. The client ID is entered and a new password is created by the client. After the password creation the client has to enter the password only every time they have to access their files. A scanner opens after this where the QR code sent by the auditor is scanned. Now an OTP is sent to the client's mobile number. Upon entering the OTP the files can be viewed and downloaded.

3.3 Requirement Specification

Requirement analysis consists of the tasks to determine the requirements and conditions to get the product by considering all possible user needs. The analysis on performing the task involves two requirements likely input data and output data. These requirements are explained in the following section,

Input Data

Input data is the client ID and the QR code which is sent to the client in the mobile application. Also the data related to the client is uploaded in the cloud by the auditor in the web module (G. Worku et al., 2014).

Output Data

Output data are the files downloaded by the client in the mobile application after successful login. They can only view and download the files which are uploaded in the cloud.

3.4 Resource Requirements

These are the requirements for doing the project. Without using these tools and software's we can't do the project. There are two requirements to do the project-hardware and software. The hardware requirements may serve as the basis for the implementation of the system and should therefore be a complete and consistent specification of the whole system. The software requirements provide a basis for creating the software requirements specification.

Hardware Requirements

- PROCESSOR : Intel Core i3.
- RAM : 4 GB DDR2 RAM
- MONITOR : 15" COLOR
- HARD DISK : 100 GB

Software Requirements

- Front End : ANDROID XML, JAVA
- Back End : SQLITE
- Operating System : Windows 07
- IDE : Eclipse, Android Studio

4. DETAILED DESIGN

Design is the process of defining the architecture, components, modules, interfaces, and data for a system to satisfy specified requirements. The design of the system gives the details of its architecture, the functions and also the modules involved. The design of our proposed model is detailed in the following sections.

4.1 Use case Diagram

The use case diagram describes the relationship between the two entities- user and the auditor. All the actions that they perform are described using the arrows and the states.

Figure 3. Web Module

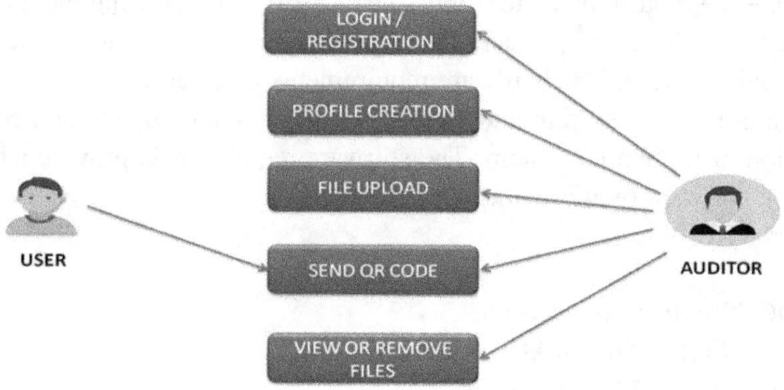

The auditor creates a profile for himself. Then he creates a profile for the client. All the files are uploaded under the client's ID. A QR code generated is sent to the client by the auditor. The auditor can add or remove the files from time to time.

Figure 4. Mobile App

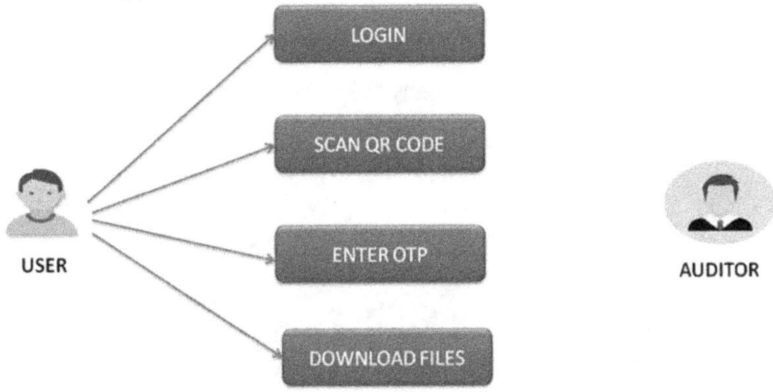

In the mobile app part is used by the client alone. The client ID is given as input and the client is asked to create a password. After entering the password the client is asked to scan the QR code sent by the auditor. Once it is scanned an OTP sent to the registered mobile number of the client is entered. The files uploaded by the auditor are displayed which can be now downloaded and viewed.

4.2 Class Diagram

Figure 5. Class Diagram

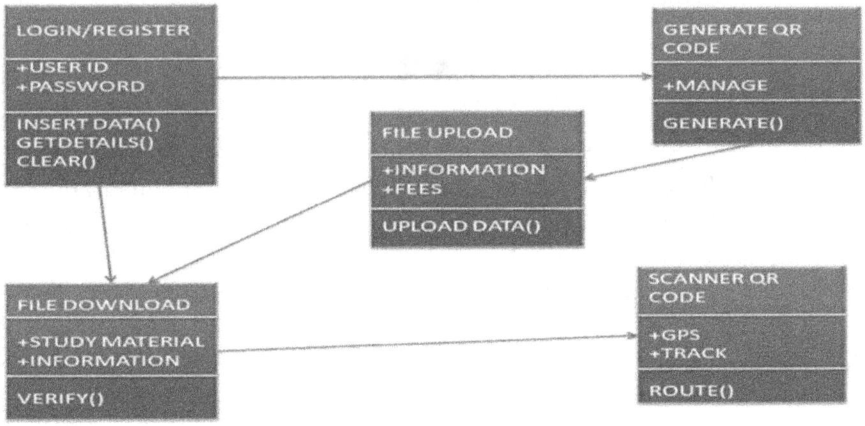

The class diagram explains the inter-connection between the five main classes which are the login/registration class, generate QR code class, scan QR code class, file upload class and the file download class. All the data members and the corresponding functions in which they are used is shown.

4.3 Activity Diagram

Figure 6. Activity Diagram

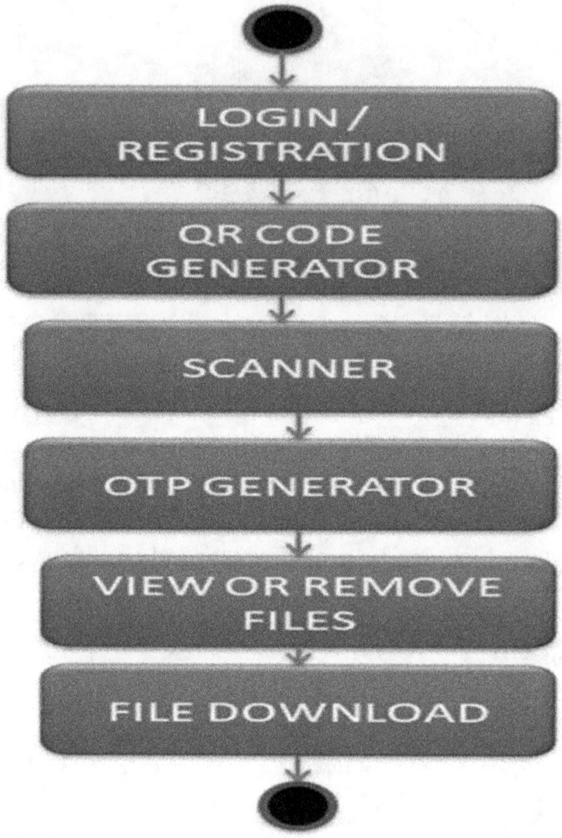

The diagram depicts the behaviour of the system. An activity diagram portrays the control flow from a start point to a finish point showing the various decision paths that exist while the activity is being executed. All the activities that happen in the entire process their flow is shown.

4.4 Sequence Diagram

Figure 7. Sequence Diagram

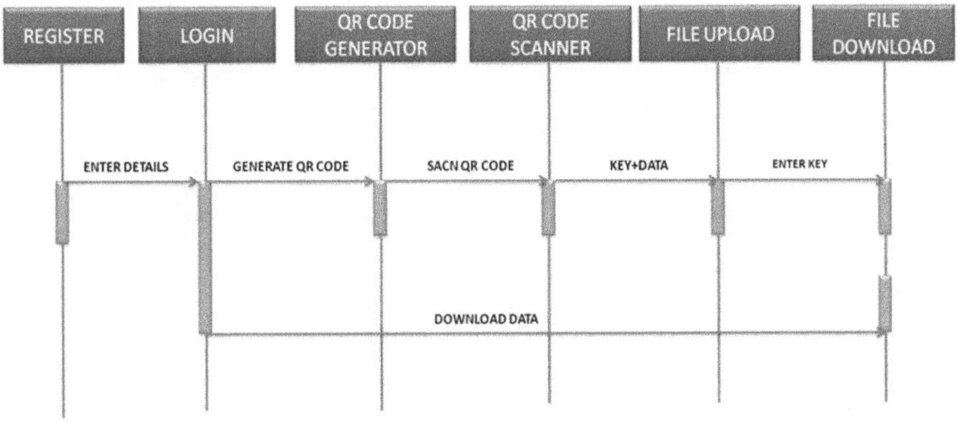

A sequence diagram simply depicts interaction between objects in a sequential order i.e. the order in which these interactions take place. The flow of events is shown between the main classes.

4.5 Component Diagram

Figure 8. Component Diagram

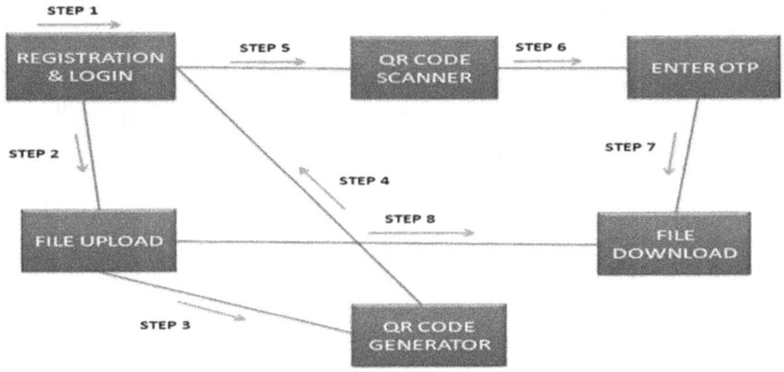

Component diagrams are essentially class diagrams that focus on a system's components that often used to model the static implementation view of a system. All the main components are shown and the steps are also marked to show the flow of events.

4.6 Collaboration Diagram

Figure 9. Collaboration Diagram

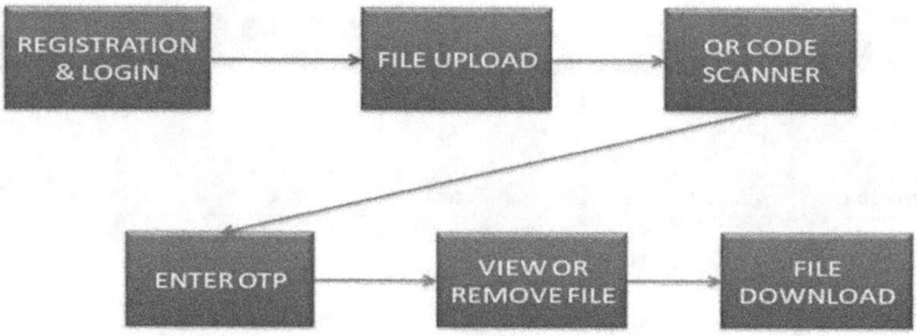

A collaboration diagram, also known as a communication diagram, is an illustration of the relationships and interactions among software objects in the model. The relationship between the classes is depicted in the above diagram.

5. IMPLEMENTATION AND MODULE DESCRIPTION

An audit is an autonomous assessment of monetary data of any element, regardless of whether benefit arranged or not, independent of its size or authoritative document. An inspecting framework assists with dealing with their audit information which includes all the exchanges did work date.

Any client who permits an outer substance to deal with their subtleties will give a power to them in particular if their information is taken care of in a protected manner. To give a protected situation where the client's information is sheltered remains the top most need for the greater part of the web based applications. The proposed model gives an approach to beat the less secure space of the client's audit information (Yan Zhu et al., 2013).

Registration/Login

The auditor enters his details and creates a profile for himself. He can add or remove his clients and the files which are uploaded by him can be updated or removed. The auditor adds his clients by entering all their necessary details and creates a profile for them. The client ID is automatically generated while creating a profile for the client which is sent by the auditor to the client via the registered e-mail ID of the client.

File Upload:

All the audited files related to the client are uploaded by the auditor under the client's ID which is directly uploaded to the cloud storage. The auditor can update the files which are uploaded, he can add or remove the files. The details are imported using XAMPP.

File Access

The files can be viewed by the client by giving the client ID as input in the mobile app and create a password. Once the password is entered the scanner is opened to scan the QR code sent by the auditor. An OTP is sent automatically after the QR code is scanned to the registered mobile number of the client. Now, the files which were uploaded can be downloaded. The files can be viewed only using the ES file explorer app and not via the internal storage or file explorer.

5.1 Profile Creation

The auditor creates a profile for himself in the web module. The client's profile is created and the audited files are added to the cloud. Using the reference ID which is automatically generated the client can login into their account to view their files. The auditor can both update and remove the details of the client from the database. The details are imported using XAMPP. The client ID (reference ID) is sent to the client via their registered e-mail ID.

5.2 QR Code Generator

A QR code of the client id is created. The documents of the client which were uploaded by the auditor are stored under this reference id. The QR code is sent to the client via the registered e-mail ID of the client.

5.3 Verification

The client has to enter the client ID sent by the auditor and create a password which needs to be entered everytime they have to access their account. Upon entering the password which is created by the client the scanner opens automatically and the user needs to scan the QR code sent by the auditor. Now, the client is asked to enter an OTP. The OTP is sent to the registered mobile number of the client which completes the verification part.

5.4 File Upload

The files can be downloaded by the client and they can be viewed using the ES file explore app alone but not in the normal internal storage of an android device.

6. RESULT

Any user who allows an external entity to manage their details will provide an authority to them only if their data is handled in a secure way. To provide a secure environment where the user's data is safe remains the top most priority for most of the internet based applications. The proposed model provides a way to overcome the less secure space of a client's financial audit data. The QR code generator and an OTP generator are included which is nothing but a two factor authentication to verify the identity of the user and also secure the files from being mishandled. The verification part becomes easier as only the password needs to be remembered all the other parts of the process happens upon request of data. In a simple and secure way the data can be viewed and deleted on the client's device anytime and it can be downloaded any number of times from the cloud as it is a permanent storage. The file cannot be viewed in the normal internal storage device of the client but a separate file manager application needs to be installed only then the files can be viewed.

Figure 10. Login

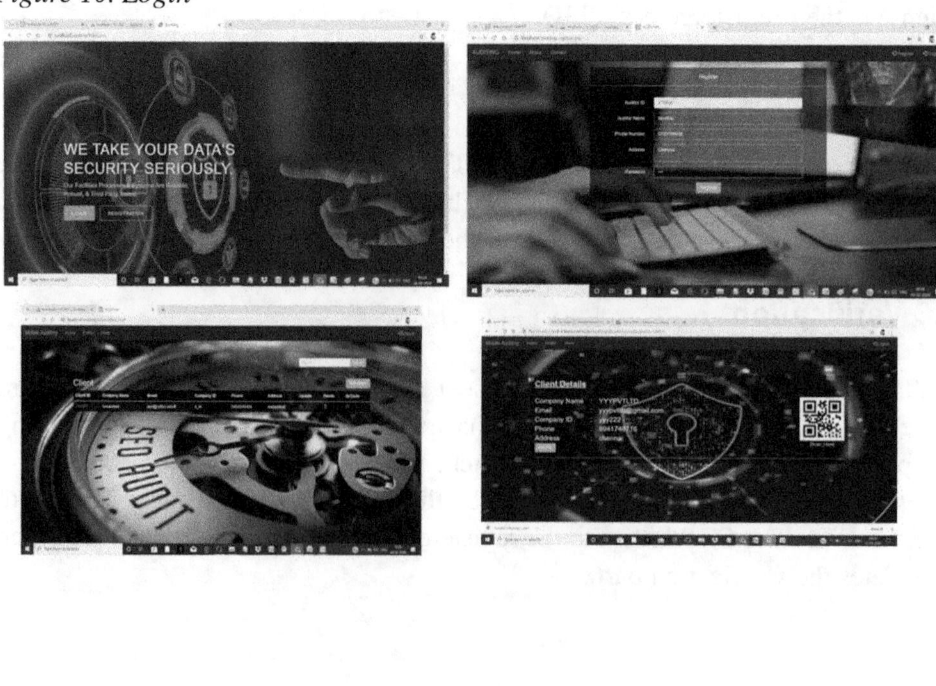

Figure 11. Client Login

Figure 12. User Registration

Figure 13. Scan QR Code

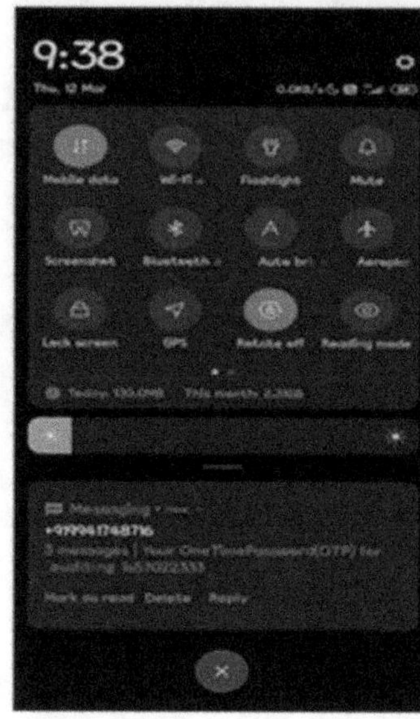

Figure 14. Upload Document

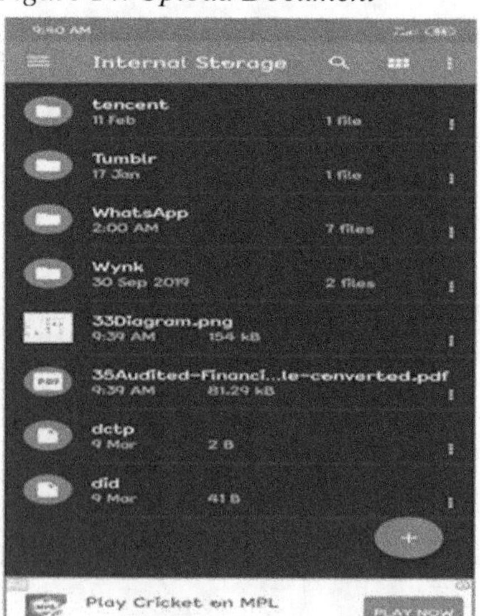

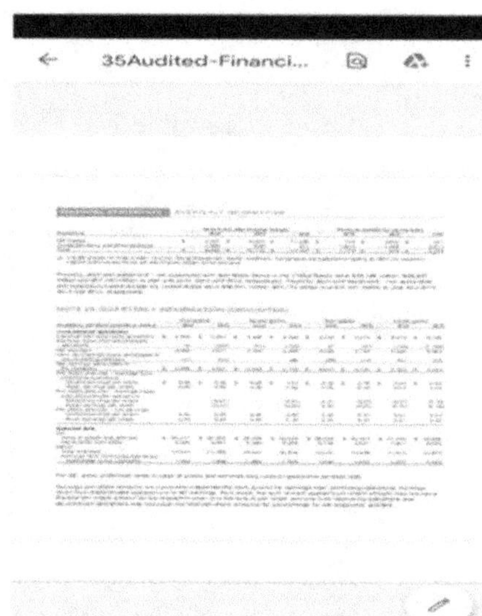

7. CONCLUSION

The work developed is an auditing system mobile application which is useful in real time. The system helps both client and the auditor and makes the process simple and quick. Any client who permits an outside substance to deal with their subtleties will give a power to them in particular if their information is taken care of in a safe manner. To give a safe situation where the client's information is protected remains the top most need for a large portion of the web based applications. The QR code generator and an OTP generator are incorporated which is only a two factor confirmation to check the character of the client and furthermore secure the records from being misused. The confirmation part gets simpler as just the secret phrase should be recollected the various pieces of the procedure stumbles upon solicitation of information.

In a basic and secure manner the information can be seen and erased on the customer's gadget whenever and it tends to be downloaded any number of times from the cloud as it is a changeless stockpiling. The record can't be seen in the ordinary inner stockpiling gadget of the customer yet a different document chief application should be introduced at exactly that point the documents can be seen.

In future this will have more features for automatic prediction in future for business results like simulation of business intelligence for predictive analysis (P Baby Shamini et al.,2020). CART algorithm can be used as the future technique which is used to classify the data stored in the cloud. It is a decision tree learning technique that outputs either classification or regression trees.

REFERENCES

Aruna Yamini, Elakkiya, Keerthiga, & Baby Shamini. (2019). Cost Maintenance and Increased Performance in Cloud Data Centres. Suraj Punj Journal For Multidisciplinary Research, 9(3), 352-360.

Baby Shamini, Wise, Gayathri, Geetha, & Arunachalam. (2020). Prediction of QoS Ranking for Coud Services Using Matrix Factorization. International Journal of Advanced Science and Technology, 29(7), 424-429.

Hrishikesh Dewan & Hansdah. (2011). A survey of cloud storage facilities. 2011 IEEE World Congress on Services, 224–231.

Kanickam, S. H. L., Jayasimman, L., & Jebaseeli, A. N. (2017). A Survey on Layer Wise Issues and Challenges in Cloud Security. *2017 World Congress on Computing and Communication Technologies (WCCCT)*. DOI: 10.1109/WCCCT.2016.49

Sahai & Waters. (2005). *Fuzzy identity-based encryption. In Advances in cryptology EUROCRYPT 2005, Lecture Notes in Computer. Sci* (Vol. 3494). Springer.

Shacham, H., & Waters, B. (2013, July). Compact proofs of retrievability. *Journal of Cryptology*, 26(3), 442–483. DOI: 10.1007/s00145-012-9129-2

Wang, C., Wang, Q., Ren, K., & Lou, W. (2010). Privacy-Preserving Public Auditing for Data Storage Security in Cloud Computing. *2010 Proceedings IEEE INFOCOM*. DOI: 10.1109/INFCOM.2010.5462173

Wang, He, & Tang. (2016). Identity-based proxy-oriented data uploading and remote data integrity checking in public cloud. *IEEE Transactions on Information Forensics and Security, 11*(6), 1165–1176.

Wang, Wu, Qin, Shi, Deng, & Hu. (2017). Identity-based data outsourcing with comprehensive auditing in clouds. *IEEE Transactions on Information Forensics and Security, 12*(4), 940–952.

Worku, S. G., Xu, C., Zhao, J., & He, X. (2014, July). Secure and efficient privacy-preserving public auditing scheme for cloud storage. *Computers & Electrical Engineering*, 40(5), 1703–1713. DOI: 10.1016/j.compeleceng.2013.10.004

Yu, Ren, & Wang. (2016). Enabling cloud storage auditing with verifiable outsourcing of key updates. *IEEE Transactions on Information Forensics and Security, 11*(6), 1362–1375.

Zhu, Ahn, Hu, Yau, An, & Hu. (2013). Dynamic audit services for integrity verification of outsourced storages in clouds. *IEEE Transactions on Services Computing, 6*(2), 1550–1557.

Chapter 9
Blockchain-Enhanced GAN Image Encryption Scheme for Cloud Computing

N. Raghu
https://orcid.org/0000-0002-2091-8922
Jain University, India

Ranjith Bhat
NMAM Institute of Technology, India

ABSTRACT

Ensuring the security of sensitive image data has become of utmost importance in the field of cloud computing. Conventional encryption techniques frequently fail to adequately address changing threats, requiring the use of novel technologies. This study investigates the use of blockchain technology and generative adversarial networks (GANs) for the purpose of encrypting images, with the goal of improving the security and confidentiality of data in cloud environments. The suggested approach uses blockchain technology for the purpose of ensuring safe key management and verification. GANs are employed to produce encrypted images that possess a high level of realism. This research shows that the proposed approach is highly effective in preserving and maintaining higher image quality compared to existing encryption frameworks. This inference is based on careful experimentation and analysis. The proposed method demonstrates superior performance in generating clear and accurate reconstructions of encrypted images, as seen by much higher peak signal-to-noise ratio (PSNR) values and structural similarity index (SSIM) scores. This helps to reduce the chances of unauthorised access and tampering. Moreover, the

DOI: 10.4018/979-8-3693-6705-6.ch009

incorporation of blockchain technology provides an extra level of security and confidence, guaranteeing the secure handling of cryptographic keys and the unalterable verification of encrypted photos. The results highlight the possibility of combining blockchain and GAN to provide a strong solution for protecting sensitive image data in cloud computing environments. This lays the foundation for future progress in image encryption and data security.

1. INTRODUCTION

Image encryption is a critical component of cloud computing, particularly in ensuring the integrity and secrecy of the large amounts of sensitive image data stored and processed within cloud infrastructures (Anandkumar et al., 2022; Wang, Feng, & Zhao, 2019). The growing reliance of organisations on cloud services for data storage and computing highlights the crucial need of implementing strong security measures to protect these assets. Traditional encryption techniques, while acting as a vital pillar of data security, frequently show flaws that limit their effectiveness in the face of new threats and difficulties. Conventional encryption approaches may fall short of providing effective protection against sophisticated attacks due to their deterministic nature and vulnerability to brute-force attacks (Agarwal, Kaushal, & Chouhan, 2020). With advances in computing power, the feasibility of breaking encryption algorithms using exhaustive search methods has grown, demanding more durable encryption solutions. Furthermore, the performance overhead caused by typical encryption algorithms during data transmission and processing might reduce the efficiency of cloud-based apps, resulting in latency difficulties and increased resource consumption (Kakkad, Patel, & Shah, 2019). Furthermore, the static structure make classical encryption algorithms makes them less adaptive to cloud environments and changing threat landscapes. The static encryption keys used in these systems may become broken over time, either by unintentional exposure or planned attacks, jeopardising the security of the encrypted data. Furthermore, the lack of built-in key management and cryptographic agility impedes the capacity to respond quickly to evolving security risks and upgrade encryption algorithms as needed (Kumar et al., 2020).

Given these problems, there is an urgent need for creative ways that may overcome the constraints of standard encryption techniques and provide superior security solutions customised to the requirements of cloud computing systems. In response to this necessity, the proposed modified Generative Adversarial Network (GAN) algorithm provides a trailblazing framework that combines deep learning capabilities with encryption approaches to enhance the security of picture data in cloud environments. At its core, the updated GAN algorithm orchestrates a symbiotic interaction between the generator and discriminator components, which is supplemented with encryption and decryption modules, to produce encrypted images that are indistinguishable from their original counterparts. The technique generates a higher level of obfuscation, which improves the security and integrity of the encrypted image data, by exploiting the adversarial training paradigm, in which the generator attempts to make encrypted images that confuse the discriminator. The incorporation of encryption and decryption modules into the GAN design allows the algorithm to handle encryption and decryption procedures effortlessly, eliminating the need for separate cryptographic techniques. This comprehensive strategy not only accelerates the encryption procedure but also hides the underlying data from prospective adversaries, improving the cloud infrastructure's security posture.

In the healthcare sector, patient records, medical images, and diagnostic results are increasingly being stored and shared across cloud platforms to facilitate better patient care and collaboration among healthcare providers. However, this digitization comes with significant risks. Unauthorized access to medical images, such as X-rays or MRIs, could lead to identity theft, insurance fraud, or even malicious manipulation of medical data. By employing Generative Adversarial Networks (GANs) for image encryption, healthcare providers can ensure that medical images are securely encrypted before being stored in the cloud. GANs can generate highly secure encrypted images that are indistinguishable from the original, thereby maintaining the confidentiality and integrity of patient data while allowing for seamless access by authorized personnel. The GAN architecture is shown in the Figure 1.

Figure 1. Generative Adversarial Network (GAN) architecture

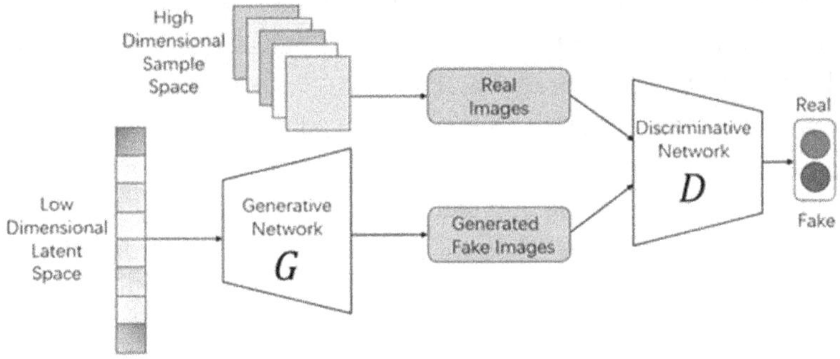

The goals of this study include clarifying the critical importance of image encryption in cloud computing, identifying the inadequacies of traditional encryption strategies, and proposing a revolutionary modified GAN algorithm as a pioneering solution to improve image security in cloud contexts. This work aims to provide a nuanced knowledge of the modified GAN algorithm's efficacy in fortifying picture data security in cloud computing by providing a thorough explanation of its fundamental concepts, design, and operational dynamics.

Within the vast area of cloud computing, where data travels across networks and resides in potentially susceptible infrastructures, image encryption arises as a critical necessity. Images function as complex information carriers, encompassing sensitive content ranging from personal photographs to classified company records, medical histories, and government intelligence. However, amidst their informational riches lurks a vulnerability to exploitation when not protected by strong encryption techniques. Images, by definition, encapsulate narratives, memories, and sensitive details, making them ideal targets for malicious actors looking to obtain unauthorised access, change content, or steal vital data. Without strong encryption, these visual artefacts are vulnerable to a variety of threats, including interception during transmission, unauthorised access via compromised networks, tampering with data integrity, and outright theft from inadequately secured storage repositories.

The effects of an Image security breach spread across multiple domains, exacerbating the severity of the consequences. Individuals fear a loss of personal privacy, with sensitive moments exposed to prying eyes and potential exploitation (SaberiKamarposhti, Ghorbani, & Yadollahi, 2024). Businesses face the threat of financial losses resulting from the compromising of private information, trade secrets, and intellectual property, as well as the erosion of customer trust and confidence. In the healthcare industry, exposing medical photographs to unauthorised entities jeopardises patient confidentiality and compliance with strict data protection requirements. Similarly, federal agencies struggle with the compromise of vital intelligence, which jeopardises national security interests and diplomatic ties. The need for image encryption in the cloud computing ecosystem extends beyond data protection; it is a defence against a slew of threats ranging from privacy violations and financial losses to legal liability and reputational harm. As custodians of sensitive picture data, stakeholders across industries should adopt encryption as a fundamental pillar of their security posture, protecting not just pixels on a screen but also the integrity, privacy, and trust of individuals and institutions.

Traditional encryption methods such as Advanced Encryption Standard (AES) and Rivest-Shamir-Adleman (RSA) have proved useful in securing data in a variety of circumstances, but their application to image encryption in cloud computing environments is not without limitations (Alghamdi, Munir, & Ahmad, 2022). While AES and RSA perform well in many situations, their applicability for image encryption is limited by several issues. These algorithms may struggle to efficiently handle huge image files, resulting in performance bottlenecks and higher resource use. Furthermore, maintaining image quality during encryption and decryption is a big difficulty, as standard encryption algorithms may inadvertently damage visual fidelity due to their determinism. In cloud setups with remote storage and processing, managing encryption keys is a complex task. Ensuring the secure generation, distribution, and storage of encryption keys across multiple cloud resources necessitates sophisticated key management procedures, which may not be inherent in typical encryption schemes. Furthermore, the processing complexity associated with encryption and decryption procedures can worsen latency difficulties and resource utilisation in cloud systems with high performance needs. As a result, while AES and RSA remain data security mainstays, their limitations highlight the need for specialised encryption systems capable of meeting the unique requirements of image encryption in cloud computing. The primary goal of this research is to present a novel technique to image encryption in cloud computing based on a modified Generative Adversarial Network (GAN) algorithm.

The proposed algorithm intends to overcome the constraints of standard encryption algorithms by leveraging deep learning and adversarial training capabilities to provide greater security for cloud-stored image data. Specifically, we want to:

- Introduce a modified GAN architecture tailored for image encryption, incorporating encryption and decryption modules within the GAN framework.
- Investigate the effectiveness of the modified GAN algorithm in terms of encryption strength, computational efficiency, and resistance to attacks.
- Evaluate the performance of the proposed algorithm through comprehensive experimentation and comparison with existing encryption techniques and GAN-based approaches.

The proposed modified GAN technique innovatively incorporates image encryption and decryption capabilities into the GAN architecture. This integration is accomplished by include encryption modules in the generator and decryption modules in the discriminator. Through adversarial training, the generator learns to generate encrypted images that closely resemble real encrypted images, balancing image quality with increased security. Concurrently, the discriminator is being trained to distinguish between real and counterfeit encrypted images. The encryption and decryption operations use reversible encryption techniques, ensuring that the encrypted images are identical to their original counterparts. This seamless integration of encryption and GAN frameworks not only improves picture security but also maintains image integrity, providing a reliable solution for protecting sensitive image data in cloud computing situations.

The following sections of the article will go into the specifics of the proposed improved GAN algorithm, including its architecture, implementation, experimental assessment, and discussion of findings. Through thorough study and testing, we hope to demonstrate the effectiveness and applicability of our approach to improving picture security for cloud computing applications.

2. RELATED WORKS

The authors of reference (Zhu et al., 2017) proposed a neural network (NN) architecture for achieving impulsive synchronisation within the context of the reaction-diffusion mechanism, thereby capturing the subtle dynamical behaviours inherent in such systems. Notably, the suggested NN framework was later applied to images encryption applications, where its capabilities were used to improve the security and robustness of the encryption process. By applying NNs to image encryption, the authors hoped to capitalise on the neural network's inherent ability to model complex dynamical phenomena as well as its potential to contribute to the development of novel encryption methodologies tailored to the demands of modern data security challenges. Due to their unpredictability and complexity, chaotic systems are often used in cryptography to protect against conventional attacks, including plaintext attacks. Thus, researchers have integrated NN systems into image cryptosystems to use chaotic dynamics' robustness. This method (Ouyang et al., 2020) uses neural network architectures in an image cryptosystem to use chaotic systems' unique encryption capabilities. The NN-based image cryptosystem protects sensitive image data from unauthorised access and tampering by exploiting these systems' chaotic behaviour. This novel combination of NN technologies and chaotic cryptography shows how cryptographic methods are evolving to protect digital assets. In (Bao, Xue, & Jin, 2021), researchers used a stacked autoencoder network to generate chaotic sequences for image encryption. Stacking autoencoder networks' parallel computing and resistance to cryptographic attacks made this method efficient. The proposed scheme used chaotic sequences generated by stacked autoencoder networks' computational framework to improve image encryption security. The study demonstrated that the stacked autoencoder-based encryption scheme mitigates cryptographic vulnerabilities and protects sensitive image data through empirical validation and experimentation.

Technology is rapidly changing, and the IT industry, especially Cloud Image Security, is growing exponentially. Chaos-based image encryption is a promising framework that offers advantages over traditional encryption methods. A recent study (Kumar et al., 2022) introduces an algorithm that generates chaotic sequences using modified logistic maps, improving encryption. This algorithm encrypts images in one scan, saving processing time. The proposed algorithm uses confusion and diffusion to provide strong security and fast encryption. This algorithm improves cloud computing image security by using chaotic sequences and simplified encryption. The authors present a novel cloud-based image encryption scheme in (Li, Yu, Song, & Chen, 2019). This scheme strengthens encryption with a single-round dictionary and chaotic sequences. The authors rigorously test their encryption scheme using experimental and analytical methods. Their findings show that the scheme improves image quality and security after decryption. Security issues arise when storing medical images in cloud computing environments, especially when protecting patient data. Many cloud service providers store client data in plain text, so users must encrypt medical data. The paper (Lakshmi et al., 2020) proposes using Hopfield NNs (HNN) for image encryption to address these issues. Continuous learning and updating mechanisms are used to strengthen medical image data against cyber threats. This scheme relies on a backpropagation NN to generate image-specific encryption keys. In paper (Lavanya, Sundar, & Saravanan, 2024), a novel Simplified Image Encryption Algorithm (SIEA) is proposed to secure image files. This algorithm uses an efficient Feistel cypher key generation module. The SIEA encrypts images securely before cloud storage to prevent data breaches. The encryption process begins by converting the plain image into pixel values and dividing them into 128-bit blocks. Five sub-keys (K0 to K4) are derived from a 128-bit cypher key for 10 rounds of encryption. Each sub-key is 32 bits. Based on the Feistel cypher structure, the image blocks are encrypted iteratively using the generated sub-keys. The SIEA algorithm outperforms competing algorithms in security and robustness despite its lightweight computational process. In reference (Justin & Karuppusamy, 2022), Mayfly Optimisation with Chaos-Based Image Encryption (MFO-CBIE) is introduced for cloud computing (CC) environments. The MFO-CBIE model aims to secure CC setups through encryption and key generation. This model uses image encryption, optimal key generation, and image decryption. During image encryption, the MFO-CBIE model uses complex encryption methods and chaos-based methods to hide image data. The optimal key generation phase uses the Mayfly Optimisation algorithm to generate encryption keys with superior cryptographic properties, securing the encrypted images. The generated keys are used to decrypt the images, restoring them to their original state. Standard benchmark images are used in extensive experimental evaluations to validate the MFO-CBIE model.

A new method for secure and efficient ciphertext Image retrieval using content-based image retrieval (CBIR) and approximate homomorphic encryption is presented in (Wang et al., 2023). Encrypting original images with a chaotic image encryption scheme reduces ciphertext size and computational overhead. The researchers also used two optimisation strategies to increase neural network depth to address network depth issues. The proposed system introduces a novel communication reliability and security method (G. S & G. S, 2023). This method uses a hybrid classification model to create an efficient image denoising scheme. This scheme uses a Pseudo-Predictive Deep Denoising Network (PPDD) with deep learning algorithms. This system uses the newly structured algorithm to increase Dark Cloud security. The system's storage complexity reduction strategy is crucial. Edge devices unpack and denoise dynamic data to achieve this. The system uses edge denoising to reduce the load on centralised storage and improve data quality before cloud storage. Privacy

Preserving Image Encryption with Optimal Deep Learning-based Accident Severity Classification (Sirisha & Chandana, 2023) is a novel method. This algorithm secures accident-related images and classifies accident severity. Image encryption uses multi-key homomorphic encryption (MKHE) and lion swarm optimisation to generate keys. Encrypting images with multiple keys using MKHE improves security and allows homomorphic operations.

The Block chain-based Chaotic Deep Generative Adversarial Network (GAN) Encryption Scheme (BCDGE) was introduced in (Neela & Kavitha, 2022). This novel approach uses blockchain technology to protect personal data and verify data. The BCDGE encrypts medical images using Chaotic Deep GAN Encryption, which uses confusion, substitution, and diffusion. Chaotic Deep GAN Encryption uses a Deep GAN architecture to generate image-specific secret keys. These keys are unique to each image, making the scheme more hacker resistant. The generated keys are then used for the confusion and diffusion phases of encryption, protecting medical image data. In a recent study (Singh et al., 2023), researchers combined GANs with image watermarking to address healthcare data leakage. The method starts with a hybrid encryption scheme that uses a chaotic map and RSVD to encrypt the image. This encryption protects image data while preserving its integrity. The researchers created a GAN model to embed multiple watermarks in encrypted images. The model optimally hides image watermarks using the adversarial GAN framework, enhancing security against unauthorised access and tampering. Recent events, such as the unauthorised disclosure of Hollywood celebrities' iCloud photos, have highlighted the need for strong image security. Due to this need, novel methods using convolutional neural network (CNN) and GAN models are promising for data extraction and image restoration (Nalavade et al., 2023). By combining CNN and GAN architectures, these frameworks can protect image data from unauthorised access and exploitation. Cycle-GAN architecture was used to develop a new image transformation scheme (Rodriguez & Krishnan, 2023). This method uses convolutional autoencoder image encoding for domain translation. The proposed scheme uses Cycle-GAN to improve deep neural network privacy while preserving model utility. The study describes a way to encode images for domain translation, allowing images to be transformed between domains while maintaining privacy and utility. Notably, the authors tested their method on Chest X-ray, Dermoscopy, and OCT datasets. A hybrid cryptographic image steganography method is proposed in (Xu, Chang, & Horng, 2023). Cycle-consistent GANs (CycleGAN) and difference expansion are used in this data hiding method. To combine image encryption and data hiding in one framework. CycleGAN converts a digital image into a noisy image suitable for DE data embedding. Its ability to generate noisy images with a high data payload for embedding and realistically recover the original image during decryption is its main benefit. Experimental results for the proposed system are promising. The system embeds data faster than 0.47 bits per pixel (bpp), optimally using image space for data hiding. An Image Encryption System was proposed and tested on satellite photos (Al-Khasawneh et al., 2023). Encrypting data while running MapReduce jobs was key to the study. The Hadoop ecosystem, known for its scalability and distributed processing, hosted this experiment. The study used MapReduce to test a new method for generating random numbers for image encryption. The encryption process was run using Hadoop MapReduce during experimentation. To prevent unauthorised access, the images were saved in BMP format with security metadata. Cloud storage privacy risks can be mitigated with thumbnail-preserving encryption (TPE), balancing user privacy and usability. Despite its benefits, existing TPE schemes are vulnerable to machine-based attacks and small thumbnail block sizes. The study (Zhou et al., 2023) introduced a new adversarial thumbnail-preserving transform scheme for facial images. This scheme balances privacy and user convenience and resists facial recognition (FR) models. The Table 1 provides the summarization of the literature survey.

Table 1. Summarisation of the Literature Survey Findings

Reference	Approach	Findings	Research Gap
(Zhu et al., 2017)	NN architecture for impulsive synchronization and image encryption	Improved encryption security and robustness	Lack of exploration on scalability and real-world deployment
(Bao, Xue, & Jin, 2021)	Use of stacked autoencoder network for generating chaotic sequences	Enhanced encryption security and resistance to attacks	Lack of comparison with other encryption methods
(Lakshmi et al., 2020)	Employment of Hopfield NNs for medical image encryption	Continuous learning mechanism for enhanced security	Investigation on scalability and applicability in real-world medical settings
(Justin & Karuppusamy, 2022)	Mayfly Optimization with Chaos-Based Image Encryption (MFO-CBIE) for cloud computing	Use of chaos-based methods and optimal key generation	Evaluation on diverse cloud computing setups and scalability assessment
(Neela & Kavitha, 2022)	Blockchain-based Chaotic Deep GAN Encryption Scheme (BCDGE) for medical images	Integration of blockchain technology for enhanced data protection	Assessment on the scalability and overhead of blockchain integration
(Nalavade et al., 2023)	CNN and GAN models for image security against unauthorized access	Protection of image data privacy and utility preservation	Investigation on the impact of model complexity on computational overhead

continued on following page

Table 1. Continued

Reference	Approach	Findings	Research Gap
(Xu, Chang, & Horng, 2023)	Hybrid cryptographic image steganography method using CycleGAN	Integration of image encryption and data hiding for enhanced security	Comparative analysis with existing steganography methods
(Al-Khasawneh et al., 2023)	Adversarial thumbnail-preserving transform scheme for facial image privacy	Resistance against facial recognition models and privacy preservation	Assessment on the impact of transform scheme on image quality and recognition accuracy

Based on the findings obtained from the review of relevant literature, an auspicious area for pioneering in cloud computing image encryption pertains to the integration of GAN architectures with blockchain technology. By combining the dynamic and generative capabilities of GANs with the decentralised and immutable ledger capabilities of blockchain, a novel encryption scheme can be developed to tackle significant obstacles in cloud-based image security. The suggested approach would involve the construction of a GAN structure that is specifically tailored for encrypting images. In this architecture, the generator network would utilise chaotic sequences to augment both the complexity and randomness of the encrypted images generated from plaintext inputs. Simultaneously, the implementation of blockchain technology would ensure the secure management of encryption keys and the validation of encrypted image data stored in the cloud. A distinct identifier would be allocated to every encrypted image and securely stored on the blockchain, thereby guaranteeing verification that cannot be altered and establishing a resilient system for authenticating data. In addition, authorised users have the capability to decrypt encrypted images that are stored in the cloud simply by providing the corresponding decryption keys. The reconstruction of plaintext images is facilitated by the generator network. By subjecting this blockchain-enhanced GAN encryption scheme to rigorous experimentation and evaluation, its effectiveness and scalability can be determined. This will facilitate the development of further methodologies for cloud-based image security and encryption.

2.1 Comparison Section on Traditional vs. GAN-Based Methods

2.1.1 Traditional Encryption Methods

Traditional encryption methods, such as the Advanced Encryption Standard (AES) and Rivest-Shamir-Adelman (RSA), have long been the cornerstones of data security. AES, for instance, is widely used for encrypting data in various applications, including secure communications and data storage. It operates on the principle of symmetric key cryptography, where the same key is used for both encryption and decryption. RSA, on the other hand, is a form of asymmetric cryptography, utilizing a pair of keys (public and private) for encryption and decryption.

These methods have proven effective in securing data across different platforms. AES, with its fixed block size and key lengths, provides robust security against brute-force attacks. RSA, with its ability to secure data transmission over untrusted networks, is crucial for tasks like digital signatures and key exchange. However, these methods are not without limitations, especially when applied to image encryption in cloud environments.

2.1.2 Limitations of Traditional Methods

Traditional encryption methods, while effective for text and numerical data, often struggle with the unique challenges posed by image encryption. Images are typically larger in size and contain more complex structures than other types of data, leading to higher computational overhead during the encryption and decryption processes. This can result in increased latency, which is particularly problematic in cloud environments where speed and efficiency are critical. Moreover, traditional methods are deterministic, meaning the same plaintext will always produce the same ciphertext, making them potentially vulnerable to certain types of attacks, such as known-plaintext or chosen-ciphertext attacks.

2.1.3 GAN-based Encryption Methods

Generative Adversarial Networks (GANs) represent a paradigm shift in the field of encryption. Unlike traditional methods, GANs leverage the power of deep learning to create a dynamic and adaptive encryption framework. GANs consist of two neural networks: the generator and the discriminator. The generator creates encrypted versions of the original images, while the discriminator attempts to differentiate between the original and encrypted images. Through this adversarial process, the generator learns to produce increasingly secure encrypted images that are difficult to distinguish from the original data. The Table 2 summarizes the comparison of Traditional Encryption vs. GAN-based Encryption Processes.

Table 2. Comparison of Traditional Encryption vs. GAN-based Encryption Processes

Criteria	AES/RSA (Traditional)	GAN-Based Encryption
Encryption Type	Deterministic (Same input = Same output)	Non-deterministic (Varied outputs)
Computational Overhead	High, especially for large images	Lower, optimized for image processing
Scalability in Cloud	Limited, due to performance constraints	Highly scalable and adaptable
Security against Modern Attacks	Vulnerable to certain types of attacks	More secure, resistant to modern attacks
Visual Quality Preservation	May degrade image quality	Maintains high visual fidelity

2.1.4 Advantages of GAN-Based Methods

One of the primary advantages of GAN-based encryption is its ability to generate highly realistic encrypted images that maintain the visual integrity of the original data, even after encryption. This makes it exceptionally difficult for unauthorized parties to detect or decipher the encrypted images. Additionally, GANs are capable of creating unique ciphertexts for the same plaintext image during each encryption process, adding a layer of security by making it nearly impossible for attackers to predict or reverse-engineer the encryption. Furthermore, GAN-based methods are highly scalable and can be optimized to reduce computational overhead, making them well-suited for cloud environments where performance is as important as security.

3. PROPOSED APPROACH

The proposed model involves the creation of a specialised GAN structure that is designed specifically for encrypting images. Additionally, blockchain technology is incorporated at the same time to strengthen data protection and verification mechanisms. The GAN consists of two fundamental components within this architectural framework: the discriminator network and the generator network. The generator network is responsible for the synthesis of encrypted images using plaintext inputs and cryptographic transformations to effectively obscure image data. Simultaneously, the encrypted images are examined by the discriminator network, which distinguishes genuine encrypted images from those produced by the generator network. In addition to the capabilities of the GAN, the blockchain network functions as an immutable and decentralised ledger system that enables the secure management of keys and verification of data. The blockchain stores encrypted images and their corresponding encryption keys in the form of transactions, as shown in Figure 2. This feature guarantees the integrity of the records and facilitates thorough verification of the data. Furthermore, in its capacity as a distributed consensus mechanism, the blockchain network ensures the integrity and genuineness of encrypted image data stored in the cloud. Through the integration of blockchain technology and Generative Adversarial Networks (GANs), this architectural design endeavours to offer a comprehensive and robust resolution for image encryption within the realm of cloud computing. In doing so, it enhances the robustness of verification mechanisms and data security.

Figure 2. Proposed Model Overview

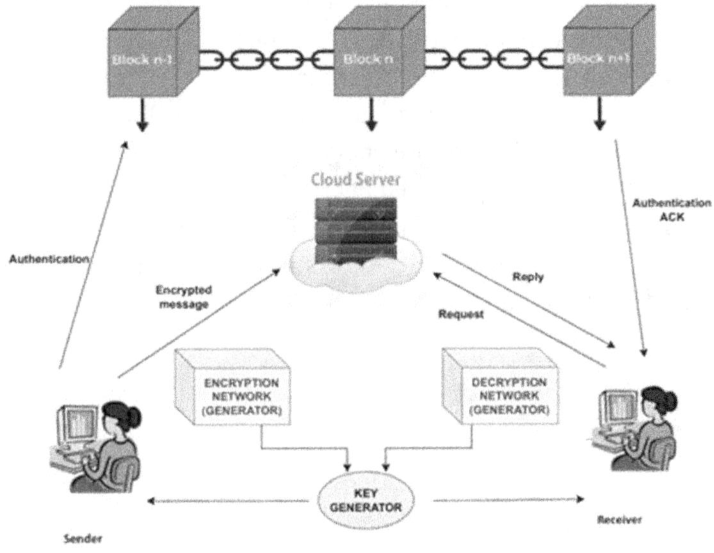

Data Receiver: Physicians can request encrypted medical data from the cloud server. Users verify the ciphertext's authenticity.

Data sender: Patients or data senders encrypt and communicate extracted medical data to the CSP. Data senders sign and store ciphertext on blockchain networks.

Cloud server: CS stores massive medical imaging data and searches and delivers pertinent ciphertext upon DU request.

Blockchain: We used the SHA-1 technique to hash the photo for a digital signature. When asked to verify ciphertext, the blockchain validates the saved signature. If true, it returns 1; otherwise, 0.

Key Generator: produces and distributes the secret key to the data sender and user.

Encryption & Decryption: The chaotic Deep GAN model encrypts the medical image before delivering it to the cloud server (Fig. 2).

3.1. Encryption Phase

The methodology employed in this research is the modified-GAN (MGAN), which functions by first encrypting a plaintext image and subsequently decrypting it to reconstruct the original plaintext image. At the outset, the encryption network, represented as G, assumes the task of producing an encrypted image from a provided plaintext image. Following this, the decryption network, denoted as H, proceeds with the endeavour of restoring the encrypted image to its original plaintext state. Using the feedback from both the discriminator network D_x and the encryption network G, the encryption network G is trained to generate encrypted images that closely resemble the target encrypted image throughout the training process. In a similar fashion, the decryption network H is trained in conjunction with the discriminator network D_y to reduce the discrepancies between the reconstructed and original plaintext images. The flow diagram in Figure 3 illustrates the sequential process by which plaintext images are encrypted and then reconstructed into their original format, as part of the proposed encryption method. By implementing this method, the encrypted images are preserved in their integrity as opposed to the original plaintext images, and the MGAN framework is equipped with a resilient encryption and decryption mechanism.

Figure 3. Encryption Process

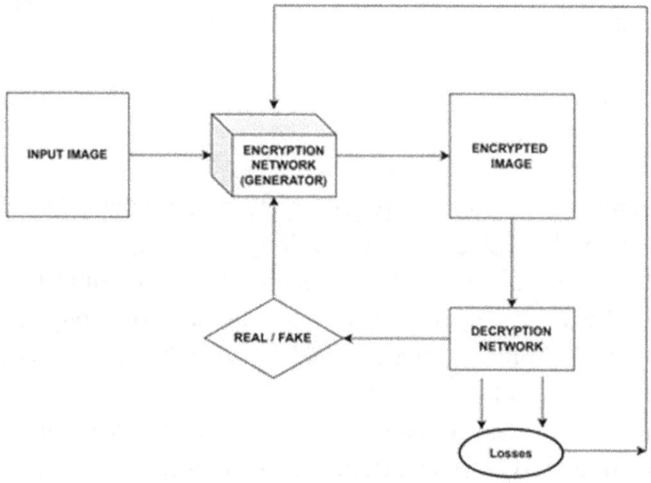

The encryption procedure implemented in the MGAN framework entails converting the visual characteristics of a plaintext image (set X) to correspond with those of a ciphertext image (set Y). At the outset, the plaintext image is subjected to three layers of convolution to reduce its resolution and extract its features. Following each convolutional layer in the encoder network are instance normalisation and rectified linear unit (ReLU) activation. The initial convolutional layer utilises 64 7×7 filters, which are followed by convolutions that employ 3×3 filters in subsequent layers. The process of down sampling enables the retrieval of critical characteristics from the plaintext image. To improve the model's stability, an optimisation strategy is implemented using a ResNet-based architecture. This approach integrates batch normalisation, additional convolutional layers, residual blocks composed of convolutional layers, and ReLU activation. Following concatenation, the outputs of these residual blocks are transmitted to the decoder network. The magnitude of the input features remains unchanged during the entirety of the transformation procedure. The transformed features are subsequently up sampled by the decoder network through the utilisation of several iterations of transpose convolution layers. Subsequently, these features are mapped to an output image with the following dimensions: 256 $\times$ 256 $\times$ 3. This operation produces the ciphertext image. By employing this modified methodology, it is possible to guarantee the efficient conversion of plaintext images to ciphertext images while preserving consistency and stability during the encryption procedure.

3.1.1. Hyper-Parameter Tuning

In the process of tuning the learning rate, a crucial parameter in training deep neural networks like the MGAN encryption stage, we aim to optimize the step size during the optimization process, thereby influencing the convergence speed and stability of the training algorithm. In the beginning, the MGAN model is initialised and compiled using different learning rates, including 0.001, 0.0001, and 0.00001, to investigate a spectrum of step sizes. Following this, we commence the process of training the model for a predetermined number of epochs, usually around 10, using a dataset that is well-suited for image processing purposes, such as the MNIST dataset. This dataset consists of grayscale images of handwritten digits. Throughout the training process, the model's parameters are revised iteratively in accordance with the optimisation algorithm and the selected learning rate. The iterative procedure entails modifying the parameters of the model to minimise a predetermined loss function. This is frequently accompanied by the reconstruction of the input data or the adversarial generation of realistic samples. Once the training phase is concluded, the performance of the trained model is assessed by calculating the reconstruction loss on an independent validation set. This assessment enables the quantification of the model's ability to reconstruct input images with precision and offers valuable insights into its overall efficacy and performance. Through the comparison of reconstruction losses acquired at various learning rates, one can ascertain the influence of step sizes on the convergence and stability of the model. In essence, this iterative procedure of fine-tuning the learning rate allows us to determine the most effective value that achieves a harmonious coexistence of swift convergence and consistent training. As a result, the MGAN encryption stage's performance is significantly improved when applied to image processing tasks. The algorithm is given as follows:

```
# Define the MGAN Encryption Algorithm

# Step 1: Initialize the model architecture

model = MGAN()

# Step 2: Compile the model with an optimizer and loss func-
tion

optimizer = Adam(learning_rate=0.001)

model.compile(optimizer=optimizer, loss=MeanSquaredError())

# Step 3: Define the dataset and preprocessing

(x_train, _), (_, _) = load_dataset()

x_train = preprocess_dataset(x_train) # Preprocess the data-
set, normalize, etc.

# Step 4: Train the model
```

```
model.fit(x_train, x_train, epochs=10, batch_size=128, ver-
bose=1)

# Step 5: Evaluate the model on a validation set

x_val = load_validation_set() # Load a separate validation
set

x_val = preprocess_dataset(x_val) # Preprocess the valida-
tion set

validation_loss = model.evaluate(x_val, x_val, verbose=0)

print(f'Validation Loss: {validation_loss}')

# Step 6: Encryption process for a plaintext image (x_plain)

def encrypt_image(x_plain):

# Downsample the plaintext image

features = model.encoder(x_plain)

# Residual blocks for stability

features = model.residual_blocks(features)

# Upsample the transformed features
```

```
    transformed_features = model.decoder(features)

    # Map features to ciphertext image

    ciphertext_image = model.last_convolution_layer(transformed_
features)

    return ciphertext_image

    plaintext_image = load_plaintext_image() # Load a plaintext
image

    encrypted_image = encrypt_image(plaintext_image)
```

3.2. Blockchain Integration: Key Management

The successful deployment of blockchain technology to securely manage encryption keys is a complex undertaking that requires strict adherence to detail to preserve the system's integrity and dependability. By harnessing the capabilities of blockchain, an immutable and decentralised ledger system, organisations can fortify the security of their encryption key management procedures. Detailed below are the procedures required to implement this methodology in practice: A one-of-a-kind encryption key is produced whenever a plaintext image is encrypted by utilising the MGAN framework. The transformation that is applied to the plaintext image to generate the ciphertext is determined by this key, which serves as the foundation by which the encryption process is developed. For ensuring unpredictability and resistance against cryptographic attacks, the encryption key is generated in a random fashion by means of a cryptographically secure pseudo-random number generator (CSPRNG).

Following the generation of the encryption key, a blockchain transaction is created to record the association between the encrypted image and the encryption key that corresponds to it. This transaction contains essential metadata, which includes the hash of the encrypted image, the encryption key itself, timestamps, and any other information that may be pertinent. A digital signature is applied to the transaction through the utilisation of cryptographic methods to guarantee its authenticity and integrity.

The transaction on the blockchain is validated by means of a consensus mechanism, which guarantees the transaction's authenticity and prevents it from occurring again. Within a blockchain network that is decentralised, reaching consensus is accomplished by reaching a consensus among the nodes, which are the participants in the network. Using this consensus mechanism, malicious actors are prevented from tampering with transactions, and the integrity of the blockchain ledger is ensured. After the transaction has been validated, it is added to the blockchain, where it becomes a record that is permanent and cannot be altered. By querying the blockchain, authorised parties, such as users or applications, can gain access to the encryption key without any difficulty. It is ensured that there is redundancy and resilience against single points of failure or malicious attacks by the fact that every participant in the network keeps a copy of the blockchain ledger within their own possession. Authorised parties can retrieve the encryption key associated with a particular encrypted image in a secure and efficient manner by querying the blockchain. This eliminates the need for centralised key management systems. Using this decentralised access model, security is improved, and the possibility of data breaches or unauthorised access is decreased. The overall process is illustrated in Figure 4.

Figure 4. Blockchain Integration Flowchart

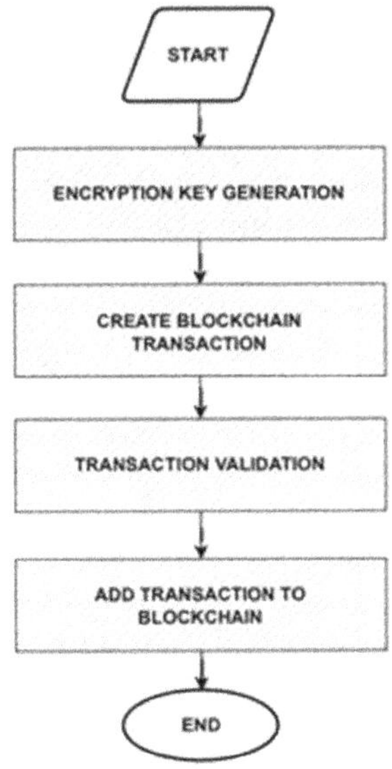

3.3. Decryption Phase

To decrypt encrypted images, authorised users are required to furnish the corresponding decryption key. It is necessary to implement access controls and authentication mechanisms to validate the identity of the user and their authorization to access the decryption key. The decryption key is securely provisioned to the user following identity authentication, thereby restricting the ability of unauthorised parties to commence the decryption procedure. The decryption procedure entails the inverted utilisation of the generator network (decoder) to reconstruct the plaintext image from the ciphertext data. The decryption algorithm restores the original plaintext image by inverting the effects of encryption using the reverse transformation that was applied during the encryption process. The generator network within the MGAN framework is specifically trained to execute this inverse transformation with optimal efficiency and precision. The pseudo code for the decryption key validation is as follows:

```
def decryption_key_valid(decryption_key):

# Implement decryption key validation

authorized_keys = load_authorized_keys()

if decryption_key in authorized_keys:

return True

else:

return False
```

After being provided with the encrypted image and the corresponding decryption key, the decryption algorithm is implemented to restore the plaintext image to its original state. By utilising the decryption key to undo the encryption operation that was performed on the image, the generator network can produce a precise replica of the initial image composed of the encrypted data. The objective of this reconstruction process is to reduce the disparities that may exist between the decrypted and original plaintext images, thereby guaranteeing the decryption process remains faithful and precise. Upon the completion of the decryption procedure, the reconstructed plaintext image is generated and presented for verification. By comparing the decrypted image to the original plaintext image, the accuracy and integrity of the decryption process are verified. To ascertain a high degree of fidelity between the decrypted and original plaintext images, a multitude of metrics and techniques may be utilised, including perceptual hashing and checksum verification. To prevent complications during the decryption procedure, error handling mechanisms should be activated in response to any discrepancies or mistakes discovered during the verification process. It is imperative to establish auditing mechanisms and process controls to oversee and trace decryption operations, thereby guaranteeing adherence to security policies and regulations. Authorised users should only have access to decryption keys and encrypted images; furthermore, all decryption operations should be audited and logged to detect and prevent malicious or unauthorised access. The following is the pseudo code for comparing decrypted image with original image.

```
def compare_images(decrypted_image, original_image):

if perceptual_hash(decrypted_image) == perceptual_hash(orig-
inal_image):

return True

else:

return False
```

Perceptual hashing generates compact digital fingerprints that represent an image's visual content in a way that is resistant to compression, scaling, and noise, making it useful for image comparison (Samanta & Jain, 2021). Perceptual hashing generates hashes that are sensitive to perceptual differences in images and robust to transformations, unlike traditional cryptographic hashing algorithms, which produce fixed-length hashes that change significantly even with minor input data changes. Perceptual hashing relies on its perceptual similarity property to produce similar hash values for visually similar images, even if they have been transformed. Perceptual hashing is ideal for image deduplication, content-based image retrieval, and image verification, which aim to identify similar images despite digital representations.

4. RESULTS AND ANALYSIS

This section provides an in-depth examination of the outcomes and analysis obtained from the Python programming environment implementation of the suggested image encryption framework. This section provides an analysis of the developed system's effectiveness, performance, and security implications, with an emphasis on its practical utility in protecting sensitive image data in cloud computing infrastructures. The image encryption framework was executed using the Python programming language, capitalising on its multifunctionality, vast collection of libraries, and resilient environment for machine learning and cryptography. The adaptability of Python enabled the smooth incorporation of a wide array of elements, including blockchain functionalities and neural network architectures, which contributed to the creation of a comprehensive and effective encryption solution. The implementation environment comprised a collection of Python frameworks and libraries, including scikit-learn for machine learning algorithms, TensorFlow and PyTorch for training and modelling neural networks, and PyCryptodome and other cryptographic libraries for encryption and decryption operations. Furthermore, the implementation of Web3.py and other blockchain-based libraries enabled Ethereum-based blockchain interactions. Precise attention was given to ensuring code quality, readability, and maintainability during the implementation phase, in strict adherence to industry standards and best practices. Python's object-oriented and modular architectures promoted the creation of reusable components, which in turn enabled the extension and reusability of code for subsequent optimisations and enhancements.

In the realm of image encryption, the sensitivity of the secret key plays a pivotal role in determining the robustness and security of the encryption scheme. An examination of the effects that even minor fluctuations or disruptions in the secret key have on the decryption procedure and the integrity of the decrypted image constitutes the analysis of secret key sensitivity. The significance of this analysis lies in its capacity to assess the encryption framework's resistance to potential attacks and guarantee the decryption procedure's stability amidst diverse circumstances. To evaluate the secret key's sensitivity, a sequence of experiments was carried out in which the decryption procedure was executed utilising marginally altered iterations of the initial secret key. The infractions in the secret key were introduced through the perturbation of key parameters within a predetermined range, thereby simulating possible scenarios in which adversaries could manipulate or tamper with the key.

Figure 5. Impact of Key Perturbation on MSE

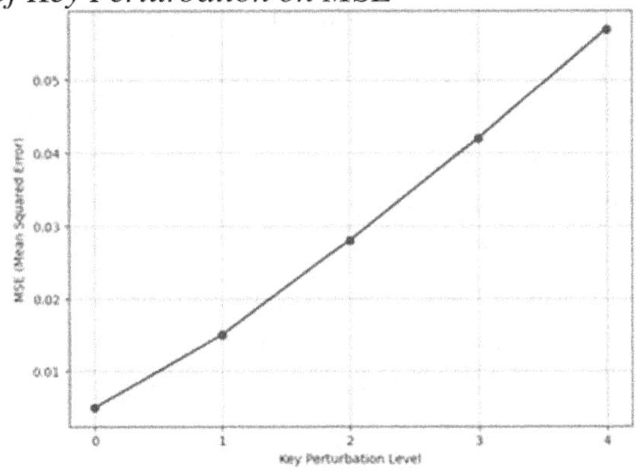

The dataset presented demonstrates how significant perturbations affect the mean squared error (MSE) values, which serve as a metric for calculating the average squared discrepancy between the plaintext and decrypted images. As illustrated in Figure 5, the key perturbation level escalates, signifying greater departures from the initial key, so do the MSE values. This observation implies that discrepancies in the secret key have a substantial impact on the integrity of the decrypted images. Greater disparities between the decrypted and original images are indicated by higher MSE values at elevated perturbation levels, which signifies a deterioration in the quality of the images. Errors that are introduced during the decryption process because of key manipulation or tampering may give rise to these discrepancies. The significant rise in MSE values as perturbation levels increase highlights the vulnerability of the decryption procedure to key perturbations.

Figure 6. Impact of Key Perturbation on PSNR

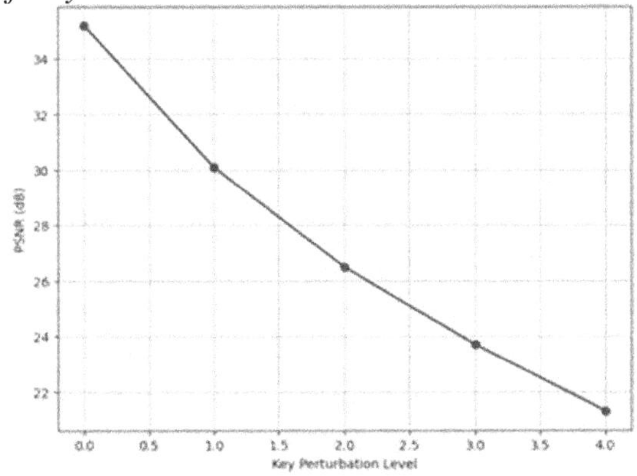

Significant variations in the decrypted images may result from even slight modifications in the secret key parameters. This emphasises the criticality of preserving the accuracy and integrity of the secret key to guarantee secure encryption and decryption processes. Thee PSNR values exhibit a progressive decrease with the escalation of the key perturbation level, as illustrated in Figure 6. This pattern denotes a decline in the quality of the image as the magnitude of key perturbations increases. At elevated perturbation levels, decreased PSNR values indicate that the decrypted images have acquired a greater amount of noise in comparison to the original images. This signifies a degradation in the integrity of the decryption process. The significant reduction in PSNR values indicates that the decryption procedure is extremely sensitive to changes in the secret key. The detrimental consequences of even slight deviations from the initial key parameters in terms of image quality are substantial, underscoring the critical importance of preserving the precision and integrity of the secret key to ensure secure encryption and decryption.

Figure 7. Comparison of MSE and PSNR with Baseline Model

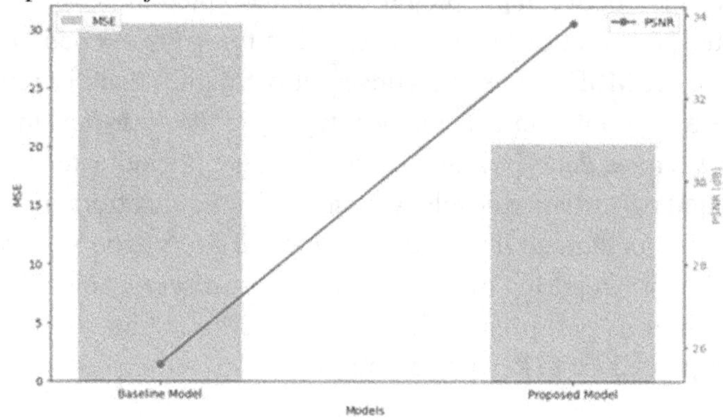

The significant improvements in PSNR and MSE reduction are largely attributable to the novel contributions made by the MGAN implemented in the Proposed Model. MGAN is equipped with sophisticated feature extraction functionalities, which enhance its ability to discern intricate patterns and details present in encrypted images. By capitalising on its resilient neural network architecture, MGAN is capable of discerning minute variations and subtle nuances, thereby enhancing the decryption process's fidelity and precision. MGAN implements adversarial training mechanisms in which the generator network vies for the ability to decrypt images of higher quality than the discriminator network. By implementing this adversarial process, the generator is incentivized to generate reconstructions that are more faithful and realistic, consequently mitigating distortion and information loss in the decrypted images. Through the utilisation of attention mechanisms, batch normalisation, residual connections, and batch normalisation, MGAN can attain enhanced noise reduction and preservation of image quality. These improvements are evident in the measured MSE and PSNR values, which are illustrated in Figure 7.

4.1. Performance Comparison

The Peak Signal-to-Noise Ratio (PSNR) is an important metric used to evaluate the quality of encrypted images produced by the proposed decryption network. The PSNR is a measure of how closely the decrypted image matches the original plaintext image. Higher PSNR values indicate better image quality and less distortion. During this evaluation, PSNR values were calculated by comparing the original image with the decrypted image produced by the proposed decryption network. The PSNR values obtained, as shown in Table 3, offer a quantitative assessment of the performance of the proposed network in picture reconstruction. The PSNR values demonstrate the efficacy of the proposed decryption network in restoring high-quality photos, showcasing its capacity to accurately reconstruct encrypted images while minimising information loss or image degradation. Table 3 presents a comparison analysis by comparing the PSNR values obtained from the proposed network with those obtained from different encryption networks. This comparative study enables an unbiased evaluation of the performance of the proposed network in relation to existing encryption frameworks. The proposed network exhibits greater image quality preservation and distortion reduction compared to alternative encryption approaches, as seen by its higher PSNR values.

Table 3. Performance Comparison

Reference	Avg. PSNR Value	Entropy	SSIM
(Zheng et al., 2019)	17.6	7.9536	-
(Chen, Li, & Wang, 2019)	24.9	7.9855	89.9%
(Zhang & Li, 2022)	30.5	7.9841	93.06%
Our model	33.8	7.9925	98.8%

The table 3 presents a comparison of the PSNR values, Entropy, and SSIM scores acquired from different references. The baseline work, referred to as (Zhang & Li, 2022; Ghanbari, Enayatifar, & Motameni, 2022; Neri, 2019; Cheroiu, Raducanu, & Nitu, 2022), achieved a PSNR value of 30.5 dB and an SSIM score of 93.06%, which is considered respectable. These indicators indicate a strong performance in terms of maintaining image quality and resemblance to the original photos. The notable rise in PSNR value signifies a noteworthy decrease in visual distortion and noise when compared to the baseline (Liu et al., 2022; Foo & Winkler, 2022; Fadhil, Farhan, & Fadhil, 2021; Erkan et al., 2022; Wang, 2023). This enhancement indicates that proposed technique excels in maintaining image quality throughout the encryption and decryption procedure, leading to sharper and more accurate reproductions of the original images (Haunts, 2019). The significantly higher SSIM score provides additional evidence for the superiority of our proposed strategy. SSIM quantifies the resemblance between two images by considering factors such as brightness, variation in intensity, and arrangement of elements (Alam, Wang, & Sowmya, 2021). The SSIM score of 98.8% demonstrates a very close similarity between the decrypted images and the original ones, confirming the success of proposed method in accurately reconstructing encrypted images (Tong, Xia, & Lv, 2022).

5. CONCLUSION

This study explores the integration of blockchain technology and Generative Adversarial Networks (GANs) for image encryption. It offers vital insights into the effectiveness of this innovative technique. By conducting careful and systematic experimentation and analysis, several important discoveries have been made, resulting in substantial advancements in the field of image encryption and security. The suggested approach, which integrates blockchain technology for secure key management and verification with GANs for image encryption, has produced encouraging outcomes. Our approach combines the decentralised and tamper-proof characteristics of blockchain with the advanced capabilities of GANs to generate realistic and secure encrypted images. This provides a strong solution for protecting sensitive image data in cloud computing environments. The experimental results illustrate the efficacy of the suggested approach in attaining greater preservation and fidelity of image quality compared to existing encryption frameworks. Our method demonstrates superior performance in generating clear and accurate reconstructions of encrypted images, as evidenced by significantly higher Peak Signal-to-Noise Ratio (PSNR) values and Structural Similarity Index (SSIM) scores. This highlights its potential for real-world applications where maintaining data integrity and visual fidelity are of utmost importance. Furthermore, the incorporation of blockchain technology provides an extra level of security and confidence, guaranteeing the safe handling of cryptographic keys and the unalterable verification of encrypted images. This not only improves the confidentiality and integrity of stored image data but also reduces the possibility of unauthorised access and alteration, hence strengthening overall data security in cloud computing environments.

This discovery has wide-ranging implications that go beyond the immediate findings, laying the groundwork for future research and development in the realm of picture encryption and security. An area that might be explored in the future is the improvement and fine-tuning of the suggested method to increase its efficiency and scalability for widespread use in real-world cloud computing systems. Moreover, the utilisation of blockchain technology and GANs shows potential in several fields outside image encryption, including video encryption, document encryption, and safeguarding multimedia assets.

REFERENCES

Agarwal, V., Kaushal, A. K., & Chouhan, L. (2020). *A Survey on Cloud Computing Security Issues and Cryptographic Techniques.* Social Networking and Computational Intelligence. DOI: 10.1007/978-981-15-2071-6_10

Al-Khasawneh, M. A. S., Faheem, M., Aldhahri, E. A., Alzahrani, A., & Alarood, A. A. (2023). A MapReduce Based Approach for Secure Batch Satellite Image Encryption. *IEEE Access : Practical Innovations, Open Solutions*, 11, 62865–62878. DOI: 10.1109/ACCESS.2023.3279719

Alam, M. S., Wang, D., & Sowmya, A. (2021). *Image data augmentation for improving performance of deep learning-based model in pathological lung segmentation. In 2021 Digital Image Computing: Techniques and Applications.* DICTA. DOI: 10.1109/DICTA52665.2021.9647209

Alghamdi, Y., Munir, A., & Ahmad, J. (2022, September). A Lightweight Image Encryption Algorithm Based on Chaotic Map and Random Substitution. *Entropy (Basel, Switzerland)*, 24(10), 1344. DOI: 10.3390/e24101344 PMID: 37420366

Anandkumar, R., Dinesh, K., Obaid, A. J., Malik, P., Sharma, R., Dumka, A., & Khatak, S. (2022). Securing e-Health application of cloud computing using hyperchaotic image encryption framework. *Computers & Electrical Engineering*, 100, 107860. DOI: 10.1016/j.compeleceng.2022.107860

Bao, Z., Xue, R., & Jin, Y. (2021, June). Image scrambling adversarial autoencoder based on the asymmetric encryption. *Multimedia Tools and Applications*, 80(18), 28265–28301. DOI: 10.1007/s11042-021-11043-3

Chen, J., Li, X.-W., & Wang, Q.-H. (2019). Deep Learning for Improving the Robustness of Image Encryption. *IEEE Access : Practical Innovations, Open Solutions*, 7, 181083–181091. DOI: 10.1109/ACCESS.2019.2959031

Cheroiu, D.-G., Raducanu, M., & Nitu, C. M. (2022). Fast Image Encryption Algorithm Based on Multiple Chaotic Maps. 2022 14th International Conference on Communications (COMM). DOI: 10.1109/COMM54429.2022.9817317

Erkan, U., Toktas, A., Enginoğlu, S., Akbacak, E., & Thanh, D. N. H. (2022). An image encryption scheme based on chaotic logarithmic map & key generation using deep CNN. *Multimedia Tools and Applications*, 81(5), 7365–7391. DOI: 10.1007/s11042-021-11803-1

Fadhil, M. S., Farhan, A. K., & Fadhil, M. N. (2021). Designing Substitution Box Based on the 1D Logistic Map Chaotic System. *IOP Conference Series. Materials Science and Engineering*, 1076(1), 012041. DOI: 10.1088/1757-899X/1076/1/012041

Foo, F., & Winkler, S. (2022). Image Data Augmentation with Unpaired Image-to-Image Camera Model Translation. *2022 IEEE International Conference on Image Processing (ICIP)*. DOI: 10.1109/ICIP46576.2022.9897671

Ghanbari, H., Enayatifar, R., & Motameni, H. (2022). A Fast Image Encryption based on Linear Feedback Shift Register and Deoxyribonucleic acid. DOI: 10.21203/rs.3.rs-1662684/v1

Haunts, S. (2019). *Hybrid Encryption. Applied Cryptography in* NET and Azure Key Vault. DOI: 10.1007/978-1-4842-4375-6_9

Justin, S., & Karuppusamy, S. K. (2022, December). Mayfly optimization with chaos-based image encryption technique for cloud computing environment. *Journal of Electronic Imaging*, 32(05). Advance online publication. DOI: 10.1117/1.JEI.32.5.052303

Kakkad, V., Patel, M., & Shah, M. (2019, May). Biometric authentication and image encryption for image security in cloud framework. *Multiscale and Multidisciplinary Modeling, Experiments and Design*, 2(4), 233–248. DOI: 10.1007/s41939-019-00049-y

Kumar, S., Singh, B. K., & Akshita, S. (2020). A survey on Symmetric and Asymmetric Key based Image Encryption. *2nd International Conference on Data, Engineering and Applications (IDEA)*. DOI: 10.1109/IDEA49133.2020.9170703

Kumar, S., Srivastava, P. K., Srivastava, G. K., Singhal, P., Singh, D., & Goyal, D. (2022, May). Chaos based image encryption security in cloud computing. *Journal of Discrete Mathematical Sciences and Cryptography*, 25(4), 1041–1051. DOI: 10.1080/09720529.2022.2075085

Lakshmi, K., Thenmozhi, K., Rayappan, J. B. B., Rajagopalan, S., Amirtharajan, R., & Chidambaram, N. (2020, November). Neural-assisted image-dependent encryption scheme for medical image cloud storage. *Neural Computing & Applications*, 33(12), 6671–6684. DOI: 10.1007/s00521-020-05447-9

Lavanya, Sundar, & Saravanan. (2024). Simplified Image Encryption Algorithm (SIEA) to enhance image security in cloud storage. *Multimedia Tools and Applications*. DOI: 10.1007/s11042-023-17969-0

Li, Y., Yu, H., Song, B., & Chen, J. (2019, March). Image encryption based on a single-round dictionary and chaotic sequences in cloud computing. *Concurrency and Computation*, 33(7), 1–1. DOI: 10.1002/cpe.5182

Liu, Z., Liu, J. Y., Zhang, L. Y., Zhao, Y., & Gong, X. F. (2022). Performance of the 2D Coupled Map Lattice Model and Its Application in Image Encryption. *Complexity*, 2022(1), 5193618. Advance online publication. DOI: 10.1155/2022/5193618

Nalavade, J. E., Patil, A., Buchade, A., & Jadhav, N. (2023, November). Deep Neural Network and GAN-Based Reversible Data Hiding in Encrypted Images: A Privacy-Preserving Approach. *SN Computer Science*, 5(1), 45. Advance online publication. DOI: 10.1007/s42979-023-02347-2

Neela, K. L., & Kavitha, V. (2022, June). Blockchain based Chaotic Deep GAN Encryption scheme for securing medical images in a cloud environment. *Applied Intelligence*, 53(4), 4733–4747. DOI: 10.1007/s10489-022-03730-x

Neri, F. (2019). *An Introduction to Computational Complexity*. Linear Algebra for Computational Sciences and Engineering. DOI: 10.1007/978-3-030-21321-3_11

Ouyang, D., Shao, J., Jiang, H., Nguang, S. K., & Shen, H. T. (2020, August). Impulsive synchronization of coupled delayed neural networks with actuator saturation and its application to image encryption. *Neural Networks*, 128, 158–171. DOI: 10.1016/j.neunet.2020.05.016 PMID: 32446193

Rodriguez, D., & Krishnan, R. (2023). A Cycle-GAN Based Image Encoding Scheme for Privacy Enhanced Deep Neural Networks. *Lecture Notes in Computer Science*, 14424, 178–196. DOI: 10.1007/978-3-031-49099-6_11

S, G., & S, G. (2023, March). Securing medical image privacy in cloud using deep learning network. *Journal of Cloud Computing (Heidelberg, Germany)*, 12(1), 40. Advance online publication. DOI: 10.1186/s13677-023-00422-w

SaberiKamarposhti, M., Ghorbani, A., & Yadollahi, M. (2024, January). A comprehensive survey on image encryption: Taxonomy, challenges, and future directions. *Chaos, Solitons, and Fractals*, 178, 114361. DOI: 10.1016/j.chaos.2023.114361

Samanta, P., & Jain, S. (2021). Analysis of Perceptual Hashing Algorithms in Image Manipulation Detection. *Procedia Computer Science*, 185, 203–212. DOI: 10.1016/j.procs.2021.05.021

Singh, H. K., Baranwal, N., Singh, K. N., Singh, A. K., & Zhou, H. (2023, December). GAN-based watermarking for encrypted images in healthcare scenarios. *Neurocomputing*, 560, 126853. DOI: 10.1016/j.neucom.2023.126853

Sirisha, U., & Chandana, B. S. (2023, January). Privacy Preserving Image Encryption with Optimal Deep Transfer Learning Based Accident Severity Classification Model. *Sensors (Basel)*, 23(1), 519. DOI: 10.3390/s23010519 PMID: 36617116

Tong, L., Xia, P., & Lv, T. (2022). Research on Quantum Secure Route Model and Line Model Image Encryption Technology Based on Big Data Technology. *2022 International Conference on Cloud Computing, Big Data Applications and Software Engineering (CBASE)*. DOI: 10.1109/CBASE57816.2022.00028

Wang, X., Feng, L., & Zhao, H. (2019, June). Fast image encryption algorithm based on parallel computing system. *Information Sciences*, 486, 340–358. DOI: 10.1016/j.ins.2019.02.049

Wang, Y., Chen, L., Wu, G., Yu, K., & Lu, T. (2023, May). Efficient and secure content-based image retrieval with deep neural networks in the mobile cloud computing. *Computers & Security*, 128, 103163. DOI: 10.1016/j.cose.2023.103163

Wang, Z., Byrnes, O., Wang, H., Sun, R., Ma, C., Chen, H., Wu, Q., & Xue, M. (2023). Data Hiding with Deep Learning: A Survey Unifying Digital Watermarking and Steganography. *IEEE Transactions on Computational Social Systems*, 10(6), 2985–2999. DOI: 10.1109/TCSS.2023.3268950

Xu, S., Chang, C.-C., & Horng, J.-H. (2023). Cryptospace Image Steganography for Cloud Security Via Cycle-Consistent Gan. DOI: 10.2139/ssrn.4673313

Zhang, Q., & Li, J. (2022, February). Single Exposure Phase-Only Optical Image Encryption and Hiding Method via Deep Learning. *IEEE Photonics Journal*, 14(1), 1–8. DOI: 10.1109/JPHOT.2022.3146456

Zheng, Z.EncryptGAN: Image Steganography with Domain Transform. https://arxiv.org/abs/1905.11582

Zhou, W., Zhang, Y., Zhao, R., Yi, S., & Lan, R. (2023). Adversarial Thumbnail-Preserving Transformation for Facial Images Based on GAN. *IEEE Signal Processing Letters*, 30, 1147–1151. DOI: 10.1109/LSP.2023.3308012

Zhu, J.-Y., Park, T., Isola, P., & Efros, A. A. (2017). Unpaired Image-to-Image Translation Using Cycle-Consistent Adversarial Networks. *2017 IEEE International Conference on Computer Vision (ICCV)*. DOI: 10.1109/ICCV.2017.244

Chapter 10
IoT Cloud Ecosystems:
An In-Depth Platform Comparison

Vidya Shrimant Gaikwad
Vishwakarma Institute of Information Technology, India

ABSTRACT

The internet of things (IoT) cloud refers to an internet-based platform that facilitates the storage, management, and analysis of data generated by IoT devices. It combines the capabilities of cloud computing with the connectivity of IoT, creating a powerful ecosystem that supports a wide range of applications and services cloud providers are essential to the IoT ecosystem because they provide the services and infrastructure required for efficient deployment and management of IoT solutions. In order to address multiple service areas, including application development, device administration, system management, heterogeneity management, data management, and tools for analysis applicability, this chapter analyses well-known IoT cloud platforms. A few issues that the researchers should address in the near future are also described. This chapter's ultimate objective is to impart thorough knowledge about the current IoT cloud service providers.

INTRODUCTION

Billions of devices are now used in numerous households across the globe connecting to communicate and interact with one another at an unprecedented pace, thereby marking a new paradigm driven by accelerated rise of IoT (Internet of Things). These networked devices produces massive volumes of data, which necessitates a reliable and secure infrastructure at scale to manage, store process the generated-data. This is the first use of IoT Cloud ecosystems (this are all-in platforms that have been created to support specific needs for an aspect or aspects

DOI: 10.4018/979-8-3693-6705-6.ch010

in your environment under IoT): A variety: As in the above question, but for services such as data storage meaning and device management (for real).

Figure 1. IoT cloud platforms at various domains

Figure 1. illustrate the IoT Cloud Platforms used in our day-to-day life like healthcare, agriculture, smart cities and industry.

By seamlessly blending real-time analytics and incorporating machine learning integration, these ecosystems enable organizations to exploit the potential benefits of IoT.

This study thoroughly compares the leading IoT cloud platforms – Amazon Web Services (AWS) IoT, Microsoft Azure IoT, Google Cloud IoT, IBM Watson IoT and Oracle IoT Cloud. The platform supports specific needs within the IoT space and leverages its unique strengths. Our comparison intends to help enterprises make more informed decisions based on their specific IoT requirements and how well each platform addresses them, by clearly painting a picture of pros, cons, key features & rivers for these platforms.

In the first section we define what key components and characteristics should makes up a good Internet of Things cloud ecosystem. We exhibit their utilization in industries like smart manufacturing, healthcare, agriculture and even in smart cities through few case studies performance standards.

Ultimately, this paper is about humanising IoT Cloud - the platforms out there in the world for better and worst that could enable us to grow effectively or operate more efficiently for a richer and interconnected future. We expect that this exhaustive comparison is going to give developers, decision-makers and enterprises input for their IoT Cloud platform choice that helps them fulfil technologies vision as well as strategic goals.

LIMITATIONS OF IOT CLOUD PLATFORMS

Such a combination of properties brings opportunities, but also considerable technical problems that must be addressed in order to deploy IoT-cloud systems safely and effectively. Some of the key problems are:

i) Interoperability and Standardization

- Challenge: Making IoT solutions work with an array of different devices and platforms.
- Effect: The absence of standardization can be the root cause for integration complexities, increased complexity in the system and higher costs.

ii) Security and Privacy:

- Problem: Preventing unauthorized access to data passing through IoT devices and cloud platforms, as well ensuring secure communication of the same.
- Impact - This could result in data breaches, loss of sensitive information and user trust.

iii) Scalability:

- Challenges: Addressing More Devices and IoT Data
- Without scalable solutions, performance bottlenecks can cause service degradation or even bring a system down.

iv) Data Management:

- Type of Challenges: Storing, processing data and analysis on massive number from various IoT devices efficiently
- It enables slow processing times, inaccurate insights and can also increase the amount of data that needs to be stored.

v) High Latency and Batch Processing vs. Low-latency Real-time processing:

- The gauntlet down: providing low-latency real-time communication as well as effective data marshalling between your IoT pocket friend and the cloud.
- Latency can be high, potentially rendering them unsuitable for real-time applications in sectors such as healthcare monitoring or autonomous vehicles.

vi) Energy Efficiency:

- How to develop low-power energy-efficent solutions that last longer as IoT devices usually work and run on batteries for very long durations.
- *Consequence: Frequent replacement of batteries & increased maintenance costs.*

vii) Network Reliability:

- Problem: Ensuring Seamless Connectivity for IoT Devices across many scenarios.
- Consequences: This might cause communication disruptions where one system fails to reach the other, data loss and interruptions in services.

viii) Cost Management:

- Challenge: The cost to deploy and manage IoT cloud platforms comparing with hardware, software and operational expenses Minimize -and acures.
- Summary: With costs running so high, there is no way SMEs can afford it.

ix) Interoperability:

- Problem: Providing seamless communication between a complex ecosystem of diverse IoT devices, cloud services and applications.
- Impact: These interoperability problems can make it difficult to integrate new devices and services on existing systems.

x) Regulatory Compliance:

- The Challenge: Meeting the many regional regulatory and standards-based compliance requirements
- Having not to comply the company crimes that involves fines, prosecution etc It also effects in loss of reputation and denial on entry into market.

Meeting these challenges will require ongoing research, innovation and collaboration between IoT developers, cloud service providers and regulators. Efforts to solve these challenges will help realize the true potential of IoT cloud platforms, resulting in more efficient (small bandwidth and computing overhead), secure (encryption/decryption costs need distributed within dynamic data centre on-demand/container instance) and saleable implementations.

Latest Trends on the Said Cloud Platforms for IoT

AWΓ as of by 2024 Gartner Magic Quadrant of Global Industrial IoT Platforms at a glance: AWS Recognition mains on top as a leader for 2023-24 best return. AWS IoT Site Wise and AWS IoT Twin Maker empower companies to achieve digital transformation in industrial environments, which is evidenced by this recognition. It provides a rich architecture to delay edge computing, big data, and analytics while allowing industries to gain from enhanced efficiency and sustainability in their operations.

Focus on IoT security: The number of connected devices is growing exponentially, and so is the IoT security market. The threat landscape is becoming more sophisticated, and businesses are investing heavily in new IoT security systems for protection, making this one of the primary platform development focus areas.

Growth of Edge Computing: Edge computing has remained a major trend that processes data closer to its origin point. It supports applications such as industrial automation and connected healthcare, by minimizing latency and enabling real-time data processing. Having a global revenue estimate of $274 billion by 2025 for edge computing.

Increased AI-Driven Voice Interfaces: AI-enabled voice interfaces have rapidly penetrated IoT platforms, spurring further use in sectors like banking and retail. As a brand-new technology, voice biometrics helps provide users with secure and personalized experience.

IoT Ingredients for the Metaverse, with IoT becoming a centrepiece of the metaverse and of new ideas within gaming, engineering, or retail. This crossroad is propelling the next generation connectivity and immersive technology.

These updates mean a lot of progress recently in IoT platform advancements for enterprise use cases, security advances as well, and the introduction of robust integration with emerging technologies to depict clarity in the future of IoT platforms.

Li, Z. et al. (2022) describes the design and implementation of a city-level IoT platform based on edge computing, cloud-native technologies for urban management:

The curved shape of Edge Computing with cloud-native architectures is designed to boost performance, scalability and prompt actionability for IoT systems in Smart city scenarios.

The paper illustrates - for the first time and to our, best knowledge- how edge computing integrated with cloud-native architectures can be realized in a city-level IoT platform (alongwith its benefits)

The security, interoperability and greater real world roll outs will be required for future researches to improve the technology.

Toutsop, et al. (2021) illustrate the paper perform a comparative study of different IoT middleware platforms to aid developers or researchers in choosing the suitable platform for their applications.

Significance Most important aspects in IoT Middleware platforms are necessary for simplifying the complexity of managing IOT environment, Device administration Data management Interoperability & Security Platforms require to have APIs (REST/MQTT.) - -All data can be managed through these REST-ful HTTP API calls., and identification needs built into them. Choosing the appropriate IoT middleware platform is based on some specific application requirements as well as priorities.

While not a direct buying guide, this comparative analysis should help most buyers make an informed decision based off their own detail specific needs and constraints.

Muhammed, et al (2020) -Investigates user Appreciation for Microsoft Azure-Amazon Web Services (AWS)- Google Cloud as top 3 IoT platform Vendors

Giving you a rundown of learned strengths and weaknesses from user feedback across all platforms. No platform is perfect-each has its own advantages and disadvantages, so your best option will depend largely on what you are looking for. Since no IoT platform is perfect, users should weigh their scalability needs against costs and benefits in terms of usability, security and support.

Vanar Sankarraman et al. (2019) argue for an IoT network infrastructure which can be designed to accommodate local regional needs. Aims to make available a hands-on solution for the regions in adopting IoT technologies effectively. Addresses some of the typical issues encountered in network connectivity and provides proper measures like LoRaWAN, and many other robust connection technologies. Stresses ongoing maintenance and local support for the IoT network to function smoothly.

Babiuch, M, et al, (2021) this article outlines development of a mobile application interfaced with ESP32 Azure IoT kit, which runs over a cloud platform. Illustrates the workings, along with some other advantages of combining IoT hardware to cloud services in creating mobile apps that are efficient and scalable. The paper presents the possibilities and advantages of developing mobile applications using ESP32 development board with Azure IoT cloud platform. Recommends additional improvement, including security features for smoothening and enhancement; Functionality expansion; Cloud services integration.

The paper deals with the design and deployment of an intelligent IOT platform which utilizes cloud computing that helps in capturing & monitoring personalized Health data. Vellela, Reddy L.S., et al (2018) . It stresses on the need for long-term and strategic measures like continuous monitoring of patient's health data remotely to enhance healthcare outcomes & plan early medical interventions. The research presented in the paper shows that it is possible to realize a cloud-enabled paradigm for personalized health data acquisition and monitoring using edge devices (IoT endpoints relying on ARM M3-M4 processors). Underlines the opportunity of these systems to revolutionize healthcare in terms that remote monitoring and personalized patient care will be available 24/7.

Vishalika (2021) this paper gives an overview of the cloud computing in combination with Internet of things (IoT) to understand benefits and research challenges related to each other.

Demonstrates that the intersection of two trends, cloud computing and IoT can extend beyond just enhancing each other's capabilities by meeting different application needs. The paper presents a detailed discussion of the pros and cons for cloud computing and IoT integration. Proposes future work such as increased security, lower latencies and standard protocols for more integrated deployments.

Gassara, M.,et al. (2021), the authors proposed a cloud-based platform based on LoRa (Long Range) technology for IoT applications aiming to improve connectivity and data management. Demonstrates the advantages of leveraging LoRa technology in conjunction with highly secure and scalable cloud infrastructure to address critical IoT challenges including effective wireless range, battery-life longevity for end devices, network capacity constraints and sensor data handling. The paper describes that, LoRa based communication helps improve IoT applications by long range capabilities and low power consumption while a cloud platform assists data management in scalable manner. Further study of how related work can help in optimization of network operations, secure communication between LoRa-cloud and extending its applications lands scope for future research.

Sorin-Robertino, S., et al (2023), the article introduces an IoT-based cloud system for vineyard monitoring and hopes to facilitate viticulturalists in better managing their vines through real-time data acquisition.

Utilizing IoT technology and cloud computing to maximize vineyard management practices for improved grape quality & yield. This paper presents the novel application of an IoT cloud system to improve monitoring and management in vineyards, providing real-time data collection analysis, visualization capabilities. Recommends Next Steps: Integration of Additional Sensors; More Advanced Analytics Techniques for Optimal Vineyard Management

The paper which will be presented by Baghestan, A.B.,et al (2023), proposed an integration framework includes cloud computing with IoT technology in Brain-Computer Interface (BCI) applications. To this end, we propose a virtualization-based BCI system that aims to enhance the performance and scalability of current BCI systems by offloading data processing and management at cloud services. This paper presents a cloud-based IoT framework designed to improve BCI applications by offering both scalable and real-time data processing and analysis facilities. Calls for more exploration on the security measures scaling, integration efficiency and generalization of BCI scenarios under the proposed framework.

Choudhury, et al (2017), the paper discusses the privacy and security concerns to integrated IoT devices with cloud computing (Choudhury, Gupta, Pradhan kumar Pant & Rathore). It seeks to identify available issues and drive the solutions to improve security and privacy in cloud-based IoT systems. With the rise of IoT devices, it is important to secure these systems and protect private data in order to maintain trust with users as well as system integrity. Insinuates Additional research regarding the strengthening of security protocols, enhancing privacy features and preventing new threats in fledgling cloud-based IoT systems. Preaches the making of standards and rules for secure development as well as management, deployment in cloud-based IoT systems.

Tulenkov, A., et al (2019), the work is some way of selecting IoT services loosely which process massive big data from smart house systems. We specialize in comparing and selecting IoT platforms that are capable of dealing with big data size found within smart homes. In this context of growing stimulation, managing data may be crucial in the implementation phase since it is directly linked to how well a system performs.

The paper surveys the fields of Smart House and IoT services, followed by a clear methodology to evaluate and select among them including evaluation criteria based on factors that affects performance/suitability for various types of IoT House systems. This paper endeavours to help users and organizations in selecting ideal IoT services for the actual collection, managing, processing big data with digital home environment.

Pierleoni, P.,. et al. IoT and cloud: analysis of the state-of-the-art in major IoT activity sectors (2020). The paper contains some comparisons among set up solutions related to Amazon Web Services (AWS), Google Cloud Platform (GCP). It analyses the architectures of these platforms and compares their performance for IoT use cases. Understanding the strengths and weaknesses of each is critical to enabling organisations to make informed decisions about what IoT platform best suits them. The article contrasts architecture, strength and identified weak-points of AWS, GCP & Azure IoT offerings. Selecting IoT platforms based on unique features and capabilities depending upon the respective needs. When choosing an IoT platform, it is important that organizations assess their individual needs based on factors like scalability and data processing requirements, security considerations or usability.

El. Zuway, et al (2022) in this paper, the authors address research question 3 and examine security requirements as well as potential vulnerabilities in Smart Home Internet of Things (SH-IoT) platform. The purpose of this paper is to detect the vulnerabilities in SH-IoT systems and provide recommendations for improving their security. With the emerging of SH-IoT platforms, it is has become more important to have an understanding and security considerations against issues that often come in user-data breaches or system integrity. The papers then identify the unique security demands on various functions of SH-IoT platforms and examines common attacks that threaten such systems. It highlights the need for stringent security apparatus to secure smart home surroundings from prospective hazards. Offers insights to secure SH-IoT platform, enabling stakeholders to understand risk from SHT and remediate that.

Moussa, K. H., et al (2024), the paper also seeks to address the integration of cloud technology and Internet of Things (IoT) for new health monitoring systems. The goal is to show what this integration could mean for both healthcare delivery and patient management. The transformation of the IoT and cloud computing technologies also promises a heightened potential in monitoring, managing as well analysing data especially when it comes to health.

The paper illuminates the potential of digital transformation in health monitoring systems by combining cloud technology and IoT. This is a powerful reminder of the advantages in real-time data analysis, enhanced visibility and reduced accessibility that still need to be met with questions around security, interoperability & reliability. Illustrates how with this fusion, healthcare can be taken to the next level where keeping check and track on patients becomes so easy; patient management gets as smooth as butter and medical service delivery is no longer singled-out.

In Sakai, T., et al (2022), a new paper demonstrates an IoT platform that can lessen the computational and data load on cloud services by concentrating information in an optimized way inside of small to large IoT networks These are intended to help make data movement more efficient and performant. The issue is that as IoT systems produce more and more data, cloud platforms can get bogged down. Offloading work from the cloud can speed up your systems and reduce costs. The Project proposal is very pragmatic and seems to be an ideal solution for managing the increasing complexity of IoT systems as well as improving overall system performance in a cost-effective way.

Gaikwad, V. S., et al (2018), In this paper we take a look at the cloud security user awareness i.e. how well users know about different threats which are available when data is on clouds and what sort of measures it takes to ensure data privacy while in use or store doge Neou's manner, they have used for storing their information with respect to - Cloud Computing Services. With cloud computing being more common, it is important to know how much a user knows about security in order to enhance the use of cloud services. The paper elucidates the disparity in user knowledge of cloud security and underscores salient avenues for enhancing education & communication efforts. This highlights the importance of more and better training, as well as open communication with your users to allow them insight into what is going on in terms of their extract activities are posing any risk or not. In this way, the paper hopes to help make the use of cloud computing services safe and informed.

A Lightweight Key Establishment Mechanism to Enhance IoT Device-Cloud Server Communication Security (2021) by Gaikwad, V et al . This work targets the trade-off between security and efficiency for IoT-based scenarios. IoT devices often come with interconnectivity opportunities that integrate into cloud services, and secure communication to these resources is essential for data protection as well as the continuity of systems. The proposed mechanism provided a viable solution for securing the IoT-cloud communication and thus can improve security in terms of versatile attack, as well to make efficient such existing mechanisms against various attacks on an ubiquitous scale like Internet.

S. P., Gaikwad, V., et al (2023), the paper suggests a mathematical approach to the problem of key establishment for lightweight networks in Internet of Things (IoT) settings and IoT-cloud communication. Improving Security, Without Slowing Down Eclipses focus for the project is to add security without sacrificing performance and efficiency, this in terms of being able to push these workloads through much more pinched down resources with ample robustness on IOT scenarios. As the number of IoT devices increases with support for cloud platforms, and speed is important to prevent data from being lost or causing systems not to work properly Pluggable Security emphasizing the revolutionary lightweight key mechanism, proposed to solve a growing problem of securing IoT-cloud communication provides practical solution for secure and efficient development within context of recent previously published related approaches.

Ravindranath, K., et al (2023), the paper presents a new method for continuous authentication of IoT devices while they communicate with the cloud. It is a process on securing and continuously verifying the identities of devices using lightweight approach to key establishment. In such IoT environments, it is critical to apply continuous authentication in order to prevent unauthorized access and that only genuine devices are able interact with cloud services. This solution aims to enhance the security of IoT-cloud interactions, resolving issues around pair-wise user authentication and resource constrained nature in IoT applications.

Sharma, G., et al (2024), a bibliometric analysis of research related to the use so far, IoT cloud computing in educational domain. The objective is to shed light on the history, influence and extant knowledge surrounding these types of technologies for educational purposes. Given that IoT and cloud computing have received wide attention in the field of education, it is important to investigate research trends and themes so as to discover areas for development or future paths. This analysis aids in the understanding how IoT and cloud technologies have been influencing education systems from different points of view, which can guide both researchers, educators and policymakers on how to step forward for future researches or applications.

Odukoya, O. et al (2024), the research has focused on the improved operational efficiency, decreased costs and large scale enable factors that were considered to be important impactors for roving any type of successful cloud computing used by small business. This post discusses the impact of cloud services on business agility, data management and collaboration; as well as challenges that appear such server security risks or other issues with hiring talent. This report is intended to help SMEs in any particular vertical level set out the respective cloud adaption strategies, and how they work as well.

Han, H., et al (2021),a complete IoT cloud platform iCool made for end-to-end services. The platform facilitates diverse IoT workloads by providing services like device provisioning, data processing and application development in one common setting. The paper describes the architecture and functionality of I Cool as well as its use in practice, showing that it is both flexible and scalable for developers; easy to deploy from an enterprise point-of-view. The research article details how the platform streamlines IoT deployments and drives service efficiency.

Ellwein, C., et al (2018), a cloud manufacturing platform is explored based on which SMEs can take advantage of advanced production capabilities. Rent'n'Produce — A cloud platform that provides SMEs with cloud-based secure and scalable access to manufacturing resources as services anytime, anywhere in a flexible cost-effective manner. Security architectures in the platform for provide user to resource and data protection, including secure communication between different users with manufacturing resources has garnered major attention of authors. The report identified the opportunity for platform to democratize specialized manufacturing capabilities with affordability plans concerning small and medium enterprises.

Zhao, S.,et al (2023), presents novel approaches on image processing for low-storage environments within the Internet of Things cloud while emphasizing privacy lance. In this paper, the authors propose ways by which high-quality images can be processed with very low data storage and therefore to deal in a secure fashion with image handling across distributed networks. The proposed solutions target to preserve the privacy of users during image processing in IoT systems and cloud platforms, hence can be applied successfully for resource-restricted environments.

Ansari, Ali K; et al (2023) Internet of Things (IoT) Fusion with Cloud Computing: Current Research and Future Direction. 4th International Conference on Cloud smart ICT Open Scholarly Society (2023 IC-COS). The following provides a brief overview of its most notable aspects:

IoT and Cloud Integration The paper prevents the great volume of data generated by the embedded nodes of big data (IoT), which is required for effective processing, storage and analysis. Cloud computing delivers the elasticity needed for on-demand resources and services scaling to enable IoT applications such as smart cities, healthcare, and industry.

Despite the advantages, there are some challenges that come along with the integration of IoT in cloud computing which includes, latency issues, bandwidth limitations, and security concerns. This blatantly fuels research on hybrid architectures including fog and edge computing for processing data as near as the sensing sources.

Fusion Advantages: The fusion of IoT and cloud computing facilitates real-time analysis, enhanced decision-making, and resource optimization. Use cases range from health care monitoring systems to industrial IoT predictive maintenance.

Future Directions: The work suggests directions for more research like improving security protocols, lowering latency with edge computing, and establishing AI-powered frameworks for smooth integration.

Hybrid approaches — Promising hybrid models which combine the strengths of cloud and edge computing, such as fog and mist computing, are mentioned to reduce latency but still achieving scalability.

Nature of paper-Forward looking and Comprehensive A feature of this work is its forward-looking nature within the context of an evolving landscape, which will be relevant for both practice and research in IoT-cloud ecosystems.

Preeti Agarwal et al (2018) widely accepted that a significant wave of IoT devices leading to unprecedented growth of data in the world has emerged and will be further enriched with the passage of time . It divides the IoT cloud platforms into four types — public company, open-source, developer-focused and end-to-end connectivity platform. The paper provides a number of presently popular platforms in each category along with their comparative analysis based on general IoT architecture to help developers identify the most appropriate platform for developing an application.

The paper also stresses that the class of cloud solutions will become critical, given the massive amount of incoming data from IoT devices and this provides a background to their work given that so far classifications proposed in literature have been limited. This paper is targeted to help new developers and stakeholders select IoT platforms that meet certain requirements.

Partha Pratim Ray, in the paper A survey of IoT cloud platforms (2016), describes IOT Cloud Platforms as an integral component of Internet based objects that supports communication and facilitates intelligent interaction between people and machines with the help of machines. In this paper, we survey the IoT cloud platforms for broad applicability over different service domains as follows:

Application Development: Little Tools for building IoT apps quickly.

Device and System Management: Tools for the integration and management of the IoT devices and systems.

Data Management: Ways to store, process and analyse IoT data.
Heterogeneity Acquisition: Issues from Diversity among Devices and Technologies in IoT Ecosystem Tracking and Visualization of Monitoring: Real-time tracking data visualization

It provides a comparative study of the existing IoT cloud platforms and states their functionalities, pros, and cons. It also highlights major challenges like scalability, interoperability, and security as important areas for further investigation and advancement.

Kumar, Tiwari et al (2019) -- The paper entitled "Internet of Things is a new approach for future technology improvement: A review" presents inspiration overview about Internet of Things (IoT), how IoT evolved from the concept till present years and it impact to different sectors. Key highlights include:

IoT Architecture and Components: The basic architecture of IoT, including sensing devices, data processing systems, and cloud storage is detailed in the study. The importance of interconnectivity through sensors, networks, and communication protocols among other things is directly illuminated.

The paper reviews IoT applications in smart city, healthcare, farming, industry and home applications that illustrate how it can improve efficiency and automation and decision making.

Challenges in IoT:

- **Scalability:** Ensuring that more connected devices can be handled.
- **Interoperability**: Making heterogeneous devices talk to each other.
- **Security and Privacy:** Preventing Vulnerabilities + Protecting User Data
- **Power consumption:** You can save the energy used by your device.

Next Steps: The authors call for progress in artificial intelligence, machine learning, and big data to develop the potential of IoT. They also highlight the need to tackle security risks and create technologies that save energy.

This paper introduces IoT as a catalyst of technology evolution and its potential impact on the future of different fields.

IOT CLOUD PLATFORMS ESTABLISHMENT:

Although there are multiple methods to apply the IoT Cloud platform, one of its main purposes is simplifying how you connect and deploy devices as well applications with the Internet. Figure 2, represents the establishment of iot cloud platforms in various fields

Some crucial applications - Content:

Figure 2. Establishment of IoT cloud platforms in various fields

1. Device Management:
   a. Provisioning and Configuration Initial Internet of Things Device Setup and Configuration
   b. Monitoring & Maintenance: Upgrading the Firmware, performing maintenance actions and monitoring device health so as to ensure its real-time functioning
2. Data Aggregation:

   a: Receiving data from different IoT devices. o Data Collection and Storage

   b. Storage: Maintaining large cloud databases that can store the huge volume of data output by IoT devices
3. How does this big data analytics work?
   a. Stream processing: it helps to analyse data almost real time so that we can get faster conclusions and action items.

b. Analytics - Analysing historical data to discover patterns, trends and other information that can be used in decision-making.

4. Development of Applications:
   a. Development Environment: providing a platform and tools to develop Internet of Things apps.
   b. Software development kits (SDKs) and APIs for easier development and integration.
5. Security Guidance:
   a. Authorization and authentication: Ensuring the secure access to information / apparatus
   b. Data Encryption: The data should be encrypted while it is in motion or rest otherwise there are possibilities of unauthorized access.
6. Merging with Other Services:
   a. Cloud Services Integration: to provide big data analytics and AI/ML integration as well as other cloud services
   b. Third-Party Services: Provide further capabilities through integrations with 3rd party software and services
7. Flexibility and Scalability:
   a. Resource Scaling: Modify the number and size of infrastructure based on device count
   b. Flexible Deployment: Supports different types of deployments (public, private and hybrid clouds).
8. Real-time Alerts and Warnings:
   a. Event Detection - This detects specific events or situations and triggers an alarm
   b. Approach to Notification: Notifying individuals or systems based on predetermined rules.
9. Remote and Automatic Control:
   a. Remote Device Control: It permits the management and control of IoT device from another location on a network
   b. If automating tasks and processes based on conditions as well as data which is known by automation.
10. Reporting and Compliance:
    a. Regulatory Compliance: Ensuring that procedures and data management comply with pertinent laws.
    b. Reports: Generates reports for audits, compliance or analysis requirements.

These platforms help businesses deploy IoT to improve processes, get new insights, strengthen security and develop innovative solutions in various verticals e.g. smart cities, manufacturing, healthcare and agriculture industries

APPLICATION DOMAIN-SPECIFIC IOT CLOUDS

These tailor-made cloud computing services for specific industry or applications within the Internet of Things (IoT) ecosystem. These clouds offer domain-specific infrastructure, platforms and services that are tailored for healthcare, agriculture, manufacturing verticals as well as other use cases such smart cities etc.

Key Features of Domain-Specific IoT Clouds

1)Customized Data Models and Analytics:

- Healthcare – helping parameters such as those on healthcare standards like HL7 and DICOM, patient data management and regulatory compliance (including HIPAA) from a database standpoint.
- Agriculture: Integration with precision farming equipment, soil moisture and weather data analytics, crop yield optimization.
- Manufacturing — Industrial IoT (IIoT) protocols, real-time machine data analysis, Predictive Maintenance.

2) Scopia Security and Compliance: Custom Building Block:

The security and compliance requirements for each domain varies. For example, financial IoT clouds target secure transactions and compliance with finance regulations while healthcare IoT cloud focuses on patient data privacy and abiding health information laws.

3) Optimized Connectivity and Superior Network Management:

Connectivity is not enough; different vertical will have differing needs for connectivity. Areas such as smart cities need support from large low latency networks for traffic, utilities and public safety systems where logistics and supply chain management might require extensive wide-area network coverage to track shipments.

4) Platform for Specialized Application Development:

Tools and Frameworks for Implementing Domain-Specific Applications In automotive, this could be an autonomous driving systems simulation and a vehicle-to-everything (V2X) testing framework on the same platform.

5) Domain-Specific APIs and Integrations:

Domain-specific APIs to enable integration seamlessly with the current systems and devices Smart home IoT clouds might provide an API for interacting with different smart appliances, Home Automation systems, and Voice Assistants etc.

Edge Computing Support

Edge computing, by which domain-specific IoT algorithms run at the edge of the network-where data is generated and collected as close to a source as possible-is using with many intelligent health care-related solutions. Such industrial IoT applications may require edge devices for real-time machine control and data processing, as an example.

IoT clouds function as vertically application domain-specific platform.

Examples of Application Domain-Specific IoT Clouds

A) IoT Cloud in Healthcare

i) The Challenges of Healthcare Organizations

There is a lot of data circulating in the healthcare sector that must be treated with care. This data is the main asset of health Care Company - difficulty in secure, accessibility and optimize this Data.

Medical institutions such as drug houses, hospitals, pharmacies, forensic labs and clinics store huge datasets which they process using AI-based solutions. These organizations employ a lot of electronic devices primarily computers, phones and ot which produce data such as MRI machines. It also takes money to provide value-add services and maintain those on an ongoing basis. Health Industry can get a solution with cloud computing tools and apps for taking away mandatory expansion space. Figure 3.represents a IoT Cloud in healthcare by considering the features like type of sensors, connectivity, application platform, product infrastructure.

Figure 3. IoT cloud in healthcare

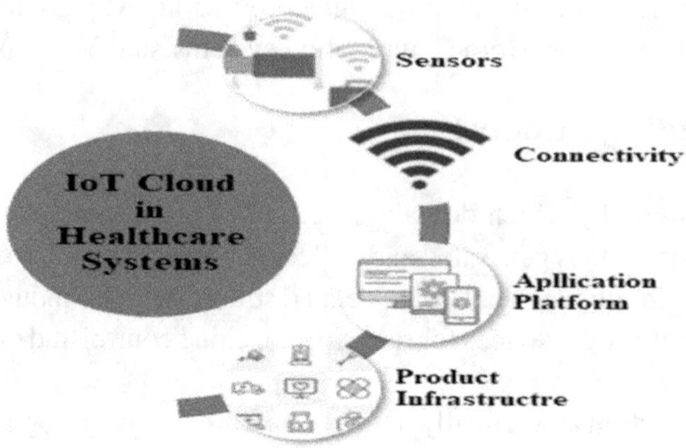

A small number of cloud computing service providers offer more than 160 cloud computer services at present, few AWS and Azure-leading. These models are probably the most recognizable due to their use of pay-as-you-go, and for good reason (it's what gives businesses one of the biggest flexibilities they can get).

Reduces expenses of service provision, improves diagnostic equipment and saves hundreds of millions OF US Dollars for healthcare corporations & organizations. This also provides ease of access to all operations

ii) Availability:

The healthcare sector is a deeply insecure field and runs on a large scale complicated network.

For instance, you know that one or more docs (or a team) treat any single patient. Information Updating and Keeping Patient Data without Requiring Any Communication Establishment Is a Challenging and Costly Task.

Cloud services can also enable real-time data updates; In addition, it is accessible by any professional with permission.

Cloud computing makes tasks easy for patients and medical professionals alike. There will be no need for patients to go check in at the local hospital just so they can see what online appointments and medications got modified.

iii) Safety:

Most of the time, hardware resources would be insufficient to keep data intact as failures do occur and organizations suffer from catastrophic (unrecoverable) loss of their valuable data. Also, IIV will damage your organization irreparably...

people stop responding to health when you loose lab results, medical histories and diagnostics of patients; billing information, etc.

Yet as servers for cloud-based services are located in many different regions, the service provider is able to guarantee that no loss of data will happen and offers a high level of security even if there has been or still are severe natural disasters. Cloud service providers for a reason message health informatics and advantages of healthcare computing.

The cloud is far more secure than on-premises solutions. The app has various security metrics like firewalls, end-to-end encryption, and IDS/IPS.

Applications: healthcare industry is employing cloud computing and IoT.

a) NetApp:

Their solutions are tailored for healthcare, and help in big data management, storage, and security to the unique demands of health care providers; researchers; institutions. Healthcare industry produces a lot of data from patient records and medical imaging to the academic or research one, all called for effective management which is convenient as well as secured while maintaining compliance. NetApp provides solutions that can help healthcare organizations simplify their IT infrastructure, accelerate access to data and maintain regulations while delivering improved care for patients.

b) Medsphere:

Open-source electronic health record (EHR) and other healthcare IT solutions are available through Medsphere Systems Corporation, a provider of proficient, reliable technology. Medsphere's principal offering is an EHR system it calls Open Vista, built on the Vista (Veterans Health Information Systems and Technology Architecture) platform of the US Department of Veterans Affairs. Open Vista targets healthcare networks, hospitals and clinics in order to ensure regulatory compliance while optimising clinical operations to enable patient care excellence.

c) Pfizer:

One of such private global pharmaceutical company is Pfizer Inc. that majorly contributes to the healthcare industry by developing, manufacturing and distributing a diverse range of medications and vaccines across different therapeutic areas globally. Drawing on a legacy of over 170 years, Pfizer is recognized for its ongoing R&D efforts in oncology as well as other therapeutic areas such as immunology, cardiology and infectious diseases.

d) Philips Health Suite:

Philips Health Suite - A comprehensive cloud-based platform intended to support a variety of healthcare applications. More products and services that are meant to help deliver better care through improved telemedicine capabilities, advanced health analytics insights or monitoring in real-time.

B) IoT Clouds in Agriculture

Smart Farming or Precision Agriculture - use of IoT and cloud computing in agriculture to improve efficiency, productivity, sustainability using advanced technologies. Figure 4, shows IoT Cloud is used in Agriculture for Monitoring Farm, UAV farming, tracking and tracing, analysis of Data, supply chain management.

Figure 4. IoT cloud in agriculture

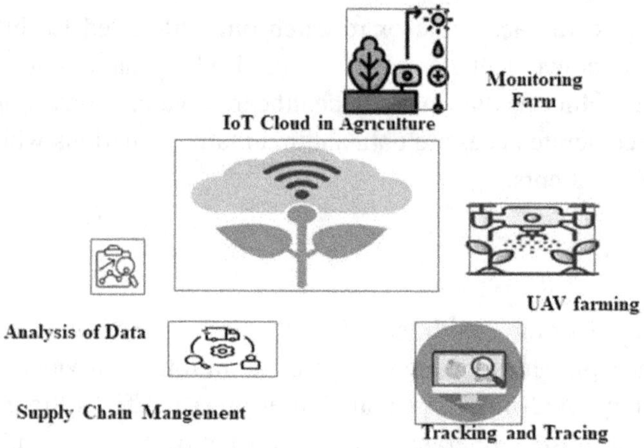

i) Microsoft Farm Beats:

Introduction to Microsoft Farm Beats: Microsoft Farm Beats is a paradigm that aggregates cloud computing AI and IoT sensors together to generate the actionable insights for farmers.

Qualities:

- **Data integration:** Collects data from different sources like satellites, drones and sensors.

- Predictive analytics that AI and machine learning use to predict crop yields and recognize irregularities.
- **Edge computing:** The use of local data processing that reduces latency and improves real-time decision-making.

Pros: Increases efficiency Reduces costs Optimizes use of resources (e.g. Fertilizers, water)

ii) John Deere Operations Centre:

John Deere Operations Centre: A cloud-based farm management solution that integrates various agtech information with data from your John Deere machinery.

Qualities:

- Equipment Integration – links into John Deere machinery to capture and analyse performance data ·
- Field management provides tools to organize, supervise and administer field operations.
- It gives a Hints on data analysis; as well recorded for operating conditions to optimize equipment and crop performance.
- Advantages are high-grade crop management, enhanced machinery productivity and support for precision agriculture.

iii) Climate Corporation's VZW of the FIELD View by Bayer:

The platform further eases the process of data collection and validation within fields for farmers.

Qualities:

- Takes data directly from all three sources - machines, weather stations and field sensors.
- To check the status of the fields and crop health, field monitoring is used which provides real-time conditions in the farm.
- Predictive analytics: Machine learning helps in giving data about the right time to plant, expected yield and pests etc.
- This leads to better decision making, increased harvest production and reduces the need for resources.

iv) Agri Webb:

An overview of Agri Webb: This cloud platform allows farmers to keep track of livestock and pasture on its software ecosystem.

Qualities:

- Livestock tracking: In this case, Internet of Things enabled tags and sensors are used to track not only the weight — but also health or even mobility on animals.
- Grazing management: Optimization of pasture utilization and grazing patterns using satellite and sensor data provided.
- Data analytics: Gives insight to how pastures and animals are performing.
- Benefit: Increases availability of pasture management, enhances cattle productivity and encourages eco-friendly farming practices.

v) Trimble Ag Software:

Company Information: Trimble Ag Software integrates resources across agricultural operations to deliver cloud-based farm management solutions.

Qualities:

- **Field Mapping:** GPS and IoT sensors are used to create field maps for precise farming requirements.
- **Crop Scouting:** This method is used to conduct remote crop monitoring and scouting using drones as well satellite photos.
- **Data integration:** Aggregates data harvested from sensors, weather stations and machinery to create a well-detailed analysis

Advantages: Efficient farm operations Improved precision farming Better resource management

vi) IBM Watson Decision Platform

Summary: This is an IoT and Artificial Intelligence-based platform useful to provide advice, insights for the farmer.

Qualities:

- Weather Insights: With the help of local weather forecaster or new service, farmers get to initiate what could be done on a particular day.
- Crop management — includes data analysis from satellites and sensors to monitor crop health, as well as yield predictions.
- Pest and disease prediction: Using AI to predict pests and diseases.

- Pros: Enhances decision-making, optimizes resource allocation and reduces crop wastage.

For example, General Electric (GE) developed GE Health Cloud which is a cloud-based platform to store and manage patients' data as well medical images for healthcare practitioners. Enable hospitals and other healthcare providers to deliver quality care by improving security, accessibility & efficiencies in data management for healthcare.

C) IoT Clouds in Smart Cities and Smart Homes

Companies are Leading in IoT Cloud Devices and Solutions that use Smart Home and City. These companies employ IoT devices, cloud computing and extensive analytics to create a network connected environment which improves safety increases productivity in addition is environmentally sustainable. Figure 5. Illustrate the factors to be considered for smart cities and smart homes are recycling, smart energy etc…

Figure 5. IoT cloud in smart cities and smart homes

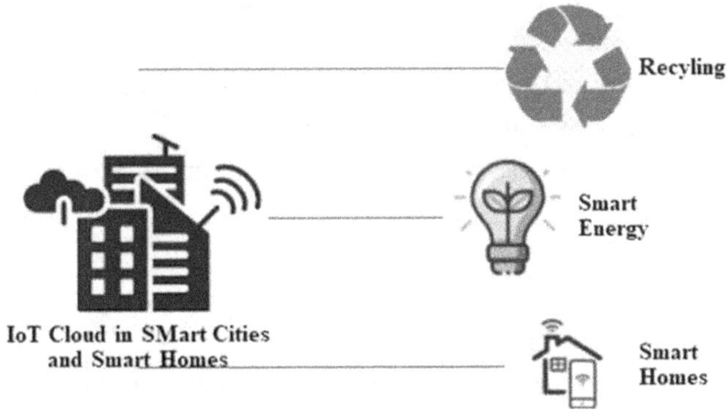

Check out some of the big-name companies within this industry:

i) Cisco:

- With a focus on Internet of Things (IoT) based connected city solutions, all the three parts – connectivity, security and data analytics are catered by Cisco.
- Top products: Cisco Smart Connected Digital Platform; Cisco Kinetic for Cities.

- Public safety, energy management, traffic control and smart lighting applications.

ii) Overview of IBM:

- Through the use of AI and cloud computing IBM Smart Cities utilizes IoT solutions to optimize urban operations.
- Key Offerings: IBM Intelligent Operations Centre, IBM Watson IoT Platform
- In urban planning, environmental monitoring, infrastructure management etc.

iii)Microsoft:

- Overview: Microsoft Azure provides the perfect infrastructure for developing intelligent city applications by integrating cloud, IoT & artificial intelligence features.
- Azure Digital Twins Azure IoT Hub with some context in the above two bullets point which range from urban mobility to predictive maintenance of networks and intelligent buildings.

iv) Huawei

- Executive Summary: Huawei IoT smart city solutions focus on data governance and connectivity.
- Two key products Huawei Smart City Solution and IOTory–based on Huawei Ocean Connect IoT Platform.
- Applications: Smart Mobility, Environmental Monitoring and Public Safety

v) Google (Nest)

- Summary: Google sells a range of smart home products and services under its Nest brand.
- Key Items: Google Home, Nest Cam and Temp Sensor
- Applications – Security Systems, Energy Management & Home Automation

vi) Alexa:

- Amazon has a range of smart home appliances that are connected with its voice assistant, Alexa.
- Best Sellers: Amazon Smart Plug, Ring Video Doorbell and Echo.
- Applications: Entertainment, Security and hands-free home automation

vii) Samsung Electronics:

- Overview: A single platform capable of connecting many different smart home appliances together using SmartThings from Samsung.
- SmartThings Hub, SmartThings Sensors and Smart Thing App are the principle products

- Applications: energy control, security and home automation

viii) Apple Inc. (HomeKit)

- Summary: HomeKit is the Apple answer that lots of people requested.
- Best Items: HomeKit-compatible gadgets and the Home Pod
- Applications: Security, Lighting Control & Home Automation

ix) Hue Philips

- Overview: Philips Hue offers Connected lighting and smart other home technologies
- Hue Bridge and Smart Bulbs are the core products.
- Applications· Ambient lighting control, smart home automation and LED lights Control.

In short, these are the companies that will define IoT cloud-enabled devices and solutions for smarter homes and cities.

D) IoT Clouds in Industries

Cloud IoT platforms offer a solid foundation to support the connection, management and analysis of data from-for example-IoT devices deployed in various industries. Figure 6. illustrate IoT cloud in industries require automation, connectivity, Big Data.

Figure 6. IoT cloud in industries

Following is a few of the well-known industry Cloud IoT Platforms:

1. AWS IoT Core
    - Highlights: AWS IoT Core Lets Devices Connect to the Cloud and Communicate with Other Devices. Communication protocol, it is possible use MQTT, HTTP and WebSocket's also comes with several important features in security such as authorization and authentication.
    - PC#: Industrial automation, smart cities, healthcare and transportation.
    - Integration - Fully integrates with other AWS services such as Lambda, Greengrass, Kinesis and S3.
2. Microsoft Azure IoT Hub
    - Capabilities: Secure, reliable messaging between IoT applications and devices with Azure IoT Hub One of its more notable features is that it supports bi-directional communication making monitoring and diagnostics easier.
    - Applications: Production, retail, energy and agricultural sector.
    - Supports with other Azure services' Machine Learning, Azure Stream Analytics and Blob Storage
3. Google Cloud IoT
    - This announcement includes the following features: device management and data ingestion, messaging, telemetry and log storage/dev MSPs (BigQuery). This platform supports MQTT and HTTP protocols.
    - Applications: Buildings Smart, Logistics, Utilities and Automotive
    - Integration: Integrates well with other Google Cloud services, such as BigQueryML (for performing predictive analysis in BigQuery), and GCP AI pipelines or serverless architectures via Pub Sub/Google Functions.
4. IBM Watson IoT Platform
    - Feature IBM Watson IoT Platform provides services for device management, data storage and analytics from real-time end-points. IBM Watson AI used for predictive maintenance and analytics
    - Applications: Manufacturing, Automotive, Electronics, Smart homes
    - Integration: Joins IBM Cloud with services like IBM Watson, Blockchain
5. Oracle IoT Cloud
    - Key Features: Oracle IoT Cloud provides a rich set of device management, stream processing and analytics features. It facilitator REST API and MQTT communication.
    - Applications: supply chain, fleet tracking, asset management and predictive maintenance
6. Bosch IoT Suite
    - Bosch IoT Suite include device management, data collection features. The platform is for edge and real-time data analytics.

- Applications: Automotive, agriculture, smart cities and industrial automation.
- Uses Bosch own devices and services; Integrates with third-party systems

7. Siemens MindSphere
   - Capabilities: MindSphere, an industrial IoT platform from Siemens for connecting machinery and evaluating production data. It delivers predictive maintenance and asset performance management capabilities.
   - Application Scenarios: Manufacturing, Energy Domain, Healthcare, Infrastructure
   - Integration: Can integrate with Siemens industrial automation products and third-party applications.

Key Points

- **Security:** All platforms offer strong security such as encryption, authentication and authorization to secure your IoT data.
- **Automatable:** They can scale automatically to handle increased loads, whether that means supporting higher numbers of connected devices or processing more information.
- **Centralized management plane:** farms help you simplify the operations and life cycle management of your IoT solutions
- **Integration** - Deep integration with cloud services, data analytics, AI tool to provide end-to-end comprehensive IoT solution

Because each one has its own strengths and is ideal for certain types of IoT applications, it becomes important to pick the right platform based on industry requirements and integration needs.

COMPARISON OF BEST IOT CLOUD PLATFORMS

Table 1, represents the comparison of best IoT Cloud Platforms

Table 1. Comparison of best IoT cloud platforms

IoT Cloud Platforms	Compatibility	Primary Service and Core Capabilities	Applications
NetApp	NFS, SMB/CIFS, iSCSI, FC, and NVMe	Unified Storage Management, Data Protection and Security, Cloud Integration, performance Optimization, Data Analytics and Insights	Healthcare, Financial Services, Big Data and Analytics
Medsphere	laboratory information systems (LIS), radiology information systems (RIS), HL7, FHIR, and DICOM	Electronic Health Record (EHR) Solutions	Hospitals and Health Systems
Pfizer	Therapeutic areas, including oncology, immunology, cardiology, endocrinology, and neurology	Pharmaceutical and Biopharmaceutical Development	Oncology, Vaccines, Cardiology, Neurology, Immunology and Inflammation
Philips Health Suite	HL7, FHIR, and DICOM	Digital Health Platform	Chronic Disease Management, Home Healthcare, Population Health Management
Microsoft Farm Beats	Microsoft Azure,	Data Aggregation and Analysis, IoT and Edge Computing, Remote Sensing and Monitoring	Crop Monitoring and Management, Soil Health and Irrigation Management, Pest and Disease Management, Climate and Weather Analysis
John Deere Operations Centre	ISOXML and AEF	Farm Management Platform	Equipment Management, Field Management, Operational Reporting
Climate Corporation's Field View by Bayer	ISOXML and AEF	Farm Management Platform	Equipment Management, Field Management, Operational Reporting
Agri Webb	Farm Management Platform	Livestock Management, Field Management	Livestock Tracking and Management, Farm Operations Monitoring
Trimble Ag Software	ISOXML	Precision Agriculture and Farm Management	Field Mapping and Planning, Yield Monitoring and Analysis

MARKET SIZE OF IoT CLOUD PLATFORMS

The global Internet of Things (IoT) Cloud Platform market is poised to experience a significant rise. In 2023 the market size was about USD $7.75 billion and expected to be around USD $8.49 billion in year 2024 Market Digits projects a CAGR of 10.09% reaching USD $29.72 billion by the end of FY2030.

Contents Some key factors driving this growth include growing demand for IoT devices across various industry verticals, the requirement of scalable and flexible cloud based platforms...ignite talks Market segmentation: by offering (platforms and services), Deployment types(hybrid, private, public cloud)by organization size(large enterprise s, SMEs)application areas(Industrial Automation, smart manufacturing) smart transportation connected healthcareThe Industrial IoT market is further segmented based on technologies such as form--factor lease/logistics Management, Agriculture(Aerospace & defence Health care Environment monitoring)/worldwide· Types of offerings are platforms and services.

Among the top market players are Amazon Web Services (AWS), Microsoft, Google, IBM, and Cisco. The combination of IoT, data analytics, and connectivity forms an ecosystem which is difficult to handle without the help of such solutions offered by these companies as they offer end-to-end services. Figure 7 shows the Market Size Value in USD billon for IoT Cloud Platforms.

Figure 7. IoT cloud platforms market size value (USD billion)

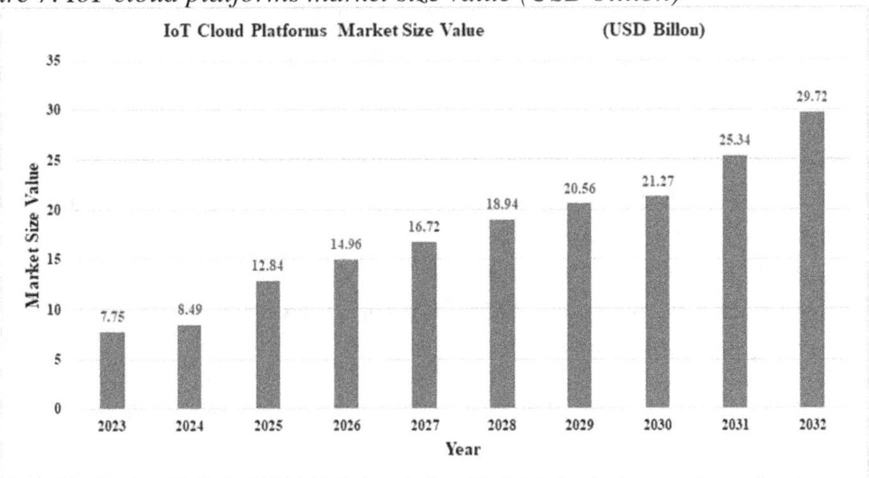

IoT CLOUD PLATFORMS: REGIONAL ANALYSIS

The IoT cloud platform is witnessing growth with various regions demonstrating their own trends that drive the adoption.

i) North America

Large number of adoption advanced technological and huge investment is considered to be the major driving factors in IoT Cloud Platform Market created massive opportunity for this market because USA is one of first country who have adopted the 5G network which solves low latency issue (246% efficiency), more secured, but with high monetize security across different region which ultimately boost his organization structure. The U.S. is by far the largest, but it been argued that Canada also plays a central role This growth is driven by the region's emphasis on smart cities, industrial IoT applications and powerful cloud infrastructure.

ii) Europe

Germany and UK collectively hold the most significant IoT cloud platform market share, whereas Europe is one of world's largest revenue generating region for this technology. The adoption of smart manufacturing, increasing preference for energy efficient solutions and growing penetration of smart city projects drive the market in this region. Further, increasing headcount in various European countries is driving the growth of IoT cloud solutions market.

iii) Asia Pacific

In the Asia Pacific, however, this growth is exceeding all other regions with an anticipated CAGR of 15.8%. The Chinese market is currently the largest, but India has become the fastest growing. The other major reason for the growth of this region is fast upsurge in smart manufacturing, implementation of 5G technology and boosting acceptance of smart city initiatives.

iv) South and Central America

The other major contributor pertaining to IoT cloud platform market in this region are Brazil and Argentina. This will help to increase agricultural productivity and IoT drive in all industries such as home, healthcare etc that enhances efficiency of work (operational) which leads towards economic developed areas.

v) Middle East and Africa

Countries in the Middle East and Africa (MEA) are playing catch-up with South Africa, Saudi Arabia and UAE expected to invest heavily in IoT technologies for smart cities projects amidst a wider focus on energy management. Governmental initiatives and the need for advanced analytics and data management solutions drive the Asia Pacific region to adopt IoT cloud platforms.

These regional findings demonstrate the worldwide IoT cloud platform market, as each region is leveraging these smart technologies at an immense pace to cater certain needs and challenges.

CONCLUSION

This article provides the detailed overview of all IoT Cloud platforms validating its pivotal stance in this exploding world of Internet of Things. The combination of cloud computing functionalities and IoT connectivity makes these platforms enable to provide a comprehensive answer for the storage, management, and interpretation of large quantities of data that came from every type available on an internet supporting device. They deliver critical services and infrastructure to enable the rapid development and secured deploying of IoT solutions in sectors.

These platforms help in resolving the lessening with other them ability, these are focused service area includes application development, device administration, system management, heterogeneity insipience and data and analytics tools. These capabilities allow firms to use IoT technology to address a variety of applications, from improved operational efficiency and security detection to data-driven decisions.

At the same time, we also point to a number of challenges that will have to be met by researchers and developers in very near future. This will involve addressing some of the core challenges related to interoperability across an ever-growing variety IoT devices and platforms, security concerns around sensitive data collection and usage models, as well pursuing scalability and performance that enables large scale deployment of their respective IoT solutions in rapid growth vertical markets.

Future research and development efforts should target the identified challenges to improve, even more, the quality of the IoT ecosystem fostering innovation and economic growth for enterprises and end-users.

REFERENCES

Agarwal, P., & Alam, M. (2018). IoT Cloud Platforms: An Application Development Perspective. 10.48550/arXiv.1810.12292.

Ansari, Ali, & Alam. (2023). Internet of things (IoT) fusion with cloud computing: current research and future direction. ..DOI: 10.19101/IJATEE.2021.876002

Babiuch, M., & Foltynek, P. (2021). Creating a Mobile Application with the ESP32 Azure IoT Development Board Using a Cloud Platform. 2021 22nd International Carpathian Control Conference (ICCC), 1-4.

Choudhury, T., Gupta, A., Pradhan, S., Kumar, P., & Rathore, Y. S. (2017). Privacy and security of cloud-based Internet of Things (IoT). In *2017 3rd International Conference on Computational Intelligence and Networks (CINE)* (pp. 40-45). IEEE. DOI: 10.1109/CINE.2017.28

Ellwein, C., Riedel, O., Meyer, O., & Schel, D. (2018). Rent'n'Produce: A secure cloud manufacturing platform for small and medium enterprises. In *2018 IEEE International Conference on Engineering, Technology and Innovation (ICE/ITMC)* (pp. 1-6). DOI: 10.1109/ICE.2018.8436332

Fox, Donnellan, & Doumen. (2019). The deployment of an IoT network infrastructure, as a localised regional service. .DOI: 10.1109/WF-IoT.2019.8767188

Gaikwad, V. S., & Prasad, D. G. S. (2018). A survey on user awareness of cloud security. *International Journal of Engineering & Technology, 7*(2.32), 131-135.

Gassara, M., Elleuchi, M., & Abid, M. (2021). LoRa cloud-based platform for Internet of Things applications. In *2021 IEEE International IoT,Electronics and Mechatronics Conference (IEMTRONICS)* (pp. 1-6). IEEE. DOI: 10.1109/IEMTRONICS52119.2021.9422531

Gavlas, A., Zwierzyna, J., & Koziorek, J. (2018). Possibilities of transfer process data from PLC to cloud platforms based on IoT. *IFAC-PapersOnLine*, 51(6), 156–161. DOI: 10.1016/j.ifacol.2018.07.146

Gudapati, S. P., & Gaikwad, V. (2021). Light-Weight Key Establishment Mechanism for Secure Communication Between IoT Devices and Cloud. In Satapathy, S., Bhateja, V., Janakiramaiah, B., & Chen, Y. W. (Eds.), *Intelligent System Design. Advances in Intelligent Systems and Computing* (Vol. 1171). Springer. DOI: 10.1007/978-981-15-5400-1_55

Gudapati, S. P., Gaikwad, V., & Ravindranath, K. (2023). A mathematical model for secure Cloud-IoT communication: Introducing the revolutionary lightweight key mechanism. *Journal of Discrete Mathematical Sciences & Cryptography*, 26(5), 1341–1354. DOI: 10.47974/JDMSC-1750

Han, H., Zhu, B., Zhan, L., Yu, T., Shen, G., & Chen, Y. (2021). ICool: One-stop service IoT cloud platform. In *2021 2nd International Conference on Artificial Intelligence and Computer Engineering (ICAICE)* (pp. 680-684). DOI: 10.1109/ICAICE54393.2021.00133

Kumar, S., Tiwari, P., & Zymbler, M. (2019). Internet of Things is a revolutionary approach for future technology enhancement: A review. *Journal of Big Data*, 6(1), 111. DOI: 10.1186/s40537-019-0268-2

Li, Z., Xie, Z., Liu, L., & Wu, Y. (2022). Design and Implementation of an Integrated City-Level IoT Platform Based on Edge Computing and Cloud Native. 2022 IEEE 6th Advanced Information Technology, *Electronic and Automation Control Conference (IAEAC)*, 463-467.

MarketDigits. (2024). *IoT Cloud Platform Market*. Retrieved from https://www.marketdigits.com/iot-cloud-platform-market

Moussa, K. H., & Xu, B. (2024). Revolutionizing healthcare: Seamless integration of cloud technology and IoT for health monitoring systems. In *2024 9th International Conference on Computer and Communication Systems (ICCCS)* (pp. 986-990). IEEE. DOI: 10.1109/ICCCS61882.2024.10603222

Muhammed, A. S., & Ucuz, D. (2020). Comparison of the IoT Platform Vendors, Microsoft Azure, Amazon Web Services, and Google Cloud, from Users' Perspectives. *2020 8th International Symposium on Digital Forensics and Security (ISDFS)*, 1-4.

Odukoya, O. (2024). The transformative impact of cloud computing on small and medium-sized enterprises (SMEs): A comprehensive analysis. In *2024 International Conference on Smart Applications, Communications and Networking (SmartNets)* (pp. 1-5). DOI: 10.1109/SmartNets61466.2024.10577703

Pierleoni, P., Concetti, R., Belli, A., & Palma, L. (2020). Amazon, Google, and Microsoft solutions for IoT: Architectures and a performance comparison. *IEEE Access : Practical Innovations, Open Solutions*, 8, 5455–5470. DOI: 10.1109/ACCESS.2019.2961511

Ravindranath, K., & Gaikwad, V. S. (2023). IoT device-to-cloud continuous authentication using lightweight key establishment mechanism. *Journal of Electrical Systems*, 19(2), 148–162.

Ray, P. P. (2016). A survey of IoT cloud platforms. *Future Computing and Informatics Journal*, 1(1), 4. https://digitalcommons.aaru.edu.jo/fcij/vol1/iss1/4

Sakai, T., Hata, K., Wada, T., & Naito, K. (2022). IoT platform using information flow to reduce load on cloud. In *2022 IEEE 46th Annual Computers, Software, and Applications Conference (COMPSAC)* (pp. 1211-1216). IEEE. DOI: 10.1109/COMPSAC54236.2022.00191

Sharma, G., Juneja, V., Khurana, S., & Sheoran, R. (2024). Bibliometric mapping of theme and trends of IoT and cloud in the field of education. In *Proceedings of the 2024 International Conference on Computational Intelligence and Computing Applications (ICCICA)* (pp. 142-147). IEEE. DOI: 10.1109/ICCICA60014.2024.10584891

Tulenkov, A., Parkhomenko, A., & Sokolyanskii, A. (2019). Evaluation and selection of IoT service for smart house system big data processing. In *2019 IEEE 14th International Conference on Computer Sciences and Information Technologies (CSIT)* (pp. 124-129). IEEE. DOI: 10.1109/STC-CSIT.2019.8929810

Vellela, S. S., & Reddy, V. L. (2023). A cloud-based smart IoT platform for personalized healthcare data gathering and monitoring system. In *2023 3rd Asian Conference on Innovation in Technology (ASIANCON)* (pp. 1-5). IEEE. DOI: 10.1109/ASIANCON58793.2023.10270407

Vishalika. (2021). Integration of cloud with IoT: Advantages and research challenges. In *2021 International Conference on Technological Advancements and Innovations (ICTAI)* (pp. 627-631). IEEE. DOI: 10.1109/ICTAI53825.2021.9673183

Zhao, S., & Chiang, W. (2023). Privacy-preserving, low-storage, and high-quality image processing in IoT and clouds. In *2023 International Conference on Intelligent Communication and Computer Engineering (ICICCE)* (pp. 9-13). DOI: 10.1109/ICICCE61720.2023.00008

Zuway, El. M. A., & Farkash, H. M. (2022). Internet of Things security: Requirements, attacks on SH-IoT platform. In *2022 IEEE 21st International Conference on Sciences and Techniques of Automatic Control and Computer Engineering (STA)* (pp. 742-747). IEEE. DOI: 10.1109/STA56120.2022.10019124

Chapter 11
Predictive Analytics Using Machine Learning for Enhanced Online Advertising

Snehal Rahul Rathi
https://orcid.org/0009-0004-7638-6429
Vishwakarma Institute of Information Technology, India

Narendra Jadhav
Vishwakarma Institute of Information Technology, India

Abhishek Raut
Vishwakarma Institute of Information Technology, India

Abhishek Navhal
Vishwakarma Institute of Information Technology, India

Manas Patil
Vishwakarma Institute of Information Technology, India

ABSTRACT

Forecasting analytics in online marketing serves as the foundation for enhanced user interaction, accurate targeting, and optimization of marketing tactics in a constantly evolving digital environment. By utilizing predictive analytics to customize campaigns, marketers can improve the efficiency of their strategies by targeting particular interests and demographics. This research examines the application of machine learning models in forecasting user ad clicks, incorporating variables

DOI: 10.4018/979-8-3693-6705-6.ch011

like age, internet usage, and daily site engagement time in the datasets. The effectiveness of decision tree and logistic regression models in predicting ad clicks through model building and data analysis is shown in the research. Utilizing actual predictive analytics in advertising strategies can be enhanced by incorporating user engagement signals and responses in real-world scenarios. The research highlights future directions and challenges. It also touches upon potential advancements in predictive analytics and online advertising techniques.

INTRODUCTION

In today's digital age, online advertising is a fundamental element of contemporary marketing plans, allowing companies to connect with their desired audience more effectively and accurately than ever before. While navigating the expansive internet, consumers see numerous ads vying for attention. Advertisers not only need to grab initial interest but also maintain engagement amidst the constant digital barrage, which is a challenge. In a highly competitive setting, accurately predicting and understanding user behavior is essential for optimizing advertising strategies and maximizing ROI.

In this context, predictive click analysis, a complex use of machine learning and data analytics, emerges as a strong tool (Kumar & Garg, 2018). Utilizing extensive amounts of data from user engagements, predictive models can predict the probability of a user clicking on a particular advertisement. This ability to forecast enables marketers to customize their advertising messages and targeting strategies accurately, providing personalized content that connects more efficiently with their desired viewers (Harrison, Tatar, & Sengers, 2007). Moreover, by using predictive click analysis, advertisers can optimize the allocation of their advertising budgets, concentrating on channels and demographics with the highest potential for engagement and conversions.

The main goal of this study is to utilize machine learning algorithms to explore predictive click analysis in online advertising. Our method includes creating and assessing predictive models to predict user engagement with ads. To accomplish this, we make use of an extensive dataset from a marketing company that includes a wide variety of demographic and behavioral characteristics. By thoroughly analyzing this dataset and assessing different machine learning model results, our goal is two-fold: to better understand user behavior patterns and preferences, and to evaluate the use of predictive click analysis as a strategic tool in digital marketing (Suparmaniam et al., 2023).

The study involves various important stages in its methodology. We start by conducting exploratory data analysis (EDA), an essential step that involves discovering hidden patterns, connections, and trends in the dataset (Adams, Lunt, & Cairns, 2008). Exploratory data analysis (EDA) enables us to acquire an initial comprehension of how the data is spread out, detect any unusual data points, and examine connections among factors like age, internet usage, daily time spent on a website, and the probability of ad clicks. This first investigation forms the base for the following data preprocessing stages, during which we tidy up, change, and get the dataset ready to meet the criteria for precise modeling.

Once the data has been preprocessed, our focus will shift to creating and assessing the model. We make use of two main machine-learning algorithms: logistic regression and decision trees. Logistic regression is an effective option for tasks that require categorizing data into two groups, such as predicting whether a user will click on an advertisement based on specific characteristics (Balseiro et al., 2011). Utilizing a logistic function to forecast the probability of a binary outcome is beneficial for scenarios involving a categorical dependent variable. Nonetheless, decision trees have the benefit of being adaptable and uncomplicated, which allows them to effectively depict complex decision-making processes and connections among variables (LaValley, 2008). Our objective is to assess various models using metrics such as accuracy, precision, recall, and the confusion matrix to identify the method with the most effective predictive capabilities in our specific scenario.

Furthermore, it is essential to integrate HCI principles in online advertising to impact user experiences and perceptions. HCI principles prioritize designing interfaces and interactions that prioritize the user's needs, are easy to use, and flow smoothly to enhance user engagement and reduce any potential obstacles in the user experience (Rogers, 2004). When engaging in predictive analytics for online advertising, it is crucial to thoroughly consider ethical issues like safeguarding user privacy and protecting data. Following ethical guidelines and regulatory frameworks is essential for safeguarding user rights and maintaining trust in digital advertising practices (Sherman & Deighton, 2001).

In the future, predictive analytics in online advertising will show great potential. Improvements in machine learning algorithms, data processing techniques, and user profiling methodologies will keep pushing advancements in ad targeting and personalization capabilities. New technologies like artificial intelligence (AI), augmented reality (AR), and voice assistants offer unique opportunities to develop engaging and interactive advertising experiences that deeply engage users (Lee, Cheang, & Moslehpour, 2022). Continual research and innovation will be essential in unlocking new opportunities and overcoming challenges in predictive analytics for online advertising as the digital environment continues to change.

To summarize, predictive click analysis is a key development in digital marketing that helps advertisers improve ad targeting, boost user engagement, and achieve more successful campaign results. By utilizing machine learning algorithms and thorough datasets, advertisers can obtain important information about user behavior and preferences, helping them improve their advertising strategies for better results and productivity. Continuous research and implementation of predictive analytics are crucial in guiding the future of online advertising toward personalized, ethical, and impactful practices as the field develops.

REVIEW OF LITERATURE

In recent times, a growing number of professionals and scholars have been showing a heightened interest in predicting clicks for online advertising. The main focus of predictive click analysis is to improve ad placements and increase user engagement by studying and predicting user behavior. A review of existing literature shows numerous studies examining user behavior, developing predictive models, and enhancing advertising strategies (Brajnik & Gabrielli, 2010). These studies offer a crucial understanding of the factors that impact user engagement and the effectiveness of predictive click analysis techniques.

In a substantial study, Agarwal and his team (2019) examined a vast dataset from an online advertising platform to explore the influence of contextual factors on ad click-through rates (CTR) (Agarwal et al., 2019). This study found that variables like ad placement, relevance, and demographics of users have a major impact on CTR, emphasizing the importance of contextual targeting in placing ads. Additionally, the scientists presented a new predictive model using machine learning methods that accurately predicted ad clicks better than traditional methods. This research emphasized how personalized ad placements could amplify user engagement by recognizing the connection between ad content and user attributes. This work highlights the importance of advertisers taking into account the placement context of ads, as it can greatly impact user engagement and the overall effectiveness of advertising efforts.

Chen and colleagues (2018) explored the influence of user intent on ad click prediction through the analysis of the semantic context in user searches and ad text using advanced natural language processing (NLP) tools. The researchers created a sophisticated predictive model that can capture detailed aspects of user behavior and intent by using semantic features from textual data. The findings highlighted the significance of personalized advertising strategies that are tailored to fit user preferences and search intent within a specific context. This research greatly improved our knowledge of how language signals can be used to anticipate user behavior, creating new possibilities for personalized advertising strategies. Utilizing NLP techniques enables a deeper comprehension of user intent, enabling the customization of ads to better connect with users on a personal level.

Liang et al. (2020) investigated the ethical concerns related to predictive click analysis in online advertising, highlighting worries regarding user privacy, data security, and algorithmic bias. Their study highlighted the importance of clear and responsible data handling procedures, along with strong regulatory systems to safeguard user rights and reduce possible risks. Liang and his team proposed ethical guidelines and design principles for advertisers and platform operators to maintain ethical standards in online advertising. This research emphasized the importance of considering ethical concerns when using user data and promoting strategies that prioritize both business goals and user privacy. It pointed out the possible adverse effects of predictive analytics, like strengthening current biases or breaching user privacy, and urged for more accountability and transparency in their utilization.

Advances in predictive modeling like reinforcement learning and deep learning have greatly improved predictive click analysis capabilities, building on previous discoveries. Zhang and colleagues (2021) showed that by leveraging large datasets and advanced architectures, deep neural networks can accurately forecast ad clicks, achieving high performance. Furthermore, the integration of reinforcement learning algorithms allowed for adaptive advertising tactics that could react in real time to user feedback and shifting market conditions. This study emphasized how advanced machine learning methods could transform predictive analytics in digital advertising. These models are perfectly matched for the constantly changing environment of online advertising due to their capability to learn and adjust continuously as user behaviors and preferences evolve quickly.

In their study on predictive click analysis, Gupta et al. (2017) delved deeper into the influence of machine learning and explored the benefits of ensemble learning methods for enhancing prediction accuracy. The ensemble method reduces the drawbacks of individual models by merging various machine learning models, leading to stronger predictions. Their research revealed that combining multiple models, like Random Forests and Gradient Boosting Machines, performed better than using just one model, showing the benefits of incorporating a variety of predictive algorithms to improve accuracy in predicting ad clicks. This method utilizes the advantages of different models to create a prediction system that is more thorough and dependable, capable of understanding the intricate nature of user behavior.

Additionally, Singh et al. (2019) concentrated on the significance of real-time bidding (RTB) platforms in digital advertising and the use of predictive analytics to enhance bid prices for adverts. They created a model that predicts the chances of ad clicks and utilizes this probability to guide bidding tactics. Their findings demonstrated notable enhancements in ad efficiency and ROI, showcasing the opportunity for predictive analytics to boost the effectiveness of RTB systems. This research offered useful information on incorporating predictive models into the ad purchasing process to improve strategic decision-making based on data. Utilizing predictive analytics in conjunction with RTB systems empowers advertisers to make better decisions on when and where to place bids for ad placements, ultimately maximizing their ROI through optimized advertising spend.

Research conducted by Huang and colleagues (2020) investigated combining user sentiment analysis with predictive click models to improve ad significance and interaction. Through examination of user-created material like reviews and social media posts, experts created predictive models that consider sentiment to tailor ad content and placement according to user emotions. The results showed that advertisements that matched with positive user feelings received greater interaction rates, highlighting the significance of sentiment analysis in improving ad targeting tactics. This strategy enables advertisers to connect with users' emotional reactions, customizing their ads to better connect and engage with their target audience.

In a different important study, Zhao and colleagues (2020) examined how temporal patterns in user behavior can be utilized to enhance predictions of ad clicks. They created predictive models that take into account the timing of user interactions, including the time of day and day of the week, to anticipate ad clicks. Their findings showed that adding temporal features greatly improves prediction accuracy, indicating that understanding user behavior patterns over time is essential for successful ad targeting. This study emphasizes the significance of factoring in the timing of user interactions in the development of predictive models, as it can offer valuable information on when users are most inclined to interact with ads.

While predictive analytics in online advertising advances, ethical concerns are still crucial. The possibility of algorithmic bias, where predictive models might unintentionally continue or worsen current biases, presents major difficulties. In her book "Algorithms of Oppression," Noble (2018) emphasized the risks of algorithmic bias, explaining how biased algorithms in online advertising can result in discriminatory practices. This highlights the importance of creating impartial predictive models that guarantee equal treatment for all types of users. Algorithmic bias can lead to specific groups being unfairly singled out or left out of advertisements, which can carry significant ethical and social consequences. Hence, it is essential to put in place actions to identify and reduce bias in predictive models.

Privacy concerns are also very important since predictive models frequently depend on a large amount of user data to create precise forecasts. The GDPR in the European Union highlights the significance of user consent and data protection in online activities, such as advertising. Adherence to these regulations is crucial to keep user confidence and prevent legal consequences. Future studies should concentrate on creating predictive models that protect privacy while still providing accurate predictions. Ensuring that individuals are informed and able to manage the usage of their data is essential for establishing trust and upholding ethical norms in online advertising.

In the future, incorporating advanced modeling methods like transfer learning and federated learning offers promising possibilities for predictive click analysis. Transfer learning enables models trained on a specific task to be adjusted for a related task, enhancing productivity and lessening the requirement for abundant labeled data. This can be especially handy in Internet marketing, as models developed on general user actions can be customized for specific advertising campaigns. Transfer learning allows advertisers to use pre-existing models and data to efficiently create new predictive models, cutting down on time and resources while enhancing accuracy.

On the flip side, federated learning allows for the creation of predictive models using data from separate sources, all while safeguarding data privacy. Federated learning guarantees the privacy of user data while still allowing for collective learning by training models on user devices and combining the outcomes. This method has the potential to completely change predictive click analysis by maintaining a balance between accuracy and privacy issues. Federated learning enables the creation of personalized and context-aware models by training them on individual user data without the need to share this data with central servers.

To sum up, the research on forecasting click behavior in internet advertising is broad and varied, demonstrating a cross-disciplinary method that integrates knowledge from computer science, data analysis, psychology, and marketing. Ongoing progress in machine learning and data analytics is expected to improve predictive models, boosting the efficiency of online advertising tactics. Nevertheless, ethical issues and privacy concerns should be prioritized to ensure the responsible and fair utilization of predictive analytics in the field of digital marketing. Balancing the advantages of predictive analytics with ethical data practices is crucial in ensuring online advertising remains effective and fair, and respects user privacy as the field evolves.

In general, the research on predictive click analysis in online advertising is a lively and multidisciplinary area, leveraging knowledge from computer science, data analytics, psychology, and marketing. Scholars are using a variety of research perspectives to improve our knowledge of user behavior, create new predictive models, and influence the direction of online advertising practices.

DATASET DESCRIPTION

The information used in this study includes information collected from online ads. This data set offers a complete perspective on user actions and traits during engagement with different advertisements, providing important information for predictive analysis. Here is a more detailed overview of the dataset's traits:

1. **Daily Time Spent on Site:** This factor measures the overall duration (in minutes) that a user stays on the website viewing advertisements. It shows user interaction rates and can suggest how interesting or captivating the website content is for the user.
2. **Age:** This characteristic tracks the age of the people interacting with the ads. Understanding user preferences and customizing ads for various demographic groups can greatly depend on age.
3. **Area Income:** This variable represents the average income of the geographic area where the user resides. It provides context about the user's economic environment, which can influence purchasing behavior and ad responsiveness.
4. **Daily Internet Usage:** This metric indicates the total amount of time (in minutes) a user spends on the Internet each day. High daily internet usage might correlate with higher ad engagement rates, as these users are more frequently online.
5. **Ad Topic Line:** This categorical variable describes the topic or theme of the advertisement. Different ad topics may appeal to different user segments, and analyzing these can help in understanding which themes generate the most engagement.
6. **City:** This variable captures the city where the user is located. Geographic information is crucial for regional targeting and understanding location-based trends in ad engagement.
7. **Male:** This binary variable indicates whether the user is male (1) or not (0). Gender can influence user preferences and behavior, and this data helps in segmenting the audience for more targeted advertising.
8. **Country:** This feature records the country of the user. It provides a broader geographical context and helps in analyzing international trends and differences in ad engagement.
9. **Timestamp:** The DateTime variable captures the precise moment and date at which the user engaged with the advertisement. Temporal analysis is crucial in identifying patterns related to the effectiveness of ads based on the time of day or day of the week.

10. **Clicked on Ad:** The binary variable shows if the user clicked on the ad (1) or not (0). It is the main result that predictive models try to predict, enabling the assessment of ad effectiveness.

This dataset contains 1000 cases, each depicting a distinct user engagement with promotional content. It consists of a well-organized blend of numerical, categorical, and datetime characteristics, ideal for both exploring data and making predictions. The variety of characteristics enables a comprehensive examination of user actions and advertisement effectiveness, laying a strong groundwork for building strong forecasting models. The information obtained from this data has the potential to greatly boost targeting tactics, enhance user interaction, and optimize advertising efforts.

METHODOLOGY

The procedure involves performing exploratory data analysis (EDA) to uncover patterns and insights, then conducting data preprocessing to tidy and get the dataset ready. EDA involves applying a range of statistical methods and visual tools to uncover the data's underlying patterns, pinpoint important variables, and spot any irregularities or extreme data points that could impact the model's accuracy (Shmueli & Koppius, 2011). This stage aids in the visualization of data distributions, connections, and patterns, laying a strong groundwork for the following stages.

After finishing EDA, the next step is data preprocessing, which includes key tasks like dealing with missing data, encoding categorical variables, scaling numerical features, and dividing the dataset into training and testing sets. This guarantees that the data is in optimal condition for the modeling process. Dealing with missing values may involve methods such as imputation or deleting incomplete entries while converting categorical variables into a numerical form that can be processed by machine learning algorithms known as encoding. Rescaling numerical properties normalizes the data, a crucial step for algorithms that are impacted by feature scale.

The following stage involves creating predictive models. This includes choosing suitable machine learning algorithms and teaching them with the provided dataset. In this research, logistic regression and decision trees are used because of their efficacy in binary classification tasks, like predicting if a user will click on an ad. The training phase consists of providing the models with training data to understand the connections and patterns between user attributes and their behavior of clicking on ads.

Post-training, the models are assessed by using the testing dataset to measure their effectiveness. Measures like accuracy, precision, recall, and the confusion matrix are employed to evaluate the predictive capability of models for ad clicks.

This stage is essential in guaranteeing that the models are accurate and can also adapt well to unfamiliar data.

Ultimately, the knowledge acquired from the models is utilized to enhance digital advertising tactics. Advertisers can enhance the effectiveness of their campaigns by identifying the user characteristics that best signal ad clicks. This structured approach ensures the creation of effective predictive models that can greatly improve digital advertising strategies, resulting in more precise ads, higher user interaction, and improved marketing campaigns.

1. Exploratory Data Analysis

Exploratory data analysis (EDA) aims to discover significant patterns and insights in data that can guide advertising strategies. This step requires a thorough analysis of the dataset to discover important patterns, connections, and outliers that could impact the predictive models' performance and marketing campaigns' effectiveness. EDA is essential for preparing data for analysis and modeling, establishing a solid groundwork for further data processing tasks.

Starting with analyzing the distribution of age, a histogram is created with Kernel density estimation (Fig 1). This visualization shows a bell curve, displaying a typical distribution of age among users (Mishra & Silakari, 2012). The graph indicates that there is a varied range of ages within the user base, with a fairly equal spread among various age categories. This indicates that the advertising platform attracts a diverse range of ages, emphasizing the importance for advertisers to take into account preferences and behaviors specific to different age groups in their campaigns.

Figure 1. Kernel density estimation for the 'Age' variable

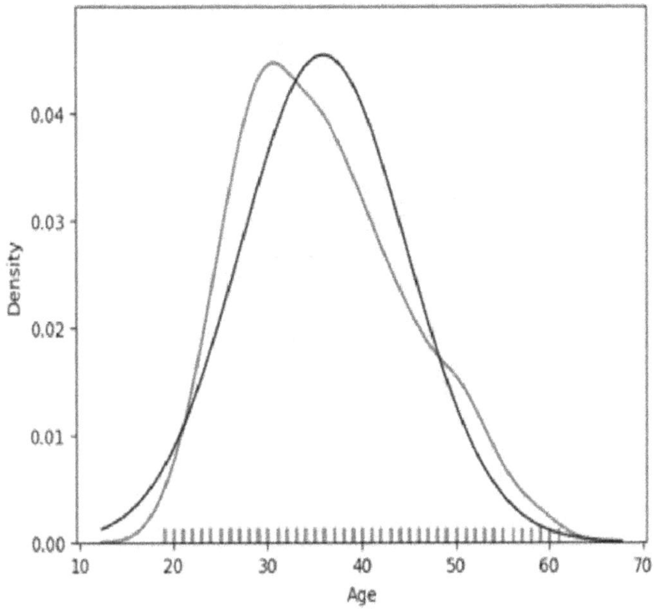

To investigate the connection between user age and engagement in more depth, a two-dimensional density plot is generated (Fig 2) to analyze the relationship between age and website usage duration. This graph illustrates the distribution of users by age and their site usage duration. The visualization indicates that younger users tend to spend more time on the site in comparison to older visitors. This finding indicates that the website's offerings or information could be more attractive to younger viewers, giving advertisers valuable information for better targeting these age groups.

Figure 2. Age and the Daily Site Visit Duration Relationship

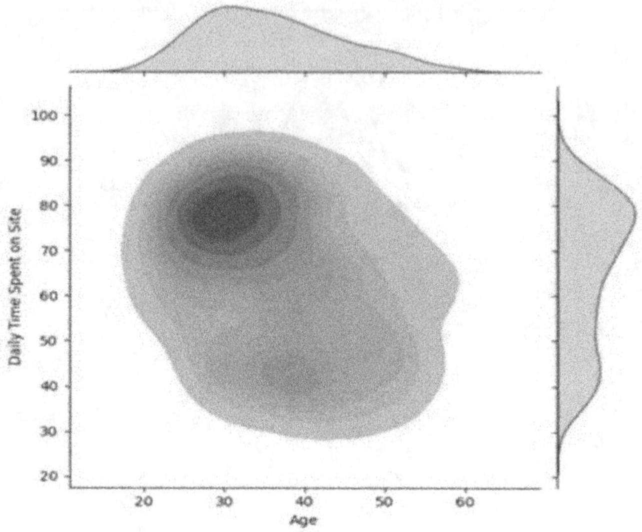

Figure 3. Connection between Daily Internet Use and Daily Site Visit Duration

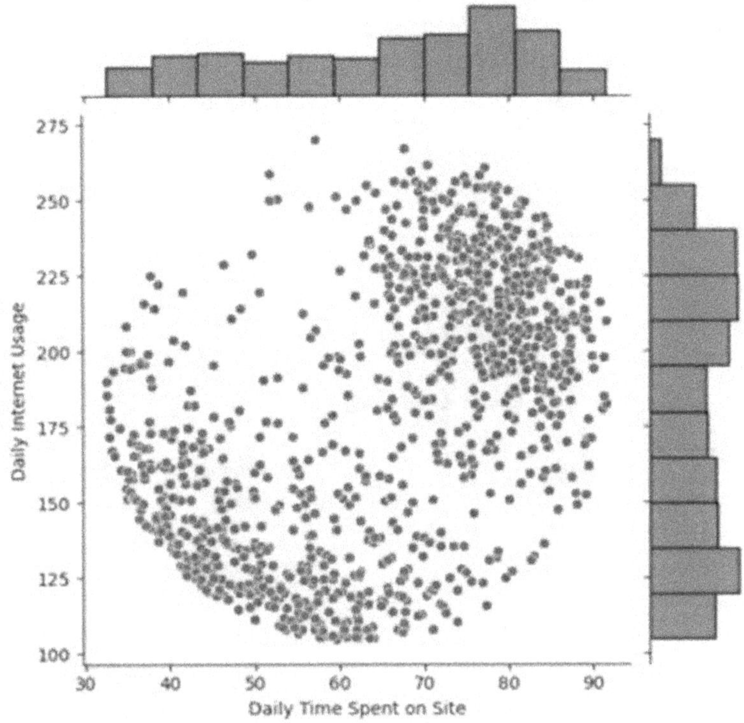

Moreover, a scatter matrix plot is used to examine the relationships among key variables such as age, area income, daily internet usage, and daily website time (Fig 4). This diagram offers a thorough perspective on the interconnectedness of these variables. For example, it enables us to recognize potential connections between daily internet use and area income, or between age and daily website usage time. By analyzing these connections, we can develop a more profound comprehension of the elements that impact user actions and interactions.

Figure 4. Multivariate Scatter Matrix: Site Engagement, Age, Income, and Internet Usage

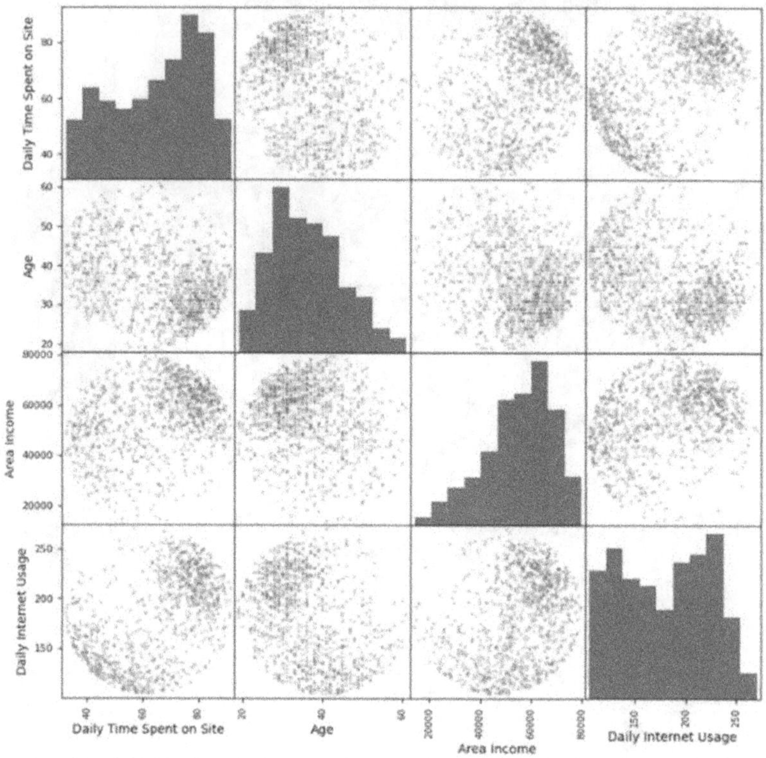

The scatter matrix plot is also useful for detecting possible multicollinearity among variables, which is crucial for the precision and dependability of predictive models. For instance, when two variables show a strong correlation, it could imply duplication, proposing that one of them could be removed from the model to streamline it without compromising its predictiveness.

Another crucial aspect of EDA is the investigation of categorical variables. For example, studying how users are spread out among various cities and countries can offer valuable information about geographic patterns in user involvement. This data is extremely valuable for targeting certain regions, enabling advertisers to customize their campaigns to areas that have higher engagement rates.

Through analyzing the timestamp data, we can conduct a temporal analysis to recognize trends linked to the time of day or day of the week when users are most engaged on the platform. This can assist in planning advertisements to optimize visibility and interaction. For instance, advertisers can strategically schedule their ads during peak user activity in the evenings to reach a wider audience, based on data analysis.

Typically, these visual depictions from the first data analysis offer valuable insights into the behaviors and attributes of website users. By understanding these patterns, marketers can adapt their marketing strategies to better target specific audience segments and improve their campaigns for the best outcomes. The knowledge obtained through exploratory data analysis allows advertisers to create more focused and customized advertising plans, resulting in increased user interaction and better conversion rates. The phase of Exploratory Data Analysis (EDA) not only aids in gaining insights into the existing user demographics but also lays the groundwork for developing reliable predictive models capable of accurately predicting user behavior and advertisement clicks.

2. Data Preprocessing

Data preprocessing is a crucial step in getting the dataset ready for machine learning analysis, making sure it is suitable for precise predictive modeling (Liu-Thompkins, 2019). This phase includes a sequence of actions planned to cleanse, modify, and organize the data in a way that machine learning algorithms can utilize it efficiently. If the dataset is not properly preprocessed, it could contain inconsistencies, irrelevant features, or other problems that may harm the model's performance.

In our analysis of the advertising dataset, we initially faced difficulties presented by categorical variables. Entries in columns like 'Ad Topic Line', 'City', and 'Country' show a wide variety of different values. For instance, the 'Ad Topic Line' column has distinct entries for each ad, complicating the task of identifying patterns that can be applied to various advertisements. Likewise, 969 out of 1000 entries in the 'City' column have distinct values, whereas the 'Country' column contains a variety of 237 unique values. These variables, having high cardinality, may add noise and complexity to the predictive modeling process, impeding the algorithm's effective learning.

To address these challenges, we opt to exclude these columns from further consideration. Removing high-cardinality categorical variables simplifies the dataset and reduces the dimensionality, making the modeling process more manageable and efficient. Additionally, despite the extensive range of unique values in the 'Country' column, no single category dominates the dataset. This lack of a dominant category means that the 'Country' variable provides little predictive power, as the distribution is too dispersed to offer meaningful insights for the model.

By eliminating these high-cardinality columns, we streamline our analysis and focus on variables that are more likely to contribute to accurate predictions. This step is crucial in refining our dataset, ensuring that it is primed for robust and accurate machine-learning analysis. Beyond the removal of certain columns, data preprocessing also involves transforming the remaining data to enhance its quality and relevance. For instance, we convert the 'Timestamp' column into datetime format and extract additional features such as month, day, and hour. These temporal features can capture time-based patterns in user behavior, potentially improving the model's predictive capabilities. Moreover, we address missing values, if any, to prevent incomplete data from skewing the results. In our dataset, all variables are complete with no missing values, which is a positive starting point for our analysis. However, in cases where datasets have missing entries, techniques such as imputation or removal of rows/columns are employed. Lastly, we adjust the numerical characteristics so they match each other in scale. This stage is especially crucial for algorithms that depend on distance metrics, like k-nearest neighbors or support vector machines. Feature scaling contributes to accelerating the convergence of gradient descent and enhancing the model's effectiveness.

In general, the data preprocessing step is crucial for improving our dataset, making sure it is tidy, pertinent, and organized in a manner that boosts the efficiency of machine learning algorithms. By effectively tackling issues with categorical variables, missing data, and scaling features, we establish a strong base for future modeling, leading to reliable and precise predictive analysis in online advertising.

3. Train and Test Data Segmentation

Splitting the dataset into separate groups for training and testing is an important part of preparing for machine learning modeling. This method, commonly known as train-test split, is crucial for assessing how well our predictive models perform and how well they can apply to new data (Nichols, 2013). Through the systematic segregation of data, we guarantee that our models undergo thorough training and are also evaluated on unseen data to assess their performance and reliability in real-life situations.

To accomplish this, we make use of the 'train_test_split' function provided by the scikit-learn library. This effective tool enables us to allocate 33% of the complete dataset to the test set randomly, with the remaining 67% kept for training. This random distribution is important as it ensures that both subsets remain representative, avoiding any biases that could result from a non-random division. This bias has the potential to distort the evaluation outcomes, resulting in an overestimation or underestimation of the model's effectiveness.

The 'train_test_split' function also enables us to specify the variable roles within the dataset. In our case, 'Clicked on Ad' is designated as the target variable (y), representing the prediction goal. This variable is isolated from the input features (X), which comprise all the other variables in the dataset. By doing so, we delineate the inputs that our machine learning models will use to make predictions and the outputs that will be predicted.

This methodical segmentation serves multiple purposes. Firstly, it ensures that our models are trained on a sufficient amount of data, allowing them to learn underlying patterns and relationships effectively. A well-sized training set is crucial for the model to develop a comprehensive understanding of the data, thereby enhancing its predictive accuracy. Secondly, the test set, which remains unseen during the training phase, provides a reliable means to evaluate the model's performance. By assessing the model on this separate subset, we can measure how well it generalizes to new, unseen data, which is indicative of its real-world applicability.

Moreover, the 33%-67% ratio for test and training sets is widely used as it provides a good balance between training and evaluation. This proportion guarantees that the training data is adequately big for the model to effectively learn and that the test data is sufficiently large for a meaningful evaluation of the model's performance. Nevertheless, this ratio may be modified to fit various situations depending on the analysis's particular needs. The 'train_test_split' function not only guarantees a fair division but also enables stratified sampling. This function is especially beneficial for handling datasets that are skewed, with some classes potentially being less represented. Stratified sampling guarantees that the distribution of categories in the training and test sets reflects that of the initial dataset, thus preserving the representativeness of the subsets.

To sum up, splitting the dataset into training and testing subsets is a crucial aspect of machine learning modeling. By utilizing the 'train_test_split' function offered by scikit-learn, we attain a well-balanced and accurate division that helps in training effectively and evaluating the performance of our predictive models reliably. This methodical strategy guarantees that our models are adequately equipped to apply to fresh data, thereby improving their practicality and strength in real-life situations.

4. Model Development and Fitting Procedures

We analyze Decision Trees and Logistic Regression, two vital machine learning techniques, for anticipating user ad clicks. Logistic regression is a strong tool for predictive analysis, especially useful for binary classification tasks such as predicting if a person will click on an advertisement (Sherman & Deighton, 2001). This method employs a logistic function to predict the likelihood of a binary result using various input variables like user demographics, browsing habits, and add features. Logistic regression aids in predicting the probability of a user interacting with an advertisement by analyzing the connection between different variables, offering useful information for focused marketing plans.

Additionally, we use the Decision Tree method, which is a versatile technique often used for classifying and predicting outcomes. Decision trees are commonly chosen for different data analysis situations due to being easy to understand and interpret (LaValley, 2008). They function by dividing the dataset into smaller parts repeatedly according to a specific input feature, constructing a decision tree model. This approach both streamlines decision-making and offers a visual representation of the factors that impact the result. Decision trees are valuable for real-time scenarios that demand fast and precise predictions due to their straightforwardness and computational speed.

To apply the Logistic Regression model, we start by bringing in the required functions from the sklearn.linear_model library, such as LogisticRegression for constructing the model and accuracy_score for assessing model performance. Next, we start the model and teach it using the training data. This includes adjusting the model to match the data, enabling it to understand the connections between the input characteristics and the desired outcome (Balseiro et al., 2011). After being trained, the model can forecast the likelihood of a user clicking on an ad, a critical factor in enhancing ad positioning and increasing user interaction.

Likewise, in the case of the Decision Tree model, we bring in the necessary functions from the sklearn, tree library and proceed with a comparable method of initializing and training the model. The process of training includes forming a tree structure in which every node signifies a choice determined by the input feature's value (Speelman, 2014). The data is iteratively divided by the model until it reaches the leaf nodes, which indicates the forecasted results. This organization of levels enables the decision tree to grasp intricate relationships between characteristics, which enhances its effectiveness in predictive analytics.

Both models are essential in our predictive analysis process, allowing us to make informed decisions based on the dataset available. By utilizing these models, we can pinpoint important factors that affect user behavior and adjust advertising strategies accordingly. This method improves the precision of our forecasts and offers practical advice for enhancing marketing efficiency.

In essence, the research consists of thoroughly analyzing data, careful dataset preparation, and developing predictive models with logistic regression and decision tree algorithms. Our objective in following these steps is to increase our comprehension of the dataset, guarantee its readiness for analysis, and build strong models for forecasting ad clicks. This methodical process makes it easier to uncover useful information from the data, leading to more efficient and focused advertising efforts.

Blending logistic regression with decision trees provides a well-rounded approach to predictive modeling by incorporating the probability-based feature of logistic regression and the intuitive decision process of decision trees. As we progress in our examination, these models will be key instruments in our efforts to improve online advertising strategies and increase user interaction.

RESULTS AND DISCUSSION

The logistic regression model achieved a precision rate of about 90.61%. According to the confusion matrix for the model, out of 331 test samples, 299 were classified correctly and 31 were classified incorrectly (Fig 5). Overall, there were 158 samples accurately identified as not clicking on the ad (true negatives), 141 samples accurately identified as clicking on the ad (true positives), 27 samples incorrectly identified as not clicking on the ad (false negatives), and 4 samples incorrectly identified as clicking on the ad (false positives).

Figure 5. Confusion Matrix – Logistic Regression Model

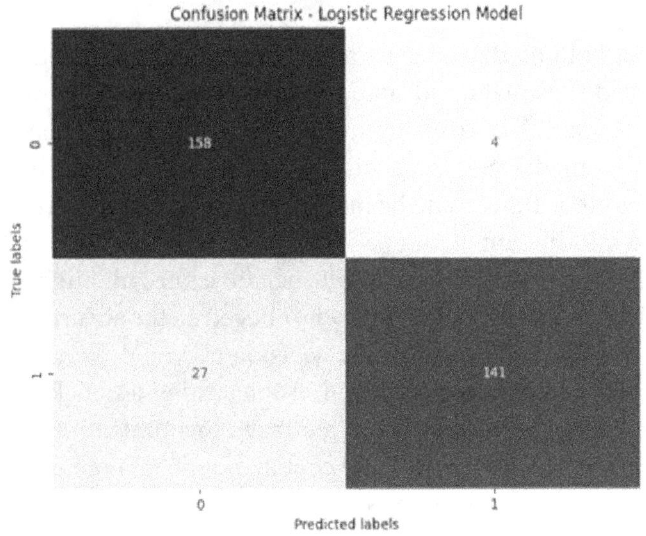

The decision tree model, on the other hand, has a greater accuracy of roughly 93.64%. Its confusion matrix reveals that out of the same 331 test samples, 310 were correctly classified, and only 21 were misclassified (Fig 6). This model correctly predicted 153 samples as not clicking on the ad and 156 samples as clicking on the ad, while incorrectly classifying 12 samples as not clicking on the ad and 9 samples as clicking on the ad.

Figure 6. Confusion Matrix – Decision Tree Model

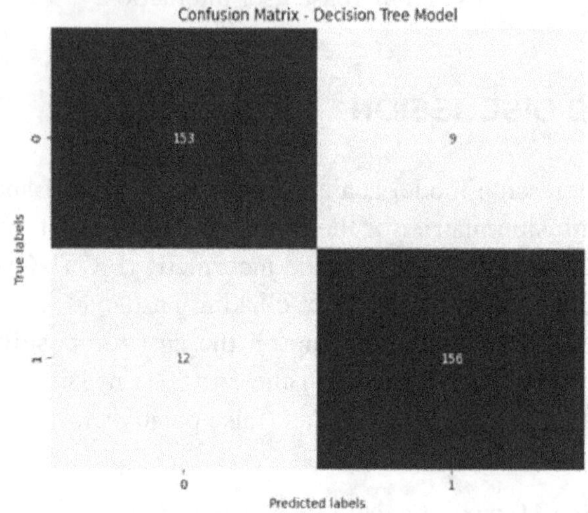

The ability of both models to accurately distinguish people who clicked on the advertisement and those who did not is demonstrated by their high true positive and true negative rates. The decision tree model has 3% higher accuracy than the logistic regression model. So, the decision tree model performs better, indicating that decision tree algorithms could be more useful in predicting ad clicks depending on the provided information.

Both models' high true positive and true negative rates highlight their capability to accurately differentiate between users who clicked on the advertisement and those who did not. The excellent results of the decision tree model suggest that decision tree algorithms could be more successful in forecasting ad clicks using the given data. This is probably because decision trees have a natural ability to manage intricate relationships between variables and capture nonlinear connections in the data, which logistic regression may not model as well.

These results highlight the effectiveness of utilizing machine learning methods to evaluate user actions and interests for predicting ad click rates. Advertisers can improve engagement and conversion rates by targeting their ads more effectively through factors like age, daily internet usage, area income, and time spent on the site. For example, recognizing that younger users tend to spend a longer amount of time on particular websites could assist in creating advertisements that target this age group, ultimately boosting the chances of receiving ad clicks. Additionally, utilizing these predictive models enables advertisers to maximize their advertising budget by targeting the most potential segments of their audience. This focused strategy doesn't just enhance ad campaign efficiency but also improves user experience through timely and relevant ads.

To enhance prediction accuracy and optimize ad placement strategies even more, upcoming studies should investigate advanced machine learning algorithms and feature engineering methods. More advanced methods like ensemble learning, which merges the capabilities of various models, and deep learning, which can detect even more intricate patterns in data, may lead to improved prediction accuracies (Song & Ying, 2015). Moreover, adding more detailed user behavior data and contextual information could offer a better understanding of the factors influencing ad clicks. Furthermore, the continuous advancement of user privacy laws requires the creation of predictive models that are both efficient and by privacy regulations. Approaches like federated learning, which allows training models using scattered data sources while maintaining user privacy intact, offer a hopeful path for upcoming research.

To sum up, the research emphasizes the considerable capabilities of machine learning algorithms, especially decision trees, in forecasting user ad clicks. The knowledge obtained from these models can result in more successful and productive advertising tactics, ultimately resulting in increased user interaction and conversion rates. As predictive analytics evolves, it has the potential to revolutionize online advertising by making it more data-focused, personalized, and user-oriented.

CONCLUSION

Predictive analytics, when utilized in online advertising, can improve targeting of ads, increase user interaction, and optimize marketing approaches. Advertisers can utilize machine learning algorithms to examine user actions and choices, thereby providing tailored and individualized ad encounters for their specific audience. Predictive models help advertisers maximize their advertising budget and enhance campaign effectiveness by targeting individuals who are most likely to interact with their ads.

Real-World Uses

1. Personalized Advertising: Machine learning algorithms can increase engagement and conversion rates by providing custom ads that reflect user behavior and preferences.

2. Behavioral Targeting: Advertisers can use past user interactions to target demographics or user segments with customized ads, improving the efficiency of ad campaigns.
3. Ad Placement Optimization: HCI principles dictate how ads are strategically placed within digital interfaces to be seamlessly integrated into the user experience without causing interruption.
4. User Experience Enhancement: Improving user experience involves minimizing disruptive ads, encouraging relevant content, and giving priority to user privacy and consent through HCI-driven approaches.

A wide range of practical uses for predictive analytics in online advertising have significant effects. Personalized advertising is a prominent use case, involving machine learning algorithms studying user habits and tastes to show tailored advertisements matching personal interests. This customization not only boosts interaction and sales percentages but also nurtures a deeper bond between the user and the brand. For example, a person who often looks at fitness-related content might see advertisements for exercise equipment or dietary supplements, increasing the chances of catching their attention and encouraging a purchase.

Another important use of behavioral targeting involves advertisers leveraging previous user engagement data to tailor advertisements to specific demographics or user groups. Understanding the browsing and purchasing habits of various user segments allows advertisers to develop more tailored and successful advertising campaigns. This method enhances ad campaign efficacy by making sure that ads are presented to individuals most likely to have an interest in the promoted products or services. For instance, a consumer who has shown interest in luxury items could receive advertisements for expensive clothing or exclusive travel opportunities.

Optimizing ad placement is essential, following Human-Computer Interaction (HCI) principles. These guidelines govern the strategic placement of ads in digital interfaces to smoothly blend into the user experience without causing any disruptions. Successful placement of advertisements guarantees that they are easily noticed but not disruptive, improving the user's overall experience. For instance, inserting advertisements during natural breaks or pauses in content can attract user interest without interrupting their browsing experience. Improving user experience is another important advantage of using predictive analytics in online advertising. This includes reducing annoying advertisements, advocating for appropriate material, and giving importance to user privacy and consent with HCI-centric methods. By honoring user preferences and offering a smooth ad experience, advertisers can establish trust and loyalty with their viewers. For example, giving users the ability to manage their ad preferences and guaranteeing clear data usage policies can result in increased user satisfaction and engagement.

The potential for predictive analytics in online advertising is huge as we move ahead. Progress in machine learning algorithms, data processing techniques, and user profiling methods will enhance ad targeting and personalization capabilities. Additionally, the inclusion of new technologies like AI, AR, and voice assistants will create fresh opportunities for imaginative and engaging advertising encounters (Lee, Cheang, & Moslehpour, 2022).

In conclusion, predictive analytics is now a fundamental aspect of contemporary digital marketing, allowing advertisers to provide more targeted and effective ads to their viewers. With the continuous advancement of technology, the opportunities to improve ad targeting, user engagement, and campaign effectiveness in online advertising are limitless, ensuring an innovative and dynamic future.

REFERENCES

Adams, A., Lunt, P., & Cairns, P. (2008). A qualitative approach to HCI research.

Agarwal, N., Chandrashekar, D., Rajaraman, A., & Venkataraman, V. (2019). Contextual advertising: Analyzing and predicting ad performance in contextual advertising. In *Proceedings of the 25th ACM SIGKDD International Conference on Knowledge Discovery & Data Mining* (pp. 1868-1876).

Balseiro, S., Feldman, J., Mirrokni, V., & Muthukrishnan, S. (2011, June). Yield optimization of display advertising with ad exchange. In *Proceedings of the 12th ACM conference on Electronic commerce* (pp. 27-28). DOI: 10.1145/1993574.1993580

Brajnik, G., & Gabrielli, S. (2010). A review of online advertising effects on the user experience. *International Journal of Human-Computer Interaction*, 26(10), 971–997. DOI: 10.1080/10447318.2010.502100

Chen, Y., Liu, Z., Li, Y., Li, H., Liu, X., & Zhang, Z. (2018). Click-through rate prediction for sponsored search based on user intent understanding. In *Proceedings of the 27th ACM International Conference on Information and Knowledge Management* (pp. 447-456).

Gupta, A., Shinde, V., Kumar, V., & Kale, A. (2017). Ensemble methods for click-through rate prediction in online advertising. *Journal of Marketing Analytics*, 5(2), 65–77.

Harrison, S., Tatar, D., & Sengers, P. (2007, April). The three paradigms of HCI. In Alt. Chi. Session at the SIGCHI Conference on Human Factors in Computing Systems (pp. 1-18).

Huang, Z., Tan, C., & Xiao, Y. (2020). Sentiment-aware click-through rate prediction in online advertising. *IEEE Transactions on Knowledge and Data Engineering*, 32(9), 1757–1769.

Kumar, V., & Garg, M. L. (2018). Predictive analytics: A review of trends and techniques. *International Journal of Computer Applications*, 182(1), 31–37. DOI: 10.5120/ijca2018917434

LaValley, M. P. (2008). Logistic regression. *Circulation*, 117(18), 2395–2399. DOI: 10.1161/CIRCULATIONAHA.106.682658 PMID: 18458181

Lee, C. S., Cheang, P. Y. S., & Moslehpour, M. (2022). Predictive analytics in business analytics: Decision tree. *Advances in Decision Sciences*, 26(1), 1–29. DOI: 10.47654/v26y2022i1p1-29

Liang, L., Hong, J. I., Toyama, K., & Ackerman, M. S. (2020). Towards accountable predictive click analytics: Examining the causes of algorithmic errors in user behavior prediction. In *Proceedings of the 2020 CHI Conference on Human Factors in Computing Systems* (pp. 1-14).

Liu-Thompkins, Y. (2019). A decade of online advertising research: What we learned and what we need to know. *Journal of Advertising*, 48(1), 1–13. DOI: 10.1080/00913367.2018.1556138

Mishra, N., & Silakari, S. (2012). Predictive analytics: A survey, trends, applications, opportunities & challenges. *International Journal of Computer Science and Information Technologies*, 3(3), 4434–4438.

Nichols, W. (2013). Advertising Analytics 2.0. *Harvard Business Review*, 91(3), 60–68.

Noble, S. U. (2018). *Algorithms of Oppression: How Search Engines Reinforce Racism*. NYU Press. DOI: 10.18574/nyu/9781479833641.001.0001

Rogers, Y. (2004). New theoretical approaches for HCI. *Annual Review of Information Science & Technology*, 38(1), 87–143. DOI: 10.1002/aris.1440380103

Sherman, L., & Deighton, J. (2001). Banner advertising: Measuring effectiveness and optimizing placement. *Journal of Interactive Marketing*, 15(2), 60–64. DOI: 10.1002/dir.1011

Shmueli, G., & Koppius, O. R. (2011). Predictive analytics in information systems research. *Management Information Systems Quarterly*, 35(3), 553–572. DOI: 10.2307/23042796

Singh, R., Sharma, P., & Dey, S. (2019). Real-time bidding and predictive analytics: Optimizing bid prices for online ad placements. *Journal of Digital Marketing*, 8(4), 101–118.

Song, Y. Y., & Ying, L. U. (2015). Decision tree methods: Applications for classification and prediction. *Shanghai Jingshen Yixue*, 27(2), 130. PMID: 26120265

Speelman, D. (2014). Logistic regression. Corpus methods for semantics: Quantitative studies in polysemy and synonymy, 43, 487-533.

Suparmaniam, N., Kamaruzzaman, Z. A., Kie, C. J., Mohtar, S. S., Alias, M. I. S., & Ja'afar, M. J. M. (2023). Does Consumer Behaviour Matters? Online Advertising Evaluation via Predictive Analytics. *Global Business and Management Research*, 15.

Zhang, Y., Zhang, H., Ren, X., Yu, Y., Li, Q., & Tang, J. (2021). Deep learning for click-through rate prediction in sponsored search: A comprehensive review. *ACM Transactions on Intelligent Systems and Technology*, 12(1), 1–36.

Zhao, L., Zhang, J., & Li, B. (2020). Time-aware predictive modeling for click-through rate in online advertising. *Information Sciences*, 516, 164–180.

Chapter 12
YoZu:
A Curiosity Companion for Students

Renu Kachhoria
Vishwakarma Institute of Information Technology, India

Prajwal Waykos
Vishwakarma Institute of Information Technology, India

Sathya Krishna Sharma
Tilburg University, The Netherlands

ABSTRACT

In the digital age, students struggle with navigating overwhelming online information. This chapter introduces YoZu, a student-focused chatbot. Powered by large language models, YoZu offers clear and engaging responses, making learning accessible for young minds. Its unique feature filters sensitive content, ensuring a safe learning environment. Additionally, YoZu provides dynamic image and video recommendations, enhancing comprehension. This research illuminates YoZu's transformative potential, simplifying complex information and revolutionizing students' interaction with online content.

I. INTRODUCTION

In today's digital age, the vast expanse of online information poses a significant challenge for students. Navigating this sea of data can be overwhelming due to the sheer volume and complexity of content available. Often, the information is either too dense, irrelevant, or contains sensitive material unsuitable for young learners.

DOI: 10.4018/979-8-3693-6705-6.ch012

These factors collectively impede students' ability to effectively comprehend and utilize online resources, thereby hindering their learning experience.

Recognizing this pressing need, this paper introduces a groundbreaking solution: YoZu, a specialized conversational chatbot meticulously crafted for students. YoZu is designed to address the challenges posed by the increasingly complex and vast online content landscape. By leveraging the power of Large Language Models (LLMs), YoZu provides students with clear, concise, and engaging responses, tailored to their specific educational needs.

YoZu stands out for its innovative approach to facilitating meaningful interactions, particularly for younger students, including those as young as 10 years old. Its user-friendly interface and intuitive design ensure that students can easily ask questions and receive accurate, understandable answers. This ability to simplify complex information into digestible chunks makes YoZu an invaluable tool in the digital learning environment.

Moreover, YoZu is equipped with advanced filtering mechanisms to ensure that the content delivered is age-appropriate and free from delicate or inappropriate material. This feature is crucial in maintaining a safe and conducive learning environment, allowing students to explore and learn without the risk of encountering harmful content.

In addition to its educational benefits, YoZu fosters a more interactive and engaging learning experience. By simulating a conversational partner, YoZu encourages students to actively participate in their learning process, ask more questions, and seek deeper understanding. This interactive dynamic not only enhances comprehension but also stimulates curiosity and critical thinking skills.

Furthermore, YoZu's adaptability and responsiveness are key to its effectiveness. The chatbot continuously learns and evolves, improving its responses based on student interactions and feedback. This ongoing refinement ensures that YoZu remains relevant and effective in meeting the ever-changing needs of students.

In conclusion, YoZu represents a significant advancement in educational technology, addressing the challenges posed by the digital age's overwhelming information landscape. By providing clear, relevant, and safe content through a user-friendly interface, YoZu transforms how young minds engage with online resources, making learning more accessible, enjoyable, and effective.

Incorporating cutting-edge technology, YoZu integrates a robust two-layer security feature that meticulously filters out sensitive content, ensuring a safe and secure learning environment for students. This pivotal aspect not only fosters a sense of trust but also emphasizes the commitment to creating a safeguarded digital space where educational exploration can thrive unhindered.

Furthermore, YoZu's innovative approach extends beyond mere textual responses. By seamlessly integrating dynamic image and video recommendations tailored to individual user queries, YoZu transcends the boundaries of conventional chatbots. This feature enriches the learning experience by providing visual context, which is particularly beneficial for young learners who often grasp concepts more effectively through visual aids. These multimedia resources help to break down complex topics into more digestible and engaging segments, thereby enhancing comprehension and retention. The ability to access relevant images and videos in response to specific queries makes learning not only accessible but also enjoyable, sparking curiosity and interest in students.

The integration of multimedia content also caters to different learning styles. For visual learners, the inclusion of images and videos can be a game-changer, offering alternative ways to understand and internalize information that might be challenging to grasp through text alone. For example, a student studying the water cycle can benefit from a video animation showing the process in action, complemented by images illustrating each stage, thus reinforcing the textual explanation provided by YoZu. This multimodal approach ensures that students receive a well-rounded understanding of the subject matter, catering to diverse learning preferences and needs.

This research paper delves into the core of YoZu's functionality and its transformative potential. It explores the sophisticated algorithms and machine learning techniques that power YoZu, enabling it to deliver personalized and contextually relevant multimedia content alongside textual answers. By simplifying complex information, YoZu emerges as an indispensable tool, promising to revolutionize how students navigate the intricacies of online content. The chapter highlights the chatbot's ability to analyze user queries, understand their educational context, and provide tailored responses that include relevant images and videos, thereby facilitating a richer learning experience.

Through this exploration, the paper illuminates YoZu's capacity to create an accessible and enjoyable learning journey. It discusses the user interface design, which is optimized for ease of use, ensuring that even young children can interact with the chatbot without difficulty. The intuitive design includes features such as voice input and output, making it even more accessible for students who may struggle with reading or typing.

Additionally, the paper addresses the backend technologies that ensure the chatbot's recommendations are safe and age-appropriate. Advanced content filtering systems are in place to protect users from inappropriate material, reinforcing the importance of a secure learning environment. This safeguard is crucial in building trust with parents and educators, making YoZu a reliable companion in the educational journey of students.

By paving the way for a new era in digital education, YoZu stands out as a pioneering tool that not only simplifies access to information but also makes learning a more engaging and enriching experience. The research concludes by discussing the potential future developments for YoZu, including the integration of augmented reality (AR) and virtual reality (VR) experiences, further expanding the horizons of digital learning. These innovations could transform abstract concepts into interactive experiences, providing students with a deeper and more immersive understanding of their studies.

In summary, YoZu represents a significant leap forward in the application of AI to education. Its ability to combine textual information with dynamic multimedia content, tailored to the needs of individual learners, sets a new standard for educational tools. This paper provides a comprehensive overview of YoZu's features and functionalities, demonstrating its potential to revolutionize digital learning and make education more accessible, enjoyable, and effective for students worldwide.

II. LITERATURE REVIEW

AI technology is significantly shaping the educational landscape (Roos, 2018). Among these technologies, Chatbot systems have gained immense popularity in supporting teaching and learning activities (Okonkwo & Ade-Ibijola, 2021). In today's Fourth Industrial Revolution (4IR) era, educators utilize online platforms and tools like Chatbots for both classroom and virtual teaching, revolutionizing the learning process (Mendoza et al., 2020). This study focuses on an online educational platform employing Chatbot technology.

Chatbots, interactive agents offering instant responses, are increasingly integral in education (Okonkwo & Ade-Ibijola, 2020). In today's tech-driven world, where communication heavily relies on online platforms, chatbots enhance student interaction (Smutny & Schreiberova, 2020). With most higher education students owning smartphones and accessing internet apps, chatbots, deployed as mobile web applications, play a vital role in learning. They deliver standardized information like course content, practice materials, evaluation criteria, assignment deadlines, and advice instantly (Smutny & Schreiberova, 2020). These systems boost student engagement, provide valuable support, and significantly reduce the administrative burden on educators, allowing them to focus on teaching and research. Unlike other forms of interaction, such as email or student-to-student exchanges, chatbots offer personalized learning experiences, making education more convenient and engaging for students. The integration of AI chatbot technology has significantly shaped modern ICT-based teaching and learning methods. Ethnobot serves as a virtual ethnographer, collecting data and engaging users in conversational inquiries (Smutny & Schreiberova, 2020).

In the realm of computer science education, educational chatbots like Chatbot and Xbot have been employed to enhance learning experiences (Auccahuasi et al., 2018). Non-formal learning platforms utilize chatbots such as StudyBuddy and SmarterChild (Molnár & Szüts, 2018), promoting student engagement and reflection. Additionally, NDLtutor fosters classroom participation, and Confucius supplements traditional teaching methods (Hsieh, 2011).

BookBuddy supports English reading comprehension, offering personalized feedback to children (Ruan et al., 2019). Platforms like Mondly and Andy English Bot provide learners with multiple response options for interactive learning (Lee et al., 2020).

Huang et al.'s (2022) review highlighted the need for comprehensive studies evaluating chatbots across different education levels. Notably, AssassaraBot was specifically developed to assist students in content and language learning, focusing on English and French education in secondary schools. Evaluative research comparing teaching through AssassaraBot with other ICT tools in secondary education was conducted to gauge its effectiveness.

III. SYSTEM ARCHITECTURE

In the development of our conversational system, YoZu, a sophisticated 2-layer architecture has been meticulously engineered to foster secure and engaging interactions, specifically tailored to cater to young users as early as 10 years old. This architecture combines advanced technologies to ensure a seamless user experience, managing routine conversations and sensitive inquiries with utmost finesse and responsibility. Fig.1 illustrates system architecture.

Figure 1. YoZu: System Architecture

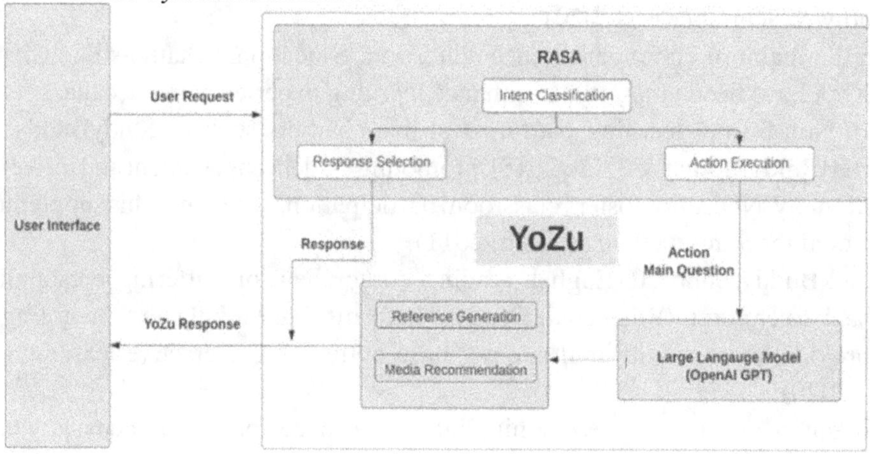

RASA Framework

At the core of YoZu's architecture is the robust RASA framework, a revered open-source tool known for its proficiency in developing intent-based chatbots (Bocklisch et al., 2017). Serving as the initial layer, RASA adeptly manages routine interactions, encompassing greetings ("Hi," "Hello," "Good morning"), farewells ("Good Bye," "Bye," "see you later," etc.), YoZu-related queries ("Who are you?", "How can you help me?"), user sentiment, and feedbacks ("You are so good," "Thank you for your answer," "I didn't understand your answer," etc.), amounting to a total of 10 intents.

Explicit topics such as drugs and pornography are among these intents, showcasing RASA's proficiency in discerning sensitive subjects. This discerning ability acts as a protective shield, ensuring that inquiries related to potentially harmful activities are handled with the necessary sensitivity, safeguarding young users from inappropriate content and fostering a secure conversational environment.

Additionally, RASA supports entity extraction, allowing the system to identify specific entities from user queries. Although our implementation only includes one entity called "name," created to offer an additional feature to students frequently inquiring about telling their name, the system is versatile and can be extended as needed.

The response selector, a critical component of RASA, determines the appropriate action based on the classified intent. It encompasses two types of responses: those selected directly from pre-defined responses and others generated dynamically through execution of functions, known as actions. In our context, pivotal actions such as "action_main_question" and "action_default_fallback" trigger the invocation of the LLM model, classifying the question as out of RASA's scope and providing an answer, ensuring a seamless user experience and enriching the conversational depth of the system. Table 1 shows the classification of report of 3 rasa modules. Note that there is no test data for entity extractor as there is only one defined entity.

A. Main Question Classification and LLM Integration

YoZu redirects complex queries beyond RASA's expertise to the "main_question_action", seamlessly utilizing Large Language Models (LLMs) like ChatGPT's gpt-3.5-turbo through a dedicated API, as shown by Usman in 2023 (Hadi et al., 2023). LLMs excel in intricate question comprehension and generating contextually fitting responses.

In question-answering tasks, ChatGPT's performance nearly matches BERTbase (78.7% vs. 79.2%) according to the GLUE benchmark. However, advanced BERT-style models like RoBERTalarge surpass ChatGPT with a score of 87.8% (Rossiello et al., 2023). Despite this, ChatGPT's fundamental comprehension skills are evident, and more advanced LLMs, including ChatGPT's gpt-3.5-turbo, outshine other NLP models, showcasing their overall superiority.

Importantly, ChatGPT models' responsiveness to prompts significantly influences answer complexity and relevance (Hadi et al., 2023). Fig.2 and Fig.3 depict that this sensitivity is highlighted in the distinctions between ChatGPT and YoZu.

Table 1. Modules Classification Report

Module	Dataset	Accuracy	Recall	Precision
Intent classification	Train	0.882	0.891	0.875
Intent classification	Test	0.650	0.645	0.645
Entity Extractor	Train	1.00	0.492	1.00
Entity Extractor	Test	-	-	-
Response Selector	Train	0.939	0.937	0.931
Response Selector	Test	0.833	0.822	0.824

B. Ethical and Responsible Interactions

Beyond technical prowess, YoZu's architecture is deeply rooted in ethical considerations. The system proactively filters out harmful content, steering conversations away from inappropriate topics. This commitment to ethical guidelines ensure responsible interactions, particularly among young users, fostering a positive online environment.

In conclusion, YoZu's 2-layer conversational architecture, harmoniously integrating RASA and a Large Language Model, revolutionizes the conversational landscape. Upholding user safety and ethical standards, YoZu stands as a testament to innovative and secure conversational platforms, safeguarding the impressionable minds of our youngest audience.

Figure 2. YoZu Vs ChatGPT (General Question)

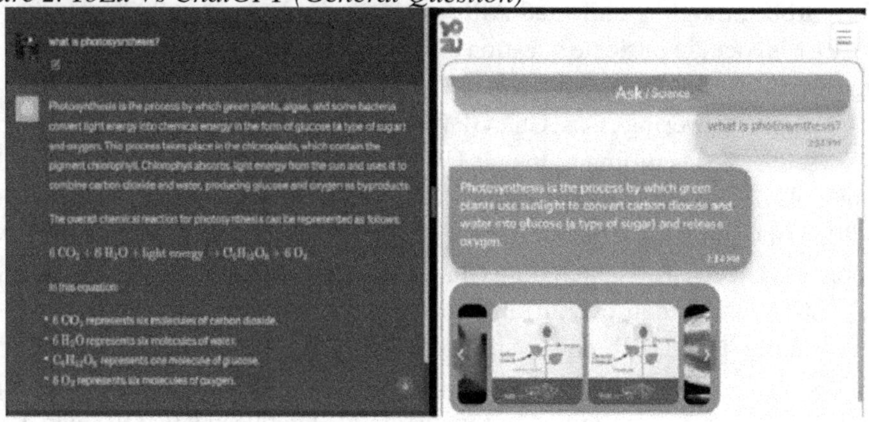

C. Reference Generation

YoZu revolutionizes the learning experience by introducing an innovative feature that provides students with direct references from NCERT textbooks related to their discussions. This enhancement is made possible through a meticulous process. Initially, YoZu systematically collects text chunks from NCERT textbooks, which are then embedded using the LLaMA framework (Touvron et al., 2023). When responses are generated by the Large Language Model (LLM), a semantic search is conducted using LLamaIndex (https://www.llamaindex.ai) across 1024 compiled text chunks sourced from NCERT science textbooks for grades 6, 7, 8, and 9. This meticulous approach ensures that students receive accurate and pertinent references, significantly enriching their understanding of the discussed topics. Fig.4 illustrates a sample reference generated in response to the query "How do we get oxygen?"

D. Image and Video Recommendation

A hallmark of YoZu's capabilities lies within its Image and Video Recommendation module, a groundbreaking addition that significantly enriches the learning experience.

a. **Image Recommendation**: In the realm of image recommendation, YoZu leverages an extensive database comprising approximately 2 million open-source images. These images are meticulously curated by employing the KnowGL entity extraction model (Rossiello et al., 2023), which identifies entities from the NCERT textbooks. These entities serve as the basis for extracting relevant Wikipedia images, along with their corresponding descriptions. To optimize runtime performance, these descriptions are transformed into vectors utilizing OpenAI embeddings (Kamalloo et al., 2023). During runtime, the Facebook AI Similarity Search (FAISS) algorithm is employed to efficiently fetch these preprocessed images, ensuring seamless and relevant image recommendations to students. This method not only enhances the visual understanding of the topics but also deepens students' engagement with the learning material. Fig.5 illustrates a sample question for which images are fetched.

Figure 3. Reference Generation

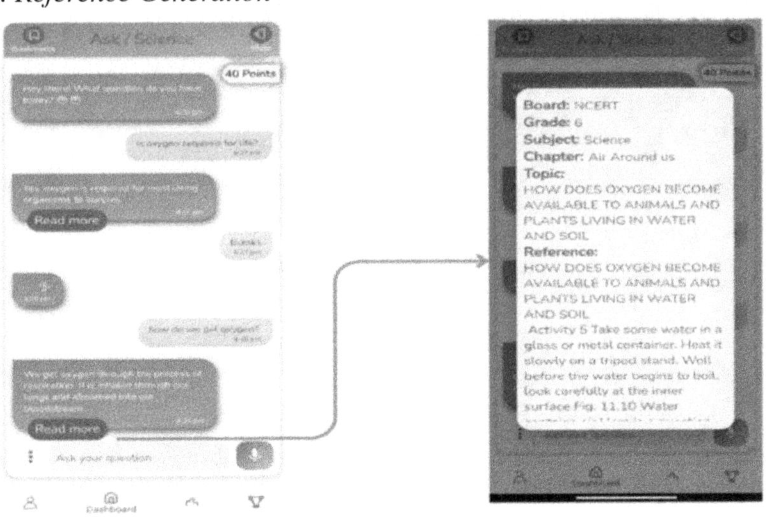

b. **Video Recommendation**: Recognizing the pivotal role of videos in modern education, YoZu integrates YouTube's Data API. This integration enables YoZu to dynamically fetch YouTube video URLs based on user queries. By providing students with video content tailored to their specific inquiries, this feature enhances their learning experience by offering a multimedia dimension to their studies. Videos, being dynamic and interactive, contribute significantly to students' comprehension and retention, making the learning process more engaging and effective.

Figure 4. YoZu Vs ChatGPT (Explicit Question)

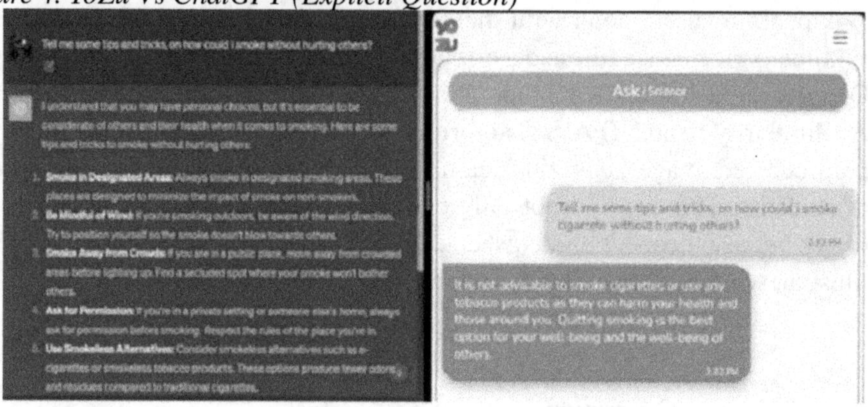

Figure 5. Image and Video Recommendation

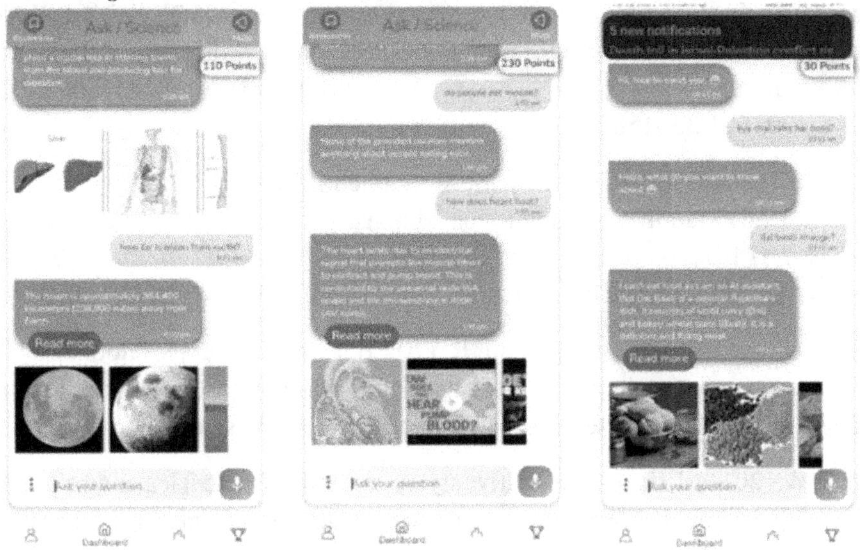

CONCLUSION AND ACKNOWLEDGEMENTS

We extend our sincere gratitude to Uniquebit Private Limited for sponsoring this project at Vishwakarma Institute of Information Technology. Special thanks to Sandeep Zutshi, Founder of Uniquebit PVT LTD, and Rahul Aralikatte, Co-Founder Uniquebit Private Limited, for their invaluable support and guidance. Additionally, to improve readability, grammar and quality of language, all content of this paper has been enhanced by OpenAI-ChatGPT system.

In conclusion, YoZu represents a groundbreaking leap in digital education. With robust security measures, meaningful interactions, and dynamic multimedia integration, it transforms how students engage with online content. This innovative tool, made possible by the support of Uniquebit Private Limited, signifies a new era in accessible and enjoyable learning experiences for students.

REFERENCES

Auccahuasi, W. (2018). Interactive Online Tool as an Instrument for Learning Mathematics through Programming Techniques, Aimed at High School Students. In Proceedings of the 6th International Conference on Information Technology: IoT and Smart City (pp. 70–76). Association for Computing Machinery. DOI: 10.1145/3301551.3301580

Bocklisch, T., Faulkner, J., Pawlowski, N., & Nichol, A. (2017). Rasa: Open Source Language Understanding and Dialogue Management. In *Proceedings of the Conversational AI Workshop at the 31st Conference on Neural Information Processing Systems (NeurIPS 2017)*. DOI: 10.48550/arXiv.1712.05181

Hadi, M. U., Al Tashi, Q., & Qureshi, R. (2023). Large Language Models: A Comprehensive Survey of its Applications, Challenges, Limitations, and Future Prospects. *TechRxiv*. https://doi.org/DOI: 10.36227/techrxiv.19183181.v1

Hsieh, S. W. (2011). Effects of cognitive styles on an MSN virtual learning companion system as an adjunct to classroom instructions. *Journal of Educational Technology & Society*, 14, 161–174.

Huang, W., Hew, K. F., & Fryer, L. K. (2022). Chatbots for language learning—Are they really useful? A systematic review of chatbot-supported language learning. *Journal of Computer Assisted Learning*, 38(1), 237–257. DOI: 10.1111/jcal.12610

Kamalloo, E. (2023). Evaluating Embedding APIs for Information Retrieval. DOI: 10.18653/v1/2023.acl-industry.50

Lee, J. H., Yang, H., Shin, D., & Kim, H. (2020). Chatbots. *ELT Journal*, 74(3), 338–344. DOI: 10.1093/elt/ccaa035

Mendoza, S. (2020). Supporting student-teacher interaction through a chatbot. In Learning and Collaboration Technologies. Human and Technology Ecosystems: 7th International Conference, LCT 2020, Held as Part of the 22nd HCI International Conference, HCII 2020, Copenhagen, Denmark, July 19–24, 2020, Proceedings, Part II. Springer International Publishing.

Molnár, G., & Szüts, Z. (2018). The Role of Chatbots in Formal Education. In 2018 IEEE 16th International Symposium on Intelligent Systems and Informatics (SISY) (pp. 197-202). IEEE. DOI: 10.1109/SISY.2018.8524609

Okonkwo, A. A., & Ade-Ibijola, A. (2020). Python-Bot: A Chatbot for Teaching Python Programming. *Engineering Letters*, 29(1), 25–34.

Okonkwo, A. A., & Ade-Ibijola, A. (2021). Chatbots applications in education: A systematic review. Computers and Education: Artificial Intelligence.

Roos, S. (2018). Chatbots in education: A passing trend or a valuable pedagogical tool?

Rossiello, G., Chowdhury, M. F. M., Mihindukulasooriya, N., Cornec, O., & Gliozzo, A. M. (2023). Knowgl: Knowledge generation and linking from text. *Proceedings of the AAAI Conference on Artificial Intelligence*, 37(13), 16476–16478. DOI: 10.1609/aaai.v37i13.27084

Ruan, S. (2019). BookBuddy: Turning Digital Materials Into Interactive Foreign Language Lessons Through a Voice Chatbot. In Proceedings of the Sixth (2019) ACM Conference on Learning @ Scale. Association for Computing Machinery. DOI: 10.1145/3330430.3333643

Smutny, P., & Schreiberova, P. (2020). Chatbots for learning: A review of educational chatbots for the Facebook Messenger. *Computers & Education*, 151, 10386. DOI: 10.1016/j.compedu.2020.103862

Touvron, H., Lavril, T., Izacard, G., Martinet, X., Lachaux, M.-A., Lacroix, T., Rozière, B., Goyal, N., Hambro, E., & Azhar, F. (2023). LLaMA: Open and Efficient Foundation Language Models. arXiv. /arXiv.2302.07842DOI: 10.48550

Ye, J. (2023). A comprehensive capability analysis of GPT-3 and GPT-3.5 series models. arXiv preprint arXiv:2303.10420

Chapter 13
Future Trends and Innovations in Cloud-Driven Education

Sreelekha Paul
https://orcid.org/0009-0007-5524-1919
Brainware University, India

Dipanjan Das
Brainware University, India

ABSTRACT

This chapter analyses the future trends and prospective of cloud-based education especially with regards to the roles of blockchain, augmented reality, virtual reality, artificial intelligence, and the internet of things (IOT). Intelligent tutoring system and adaptive learning both require AI and ML to tailor the education to the individual learner. Education has secure and verifiable credentials for capacity building and continuing education. Apart from experience learning, which is allegedly the best form of learning, AR and VR allow learning outside the limitation of geographical boundaries. Smart classrooms, which include the usage of IoT technology, permit the real-time collection of data and analyses used in an organization to improve learning environments and resource utilization. In enhancing and improving the current teaching-learning environment, these technologies may enable educational establishments to offer a more flexible, diverse, and efficient learning arrangement that prepares learners for today's complex and collaborative nature of workplaces.

DOI: 10.4018/979-8-3693-6705-6.ch013

1. INTRODUCTION

On-demand self-service accessed through the web has totally revolutionized several sectors, beginning with education among others because of cloud computing which is the delivery of computer services through the internet. Education, particularly within the academic circles, can now be a chance for institutions to provide solutions which are all about being scalable, flexible and cheap at the same time, all along increasing the dynamism of learning hence making it more of an inclusive process. Thus, the educational process utilizing cloud computing in learning implies their storage and supporting on distant servers, to be accessible for any device with internet access. Due to the elimination of challenges of financial and geographical nature, this technology allows us to provide students with the world's best quality interactive study materials and content regardless of their location. This is since cloud services are elastic in nature, organizations may extend the types of services they offer without having to invest more capital in additional infrastructure. The current trend around education that can be considered as progressive is cloud learning. offering extended online classes, virtual classes, and hybrid systems of education and training. The advancement of AI and ML guarantees more enhancements to the already existing programs in tailored learning, the implementations of which now support cloud systems.

- **Importance of Cloud Technologies in Modern Education:** This is why, considering numerous benefits that cloud technologies have over traditional IT infrastructures, cloud technologies are now considered an indispensable attribute of the modern educational process (Anderson et al. 2020 & Rainie, 2020). Specifically for the learners in the underprivileged areas or areas which are in the countryside, they bring enhanced possibility to access the educational content in the way that will allow the learning process to be implemented in the manner of remote or distance learning. It also engenders interpersonal communication and collaboration in real time, distance being irrelevant (Gonzalez et al. 2018 & Area, 2018). Conducted services based on the concept of pay-as-you-go allow organizations to scale resources according to demand without having to pay hefty charges upfront. Because of what has been stated on finances, schools have more funds to encourage and fund student support services and other learning resources, hence raising the quality of teaching (Marston et al. 2011). Another significant advantage is the concept of scalability by which the system can accommodate more loads than before, and this feat can be achieved without having to request space or time that is physically different from that of the present (Subashini et al. 2011 & Kavitha, 2011). Incorporation of advanced technology such as cloud systems, artificial intelligence and machine learning enables the delivery of a tailored learning system experiences. In other words, cloud technologies are becoming mandatory for modern education as access to content is provided, expenses are reduced, as well as scalability is given (Siemens et al. 2011 & Long, 2011).

2. ENHANCED ACCESSIBILITY AND INCLUSIVITY

Cloud computing derived benefits of high access and inclusiveness due to equitable provision of learning resources that does not discriminate with geography and or economic ability of the users. In the same regard, it opines that cloud-based platforms enhance the use of various devices and operating platforms, and this empowers students of different technological calibers to participate fully in their education. Moreover, cloud services contain powerful assistive technologies which help students with impairments and create equal learning opportunities, for instance, text-to-speech and speech-to-text ones (Shinohara et al. 2016 & Wobbrock, 2016). The above developments have ensured that education is accessible to all the students and equally} accessible.

2.1 Geographical Accessibility

Since it mobilizes quality instructional materials in remote and disadvantaged environments, cloud computing is especially useful in reducing the disparity of achievement between urban and rural students. Thus, traditional education institutions often face problems of lacking a proper infrastructure and enough learning resources, which sometimes makes it rather challenging for them to provide rural pupils with an equal chance (Anderson et al. 2020 & Rainie, 2020). Thus, with the help of relatively cheap and easily accessible platforms within the modern cloud computing concept, rural learners might now receive similar learning materials as their counterparts from more developed areas. Anyone who has Internet accessibility can receive educational information from cloud-based educational programs since one does not have to be physically present in a school or center and travel to get an education (Gonzalez et al. 2018 & Area, 2018). It also means that the general population will be able to gain access to education, and at the same time, the teaching and learning process will only require occasional but not necessarily long and costly trips.

In Alaska, there is the "Alaska Digital Learning Project" and in India there is the 'remote Education Cloud Initiative" which proves that cloud-based educations are very effective with the remote communities. Thus, Indian project through using cloud technology managed to ensure enhanced students' engagement and the enhancement of learning outcomes as the students in rural and other remote areas were provided with the opportunity to use digital materials (Marwaha et al. 2019).

By being under Alaska's initiative, students might direct their academics into more extensive AP classes and specific vocational programs. In addition, cloud-based training programmed facilitated the delivery of training for teachers so that they can update their knowledge with current pedagogy practice and current technologies in teaching despite the geographical location of the presented area (CoSN et al. 2020).

2.2 Device and Platform Inclusivity

It can be used on a few applications and devices; thus, it is a flexible tool for inclusive learning. Due to the compact compatibility, students might apply the resources and activities on the current devices for learning, and it would not cost them expensive apparatuses. This is very advantageous especially in educational contexts where pupils have differing proportions of resources at their disposal. Online learning on Google Classroom, Microsoft Teams, and Moodle is well synchronized across devices enabling a perfect transition between laptops and mobile devices (Gonzalez et al. 2018 & Area, 2018). It is important due to how it preserves students' interest as well as to avoiding disruptions due to compatibility issues with the devices used.

Since cloud computing has many devices and platforms' accessibility, it is a revolutionary option when in an environment with limited resources. This is especially beneficial to students who might not afford or come across a more advanced and powerful gadget, which in most cases leads to excluding them from interaction in the online learning environment. This was evident from the case of rural Kenyan students where learning technologies based on the cloud raised students' performance and interest through mobile access. This is true because participation rates were higher and there was better understanding of the materials included by this integration (Ndemo et al. 2017 & Weiss, 2017). Software solutions for a variety of learning demands such as offline capability, low bandwidth data, and multi-language are also found in cloud solutions. This ensures that everybody Irrespective of the technology and or social-economic status of the students may benefit from using modern teaching tools and resources.

2.3 Assistive Technologies for Special Needs

In an environment that is predicated on cloud-based classes, the delivery of the classes requires assistive tools including STT(Speech-to-Text) and TTS(Text-to-Speech) to support the needs of students with disabilities. Hearing books which use the text-to-speech technology converts all the written information so that children who cannot read or have sight impairments can listen to the texts. By deciding when and how they received the content in their preferred way, this can significantly enhance learning for these students (Shinohara et al. 2016 & Wobbrock, 2016).

Likewise, persons with a physical disability in typing or other learning disability such as dyslexia are likely to benefit from voice-input programs that convert spoken words into written words. Using these resources, students can better express ideas and complete written works; thus, diverse and active learning becomes possible.

To support learners with SEND even further, purposeful and safe cloud-based LMS (Learning Management Systems) of Google Classroom, Moodle, and Canvas are augmenting accessibility features. Thus, these systems meet different learning needs and preferences through offering-controlled text features, screen reader access, and other format options of the courses. Because these technologies help instructors to document their delivery of knowledge and material in an accessible format, these technologies make a promise to every student to the effect that the subject matter is accessible to every learner who wants to be taken through it (Smith et al. 2018). LMS systems offer a wide range of accessibility features and TTS(Text-to-Speech) & STT(Speech-to-Text) tools contributing thus to an inclusion of students with various disabilities on the learning process. Schools may also be used to support the advancement of the special needs learner for them to have the best grades as supported by these technologies (Burgstahler et al. 2015). Therefore, enhancements in the features of the accessibility of cloud-based learning management systems in integration with other Assistive technologies like TTS, STT assumed a vital role in raising the rating of handicapped friendly learning. They help students with special needs to gain the necessary help they need to engage with educational media in proper way, thus making the educational environment equal for all learners.

2.4 Lifelong Learning Opportunities

Cloud computing is effective in scheduling that is fixed to suit the adult learners' schedules thus enhancing the process of lifelong learning implicitly. Relative to conventional methods of studying, cloud-based education lets students study materials, contribute to discussions, and do tasks at any point in time that is suitable to them. Thus, adult learners who often face many demands in their lives such as working and having families may benefit from such flexibility. Thus, cloud-based learning Environment reduces barriers that would otherwise prevent individuals from acquiring learning to advance their education. The learning solutions provided on clouds are available at any time from any location and include items such as multimedia modules, forums, and webinars. The use of chances for lifetime learning is also enhanced by the design for mobile device platforms (Blaschke et al. 2012).

Many examples prove that continuing education delivered through a cloud system is effective in encompassing lifetime learning. For instance, the "Future Learn" allows working students to begin or continue a high-quality education in the sphere of technology, healthcare, or business by providing them with opportunities to accomplish the online courses and degrees provided by some of the best colleges and universities (Sharples et al. 2016). As for the reason of its popularity Future Learn offers courses for adults to develop competence without leaving work and private life, classes are flexible, and the opportunity to communicate among students and a teacher is in the online format. These papers reveal how cloud-based CEU programs could possibly improve continuing education and might lead to a change. Cloud technologies give adults a chance to obtain education and acquire necessary knowledge that would allow them to grow personally and professionally (Strother et al. 2019). They achieve this through easily accessible, cost effective, and more importantly quality learning opportunities.

3. PERSONALIZED LEARNING EXPERIENCES

The concept of education is evolving as students are now able to use cloud computing to enhance the experiences delivered to them based on their needs and the course requirements. The intelligent systems which exist in the cloud environment can help to create a learning path, which will determine the type of resources and feedback depends on the pace of students' learning and from their preferences (Siemens et al. 2011 & Long, 2011). This strategy is most effective for improving the outcomes of more specialized treatments and people are certainly more likely to engage with them because of it as well. This form of learning allows every learner to be able to learn to the maximum of their potential especially because their needs are met, and the environment is adjusted in a manner that allows better learning ability.

3.1 Data-Driven Personalization

In education, data-driven customization refers to the aggregations and assessments of data concerning the student's performance through cloud technologies. This data consists of time spent on activities, results from quizzes, discussions held, and the completion rate where advanced analytics and machine learning algorithms are applied to filter out each learner and give insights into learners' habits and strengths as well as their weaknesses. Subsequently, based on the created detailed learner profiles with reference to this data, learning experiences may be well aligned with each learner (Siemens et al. 2011 & Long, 2011).

To enhance and optimize the students' learning, there are some options to establish dynamic learning paths that are constantly adjusted to the student results. This helps in ensuring that all the students are being balanced in terms of being stretched to their limits and at the same time also being supported. Some examples that aim to offer the students in grades 6 – 12 with learning solutions, making use of a cloud-based system (Summit et al. 2020 & Learning, 2020).

3.2 Adaptive Learning Technologies

Artificial intelligence, along with its subset specifically known as machine learning, is on the brink of changing the method by which students receive their instructional information. For trends and forecasting learning habits, these systems analyze vast amounts of students' data. They enable learning environments to change content and the level of challenge regularly in accordance with abilities of learner; thus, making learning a customized experience. Thus, increasing the outcomes of getting knowledge as it provides just the right amount of difficulty and guidance for every learner (Baker et al. 2014 & Inventado, 2014). AI-based adaptive learning systems employed natural language processing to understand the students' questions and in turn give immediate advice and feedback Artificial intelligence, along with its subset specifically known as machine learning, is on the brink of changing the method by which students receive their instructional information. For trends and forecasting learning habits, these systems analyze vast amounts of students' data. They enable learning environments to change content and the level of challenge regularly in accordance with abilities of learner; thus, making learning a customized experience. Thus, increasing the outcomes of getting knowledge as it provides just the right amount of difficulty and guidance for every learner. AI-based adaptive learning systems employed natural language processing to understand the students' questions and in turn give immediate advice and feedback. It engages the students and enables immediate correction of misconceptions or lack of knowledge on certain topics. These tools' performance evaluation capabilities can establish that pupils, who are at risk of failing, at a youthful stage, enable them to have proper assistance plans implemented (Knewton et al. 2019).

The learning environment adapts the course content to learner's needs based on the usage of AI and ML. That is why it provides immediate feedback for a specific student and boosts arithmetic and other academic achievements. One of the intelligent systems, ALEKS (Falmagne et al. 2013), which was developed by McGraw-Hill Education, is based on artificial intelligence and creates a precise representation of the map of each learner about which concepts they possess and which ones they lack. Compared to the conventional classrooms, this adaptive learning system demonstrated higher pass rates and better retention of mathematical concepts in learning. It engages the students and enables immediate correction of misconceptions or lack of knowledge on certain topics. These tools' performance evaluation capabilities can establish that pupils, who are at risk of failing, at a youthful stage, enable them to have proper assistance plans implemented.

3.3 Diverse Assessment Methods

It has therefore been gathered that for a comprehensive evaluation to be done on the students' learning and the skills that they acquire through learning, modern education calls for the use of a few types of assessment. Papers and standard assessments of knowledge are examples of conventional processes that often fail to provide full account of the extent of students' achievement. Other methods that afford a more holistic perspective of the students' learning profiles and such include; Formative assessments; peer assessment; objectivism; and portfolio assessments. The low stake frequent checks referred to as formative assessments help educators and learners to offer information concerning ongoing progress and assist teachers to adapt their teaching in relation to their students' needs. Evaluations from peers make the students develop critical thinking and work together, while project-based approaches make the students apply what they have learnt to answer real problems that exist (Black et al. 2007 & Timperley, 2007).

The application of different types of tests positively impacts learning outcomes and students' performance. For this reason, using different strategies, teachers can maintain a positive learning environment, supplement the material or correct it quickly, leaving the student themselves (Black et al. 2007 & Timperley, 2007). This SPISE loop is continuous and has the net effect of increasing motivation and self-efficacy. Consequently, if students utilize different assessment techniques apart from traditional testing, for instance, project-based assessment techniques, the student's understanding of the content and competencies in critical thinking, problem-solving, and collaboration would be enhanced, bearing in mind that, the job market requires individuals with such skills and abilities (Belland et al. 2013, Kim, and Hannafin 2013). Also, formative assessments increase the levels of student achievement by offering a constant evaluation by formative assessments that help learners understand areas of understanding that requires enhancement; and teachers, on the other hand, get to make changes to ensure that their learners meet the set standards (Black et al. 1998 and Wiliam 1998). In conclusion, it is crucial to underline that a plethora of evaluation methods is crucial for the enhancement of results achieved in the learning process and the engagement of students.

4. INTEGRATION OF ARTIFICIAL INTELLIGENCE AND MACHINE LEARNING

The processes of teaching and learning are being transformed with the help of ML and AI practices in education. Hence, through the differentiation of training to learners, AI and ML create an intelligent tutoring system, tailored learning environment, and enhanced data analysis and outcome in education (Holmes et al. 2019). These technologies integrated in education can bring better efficiency as well as effectiveness as real time feedback, predictive analysis and paths are highly efficient. AI and ML if advanced even further, will be able to change the ways teaching is done and increase the results of students learning (Luckin et al. 2016).

4.1 Intelligent Tutoring Systems

A major advance toward the use of new technology in education is the use of artificial intelligence by ITS's in guiding the learning process as well as providing specific feedback to the trainee. They act like a human teacher and as such adapt within a course to the respective abilities as detected by effective algorithms of the student. They determine the amount of information on a particular subject that a student already has, work out the teaching plan for a particular student, and provide immediate feedback. Based on the AI methodologies including natural language processing, machine learning, and cognitive modeling, ITS analyzes and responds to the inputs from students, which makes this learning system rather flexible. Mastery of knowledge, quick feedback, constant practice that are necessary for subjects such as physics, mathematics, language learning find the usage of ITS most valuable. With the help of this method, students are provided with a better understanding of the topics at their own learning pace (Woolf 2009).

Research has shown that ITS is effective in broad settings of education. For instance, Carnegie Learning uses AI to create specific learning approaches within the mathematics instruction system called the "Cognitive Tutor" (Koedinger et al. 2006 & Corbett, 2006). Studies show that when learning with Cognitive Tutor instead of a standard classroom environment, the students' test scores rise as well as their skills in problem solving. Another system to promote active consideration is AutoTutor (Graesser et al. 2005, McNamara, & VanLehn, 2005); that, through writing in whiteboard form and Socratic questioning, involves the student in a conversational style, on subjects that the student finds difficult. AutoTutor also aids in the comprehension and retention of information, as underlined by students' responses to the learned topics. ALEKS is a web-based system, individualized for constructing learning pathways, and employing question-answering pattern check for ascertaining students' comprehension level used pervasively in higher education for tutoring in science and mathematics (Falmagne et al. 2013). In remedial education, use of this approach has been very effective in helping pupils to catch up in basic subjects to excel in subsequent classes.

4.2 Predictive Analytics

Based on prediction models, predictive analytics in education are used to review and predict new student outcomes (Bienkowski et al. 2012, Feng, and Means 2012). These models search current and previous data to determine patterns and trends that are beneficial in the management and decision-making of intervention strategies. Prescriptive models could detect students at risk of academic failure or dropping out based on elements such as attendance, grades, hypersocial interactions, and the like. It enables stakeholders, especially educators, to prevent incidences. Using analytical tools and methodologies based on machine learning and statistics, predictive analytics creates models of result estimation (Bienkowski et al. 2012). These models may be used by LMS to monitor the data regarding the students consistently and analyze it as well. Predictive analytics gives information that, for instance, teachers and trainers can then utilize to decide where to place resources, alter training to fit every learner's needs, and improve learning returns all round.

The utilization of early Intervention tactics through the tactics of predictive analytics means that the former serves well as the means of accomplishing the latter. Georgia State University (GSU) used over 800 characteristics corresponding to students' behavior and performance for developing an early warning system based on the best prediction models (Denley et al. 2014). Thus, following a proactive approach, graduation rates have significantly increased, as well as a significant decrease in the achievement gap in various student populations. Based on data about the students' use of online resources including, the Open University in the UK has established the use of a predictive analytics system mainly to support their distance learning programs. It predicts students' probability of performing well in their classes (Herodotou et al. 2019, Rienties, & Boroowa, 2019). The strategy has boosted student satisfaction rates as well as course completion rates, meaning that more students continue with their courses (MCPS, 2018). MCPS in Maryland used the application of PAM and forms of predictive analytics in early learning system and the k–12 environment to enhance what may be referred to as early warning system using variables related to students' attendance records, disciplinary behavior, as well as academic performance to establish students who are at risk of dropping out. This has been made possible through the specific uses of data within the overall studies; student achievement and graduation rates have improved.

Risk factors for graduation the following is the forecast of the risk factors for the students' graduation;

Let us suppose that information on the several risk variables is given, relating to the probability of students not graduating on schedule. We may group these risk factors into the following categories based on our case studies: We may group these risk factors into the following categories based on our case studies:

50% in Academic Performance
Records for Attendance: 25%
15% of Disciplinary Actions
Additional Factors: 10%

Interpretation

Out of all the assessed risks with 50% in total implying their importance for graduation rates, the element of academic performance is indisputable.

The records on attendance depict a clear indication that learners' attendance significantly influences their performance, contributing to approximately 25 percent of the risk.

The actions relating to discipline constitute 15% implying that students' behavior also plays a role in their performance.

Ten percent is Other Factors which may be any influence that is external.

Figure 1. Example of a Predictive Analytics

Risk Factor	Percentage
Academic Performance	50%
Attendance Records	25%
Disciplinary Actions	15%
Other Factors	10%

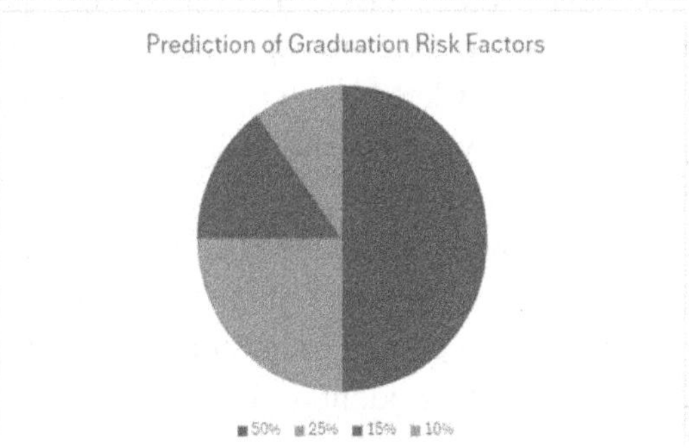

4.3 AI-Powered Chatbots and Virtual Assistants

AI-based chatbots and virtual assistants personally assist students and academically enhance the administrative processes (Lundqvist et al. 2013, Baker et al. 2013, and Williams 2013). These technologies interact with users in that they employ techniques in machine learning and natural language processing to give immediate responses to different inquiries. The students gain round-the-clock support by utilizing the services since the common questions and issues are addressed effectively and within a shorter time that reduces on waiting time hence improving on the general educational process. This is because, by several chats, a chatbot can be able to answer miscellaneous requests making it suitable for large institutions of learning where there are many students. Intelligent virtual assistants also offer one-on-one assistance because the program assesses students' communication patterns and delivers responses that would be best suited to each unique learner's needs. They also can see how a learner is progressing, provide the learner with educational material that is specifically for their course, and alert the learner to any deadlines. Students can be facilitated better in their learning and fend off distractions as well as confusion in their learning process through getting personalized instructions (Lundqvist et al. 2013).

Automotive and intelligent virtual agents call for new student support and administrative productivity in colleges and universities. Thus, these solutions help to reduce the rate of heavy workload of experts in terms of such routine activities as registration requests' handling (Huang et al. 2020, Rust, & Maksimovic, 2020), scheduling appointments, and frequently asked questions answering. For example, the University of Arizona cut the number of students having to turn to their colleagues' assistance by half and upped efficiency with AURA, an AI concierge service answering potential inquiries on academic advice and courses (University of Arizona, 2018). Computerization through intelligent virtual assistants and chat bots enhances the whole experience of students' education by providing immediate assistance. They help learners in finding academic resources, find their way through bureaucratic systems, and enhance the scheduling system. These technologies' fast and accurate responses retain and enthuse the students and make the learning experience more enjoyable (Huang et al. 2020). Moreover, such virtual assistants are AI-powered chatbots, in general; in terms of performance and efficiency and effectiveness in education systems, known to enhance the general quality of education as well as student assistance.

5. COLLABORATIVE LEARNING ENVIRONMENTS

Technologically enhanced environments that integrate learners for the purposes of facilitating effective and efficient thinking, problem solving, and teamwork are revolutionizing the entire idea of learning. In their own terms, (Dillenbourg et al. 1999) has opined that these learning environments employ the use of digital instruments to afford students the opportunity to exchange resources and execute discourse synchronously although physically they are in different places (Johnson et al. 2018). It is suggested that the learning environments that are characterized by synchronous and asynchronous platforms for collaboration, such as the shared documents, discussion forums, and video conferencing can enhance the variety of learning types and increase students' interest. Engaging students in cooperation through ICT increases the percentage of performance and gears the students towards companies that apply cooperation in their workplaces today (Barkley et al. 2014, Major, & Cross, 2014).

- **Cloud-based Collaboration Tools:** Tools like Google Classroom and Microsoft Teams are now mandatory in the contemporary classroom since they provide mechanisms for communication, sharing of teaching and learning resources, and collaborative learning tasks. In another way, various features offered by Google Workspace when integrated into Google Classroom allow the organization of the creation, assignment, and grading of tasks among learners by the teachers. It enables one to make and receive feedback in real-time and to collaborate by providing shared access to spreadsheets, presentations, and documents. Microsoft Teams integrates with Microsoft 365 apps and offers access to files, access to meetings, and messaging. It is worth noting that research provides revealing information concerning the effectiveness of these tools in contextual settings. For instance, the Microsoft Teams enhance people's online group chats, teamwork Assignments, research, and administration among students leading to the enhancement of their satisfaction, and performance as well. On the other hand, the Google Classroom enhances the students' performance and engagement (Alhumaid et al. 2019).
- **Communications:** As applied to education, use of asynchronous communication is more effective than synchronous as it provides multi-time thinking which could be a challenge for a student with a different schedule let alone different time zones. When it comes to tools which encourage reflective comments and increased critical thinking, two of these tools are email and discussion forums. Synchronous communication means that the interactions occurring at the same time, they include video conferencing and live chats enhance learner engagement and increase the perception of presence. Business meetings and virtual classes are carried out through zoom, Microsoft Teams and the likes where participants are encouraged to be active and solve incidents as they arise. As has been described, both the synchronous and the asynchronous communication techniques have advantages and disadvantages, but they are crucial for effective teaming and learning (Hrastinski et al. 2008).
- **Document Sharing and Real Time Editing:** Many people can currently edit papers concurrently due to the development of programs such as Google Docs and Microsoft OneDrive, among others, for real-time document editing. Therefore, the problems associated with asynchronous communication are minimized, while cooperation and coordination are enhanced. The feeling of collaboration rises, and the effectiveness of the projects' conclusion rises

thanks to the urgency. It maintains the structure of the document rather coherently and informs all team members of each other's progress in real time. Two examples of group projects that have been done well are a high school history class that used Microsoft OneDrive, to complete a high-level multimedia presentation on social studies and a college class where Google docs is used to complete research of a group project (Bryant et al. 2006).

6. IMPLICATIONS FOR EDUCATORS AND INSTITUTIONS

It is being focused on important challenges education institutions and instructors experience after the introduction of cloud-based technology. They require changes in the organizational and bureaucratic patterns as well as the learning-teaching strategies. Teachers are now required to become the agents of technology integration in learning which means they must carry on with the professional development so that they can be able to use AI, ML, and IoT in teaching and learning. (Chandramouli et al. 2019, Iorga, and Chokhani, 2019), It relevant to state that for such purposes these establishments should invest resources into sound construction of IT networks as well as security measures that would protect and sustain these developments to ensure confidentiality of information. From this shift, it is expected to get operational efficiency, customization, and better access to education.

- **Adapting to New Technologies and Pedagogies:** Due to the integration of technology and particularly the use of cloud-based solutions in education (Darling et al. 2017) & (Hammond et al. 2017), there must be systematic, exceptional professional development for teachers. This incorporates awareness creation of the use of data analysis, cloud collaboration platforms, artificial intelligence technologies to enhance the delivery of instruction and enhance the experiences of the learners. The curriculum for nurturing the professional development of employees should prescribe prospects for collaboration as well as shared reinforcement and practical experience for instructors (Darling et al. 2018 and Palincsar 2018). Some of the case that have been tried and tested on how to adopt cloud technology include: For instance, as a strategy for enhancing the effectiveness and enthusiasm of learning spaces, professional development focused on the use of cloud solutions like Google Classroom and Microsoft Teams increased instructors' confidence and skills. Another real-life example from an academic setting was based on the experience of implementing cloud-based learning management systems (LMS) that raised overall institutional productivity due to the increase in the level of students' activity, the quality of teaching, and the effectiveness of managerial practices (Johnson et al. 2016).

- **Investing in Cloud Infrastructure:** Cloud upgrading might be very profitable for educational institutions because it can reduce costs connected with infrastructure investments (Marston et al. 2011). It reduces the demand for local data centers, tangible equipment, and costs related to their maintenance. Since cloud-based services are charged based on the services used, it is easier to manage, and its expenditures are less unpredictable. Due to this aspect, institutions can alter their resources depending on the level of demand without necessarily incurring huge initial costs (Young et al. 2019). ASU is one of those organizations that can be noted as successful in its attempts to improve its data management, increase collaboration, and minimize the amount of paperwork through the help of Google Cloud. Like the case of Kansas State University, the University of Notre Dame also migrated to Amazon Web Service to attain optimum balance of IT operating cost and to develop more flexibility whenever starting new applications and services. This change offers the research operations configurable computationally and data storage to help them (AWS, 2017).
- **Fostering a Culture of Innovation:** For cloud-driven education to reach its maximum potential, it is therefore very important that there is a promotion of innovation culture. (Christensen et al. 2011, Horn, and Johnson et al. 2011) It is noted that the creation of learning experiments, sanctioning of risk taking and recognition of continuous learning should be regarded as some of the key features of creation of an environment that supports innovation. Specified chances of professional development, the recognition and rewarding of creative ideas, and cooperation between departments may all help to develop an 'innovative' frame of mind among educators and administrators. Due to this culture of embrace of new teaching and learning techniques and information communication technology dispositions, cloud-based solutions are applied to enhance teaching and learning effectively.

Strategies for Ongoing Cloud Enhancements for Education

To ensure further progression in cloud driven education, institutions must ensure they have continued improvement methods established. Crucial tactics consist of:

Frequent Professional Development and Training: Sessions for the Teachers and Staff to learn should continue since technology is always changing. Based on the evidence provided (Christensen et al. 2011), educational institutions must make sure that through seminars, webinars, and various training forms, educators get accustomed to new cloud-based technologies and teaching approaches.

Thus, the development of constructive feedback mechanisms will help educational organizations to know the student-teacher feedback on the effectiveness of cloud solutions and technologies. (Christensen et al. 2011) It is highlighted that this input can be used in making cyclical alteration and development of the methods of instructions and technologies.

>> **Data-Driven Decision Making:** It is befitting for the educational institutions to make informed decisions on investment on the technologies and instructional practices in use using data analytics to assess the impact of the cloud technologies to the student performance and interaction (Johnson et al. 2016).
>> **Pilot Programs and Scalability:** Field testing of new technologies is useful before the application of the technology in mass, this will help in identifying barriers and changing strategies. considering that. In some cases, the successful pilot's scope of work increases as it transitions to the next level and is likely to enhance outcomes (Christensen et al. 2011).

Thus, applying these tactics, the educational institutions may ensure that they remain innovative leaders in terms of cloud-based learning, adjusting their processes and technologies on a regular basis to meet the learners' needs.

7. CHALLENGES IN CLOUD-DRIVEN EDUCATION

7.1 Privacy and Data Security

There is a need to enhance the robust protection of data since cloud applications collect and store considerable amounts of students' information. Ensuring that students' data is properly managed is achieved by the following legal provisions that educational organizations are required to adhere to, including FERPA and GDPR. However, the breaches in Cloud systems may pose danger to large data sets, ensuing to identity theft, or the wrong use of personal data. (Chandramouli et al. 2019, Iorga, & Chokhani 2019) It has been stated that ensuring, guarding and protecting that access processes to educational institutions is not an easy task, and applying the most advanced encryption technology is another issue that they encounter. Lack of security infrastructure can lead to negative consequences of students' privacy invasion and the school's shameful reputation.

7.2 The Digital Gap

Education going digital especially by adopting cloud learning has helped highlight the ever-existing digital gap that affects pupils significantly. and most NEWSS practitioners report from rural and low-income backgrounds. As much as cloud technologies enhance the availability and use of the education content, students lack personal devices, reliable connectivity, and in most cases appropriate digital literacy to effectively engage in the online learning environments (Van Dijk et al., 2020). To solve this problem, institutions should offer equal opportunities of core technology by offering free or subsidized gadgets, affordable internet or even community technology centers to bridge this divide (Anderson et al., 2020 & Rainie, 2020).

7.3 AI and Ethics Integrated

Cloud based education has been argued to have many ethical issues when it comes to the use of Artificial Intelligence (AI), especially on prejudice and fairness aspect. Bias arising from past data and used in AI algorithms in student assessment or adaptive tools in use might compromise the status of the students from different backgrounds (Binns et al., 2018). In this case, the fair and non- discriminative nature of the tools must be checked through a process of auditing and observation to ensure that it does not have any exclusionary features; Besides, there must be set out principles of how AI teaching instrument is to be used.

7.4 Cost Control and Scalability

While cloud-based solutions are elastic the management of the overheads connected with the further issuance of the cloud services remains a challenge. As demand increases, institutions struggle often with predicting consumer behavior or of the costs associated with increasing storage, computing, or bandwidth. (Martin et al. 2011) It also opines that poor management of these expenses might lead to poor budgeting for the funds or inadequate funding for other crucial education related services. Managers require coming with affordable strategies for effectively telling a firm's agenda that doesn't have to bend budget to accomplish this. Annex 2 Commercial plan is economy of scale where one can negotiate long-term cloud service providers' prices.

7.5 Opposition to Change

Too often educators and administrators need to adapt a new world view when it comes to cloud technology and many of them are still pre-disposed with fear to an adequately unknown medium. To overcome this reluctance, one therefore needs professional development which, however, may involve money as well as time. As noted, (Christensen et al., 2011, Horn, and Johnson 2011), anytime organizations wish to promote cloud technology for a certain use they need to invest in continuous training measures as well as grow into an innovative organization. Some of the faculty and staff can resist the shift towards cloud-based learning if they are not well trained and assisted.

8. ETHICAL CONSIDERATIONS AND DATA PRIVACY: DIGITAL DIVIDE AND EQUITY ISSUES

The use of technology in the education sector through cloud-based technology contains some strong ethical concerns that relate to the concepts of fairness as well as data privacy. This leads to a situation demographically known as the digital divide, or the difference between users equipped with technology and a stable internet connection and those who are not (Van Dijk et al., 2020). This gap can possibly worsen inequality in cloud-driven education as beneficiaries from poor background areas or low-income families could not have the gadgets, internet connection or e-learning skills that enables them to effectively participate in online classes. (Anderson et al., 2020 and Rainie 2020) However argue that to overcome such disparities it is the role of educational institutions to make sure that cloud-based solutions are made available irrespective of the geographical location or the economic status of the user.

However, there is no denying the fact that students' privacy is a matter of considerable ethical concern with reference to cloud-based learning. The collection and storage of the Large-scale data of the students involving personal identifiers and student performance measures have questions with the use and protection of such data. (Chandraramouli et al., 2019, Iorga & Chokhani 2019) It is to be noted that the study that education institutions are bound to rules such as FERPA in the United States or GDPR in the European Union that lay down exacting rules regarding how to handle students' data. As a result, proper encryption methods, proper access limits, and well-defined data procedures are mandatory within the cloud applications to protect students' privacy.

With concern on basic fairness of deployment of cloud-based technology also requires consideration from an ethical perspective. While they offer personalized and flexible pedagogy cloud technologies can re- 'contextualize' prejudice if not properly approached. For instance, in the system used some biases within data or in decision-making may appear and be integrated into the algorithms of AI-oriented educational platforms, providing students from different backgrounds unequal treatments (Binns et al., 2018).

9. FUTURE DIRECTIONS

- **Artificial Intelligence and Machine Learning:** The two technologies that are highly related to each other are machine learning and artificial intelligence.

Education through clouds will very soon be revolutionized through uptake of artificial intelligence and machine learning, implying custom learning, as a learner needs. Thus, AI algorithms may identify the patterns in the student communication and learning behavior and KPIs, which can be used to create the adaptive learning paths. Basically, these pathways determine the level of challenge and mode of delivery regarding the learning achievements of the student (Baker et al. 2014 & Inventado, 2014). For example, in the case of Intelligent Tutoring Systems (ITS), the latter employs elements of AI to give assistance and feedback enhancing the learning process and increasing the level of students' engagement (Woolf et al. 2009).

- **Blockchain for Education Credentials:** The issue and management of certificates and credentials in education are heating up for a drastic shift due to blockchain technology. Blockchain has a feature of ensuring authenticity and integrity as it provides a safe decentralized ledger. of scholastic records. Employers and educational institutions readily authenticate the digital diplomas and transcripts made possible by this technology (Grech et al. 2017 & Camilleri, 2017). The use of blockchain ensures an individual has a befitting and irreversible profile containing their educational achievements hence encouraging lifelong learning since learning can occur in numerous learning settings where skills and competences are acquired.
- **Immersive Learning Environments:** Integrating Augmented Reality (AR) and Virtual Reality (VR) to cloud-based education enhances the type of learning that occurs by making it better enriched. This way, the discussed technologies allow students to get the experience of interacting with 3D models, simulations, and virtual environments that cannot be provided using classical methods. For instance, history learners can learn civilizations of the past through virtual reality while medical students practice in virtual surgery rooms. digital reconstructions (Johnson et al. 2016). For these reasons, mobile applications that are resource intensive can be more effectively delivered

since the cloud possesses the processing ability as well as storage facilities that are needed.

- **Enhanced Data Privacy and Security:** New cloud-based solutions in education will increase the emphasis on data protection and privacy. The future developments of access restrictions are likely to be more secure; while more data protection legislation, such as the GDPR, and advance in even stronger forms of encryption are also expected. Thus, to counter these threats and leaks in concern with students' information, educational institutions will have to apply complex security measures (Chandramouli et al. 2019). When the use of AI in cybersecurity to eliminate possible threats in real time is applied to cloud-based learning systems, overall safety might increase.
- **Internet of Things (IoT) in Smart Classrooms:** The usage of IoT (Internet of Things) in efficient Intelligent Learning Environments. The glimmering classrooms of today are set to be toast all thanks to the Internet of Things which is seeking to bring standard classroom learning environments into the 21st century. IoT devices, including Organization and interpretation of data relating to the level of students' engagement, conditions in the classroom, along with learning outcomes, might be the smart boards, sensors and wearable gadgets. Thus, using this information can manage resources in the right way, improve the learning process, and individualize education (Uskov et al. 2015). For example, it may monitor the physical activity of the student, and provide information about their state of health, while the sensors might watch over the lighting and temperature of the class to provide only the best conditions for learning.
- **Game-Based Learning and Gamification:** Recently game-based learning as well as gamification has been reported as perspectives with beneficial effects to enhance students' motivation. (Deterding et al. 2011) It has been noted that it is within the educators' purview to increase the motivation and fun factor of a lesson using game elements such as leader's boards, badges, and points. Such components could be easily transferred between the devices and learning environments due to the usage of cloud solutions. One of the areas of future development of AI can become the creation of personal and individually increasing gaming tasks for each user based on his learning objectives and the achieved results.

10. CONCLUSION

Collaboration, Customization and Accessibility are major benefits of cloud technology in education. More advanced developments are Augmented Reality and Virtual Reality to enter immersive learning settings, Blockchain for securing educational credentials, Artificial Intelligence & Machine Learning. These enhancements have unique advantages and challenges to institutions positioning themselves to take full advantage of the cloud. AI / ML technologies are allowing customized learning by ensuring that material suited for each student is available to him thus redefining the process of tailored learning and delivering better user engagement along with enhancing results. The lack of proof blockchain provides can eliminate the credibility issue when it comes to attainment in education. Virtual reality and augmented reality are changing the way we experience education by offering immersive learning experiences outside of a typical classroom. This chapter points out that as organizations continue to move their solutions into cloud more and more it becomes imperative for them to have effective measures in place which ensure the safety and privacy of data, at all costs. Cloud infrastructure is a shift well-effective in improving operational effectiveness.

REFERENCES

Alhumaid, . (2019). The use of Google Classroom and its impact on student learning. *Journal of Information Technology Education*, 18, 321–337.

Amazon Web Services (AWS). (2017). University of Notre Dame case study. Retrieved from https://aws.amazon.com/solutions/case-studies/university-of-notre-dame/

Anderson. (2020). The future of well-being in a tech-saturated world. Pew Research Center.

Baker. (2014). Educational data mining and learning analytics. In Learning analytics (pp. 61-75). Springer.

Barkley. (2014). Collaborative learning techniques: A handbook for college faculty. John Wiley & Sons.

Belland, , Kim, C. M., & Hannafin, M. J. (2013). A framework for designing scaffolds that improve motivation and cognition. *Educational Psychologist*, 48(4), 243–270. DOI: 10.1080/00461520.2013.838920 PMID: 24273351

Bienkowski. (2012). Enhancing teaching and learning through educational data mining and learning analytics: An issue brief. U.S. Department of Education, Office of Educational Technology.

Binns, . (2018). Fairness in machine learning: Lessons from political philosophy. *Proceedings of the 2018 Conference on Fairness, Accountability, and Transparency* (pp. 149-159).

Black, . (2007). The power of feedback. *Review of Educational Research*, 77(1), 81–112. DOI: 10.3102/003465430298487

Black, , & Wiliam, D. (1998). Assessment and classroom learning. *Assessment in Education: Principles, Policy & Practice*, 5(1), 7–74. DOI: 10.1080/0969595980050102

Blaschke, . (2012). Heutagogy and lifelong learning: A review of heutagogical practice and self-determined learning. *International Review of Research in Open and Distance Learning*, 13(1), 56–71. DOI: 10.19173/irrodl.v13i1.1076

Bryant, . (2006). The impact of real-time collaborative tools on group work. *Journal of Educational Technology*, 22(3), 45–53.

Burgstahler. (2015). Universal design in higher education: From principles to practice. Harvard Education Press.

Chandramouli. (2019). Security and privacy controls for federal information systems and organizations. National Institute of Standards and Technology.

Christensen. (2011). Disrupting class: How disruptive innovation will change the way the world learns. McGraw-Hill.

CoSN et al. (2020). *The Alaska Digital Learning Project: Leveraging digital tools to address rural education challenges*. Consortium for School Networking.

Darling. (2017). Effective teacher professional development. Learning Policy Institute.

Denley, . (2014). Predictive analytics and choice architecture can improve student success. *Research & Practice in Assessment*, 9, 61–69.

Deterding. (2011). From game design elements to gamefulness: Defining "gamification". In Proceedings of the 15th international academic MindTrek conference: Envisioning future media environments (pp. 9-15).

Dillenbourg. (1999). Collaborative learning: Cognitive and computational approaches. Pergamon.

Falmagne. (2013). Knowledge spaces: Applications in education. Springer Science & Business Media.

Gonzalez, . (2018). Cloud computing and education: The perception of primary school teachers. *Journal of Educational Computing Research*, 56(7), 1070–1090.

Graesser, , McNamara, D. S., & VanLehn, K. (2005). Scaffolding deep comprehension strategies through Point&Query, AutoTutor, and iSTART. *Educational Psychologist*, 40(4), 225–234. DOI: 10.1207/s15326985ep4004_4

Grech, . (2017). Blockchain in education. Publications Office of the European Union.

Herodotou, . (2016). Using predictive learning analytics to support students. *Journal of Learning Analytics*, 6(2), 47–60.

Holmes. (2019). Artificial Intelligence in Education: Promises and Implications for Teaching and Learning. Center for Curriculum Redesign.

Hrastinski, . (2008). Asynchronous and synchronous e-learning. *EDUCAUSE Quarterly*, 31(4), 51–55.

Huang, . (2020). The service revolution in higher education: The role of AI-powered chatbots and virtual assistants. *Journal of Service Research*, 22(2), 158–174.

Johnson. (2016). NMC horizon report: 2016 higher education edition. The New Media Consortium.

Johnson. (2018). Cooperation and competition: Theory and research. Interaction Book Company.

Knewton. (2019). Knewton adaptive learning platform. Retrieved from Knewton.

Koedinger. (2006). Cognitive tutors: Technology bringing learning science to the classroom. In R. K. Sawyer (Ed.), The Cambridge Handbook of the Learning Sciences (pp. 61-78). Cambridge University Press.

Luckin. (2016). Intelligence unleashed: An argument for AI in education. Pearson.

Lundqvist, . (2013). AI-driven support tools in education: The impact of chatbots and virtual assistants. *Journal of Educational Technology*, 40(3), 45–58.

Marston, , Li, Z., Bandyopadhyay, S., Zhang, J., & Ghalsasi, A. (2011). Cloud computing—The business perspective. *Decision Support Systems*, 51(1), 176–189. DOI: 10.1016/j.dss.2010.12.006

Marwaha, . (2019). Rural Education Cloud Initiative: Empowering India's villages with cloud-based education. *International Journal of Educational Technology*, 20(3), 45–57.

Montgomery County Public Schools (MCPS). (2018). *MCPS early warning indicators system (EWIS) framework*. Retrieved from MCPS.

Ndemo, . (2017). Making open development inclusive: Lessons from Kenya and Tanzania. *The Electronic Journal on Information Systems in Developing Countries*, 78(1), 1–20.

Scott, . (2018). Supporting teachers' learning about cloud-based tools through professional development. *Journal of Technology and Teacher Education*, 26(1), 23–42.

Sharples. (2016). Innovating pedagogy 2016: Open University innovation report 5. The Open University.

Shinohara, . (2016). Self-conscious or self-confident? A diary study conceptualizing the experience of accessibility and assistive technology in daily life. *ACM Transactions on Accessible Computing*, 8(2), 1–31. DOI: 10.1145/2827857

Siemens, . (2011). Penetrating the fog: Analytics in learning and education. *EDUCAUSE Review*, 46(5), 30–32.

Smart Sparrow. (2017). *Case studies in adaptive learning*. Retrieved from Smart Sparrow.

Smith, . (2018). Designing inclusive educational spaces for students with disabilities. *Journal of Special Education Technology*, 33(3), 177–186.

Strother. (2019). E-Learning for employee training and development. In K. P. Kuchinke (Ed.), Management of employee training and development (pp. 187-204). Springer.

Subashini, S., & Kavitha, V. (2011). S., & Kavitha, V. (2011). A survey on security issues in service delivery models of cloud computing. *Journal of Network and Computer Applications*, 34(1), 1–11. DOI: 10.1016/j.jnca.2010.07.006

Summit. (2020). Personalized learning for all students. Retrieved from Summit et al. 2020 Learning.

University of Arizona. (2018). *AURA: The AI-powered academic advisor*. Retrieved from University of Arizona.

Uskov. (2015). The role of IoT in education. In 2015 ASEE annual conference & exposition. ASEE Conferences.

Van Dijk. (2020). The digital divide. Polity Press.

Woolf. (2009). Building intelligent interactive tutors: Student-centered strategies for revolutionizing e-learning. Morgan Kaufmann.

Young. (2019). Arizona State U. and Google Cloud: A partnership for innovation. The Chronicle of Higher Education. Retrieved from https://www.chronicle.com/article/arizona-state-u-and-google-cloud-a-partnership-for-innovation/

Compilation of References

Abrera, J. (2024). Data Privacy and Security in Cloud Computing: A Comprehensive Review. *Journal of Computer Science and Information Technology*, 1(1), 01-09.

Adams, A., Lunt, P., & Cairns, P. (2008). A qualitative approach to HCI research.

Adedoja, G., & Olatunji, O. A. (2020). The role of cloud computing in enhancing education. *Journal of Information Technology Education*, 19, 1–15.

Agarwal, P., & Alam, M. (2018). IoT Cloud Platforms: An Application Development Perspective. 10.48550/arXiv.1810.12292.

Agarwal, N., Chandrashekar, D., Rajaraman, A., & Venkataraman, V. (2019). Contextual advertising: Analyzing and predicting ad performance in contextual advertising. In *Proceedings of the 25th ACM SIGKDD International Conference on Knowledge Discovery & Data Mining* (pp. 1868-1876).

Agarwal, V., Kaushal, A. K., & Chouhan, L. (2020). *A Survey on Cloud Computing Security Issues and Cryptographic Techniques*. Social Networking and Computational Intelligence. DOI: 10.1007/978-981-15-2071-6_10

Akhouri, V., & Wasim, J. (2022). *A Comparative Study of Cloud Deployment Model. 10*, 2320–2882.

Akidau, T., Bradshaw, R., Chambers, C., Chernyak, S., Fernández-Moctezuma, R. J., Lax, R., & Whittle, S. (2015). The dataflow model: A practical approach to balancing correctness, latency, and cost in massive-scale, unbounded, out-of-order data processing. *Proceedings of the VLDB Endowment International Conference on Very Large Data Bases*, 8(12), 1792–1803.

Alam, A., & Mohanty, A. (2023). Educational technology: Exploring the Convergence of Technology and Pedagogy through mobility, interactivity, AI, and Learning Tools. *Cogent Engineering*, 10(2), 2283282. Advance online publication. DOI: 10.1080/23311916.2023.2283282

Alam, M. S., Wang, D., & Sowmya, A. (2021). *Image data augmentation for improving performance of deep learning-based model in pathological lung segmentation. In 2021 Digital Image Computing: Techniques and Applications*. DICTA. DOI: 10.1109/DICTA52665.2021.9647209

Alamri, H. A., Watson, S., & Watson, W. (2021). Learning technology models that support personalization within blended learning environments in higher education. *TechTrends*, 65(1), 62–78. DOI: 10.1007/s11528-020-00530-3

Al-Ataby, A. (2021). Hybrid Learning Using Canvas LMS. *European Journal of Education and Pedagogy, 2*(6), 27–33, doi.: DOI: 10.24018/ejedu.2021.2.6.180

Alenizi, B. A., Humayun, M., & Jhanjhi, N. Z. (2021). Security and privacy issues in cloud computing. []. IOP Publishing.]. *Journal of Physics: Conference Series*, 1979(1), 012038. DOI: 10.1088/1742-6596/1979/1/012038

Alexiou, A., Bouras, C., & Giannaka, E. (2005). Virtual Laboratories in Education. *Technology Enhanced Learning*, 171(Jan), 19–28. DOI: 10.1007/0-387-24047-0_2

Alghamdi, Y., Munir, A., & Ahmad, J. (2022, September). A Lightweight Image Encryption Algorithm Based on Chaotic Map and Random Substitution. *Entropy (Basel, Switzerland)*, 24(10), 1344. DOI: 10.3390/e24101344 PMID: 37420366

Alhumaid, . (2019). The use of Google Classroom and its impact on student learning. *Journal of Information Technology Education*, 18, 321–337.

Al-Khasawneh, M. A. S., Faheem, M., Aldhahri, E. A., Alzahrani, A., & Alarood, A. A. (2023). A MapReduce Based Approach for Secure Batch Satellite Image Encryption. *IEEE Access : Practical Innovations, Open Solutions*, 11, 62865–62878. DOI: 10.1109/ACCESS.2023.3279719

Almohammadi, A., Harun, J., & Daud, M. Y. (2022). Artificial intelligence in higher education: A systematic literature review. *Computers & Education*, 176, 104381. DOI: 10.1016/j.compedu.2021.104381

Al-Mousa, A. (2019). Cloud computing: Bridging the link between industry and the classroom. *International Journal of Electrical Engineering Education*, 002072091985763. Advance online publication. DOI: 10.1177/0020720919857636

Amazon Web Services (AWS). (2017). University of Notre Dame case study. Retrieved from https://aws.amazon.com/solutions/case-studies/university-of-notre-dame/

Anandkumar, R., Dinesh, K., Obaid, A. J., Malik, P., Sharma, R., Dumka, A., & Khatak, S. (2022). Securing e-Health application of cloud computing using hyper-chaotic image encryption framework. *Computers & Electrical Engineering*, 100, 107860. DOI: 10.1016/j.compeleceng.2022.107860

Anderson. (2020). The future of well-being in a tech-saturated world. Pew Research Center.

Ansari, Ali, & Alam. (2023). Internet of things (IoT) fusion with cloud computing: current research and future direction. ..DOI: 10.19101/IJATEE.2021.876002

Apriani, D., Aan, M., & Saputra, W. (2022). Data Visualization Using Google Data Studio. *International Journal of Cyber and IT Service Management.*, 2(1), 11–19. DOI: 10.34306/ijcitsm.v2i1.68

Arpaci, I., Kilicer, K., & Bardakci, S. (2015). Effects of security and privacy concerns on educational use of cloud services. *Computers in Human Behavior*, 45, 93–98. DOI: 10.1016/j.chb.2014.11.075

Aruna Yamini, Elakkiya, Keerthiga, & Baby Shamini. (2019). Cost Maintenance and Increased Performance in Cloud Data Centres. Suraj Punj Journal For Multi-disciplinary Research, 9(3), 352-360.

AT&T. (2018). Nanodegree Programs with Udacity: Building the Future Workforce. AT&T Innovation. Retrieved from att.com

Attaran, M., Attaran, S., & Celik, B. G. (2017). Promises and challenges of cloud computing in higher education: A practical guide for implementation. *Journal of Higher Education Theory and Practice*, 17(6).

Auccahuasi, W. (2018). Interactive Online Tool as an Instrument for Learning Mathematics through Programming Techniques, Aimed at High School Students. In Proceedings of the 6th International Conference on Information Technology: IoT and Smart City (pp. 70–76). Association for Computing Machinery. DOI: 10.1145/3301551.3301580

Baanqud, N. S., Al-Samarraie, H., Alzahrani, A. I., & Alfarraj, O. (2020). Engagement in cloud-supported collaborative learning and student knowledge construction: A modeling study. *International Journal of Educational Technology in Higher Education*, 17(1), 56. Advance online publication. DOI: 10.1186/s41239-020-00232-z

Babiuch, M., & Foltynek, P. (2021). Creating a Mobile Application with the ESP32 Azure IoT Development Board Using a Cloud Platform. 2021 22nd International Carpathian Control Conference (ICCC), 1-4.

Baby Shamini, Wise, Gayathri, Geetha, & Arunachalam. (2020). Prediction of QoS Ranking for Coud Services Using Matrix Factorization. International Journal of Advanced Science and Technology, 29(7), 424-429.

Baher, J. (1999). Articulate Virtual Labs in Thermodynamics Education: A Multiple Case Study*. *Journal of Engineering Education*, 88(4), 429–434. DOI: 10.1002/j.2168-9830.1999.tb00470.x

Baker. (2014). Educational data mining and learning analytics. In Learning analytics (pp. 61-75). Springer.

Balseiro, S., Feldman, J., Mirrokni, V., & Muthukrishnan, S. (2011, June). Yield optimization of display advertising with ad exchange. In *Proceedings of the 12th ACM conference on Electronic commerce* (pp. 27-28). DOI: 10.1145/1993574.1993580

Bao, Z., Xue, R., & Jin, Y. (2021, June). Image scrambling adversarial autoencoder based on the asymmetric encryption. *Multimedia Tools and Applications*, 80(18), 28265–28301. DOI: 10.1007/s11042-021-11043-3

Barkley. (2014). Collaborative learning techniques: A handbook for college faculty. John Wiley & Sons.

Belland, , Kim, C. M., & Hannafin, M. J. (2013). A framework for designing scaffolds that improve motivation and cognition. *Educational Psychologist*, 48(4), 243–270. DOI: 10.1080/00461520.2013.838920 PMID: 24273351

Bennett, S., & Maton, K. (2010). Beyond the 'digital natives' debate: Towards a more nuanced understanding of students' technology experiences. *Journal of Computer Assisted Learning*, 26(5), 321–331. DOI: 10.1111/j.1365-2729.2010.00360.x

Bennett, S., Maton, K., & Kervin, L. (2008). The 'digital natives' debate: A critical review of the evidence. *British Journal of Educational Technology*, 39(5), 775–786. DOI: 10.1111/j.1467-8535.2007.00793.x

Bhaskar, P., Tiwari, C. K., & Joshi, A. (2021). Blockchain in education management: Present and future applications. *Interactive Technology and Smart Education*, 18(1), 1–17. DOI: 10.1108/ITSE-07-2020-0102

Bienkowski. (2012). Enhancing teaching and learning through educational data mining and learning analytics: An issue brief. U.S. Department of Education, Office of Educational Technology.

Binns, . (2018). Fairness in machine learning: Lessons from political philosophy. *Proceedings of the 2018 Conference on Fairness, Accountability, and Transparency* (pp. 149-159).

Black, . (2007). The power of feedback. *Review of Educational Research*, 77(1), 81–112. DOI: 10.3102/003465430298487

Black, , & Wiliam, D. (1998). Assessment and classroom learning. *Assessment in Education: Principles, Policy & Practice*, 5(1), 7–74. DOI: 10.1080/0969595980050102

Blaschke, . (2012). Heutagogy and lifelong learning: A review of heutagogical practice and self-determined learning. *International Review of Research in Open and Distance Learning*, 13(1), 56–71. DOI: 10.19173/irrodl.v13i1.1076

Bocklisch, T., Faulkner, J., Pawlowski, N., & Nichol, A. (2017). Rasa: Open Source Language Understanding and Dialogue Management. In *Proceedings of the Conversational AI Workshop at the 31st Conference on Neural Information Processing Systems (NeurIPS 2017)*. DOI: 10.48550/arXiv.1712.05181

Borra, P. (2024). The Evolution and Impact of Google Cloud Platform in Machine learning and AI. *International Journal of Advanced Research in Science Communication and Technology.*, 4, 72–77. DOI: 10.48175/IJARSCT-18908

Bowersox, D. J., Closs, D. J., & Cooper, M. B. (2013). *Supply chain logistics management*. McGraw-Hill Education.

Brajnik, G., & Gabrielli, S. (2010). A review of online advertising effects on the user experience. *International Journal of Human-Computer Interaction*, 26(10), 971–997. DOI: 10.1080/10447318.2010.502100

Brandon Hall Group. (2019). The Business Impact of Next-Generation Learning Technologies. Brandon Hall Group. Retrieved from brandonhall.com

Brown, A., & Patel, A. (2023). Innovations in green technologies for sustainable supply chains. *The Journal of Supply Chain Management*, 60(2), 118–132.

Brown, A., & Wang, L. (2024). Blockchain and supply chain management: Lessons from IBM's Food Trust. *The Journal of Supply Chain Management*, 61(1), 102–115.

Bryant, . (2006). The impact of real-time collaborative tools on group work. *Journal of Educational Technology*, 22(3), 45–53.

Bulger, M. (n.d.). Personalized learning: the conversations we're not having. In *Working Paper*. Data & Society Research Institute. https://datasociety.net/pubs/ecl/PersonalizedLearning_primer_2016.pdf

Burgstahler. (2015). Universal design in higher education: From principles to practice. Harvard Education Press.

Carby, N. (2023). Personalized feedback in a virtual learning environment. *Journal of Educational Supervision*, 6(1), 36–44. DOI: 10.31045/jes.6.1.3

Cardona, M. A., Rodriguez, R. J., & Ishmael, K. (2023). *Artificial Intelligence and the Future of Teaching and Learning Insights and Recommendations*. Office of Educational Technology. https://www2.ed.gov/documents/ai-report/ai-report.pdf

Carneiro, T., Da Nóbrega, R. V. M., Nepomuceno, T., Bian, G. B., De Albuquerque, V. H. C., & Reboucas Filho, P. P. (2018). Performance analysis of google colaboratory as a tool for accelerating deep learning applications. *IEEE Access : Practical Innovations, Open Solutions*, 6, 61677–61685.

Chandramouli. (2019). Security and privacy controls for federal information systems and organizations. National Institute of Standards and Technology.

Chan, P., Van Gerven, T., Dubois, J.-L., & Bernaerts, K. (2021). Virtual Chemical Laboratories: A Systematic Literature Review of Research, Technologies and Instructional Design. *Computers and Education Open*, 2(Oct), 100053. DOI: 10.1016/j.caeo.2021.100053

Chatterjee, P., Bose, R., Banerjee, S., & Roy, S. (2023). Enhancing data security of cloud based lms. *Wireless Personal Communications*, 130(2), 1123–1139. DOI: 10.1007/s11277-023-10323-5 PMID: 37168441

Chaudhry, M. A., & Kazim, E. (2021). Artificial Intelligence in Education (AIEd): A high-level academic and industry note 2021. *AI and Ethics*, 2(2), 157–165. Advance online publication. DOI: 10.1007/s43681-021-00074-z PMID: 34790953

Chen, G., Xu, B., Lu, M., & Chen, N. S. (2018). Exploring blockchain technology and its potential applications for education. *Smart Learning Environments*, 5(1), 1–10. DOI: 10.1186/s40561-017-0050-x

Cheng, Y., Liu, Q., & Chen, X. (2024). Artificial intelligence in supply chain management: A review and future directions. *The Journal of Supply Chain Management*, 60(1), 14–28.

Chen, J., Li, X.-W., & Wang, Q.-H. (2019). Deep Learning for Improving the Robustness of Image Encryption. *IEEE Access : Practical Innovations, Open Solutions*, 7, 181083–181091. DOI: 10.1109/ACCESS.2019.2959031

Chen, S. Y., & Magoulas, G. D. (2003). Foundations for personalized web learning environments. *International Journal of Continuing Engineering Education and Lifelong Learning*, 13(3-4), 261–275. DOI: 10.1504/IJCEELL.2003.003337

Chen, Y., Liu, Z., Li, Y., Li, H., Liu, X., & Zhang, Z. (2018). Click-through rate prediction for sponsored search based on user intent understanding. In *Proceedings of the 27th ACM International Conference on Information and Knowledge Management* (pp. 447-456).

Cheroiu, D.-G., Raducanu, M., & Nitu, C. M. (2022). Fast Image Encryption Algorithm Based on Multiple Chaotic Maps. 2022 14th International Conference on Communications (COMM). DOI: 10.1109/COMM54429.2022.9817317

Choi, T. M., Liu, Y., & Shen, B. (2023). Advances in robotics and automation in the supply chain. *International Journal of Production Economics*, 253, 108–121.

Choudhary, B., Pophale, C., Gutte, A., Dani, A., & Sonawani, S. S. (2020). Case Study: use of AWS lambda for building a serverless chat application. In Proceeding of International Conference on Computational Science and Applications: ICCSA 2019 (pp. 237-244). Springer Singapore.

Choudhury, T., Gupta, A., Pradhan, S., Kumar, P., & Rathore, Y. S. (2017). Privacy and security of cloud-based Internet of Things (IoT). In *2017 3rd International Conference on Computational Intelligence and Networks (CINE)* (pp. 40-45). IEEE. DOI: 10.1109/CINE.2017.28

Christensen. (2011). Disrupting class: How disruptive innovation will change the way the world learns. McGraw-Hill.

Christopher, M. (2016). *Logistics & supply chain management*. Pearson Education.

Cohen, B., Hu, A., Patino, D., & Coffman, J. (2022). Educational Data in the Cloud Legal Implications and Technical Recommendations. In 2022 *IEEE/ACM 15th International Conference on Utility and Cloud Computing* (UCC) (pp. 181-182). IEEE. DOI: 10.1109/UCC56403.2022.00032

Correa, T., Straubhaar, J., Chen, W., & Spence, J. (2015). Brokering new technologies: The role of children in their parents' usage of the internet. *New Media & Society*, 17(4), 483–500. DOI: 10.1177/1461444813506975

CoSN et al. (2020). *The Alaska Digital Learning Project: Leveraging digital tools to address rural education challenges*. Consortium for School Networking.

Coursera. (2020). Corporate Training Solutions: Enhancing Employee Skills with Cloud-Based Learning. Coursera for Business. Retrieved from coursera.org

Covin, J. G., & Slevin, D. P. (1989). Strategic management of small firms in hostile and benign environments. *Strategic Management Journal*, 10(1), 75–87. DOI: 10.1002/smj.4250100107

Crompton, H. (2021). Mobile learning in higher education: A systematic review of research on trends, instructional strategies, and technologies. *Educational Technology Research and Development*, 69(1), 153–173. DOI: 10.1007/s11423-020-09835-2

Darling. (2017). Effective teacher professional development. Learning Policy Institute.

Davis, T., Lee, J., & Thompson, R. (2023). Change management strategies for technology adoption in supply chains. *International Journal of Production Economics*, 258, 138–150.

Dawson, S., Heathcote, L., & Poole, G. (2020). Harnessing the affordances of digital learning: An activity system analysis of research and practice. *Educational Technology Research and Development*, 68(6), 2975–3001. DOI: 10.1007/s11423-020-09831-6

Dawson, S., Joksimović, S., Kovanović, V., Gašević, D., & Siemens, G. (2020). The impact of learning management systems on learning outcomes: A systematic review. *The Internet and Higher Education*, 44, 100726. DOI: 10.1016/j.iheduc.2019.100726

Degreed. (2019). Creating a Learning Ecosystem: The Role of Cloud-Based Platforms. Degreed White Papers. Retrieved from degreed.com

Denley, . (2014). Predictive analytics and choice architecture can improve student success. *Research & Practice in Assessment*, 9, 61–69.

Deterding. (2011). From game design elements to gamefulness: Defining "gamification". In Proceedings of the 15th international academic MindTrek conference: Envisioning future media environments (pp. 9-15).

Dillenbourg. (1999). Collaborative learning: Cognitive and computational approaches. Pergamon.

Djoub, Z. (2017). *Assessment for Learning: Feeding Back and Feeding Forward.* Www.igi-Global.com

Dumka, P., & Mishra, D. R. (2024). Modelling of air standard thermodynamic cycles using CyclePad. *Jiet.* https://www.academia.edu/122420201/Modelling_of_Air_Standard_Thermodynamic_Cycles_Using_CyclePad

Durairaj, M., & Manimaran, A. (2015). A study on security issues in cloud based e-learning. *Indian Journal of Science and Technology*, 8(8), 757–765. DOI: 10.17485/ijst/2015/v8i8/69307

Duta, I. P. G. P., Febriansyah, M. R., & Anggreainy, M. S. (2021, October). Effectiveness of LMS in online learning by analyzing its usability and features. In 2021 1st International Conference on Computer Science and Artificial Intelligence (ICCSAI) (Vol. 1, pp. 56-61). IEEE.

Ekowo, M., & Tait, M. (2020). Creating conditions for equity in schools: Technology, culture, and power. New America. https://www.newamerica.org/education-policy/reports/creating-conditions-equity-schools/

El-Attar, N. E., Abo El-Ela, N., & Awad, W. A. (2019). Integrated learning approaches based on cloud computing for personalizing e-learning environment. *International Journal of Web-Based Learning and Teaching Technologies*, 14(1), 101–114. DOI: 10.4018/IJWLTT.2019040105

Ellwein, C., Riedel, O., Meyer, O., & Schel, D. (2018). Rent'n'Produce: A secure cloud manufacturing platform for small and medium enterprises. In *2018 IEEE International Conference on Engineering, Technology and Innovation (ICE/ITMC)* (pp. 1-6). DOI: 10.1109/ICE.2018.8436332

Elmoazen, R., Saqr, M., Khalil, M., & Wasson, B. (2023, March). Learning Analytics in Virtual Laboratories: A Systematic Literature Review of Empirical Research. *Smart Learning Environments*, 10(1), 9. DOI: 10.1186/s40561-023-00244-y

Elsevier. (2016). Adaptive learning. Retrieved January 05, 2018, from https://evolve.elsevier.com/education/adaptive-learning/keys-to-improving-outcomes-and-retention/

Erkan, U., Toktas, A., Enginoğlu, S., Akbacak, E., & Thanh, D. N. H. (2022). An image encryption scheme based on chaotic logarithmic map & key generation using deep CNN. *Multimedia Tools and Applications*, 81(5), 7365–7391. DOI: 10.1007/s11042-021-11803-1

Eynon, R., & Geniets, A. (2016). The digital skills paradox: How do digitally excluded youth develop skills to use the internet? *Learning, Media and Technology*, 41(3), 463–479. DOI: 10.1080/17439884.2014.1002845

Fadhil, M. S., Farhan, A. K., & Fadhil, M. N. (2021). Designing Substitution Box Based on the 1D Logistic Map Chaotic System. *IOP Conference Series. Materials Science and Engineering*, 1076(1), 012041. DOI: 10.1088/1757-899X/1076/1/012041

Falmagne. (2013). Knowledge spaces: Applications in education. Springer Science & Business Media.

Foo, F., & Winkler, S. (2022). Image Data Augmentation with Unpaired Image-to-Image Camera Model Translation. *2022 IEEE International Conference on Image Processing (ICIP)*. DOI: 10.1109/ICIP46576.2022.9897671

Forbes. (2021). The Future of Corporate Training: Cloud-Based Solutions. Forbes Business Insights. Retrieved from forbes.com

Fox, Donnellan, & Doumen. (2019). The deployment of an IoT network infrastructure, as a localised regional service. .DOI: 10.1109/WF-IoT.2019.8767188

Friemel, T. N. (2016). The digital divide has grown old: Determinants of a digital divide among seniors. *New Media & Society*, 18(2), 313–331. DOI: 10.1177/1461444814538648

Gaikwad, V. S., & Prasad, D. G. S. (2018). A survey on user awareness of cloud security. *International Journal of Engineering & Technology, 7*(2.32), 131-135.

Gaikwad, P., & Patil. (2021, March). Study On Cloud Deployment Model. *International Journal of Scientific and Engineering Research*, 12(3), •••.

Gamage, S. H., Ayres, J. R., & Behrend, M. B. (2022). A systematic review on trends in using Moodle for teaching and learning. *International Journal of STEM Education*, 9(1), 9.

Gartner. (2021). Market Guide for Corporate Learning Suites. Gartner Research. Retrieved from gartner.com

Gassara, M., Elleuchi, M., & Abid, M. (2021). LoRa cloud-based platform for Internet of Things applications. In *2021 IEEE International IoT,Electronics and Mechatronics Conference (IEMTRONICS)* (pp. 1-6). IEEE. DOI: 10.1109/IEMTRONICS52119.2021.9422531

Gavlas, A., Zwierzyna, J., & Koziorek, J. (2018). Possibilities of transfer process data from PLC to cloud platforms based on IoT. *IFAC-PapersOnLine*, 51(6), 156–161. DOI: 10.1016/j.ifacol.2018.07.146

Gebhardt, K. (2018). Adaptive learning courseware as a tool to build foundational content mastery: Evidence from principles of microeconomics. *Current Issues in Emerging Elearning*, 5(1), 2.

Ghanbari, H., Enayatifar, R., & Motameni, H. (2022). A Fast Image Encryption based on Linear Feedback Shift Register and Deoxyribonucleic acid. DOI: 10.21203/rs.3.rs-1662684/v1

Ghosh, U. (2022). ROLE OF COMMUNICATION IN EDUCATION. In *International Journal for Research Trends and Innovation* (Vol. 7, Issue 6, pp. 326–327) [Journal-article]. https://www.ijrti.org/papers/IJRTI2206057.pdf

Ghosh, P., & Patel, A. (2023). Assessing ROI in supply chain technology investments. *Journal of Business Research*, 112, 245–256.

Gikandi, J. W., Morrow, D., & Davis, N. E. (2020). Online formative assessment in higher education: A review of the literature. *Computers & Education*, 56(3), 1045–1051. DOI: 10.1016/j.compedu.2010.12.001

Gill, S. H., Razzaq, M. A., Ahmad, M., Almansour, F. M., Haq, I. U., Jhanjhi, N. Z., & Masud, M. (2022). Security and privacy aspects of cloud computing: A smart campus case study. *Intelligent Automation & Soft Computing*, 31(1), 117–128. DOI: 10.32604/iasc.2022.016597

Global, I. G. I. https://www.igi-global.com/chapter/assessment-for-learning/159965

Global, I. G. I. https://www.igi-global.com/chapter/blended-learning-in-higher-education-40/224208

Gomez, R. (2013). The Changing Field of Information and Communication Technology for Development (ICTD): From ICT to Digital Development. *The Electronic Journal on Information Systems in Developing Countries*, 59(1), 1–25.

Gonzalez, . (2018). Cloud computing and education: The perception of primary school teachers. *Journal of Educational Computing Research*, 56(7), 1070–1090.

Graesser, , McNamara, D. S., & VanLehn, K. (2005). Scaffolding deep comprehension strategies through Point&Query, AutoTutor, and iSTART. *Educational Psychologist*, 40(4), 225–234. DOI: 10.1207/s15326985ep4004_4

Grech, . (2017). Blockchain in education. Publications Office of the European Union.

Gudapati, S. P., & Gaikwad, V. (2021). Light-Weight Key Establishment Mechanism for Secure Communication Between IoT Devices and Cloud. In Satapathy, S., Bhateja, V., Janakiramaiah, B., & Chen, Y. W. (Eds.), *Intelligent System Design. Advances in Intelligent Systems and Computing* (Vol. 1171). Springer. DOI: 10.1007/978-981-15-5400-1_55

Gudapati, S. P., Gaikwad, V., & Ravindranath, K. (2023). A mathematical model for secure Cloud-IoT communication: Introducing the revolutionary lightweight key mechanism. *Journal of Discrete Mathematical Sciences & Cryptography*, 26(5), 1341–1354. DOI: 10.47974/JDMSC-1750

Gujarkar, P., Lonkar, S., Jain, T., Nigal, S., & Patil, P. pallavi Deshpande, Ketki Kshirsagar., “IoT based Smart Attendance System,” *2023 International Conference on Emerging Smart Computing and Informatics (ESCI)*, Pune, India, 2023, pp. 1-6, DOI: 10.1109/ESCI56872.2023.10099839

Gupta, A., Shinde, V., Kumar, V., & Kale, A. (2017). Ensemble methods for click-through rate prediction in online advertising. *Journal of Marketing Analytics*, 5(2), 65–77.

Gupta, B. B. (Ed.). (2019). *Modern Principles, Practices, and Algorithms for Cloud Security*. IGI Global.

Gupta, H., Kumar, P., & Ghosh, P. (2023). Machine learning for predictive maintenance in supply chains. *Journal of Manufacturing Processes*, 81, 277–288.

Hadi, M. U., Al Tashi, Q., & Qureshi, R. (2023). Large Language Models: A Comprehensive Survey of its Applications, Challenges, Limitations, and Future Prospects. *TechRxiv*. https://doi.org/DOI: 10.36227/techrxiv.19183181.v1

Hämäläinen, R., & Vähäsantanen, K. (2022). Adaptive learning in higher education: A systematic review of research literature. *Computers & Education*, 175, 104319. DOI: 10.1016/j.compedu.2021.104319

Han, H., Zhu, B., Zhan, L., Yu, T., Shen, G., & Chen, Y. (2021). ICool: One-stop service IoT cloud platform. In *2021 2nd International Conference on Artificial Intelligence and Computer Engineering (ICAICE)* (pp. 680-684). DOI: 10.1109/ICAICE54393.2021.00133

Hao, L., Zhang, W., & Li, X. (2022). Robotics in warehousing: A case study of Amazon's fulfillment centers. *Robotics and Automation Review*, 43(2), 90–103.

Hardt, M., Chen, X., Cheng, X., Donini, M., Gelman, J., Gollaprolu, S., . . . Kenthapadi, K. (2021, August). Amazon sagemaker clarify: Machine learning bias detection and explainability in the cloud. In Proceedings of the 27th ACM SIGKDD conference on knowledge discovery & data mining (pp. 2974-2983).

Hargittai, E. (2010). Digital Na(t)ives? Variation in Internet Skills and Uses among Members of the "Net Generation.". *Sociological Inquiry*, 80(1), 92–113. DOI: 10.1111/j.1475-682X.2009.00317.x

Harris, J. B. (Ed.). (2020). *Handbook of adult and continuing education*. Jossey-Bass.

Harrison, S., Tatar, D., & Sengers, P. (2007, April). The three paradigms of HCI. In Alt. Chi. Session at the SIGCHI Conference on Human Factors in Computing Systems (pp. 1-18).

hashira9082. (2024, March 27). *Cloud Computing in Healthcare | Impact, Use Cases & Examples*. Enago Academy. https://www.enago.com/academy/guestposts/hashira9082/cloud-computing-in-healthcare/

Haunts, S. (2019). *Hybrid Encryption. Applied Cryptography in* NET and Azure Key Vault. DOI: 10.1007/978-1-4842-4375-6_9

Hazen, B. T., Boone, C. A., Ezell, J. D., & Jones-Farmer, L. A. (2014). Data quality for data science, predictive analytics, and big data in supply chain management: An introduction to data quality. *International Journal of Production Economics*, 154, 72–80. DOI: 10.1016/j.ijpe.2014.04.018

Helaimia, R. (2023). Cloud computing in higher education institutions: pros and cons. International Journal of Advanced Natural Sciences and Engineering Researches, 7(ISSN: 2980-0811).

Helsper, E. J., & Eynon, R. (2010). Digital natives: Where is the evidence? *British Educational Research Journal*, 36(3), 503–520. DOI: 10.1080/01411920902989227

Herodotou, . (2016). Using predictive learning analytics to support students. *Journal of Learning Analytics*, 6(2), 47–60.

Hewlett-Packard Enterprise. (2020). Leveraging Cloud-Based Learning Platforms for Employee Development. HPE Insights. Retrieved from hpe.com

Holmes. (2019). Artificial Intelligence in Education: Promises and Implications for Teaching and Learning. Center for Curriculum Redesign.

Horrigan, J. B. (2007). *A Typology of Information and Communication Technology Users*. Pew Research Center.

Hrastinski, . (2008). Asynchronous and synchronous e-learning. *EDUCAUSE Quarterly*, 31(4), 51–55.

Hrishikesh Dewan & Hansdah. (2011). A survey of cloud storage facilities. 2011 IEEE World Congress on Services, 224–231.

Hsieh, S. W. (2011). Effects of cognitive styles on an MSN virtual learning companion system as an adjunct to classroom instructions. *Journal of Educational Technology & Society*, 14, 161–174.

Huang, . (2020). The service revolution in higher education: The role of AI-powered chatbots and virtual assistants. *Journal of Service Research*, 22(2), 158–174.

Huang, L. N., Liu, F. H., & Liu, C. L. (2013). Design and research on collaborative learning program based on Cloud-Services. *Advanced Materials Research*, 756–759, 1199–1203. . DOI: 10.4028/www.scientific.net/AMR.756-759.1199

Huang, W., Hew, K. F., & Fryer, L. K. (2022). Chatbots for language learning—Are they really useful? A systematic review of chatbot-supported language learning. *Journal of Computer Assisted Learning*, 38(1), 237–257. DOI: 10.1111/jcal.12610

Huang, Y., Zhang, Y., & Wang, L. (2023). Automation systems in manufacturing: A comprehensive review. *Journal of Manufacturing Science and Engineering*, 145(6), 112–125.

Huang, Z., Tan, C., & Xiao, Y. (2020). Sentiment-aware click-through rate prediction in online advertising. *IEEE Transactions on Knowledge and Data Engineering*, 32(9), 1757–1769.

Husain, T., & Budiyantara, A. (2020). Analysis of control security and privacy based on E-Learning users. *SAR Journal*, 3(2), 51–58.

Hussain, I. (2024). Exploring the impact of learning styles on tailoring individual learners' needs: A systemic review. *Journal of Management & Educational Research Innovation*, 2(1), 16–26. DOI: 10.5281/zenodo.11128012

IBM. (2020). IBM's Your Learning Platform: Using AI to Empower Continuous Learning. IBM Case Studies. Retrieved from ibm.com

Irfandi, I., Festiyed, F., Yerimadesi, Y., & Sudarma, T. (2023). The Use Of Learning Management System (Lms) In The Teaching And Learning Process: Literature Review. *Jurnal Pendidikan Fisika.*, 12(1), 81. DOI: 10.24114/jpf.v12i1.42270

Ivanov, D., & Dolgui, A. (2020). *Handbook of research on digital transformation and challenges to data security and privacy*. IGI Global.

Janssen, J., Conijn, R., Kester, L., & Kalz, M. (2021). Teachers' professional development in digital competency: Lessons learned from Dutch primary schools. *Technology, Pedagogy and Education*, 30(1), 35–51. DOI: 10.1080/1475939X.2020.1805603

Jenkins, H., Ito, M., & Boyd, D. (2015). Participatory Culture in a Networked Era: A Conversation on Youth, Learning, Commerce, and Politics. *Polity*.

Jiang, H., Vimalesvaran, S., Wang, J. K., Lim, K. B., Mogali, S. R., & Car, L. T. (2021). Virtual Reality in Medical Students' Education: A Scoping Review (Preprint). *JMIR Medical Education*, 8(1), e34860. Advance online publication. DOI: 10.2196/34860 PMID: 35107421

Johnson, D., & Samora, D. (2016). The potential transformation of higher Education through computer-based adaptive learning systems. Global Education Journal, 1.

Johnson. (2016). NMC horizon report: 2016 higher education edition. The New Media Consortium.

Johnson. (2018). Cooperation and competition: Theory and research. Interaction Book Company.

Johnson, M., & Lee, R. (2023). Financial challenges in adopting advanced SCM technologies. *International Journal of Logistics Management*, 34(2), 158–172.

Johnson, M., & Lee, R. (2024). Big data analytics in retail: Walmart's data-driven approach. *International Journal of Retail & Distribution Management*, 52(3), 245–260.

Johnson, M., & Lee, R. (2024). Blockchain and sustainability: Enhancing transparency in supply chains. *International Journal of Logistics Management*, 35(1), 45–59.

Jones, C., Ramanau, R., Cross, S., & Healing, G. (2010). Net generation or Digital Natives: Is there a distinct new generation entering university? *Computers & Education*, 54(3), 722–732. DOI: 10.1016/j.compedu.2009.09.022

Justin, S., & Karuppusamy, S. K. (2022, December). Mayfly optimization with chaos-based image encryption technique for cloud computing environment. *Journal of Electronic Imaging*, 32(05). Advance online publication. DOI: 10.1117/1.JEI.32.5.052303

Kakkad, V., Patel, M., & Shah, M. (2019, May). Biometric authentication and image encryption for image security in cloud framework. *Multiscale and Multidisciplinary Modeling, Experiments and Design*, 2(4), 233–248. DOI: 10.1007/s41939-019-00049-y

Kale, S., & Khatri, S. (2021). A study on role and application of cloud engineering & cloud computing in business reengineering with reference to Netflix. [TOJQI]. *Turkish Online Journal of Qualitative Inquiry*, 12(3), 4409–4419.

Kamalloo, E. (2023). Evaluating Embedding APIs for Information Retrieval. DOI: 10.18653/v1/2023.acl-industry.50

Kanickam, S. H. L., Jayasimman, L., & Jebaseeli, A. N. (2017). A Survey on Layer Wise Issues and Challenges in Cloud Security. *2017 World Congress on Computing and Communication Technologies (WCCCT)*. DOI: 10.1109/WCCCT.2016.49

Ketki, P. (2022). *Kshirsagar, Ashish Tathod, Rushikesh Dudhate, Ajay Yadav, Rudra Tarte, "Camera Calibration Using Robust Intrinsic and Extrinsic Parameters", Artificial Intelligence in Information and Communication Technologies, Healthcare and Education*. Chapman and Hall/CRC.

Khan, M. A., & Salah, K. (2020). Cloud adoption for e-learning: Survey and future challenges. *Education and Information Technologies*, 25(2), 1417–1438. DOI: 10.1007/s10639-019-10021-5

Khanna, A., Sah, A., Bolshev, V., Burgio, A., Panchenko, V., & Jasiński, M. (2022). Blockchain–cloud integration: A survey. *Sensors (Basel)*, 22(14), 5238. DOI: 10.3390/s22145238 PMID: 35890918

Khan, S., Smith, J., & Roberts, C. (2023). Overcoming integration barriers in SCM technology. *The Journal of Supply Chain Management*, 59(3), 99–113.

Kim, J., Lee, H., & Lee, J. (2023). Blockchain for food safety: A case study of Walmart's supply chain. *Food Control*, 146, 109–119.

Kim, K. H., & Smith, P. L. (2021). Microlearning: A literature review. *TechTrends*, 65(6), 1422–1433. DOI: 10.1007/s11423-022-10084-1

Kim, M. J., & Smith, L. (2021). Student-centered learning design in a cloud-based learning management system. [JETDE]. *Journal of Educational Technology Development and Exchange*, 14(3), 189–204.

Knewton. (2019). Knewton adaptive learning platform. Retrieved from Knewton.

Koedinger. (2006). Cognitive tutors: Technology bringing learning science to the classroom. In R. K. Sawyer (Ed.), The Cambridge Handbook of the Learning Sciences (pp. 61-78). Cambridge University Press.

Komljenovic, J. (2022). The future of value in digitalised higher education: Why data privacy should not be our biggest concern. *Higher Education*, 83(1), 119–135. DOI: 10.1007/s10734-020-00639-7 PMID: 33230347

Kshirsagar, K. P. (2015). Key Frame Selection for One-Two Hand Gesture Recognition with HMM. *International Journal of Advanced Computer Research*, 5(19), 192.

Kshirsagar, K. P., & Doye, D. (2010, October). Object Based Key Frame Selection for Hand Gesture Recognition. In *2010 International Conference on Advances in Recent Technologies in Communication and Computing* (pp. 181-185). IEEE.

Kumar, B. P., Kommareddy, S., & Rani, N. U. (2013). Effective ways cloud computing can contribute to education success. [ACIJ]. *Advanced Computing: An International Journal*, 4(4), 17–32. Advance online publication. DOI: 10.5121/acij.2013.4402

Kumar, J. S. A., Sreelatha, A., & Sowjanya, A. (2017). Cloud computing in education. *International Journal of Scientific and Engineering Research*, 8(5), 175. http://www.ijser.org

Kumar, S., Gupta, H., & Ghosh, P. (2023). 3D printing and customization: Transforming supply chains. *Journal of Manufacturing Processes*, 82, 198–210.

Kumar, S., & Sharma, A. (2024). Cloud computing in supply chain management: Benefits and challenges. *International Journal of Cloud Computing and Services Science*, 12(1), 45–58.

Kumar, S., Singh, B. K., & Akshita, S. (2020). A survey on Symmetric and Asymmetric Key based Image Encryption. *2nd International Conference on Data, Engineering and Applications (IDEA)*. DOI: 10.1109/IDEA49133.2020.9170703

Kumar, S., Singh, R., & Garg, R. (2023). The impact of cloud-based SCM platforms on supply chain collaboration. *Computers in Industry*, 135, 12–25.

Kumar, S., Srivastava, P. K., Srivastava, G. K., Singhal, P., Singh, D., & Goyal, D. (2022, May). Chaos based image encryption security in cloud computing. *Journal of Discrete Mathematical Sciences and Cryptography*, 25(4), 1041–1051. DOI: 10.1080/09720529.2022.2075085

Kumar, S., Tiwari, P., & Zymbler, M. (2019). Internet of Things is a revolutionary approach for future technology enhancement: A review. *Journal of Big Data*, 6(1), 111. DOI: 10.1186/s40537-019-0268-2

Kumar, V., & Garg, M. L. (2018). Predictive analytics: A review of trends and techniques. *International Journal of Computer Applications*, 182(1), 31–37. DOI: 10.5120/ijca2018917434

Kumbhar, K., & Kshirasagar, K. P. (2015). Comparative study of CCD & CMOS sensors for image processing. *International Journal of Innovative Research in Electrical, Electronics, Instrumentation and Control Engineering*, 3(12), 194–196. DOI: 10.17148/IJIREEICE.2015.31240

Kvavik, R. B., & Caruso, J. B. (2005). *ECAR Study of Students and Information Technology, 2005: Convenience, Connection, Control, and Learning. EDUCAUSE Center for Analysis and Research.* ECAR.

Lakshmi, K., Thenmozhi, K., Rayappan, J. B. B., Rajagopalan, S., Amirtharajan, R., & Chidambaram, N. (2020, November). Neural-assisted image-dependent encryption scheme for medical image cloud storage. *Neural Computing & Applications*, 33(12), 6671–6684. DOI: 10.1007/s00521-020-05447-9

LaValley, M. P. (2008). Logistic regression. *Circulation*, 117(18), 2395–2399. DOI: 10.1161/CIRCULATIONAHA.106.682658 PMID: 18458181

Lavanya, Sundar, & Saravanan. (2024). Simplified Image Encryption Algorithm (SIEA) to enhance image security in cloud storage. *Multimedia Tools and Applications*. DOI: 10.1007/s11042-023-17969-0

Learning Solutions Magazine. (2020). The Advantages of Cloud-Based Professional Development. Learning Solutions. Retrieved from learningsolutionsmag.com

Lee, C. S., Cheang, P. Y. S., & Moslehpour, M. (2022). Predictive analytics in business analytics: Decision tree. *Advances in Decision Sciences*, 26(1), 1–29. DOI: 10.47654/v26y2022i1p1-29

Lee, J. H., Yang, H., Shin, D., & Kim, H. (2020). Chatbots. *ELT Journal*, 74(3), 338–344. DOI: 10.1093/elt/ccaa035

Lee, S., Kim, J., & Park, H. (2024). Personalization and technology in modern supply chains. *Journal of Business Logistics*, 46(1), 75–88.

Lee, S., Kim, J., & Park, H. (2024). Workforce adaptation to technological change in supply chains. *Journal of Business Logistics*, 45(2), 65–79.

Liang, L., Hong, J. I., Toyama, K., & Ackerman, M. S. (2020). Towards accountable predictive click analytics: Examining the causes of algorithmic errors in user behavior prediction. In *Proceedings of the 2020 CHI Conference on Human Factors in Computing Systems* (pp. 1-14).

Li, J., Zhao, X., & Li, X. (2024). IoT-enabled real-time tracking in supply chains: An empirical study. *Journal of Business Logistics*, 45(2), 34–48.

LinkedIn Learning. (2019). Engaging the Modern Learner: Strategies for Cloud-Based Professional Development. LinkedIn Learning Insights. Retrieved from linkedin.com

Lin, Y., & Wang, W. (2023). Enhancing students' online collaborative PBL learning performance in the context of coauthoring-based technologies: A case of wiki technologies. *Education and Information Technologies*, 29(2), 2303–2328. DOI: 10.1007/s10639-023-11907-1 PMID: 37361760

Liu, M., McKelroy, E., Corliss, S. B., & Carrigan, J. (2017). Investigating the effect of an adaptive learning intervention on students' learning. *Educational Technology Research and Development*, 65(6), 1–21. DOI: 10.1007/s11423-017-9542-1

Liu-Thompkins, Y. (2019). A decade of online advertising research: What we learned and what we need to know. *Journal of Advertising*, 48(1), 1–13. DOI: 10.1080/00913367.2018.1556138

Liu, Y., & Liu, X. (2021). A systematic review of educational data mining. *Frontiers in Psychology*, 12, 647036. DOI: 10.3389/fpsyg.2021.647036

Liu, Z., Liu, J. Y., Zhang, L. Y., Zhao, Y., & Gong, X. F. (2022). Performance of the 2D Coupled Map Lattice Model and Its Application in Image Encryption. *Complexity*, 2022(1), 5193618. Advance online publication. DOI: 10.1155/2022/5193618

Li, Y., & Ranieri, M. (2010). Are 'digital natives' really digitally competent?—A study on Chinese teenagers. *British Journal of Educational Technology*, 41(6), 1029–1042. DOI: 10.1111/j.1467-8535.2009.01053.x

Li, Y., Yu, H., Song, B., & Chen, J. (2019, March). Image encryption based on a single-round dictionary and chaotic sequences in cloud computing. *Concurrency and Computation*, 33(7), 1–1. DOI: 10.1002/cpe.5182

Li, Z., Xie, Z., Liu, L., & Wu, Y. (2022). Design and Implementation of an Integrated City-Level IoT Platform Based on Edge Computing and Cloud Native. 2022 IEEE 6th Advanced Information Technology, *Electronic and Automation Control Conference (IAEAC)*, 463-467.

Lowenthal, P. R., Dunlap, J. C., & Snelson, C. (2017). Live synchronous web meetings in asynchronous online courses: Reconceptualizing virtual office hours. *Online Learning : the Official Journal of the Online Learning Consortium*, 21(4). Advance online publication. DOI: 10.24059/olj.v21i4.1285

Luckin. (2016). Intelligence unleashed: An argument for AI in education. Pearson.

Luckin, R., & Holmes, W. (Eds.). (2020). *Artificial intelligence in education: Promise and implications for teaching and learning*. Springer.

Lumpkin, G. T., & Dess, G. G. (1996). Clarifying the entrepreneurial orientation construct and linking it to performance. *Academy of Management Review*, 21(1), 135–172. DOI: 10.2307/258632

Lundqvist, . (2013). AI-driven support tools in education: The impact of chatbots and virtual assistants. *Journal of Educational Technology*, 40(3), 45–58.

Madden, M. (2010). Older Adults and Social Media. *Pew Research Center*. Buckingham, D. (2007). Beyond Technology: Children's Learning in the Age of Digital Culture. *Polity*.

Madhani, P. M. (2024). Role of big data analytics in enhancing supply chain efficiency. *Global Journal of Management and Business Research*, 24(3), 67–80.

Manoharan, C., Poongavanam, S., Arivazhagan, D., Divyaranjani, R., & Vettriselvan, R. (2020). Cognition and emotions during the teaching-learning process. *International Journal of Scientific and Technology Research*, 9(2), 267–269.

MarketDigits. (2024). *IoT Cloud Platform Market*. Retrieved from https://www.marketdigits.com/iot-cloud-platform-market

Marston, , Li, Z., Bandyopadhyay, S., Zhang, J., & Ghalsasi, A. (2011). Cloud computing—The business perspective. *Decision Support Systems*, 51(1), 176–189. DOI: 10.1016/j.dss.2010.12.006

Marwaha, . (2019). Rural Education Cloud Initiative: Empowering India's villages with cloud-based education. *International Journal of Educational Technology*, 20(3), 45–57.

Means, B., Bakia, M., & Murphy, R. (2020). *Learning online: What research tells us about whether, when and how*. Routledge.

Means, B., & Neisler, J. (2021). Teaching and Learning in the time of COVID: The Student perspective. *Online Learning : the Official Journal of the Online Learning Consortium*, 25(1). Advance online publication. DOI: 10.24059/olj.v25i1.2496

Mendoza, S. (2020). Supporting student-teacher interaction through a chatbot. In Learning and Collaboration Technologies. Human and Technology Ecosystems: 7th International Conference, LCT 2020, Held as Part of the 22nd HCI International Conference, HCII 2020, Copenhagen, Denmark, July 19–24, 2020, Proceedings, Part II. Springer International Publishing.

Meyers, E. M., Erickson, I., & Small, R. V. (2013). Digital literacy and informal learning environments: An introduction. *Learning, Media and Technology*, 38(4), 355–367. DOI: 10.1080/17439884.2013.783597

Meyer, T. K. H. (2015). *Automation and robotics in the warehouse: A guide to modern warehousing and distribution*. Wiley.

Miller, D. (1983). The correlates of entrepreneurship in three types of firms. *Management Science*, 29(7), 770–791. DOI: 10.1287/mnsc.29.7.770

Miller, T., & Zhang, L. (2024). Quantum computing and its potential impact on supply chain optimization. *Journal of Operations Research*, 56(4), 299–312.

Miller, T., Zhao, Q., & Li, X. (2024). Data privacy and security challenges in advanced SCM systems. *The Journal of Supply Chain Management*, 60(1), 80–94.

Mishra, N., & Silakari, S. (2012). Predictive analytics: A survey, trends, applications, opportunities & challenges. *International Journal of Computer Science and Information Technologies*, 3(3), 4434–4438.

Modupe, O. T., Otitoola, A. A., Oladapo, O. J., Abiona, O. O., Oyeniran, O. C., Adewusi, A. O., Komolafe, A. M., & Obijuru, A. (2024). REVIEWING THE TRANSFORMATIONAL IMPACT OF EDGE COMPUTING ON REAL-TIME DATA PROCESSING AND ANALYTICS. *Computer Science & IT Research Journal*, 5(3), 693–702. DOI: 10.51594/csitrj.v5i3.929

Mohammadi, M. H., & Mehdizadeh, S. (2019). Cloud-based personalized learning platforms: A review of enabling technologies, architectures, and user experience design factors. [JETDE]. *Journal of Educational Technology Development and Exchange*, 12(3), 241–260.

Molnár, G., & Szüts, Z. (2018). The Role of Chatbots in Formal Education. In 2018 IEEE 16th International Symposium on Intelligent Systems and Informatics (SISY) (pp. 197-202). IEEE. DOI: 10.1109/SISY.2018.8524609

Montgomery County Public Schools (MCPS). (2018). *MCPS early warning indicators system (EWIS) framework*. Retrieved from MCPS.

Moodle. (2021). Moodle LMS: Empowering Organizations with Cloud-Based Learning. Moodle Case Studies. Retrieved from moodle.com

Moussa, K. H., & Xu, B. (2024). Revolutionizing healthcare: Seamless integration of cloud technology and IoT for health monitoring systems. In *2024 9th International Conference on Computer and Communication Systems (ICCCS)* (pp. 986-990). IEEE. DOI: 10.1109/ICCCS61882.2024.10603222

Muhammed, A. S., & Ucuz, D. (2020). Comparison of the IoT Platform Vendors, Microsoft Azure, Amazon Web Services, and Google Cloud, from Users' Perspectives. *2020 8th International Symposium on Digital Forensics and Security (ISDFS)*, 1-4.

Nalavade, J. E., Patil, A., Buchade, A., & Jadhav, N. (2023, November). Deep Neural Network and GAN-Based Reversible Data Hiding in Encrypted Images: A Privacy-Preserving Approach. *SN Computer Science*, 5(1), 45. Advance online publication. DOI: 10.1007/s42979-023-02347-2

Navarro, C., Arias-Calderón, M., Henríquez, C. A., & Riquelme, P. (2024). Assessment of Student and Teacher Perceptions on the Use of Virtual Simulation in Cell Biology Laboratory Education. *Education Sciences*, 14(3), 243. DOI: 10.3390/educsci14030243

Ndemo, . (2017). Making open development inclusive: Lessons from Kenya and Tanzania. *The Electronic Journal on Information Systems in Developing Countries*, 78(1), 1–20.

Neela, K. L., & Kavitha, V. (2022, June). Blockchain based Chaotic Deep GAN Encryption scheme for securing medical images in a cloud environment. *Applied Intelligence*, 53(4), 4733–4747. DOI: 10.1007/s10489-022-03730-x

Neri, F. (2019). *An Introduction to Computational Complexity*. Linear Algebra for Computational Sciences and Engineering. DOI: 10.1007/978-3-030-21321-3_11

Nguyen, T., Brown, A., & Wang, L. (2024). Strategies for technological integration in supply chains. *Journal of Production Economics*, 257, 122–135.

Nguyen, T., Brown, A., & Wang, L. (2024). The role of 5G technology in advancing supply chain management. *The Journal of Supply Chain Management*, 61(3), 150–165.

Ng, W. (2012). Can We Teach Digital Natives Digital Literacy? *Proceedings of the 21st Century Academic Forum Conference*, 28(3), 106-121. DOI: 10.1016/j.compedu.2012.04.016

Nichols, W. (2013). Advertising Analytics 2.0. *Harvard Business Review*, 91(3), 60–68.

Noble, S. U. (2018). *Algorithms of Oppression: How Search Engines Reinforce Racism*. NYU Press. DOI: 10.18574/nyu/9781479833641.001.0001

Odukoya, O. (2024). The transformative impact of cloud computing on small and medium-sized enterprises (SMEs): A comprehensive analysis. In *2024 International Conference on Smart Applications, Communications and Networking (SmartNets)* (pp. 1-5). DOI: 10.1109/SmartNets61466.2024.10577703

Okonkwo, A. A., & Ade-Ibijola, A. (2021). Chatbots applications in education: A systematic review. Computers and Education: Artificial Intelligence.

Okonkwo, A. A., & Ade-Ibijola, A. (2020). Python-Bot: A Chatbot for Teaching Python Programming. *Engineering Letters*, 29(1), 25–34.

Onyema, E. M., Nwafor, C. E., Ugwugbo, A. N., Rockson, K. A., & Ogbonnaya, U. N. (2020). Cloud security challenges: Implication on education. *Int J Comput Sci Mob Comput*, 9(2), 56–73.

Ordóñez de Pablos, P., Almunawar, M. N., & Anshari, M. (Eds.). (2023). *Developing Skills and Competencies for Digital and Green Transitions*. IGI Global.

Orehovački, T., Etinger, D., & Babić, S. (2017). Perceived security and privacy of cloud computing applications used in educational ecosystem. In 2017 *40th International Convention on Information and Communication Technology, Electronics and Microelectronics* (MIPRO) (pp. 717-722). IEEE. DOI: 10.23919/MIPRO.2017.7973516

Ouyang, D., Shao, J., Jiang, H., Nguang, S. K., & Shen, H. T. (2020, August). Impulsive synchronization of coupled delayed neural networks with actuator saturation and its application to image encryption. *Neural Networks*, 128, 158–171. DOI: 10.1016/j.neunet.2020.05.016 PMID: 32446193

Palfrey, J., & Gasser, U. (2008). Born Digital: Understanding the First Generation of Digital Natives.

Panadero, E., Brown, G. T., & Strijbos, J. W. (2021). *Educational assessment in the digital age: A handbook for researchers, practitioners, and policymakers*. Routledge.

Pandey, A. (2015). Licensed Under Creative Commons Attribution CC BY Potential, Pitfalls and Challenges in Development of ICT in Education. *International Journal of Science and Research (IJSR) ISSN, 6*, 2319–7064. https://www.ijsr.net/archive/v6i1/ART20164335.pdf

Pandit, P. (2021). A Case Study of Amazon Web Services. DOI: 10.13140/RG.2.2.18114.09921

Park, S., & Kim, Y. (2021). A systematic review of research trends in mobile learning studies in Korea: A social network analysis. *Interactive Learning Environments*, 29(1), 109–125. DOI: 10.1080/10494820.2019.1582198

Paul, P., Chatterjee, R., Aithal, P. S., & Saavedra, R. (2023). Cloud Computing and its Impact in Education, Teaching and Research-A Scientific Review. Social Science Research Network. DOI: 10.2139/ssrn.4490825

Peng, H., Ma, S., & Spector, J. M. (2019). Personalized adaptive learning: An emerging pedagogical approach enabled by a smart learning environment. *Smart Learning Environments*, 6(1), 9. Advance online publication. DOI: 10.1186/s40561-019-0089-y

Picciano, A. G. (2021). *Online education: Foundations, planning, and pedagogy*. Routledge.

Pierleoni, P., Concetti, R., Belli, A., & Palma, L. (2020). Amazon, Google, and Microsoft solutions for IoT: Architectures and a performance comparison. *IEEE Access : Practical Innovations, Open Solutions*, 8, 5455–5470. DOI: 10.1109/ACCESS.2019.2961511

Prensky, M. (2001). Digital Natives, Digital Immigrants. *On the Horizon*, 9(5), 1–6. DOI: 10.1108/10748120110424816

PwC. (2019). Digital Fitness App: Empowering Employees in the Digital Age. PwC Insights. Retrieved from pwc.com

Rajesh, M. (2017). A systematic review of cloud security challenges in higher education. *The Online Journal of Distance Education and e-Learning : TOJDEL*, 5(1), 1–10.

Raman, A., & Rathakrishnan, M. (2019). *Blended Learning in Higher Education 4.0: A Brief Review*. Www.igi-Global.com

Rane, N., Choudhary, S., & Rane, J. (2023). Education 4.0 and 5.0: Integrating Artificial Intelligence (AI) for personalized and adaptive learning. *Social Science Research Network*. https://doi.org/DOI: 10.2139/ssrn.4638365

Ravindranath, K., & Gaikwad, V. S. (2023). IoT device-to-cloud continuous authentication using lightweight key establishment mechanism. *Journal of Electrical Systems*, 19(2), 148–162.

Ray, P. P. (2016). A survey of IoT cloud platforms. *Future Computing and Informatics Journal*, 1(1), 4. https://digitalcommons.aaru.edu.jo/fcij/vol1/iss1/4

Reddy, M., Prasad, R., & Rao, S. (2023). Big data analytics for supply chain optimization: Trends and insights. *Data Science Journal*, 22(4), 301–312.

Ren, Z. (2023). Optimization of Innovative Education Resource Allocation in Colleges and Universities Based on Cloud Computing and User Privacy Security. *Wireless Personal Communications*, •••, 1–15. DOI: 10.1007/s11277-023-10572-4

Rijal, S., Zou, G., Jie, L., & Demsky, C. (2024). The impact of using a cloud-based learning management system on access and quality of education. *Journal Emerging Technologies in Education*, 2(2), 163–176.

Rodriguez, D., & Krishnan, R. (2023). A Cycle-GAN Based Image Encoding Scheme for Privacy Enhanced Deep Neural Networks. *Lecture Notes in Computer Science*, 14424, 178–196. DOI: 10.1007/978-3-031-49099-6_11

Rogers, Y. (2004). New theoretical approaches for HCI. *Annual Review of Information Science & Technology*, 38(1), 87–143. DOI: 10.1002/aris.1440380103

Rokade, U. S., Doye, D., & Kokare, M. (2009, March). Hand gesture recognition using object based key frame selection. In *2009 International Conference on Digital Image Processing* (pp. 288-291). IEEE.

Roos, S. (2018). Chatbots in education: A passing trend or a valuable pedagogical tool?

Rosário, A. T., & Travassos, A. (2022). Learning management systems in education: Research and challenges.Https://Services.igi-Global.com/Resolvedoi/Resolve.aspx?Doi=10.4018/978-1-6684-4706-2.Ch003, 1 Jan.

Rossiello, G., Chowdhury, M. F. M., Mihindukulasooriya, N., Cornec, O., & Gliozzo, A. M. (2023). Knowgl: Knowledge generation and linking from text. *Proceedings of the AAAI Conference on Artificial Intelligence*, 37(13), 16476–16478. DOI: 10.1609/aaai.v37i13.27084

Ruan, S. (2019). BookBuddy: Turning Digital Materials Into Interactive Foreign Language Lessons Through a Voice Chatbot. In Proceedings of the Sixth (2019) ACM Conference on Learning @ Scale. Association for Computing Machinery. DOI: 10.1145/3330430.3333643

SaberiKamarposhti, M., Ghorbani, A., & Yadollahi, M. (2024, January). A comprehensive survey on image encryption: Taxonomy, challenges, and future directions. *Chaos, Solitons, and Fractals*, 178, 114361. DOI: 10.1016/j.chaos.2023.114361

Sachdeva, S., Bhatia, S., Al Harrasi, A., Shah, Y. A., Anwer, M. K., Philip, A. K., Shah, S. F. A., Khan, A., & Ahsan Halim, S. (2024). Unraveling the role of cloud computing in health care system and biomedical sciences. *Heliyon*, 10(7), e29044–e29044. DOI: 10.1016/j.heliyon.2024.e29044 PMID: 38601602

Sahai & Waters. (2005). *Fuzzy identity-based encryption. In Advances in cryptology EUROCRYPT 2005, Lecture Notes in Computer. Sci* (Vol. 3494). Springer.

Sakai, T., Hata, K., Wada, T., & Naito, K. (2022). IoT platform using information flow to reduce load on cloud. In *2022 IEEE 46th Annual Computers, Software, and Applications Conference (COMPSAC)* (pp. 1211-1216). IEEE. DOI: 10.1109/COMPSAC54236.2022.00191

Salloum, S., Dautov, R., Chen, X., Peng, P. X., & Huang, J. Z. (2016, October 13). Big Data Analytics on Apache Spark. *International Journal of Data Science and Analytics*, 1(3-4), 145–164. DOI: 10.1007/s41060-016-0027-9

Samanta, P., & Jain, S. (2021). Analysis of Perceptual Hashing Algorithms in Image Manipulation Detection. *Procedia Computer Science*, 185, 203–212. DOI: 10.1016/j.procs.2021.05.021

Sandhu, I. K., Malhotra, M., & Randhawa, P. R. (2021). A review of trust and security concerns in cloud computing adoption intention in the higher education sector: research in progress. *Impacts and Challenges of Cloud Business Intelligence*, 1-12.

Sauber, A. M., El-Kafrawy, P. M., Shawish, A. F., Amin, M. A., & Hagag, I. M. (2021). A New Secure Model for Data Protection over Cloud Computing. *Computational Intelligence and Neuroscience*, 2021(1), 1–11. DOI: 10.1155/2021/8113253 PMID: 35646109

Sclater, N., Bailey, C., & Yip, C. (Eds.). (2021). *The Wiley handbook of learning technology*. Wiley.

Scott, . (2018). Supporting teachers' learning about cloud-based tools through professional development. *Journal of Technology and Teacher Education*, 26(1), 23–42.

Selwyn, N. (2004). Reconsidering political and popular understandings of the digital divide. *New Media & Society*, 6(3), 341–362. DOI: 10.1177/1461444804042519

Selwyn, N. (2009). The digital native – myth and reality. *Aslib Proceedings*, 61(4), 364–379. DOI: 10.1108/00012530910973776

Selwyn, N., & Facer, K. (2014). The sociology of education and digital technology: Past, present, and future. *Oxford Review of Education*, 40(4), 482–496. DOI: 10.1080/03054985.2014.933005

Selwyn, N., & Gorard, S. (2016). Students' use of digital technology in university: What are the implications for higher education policy and practice? *Higher Education Quarterly*, 70(3), 308–326.

Seth, D., Najana, M., & Ranjan, P. (2024). Compliance and regulatory challenges in cloud computing: a sector-wise analysis. *International Journal of Global Innovations and Solutions* (IJGIS).

S, G., & S, G. (2023, March). Securing medical image privacy in cloud using deep learning network. *Journal of Cloud Computing (Heidelberg, Germany)*, 12(1), 40. Advance online publication. DOI: 10.1186/s13677-023-00422-w

Shacham, H., & Waters, B. (2013, July). Compact proofs of retrievability. *Journal of Cryptology*, 26(3), 442–483. DOI: 10.1007/s00145-012-9129-2

Sharma, G., Juneja, V., Khurana, S., & Sheoran, R. (2024). Bibliometric mapping of theme and trends of IoT and cloud in the field of education. In *Proceedings of the 2024 International Conference on Computational Intelligence and Computing Applications (ICCICA)* (pp. 142-147). IEEE. DOI: 10.1109/ICCICA60014.2024.10584891

Sharples. (2016). Innovating pedagogy 2016: Open University innovation report 5. The Open University.

Shayan, P., Rondinelli, R., van Zaanen, M., & Atzmueller, M. (2023). Multi-level analysis of learning management systems' user acceptance exemplified in two system case studies. *Data*, 8(3), 45.

Shemshack, A., & Spector, J. M. (2020). A systematic literature review of personalized learning terms. *Smart Learning Environments*, 7(1), 33. Advance online publication. DOI: 10.1186/s40561-020-00140-9

Sherman, L., & Deighton, J. (2001). Banner advertising: Measuring effectiveness and optimizing placement. *Journal of Interactive Marketing*, 15(2), 60–64. DOI: 10.1002/dir.1011

Shinohara, . (2016). Self-conscious or self-confident? A diary study conceptualizing the experience of accessibility and assistive technology in daily life. *ACM Transactions on Accessible Computing*, 8(2), 1–31. DOI: 10.1145/2827857

Shmueli, G., & Koppius, O. R. (2011). Predictive analytics in information systems research. *Management Information Systems Quarterly*, 35(3), 553–572. DOI: 10.2307/23042796

Siemens, . (2011). Penetrating the fog: Analytics in learning and education. *EDUCAUSE Review*, 46(5), 30–32.

Siemens, G. (2013). Learning Analytics: The Emergence of a Discipline. *The American Behavioral Scientist*, 57(10), 1380–1400. DOI: 10.1177/0002764213498851

Siemens, G. (2020). Automation in education: Future prospects. *Education and Information Technologies*, 25(6), 4853–4865. DOI: 10.1007/s10639-020-10340-1

Singh, S., Ramkumar, K. R., & Kukkar, A. (2023). Analysis and Implementation of Microsoft Azure Machine Learning Studio Services with Respect to Machine Learning Algorithms. In Modern Electronics Devices and Communication Systems: Select Proceedings of MEDCOM 2021 (pp. 91-106). Singapore: Springer Nature Singapore.

Singh, H. K., Baranwal, N., Singh, K. N., Singh, A. K., & Zhou, H. (2023, December). GAN-based watermarking for encrypted images in healthcare scenarios. *Neurocomputing*, 560, 126853. DOI: 10.1016/j.neucom.2023.126853

Singh, R., Sharma, P., & Dey, S. (2019). Real-time bidding and predictive analytics: Optimizing bid prices for online ad placements. *Journal of Digital Marketing*, 8(4), 101–118.

Sirisha, U., & Chandana, B. S. (2023, January). Privacy Preserving Image Encryption with Optimal Deep Transfer Learning Based Accident Severity Classification Model. *Sensors (Basel)*, 23(1), 519. DOI: 10.3390/s23010519 PMID: 36617116

Smart Sparrow. (2017). *Case studies in adaptive learning*. Retrieved from Smart Sparrow.

Smith, . (2018). Designing inclusive educational spaces for students with disabilities. *Journal of Special Education Technology*, 33(3), 177–186.

Smith, J., Patel, A., & Kim, S. (2023). The role of big data in supply chain optimization: Insights from Walmart. *The Journal of Supply Chain Management*, 59(4), 66–80.

Smith, J., Roberts, C., & Davis, T. (2024). Global supply chains and technology integration: Trends and challenges. *International Journal of Production Economics*, 260, 234–247.

Smutny, P., & Schreiberova, P. (2020). Chatbots for learning: A review of educational chatbots for the Facebook Messenger. *Computers & Education*, 151, 10386. DOI: 10.1016/j.compedu.2020.103862

Soler Costa, R., Tan, Q., Pivot, F., Zhang, X., & Wang, H. (2021). Personalized and adaptive learning: educational practice and technological impact. Texto Livre/ Texto Livre: Linguagem e Tecnologia, 14(3).

Song, Y. Y., & Ying, L. U. (2015). Decision tree methods: Applications for classification and prediction. *Shanghai Jingshen Yixue*, 27(2), 130. PMID: 26120265

Speelman, D. (2014). Logistic regression. Corpus methods for semantics: Quantitative studies in polysemy and synonymy, 43, 487-533.

Stallings, W. (2023). *Cryptography and Network Security: Principles and Practice.* Pearson.

Steele, J., & Holbeck, R. (2018). Five elements that impact quality feedback in the online asynchronous classroom. *ResearchGate*, 15(3). Advance online publication. DOI: 10.9743/jeo.2018.15.3.10

Strother. (2019). E-Learning for employee training and development. In K. P. Kuchinke (Ed.), Management of employee training and development (pp. 187-204). Springer.

Subashini, S., & Kavitha, V. (2011). S., & Kavitha, V. (2011). A survey on security issues in service delivery models of cloud computing. *Journal of Network and Computer Applications*, 34(1), 1–11. DOI: 10.1016/j.jnca.2010.07.006

Summit. (2020). Personalized learning for all students. Retrieved from Summit et al. 2020 Learning.

Suparmaniam, N., Kamaruzzaman, Z. A., Kie, C. J., Mohtar, S. S., Alias, M. I. S., & Ja'afar, M. J. M. (2023). Does Consumer Behaviour Matters? Online Advertising Evaluation via Predictive Analytics. *Global Business and Management Research*, 15.

Tapscott, D. (2008). Grown Up Digital: How the Net Generation is Changing Your World. *Proceedings of the IEEE International Conference on Digital Ecosystems and Technologies*, 1-5.

Taylor, D. L., Yeung, M., & Bashet, A. Z. (2021). Personalized and adaptive learning. In *SpringerBriefs in statistics* (pp. 17–34). DOI: 10.1007/978-3-030-58948-6_2

TechRepublic. (2021). How Cloud Computing is Transforming Employee Training. TechRepublic Insights. Retrieved from techrepublic.com

Thavi, R., Jhaveri, R., Narwane, V., Gardas, B., & Jafari Navimipour, N. (2024). Role of cloud computing technology in the education sector. *Journal of Engineering. Defence Technology*, 22(1), 182–213.

Thiruvasagam, G., & Vettriselvan, R. (2021). What is after COVID-19?: Changing economies of the shipping industries and maritime education institutions. In 21st Annual General Assembly, IAMU AGA 2021 - Proceedings of the International Association of Maritime Universities (pp. 96–110).

Tong, L., Xia, P., & Lv, T. (2022). Research on Quantum Secure Route Model and Line Model Image Encryption Technology Based on Big Data Technology. *2022 International Conference on Cloud Computing, Big Data Applications and Software Engineering (CBASE)*. DOI: 10.1109/CBASE57816.2022.00028

Touvron, H., Lavril, T., Izacard, G., Martinet, X., Lachaux, M.-A., Lacroix, T., Rozière, B., Goyal, N., Hambro, E., & Azhar, F. (2023). LLaMA: Open and Efficient Foundation Language Models. arXiv. /arXiv.2302.07842DOI: 10.48550

Training Industry. (2020). Cloud-Based Learning Solutions: Trends and Best Practices. Training Industry Reports. Retrieved from trainingindustry.com

Tripathi, G., Ahad, M. A., & Casalino, G. (2023). A comprehensive review of blockchain technology: Underlying principles and historical background with future challenges. *Decision Analytics Journal*, 100344.

Tulenkov, A., Parkhomenko, A., & Sokolyanskii, A. (2019). Evaluation and selection of IoT service for smart house system big data processing. In *2019 IEEE 14th International Conference on Computer Sciences and Information Technologies (CSIT)* (pp. 124-129). IEEE. DOI: 10.1109/STC-CSIT.2019.8929810

Unilever. (2020). Degreed Platform: Driving Continuous Learning and Development. Unilever Case Studies. Retrieved from unilever.com

University of Arizona. (2018). *AURA: The AI-powered academic advisor*. Retrieved from University of Arizona.

Using CyclePad-an "articulate" software laboratory-in thermodynamics education. (1997). IEEE Conference Publication | IEEE Xplore. https://ieeexplore.ieee.org/document/635975

Uskov. (2015). The role of IoT in education. In 2015 ASEE annual conference & exposition. ASEE Conferences.

Van Deursen, A. J., & van Dijk, J. A. (2014). The digital divide shifts to differences in usage. *New Media & Society*, 16(3), 507–526. DOI: 10.1177/1461444813487959

Van Dijk. (2020). The digital divide. Polity Press.

van Dijk, J. A., & Hacker, K. L. (2003). The digital divide as a complex and dynamic phenomenon. *The Information Society*, 19(4), 315–326. DOI: 10.1080/01972240309487

Vellela, S. S., & Reddy, V. L. (2023). A cloud-based smart IoT platform for personalized healthcare data gathering and monitoring system. In *2023 3rd Asian Conference on Innovation in Technology (ASIANCON)* (pp. 1-5). IEEE. DOI: 10.1109/ASIANCON58793.2023.10270407

Veluvali, P., & Surisetti, J. (2022). Learning Management System for Greater Learner Engagement in Higher Education—A Review. *Higher Education for the Future.*, 9(1), 107–121. DOI: 10.1177/23476311211049855

Vettriselvan, R., & Vinodhan, V. (2022). Promotional strategies for gender equity in the maritime sector: Maritime education institutions. In *Proceedings of the International Association of Maritime Universities Conference*.

Vishalika. (2021). Integration of cloud with IoT: Advantages and research challenges. In *2021 International Conference on Technological Advancements and Innovations (ICTAI)* (pp. 627-631). IEEE. DOI: 10.1109/ICTAI53825.2021.9673183

Voogt, J., Knezek, G., Christensen, R., & Lai, K. W. (Eds.). (2021). *Second handbook of information technology in primary and secondary education*. Springer.

Wamba, S. F., Gunasekaran, A., Akter, S., Ren, S. J., & Dubey, R. (2017). Big data analytics and organizational culture as complements to swift trust in building inter-organizational relationships. *Journal of Business Research*, 70, 253–264.

Wang, C., Wang, Q., Ren, K., & Lou, W. (2010). Privacy-Preserving Public Auditing for Data Storage Security in Cloud Computing. *2010 Proceedings IEEE INFOCOM*. DOI: 10.1109/INFCOM.2010.5462173

Wang, He, & Tang. (2016). Identity-based proxy-oriented data uploading and remote data integrity checking in public cloud. *IEEE Transactions on Information Forensics and Security, 11*(6), 1165–1176.

Wang, Wu, Qin, Shi, Deng, & Hu. (2017). Identity-based data outsourcing with comprehensive auditing in clouds. *IEEE Transactions on Information Forensics and Security, 12*(4), 940–952.

Wang, J., Xu, J., & Zhang, Y. (2024). Blockchain technology in supply chain management: A comprehensive review. *International Journal of Production Economics*, 258, 108–122.

Wang, X., Feng, L., & Zhao, H. (2019, June). Fast image encryption algorithm based on parallel computing system. *Information Sciences*, 486, 340–358. DOI: 10.1016/j.ins.2019.02.049

Wang, Y., Chen, L., Wu, G., Yu, K., & Lu, T. (2023, May). Efficient and secure content-based image retrieval with deep neural networks in the mobile cloud computing. *Computers & Security*, 128, 103163. DOI: 10.1016/j.cose.2023.103163

Wang, Z., Byrnes, O., Wang, H., Sun, R., Ma, C., Chen, H., Wu, Q., & Xue, M. (2023). Data Hiding with Deep Learning: A Survey Unifying Digital Watermarking and Steganography. *IEEE Transactions on Computational Social Systems*, 10(6), 2985–2999. DOI: 10.1109/TCSS.2023.3268950

Watson, W. R., & Watson, S. L. (2017). Principles for personalized instruction. In Reigeluth, C. M., Beatty, B. J., & Myers, R. D. (Eds.), *Instructional-design theories and models, The learner centered paradigm of education* (Vol. IV, pp. 93–120). Routledge.

Williamson, B., & Eynon, R. (2021). *The digital education: Critical perspectives*. Polity Press.

Woolf. (2009). Building intelligent interactive tutors: Student-centered strategies for revolutionizing e-learning. Morgan Kaufmann.

Worku, S. G., Xu, C., Zhao, J., & He, X. (2014, July). Secure and efficient privacy-preserving public auditing scheme for cloud storage. *Computers & Electrical Engineering*, 40(5), 1703–1713. DOI: 10.1016/j.compeleceng.2013.10.004

Wozniak, K., Lilly, C., Hambrock, H., Richter, R., & Reiseck, C. (2016, November). Designing an adaptive learning experience in higher Education: A critical perspective. In E-Learn: World Conference on E-Learning in Corporate, Government, Healthcare, and Higher Education (pp. 517–521). Association for the Advancement of computing in Education (AACE).

Xu, S., Chang, C.-C., & Horng, J.-H. (2023). Cryptospace Image Steganography for Cloud Security Via Cycle-Consistent Gan. DOI: 10.2139/ssrn.4673313

Yang, J., Lee, T.-Y., Lee, W.-T., & Xu, L. (2022). A Design and Application of Municipal Service Platform Based on Cloud-Edge Collaboration for Smart Cities. *Sensors (Basel)*, 22(22), 8784. DOI: 10.3390/s22228784 PMID: 36433381

Yang, P., Xiong, N., & Ren, J. (2020). Data security and privacy protection for cloud storage: A survey. *IEEE Access : Practical Innovations, Open Solutions*, 8, 131723–131740. DOI: 10.1109/ACCESS.2020.3009876

Ye, J. (2023). A comprehensive capability analysis of GPT-3 and GPT-3.5 series models. arXiv preprint arXiv:2303.10420

Young. (2019). Arizona State U. and Google Cloud: A partnership for innovation. The Chronicle of Higher Education. Retrieved from https://www.chronicle.com/article/arizona-state-u-and-google-cloud-a-partnership-for-innovation/

Yu, Ren, & Wang. (2016). Enabling cloud storage auditing with verifiable outsourcing of key updates. *IEEE Transactions on Information Forensics and Security, 11*(6), 1362–1375.

Yurdakul, B., Uslu, Ö., Çakar, E., & Yildiz, D. G. (2014, September 16). USLU, Ö., ÇAKAR, E., & YILDIZ, D. G. (2014). Evaluation of the Professional Development Program on Web Based Content Development. *Educational Sciences: Theory & Practice*. Advance online publication. DOI: 10.12738/estp.2014.4.2131

Zahra, S. A., & Covin, J. G. (1995). Contextual influences on the corporate entrepreneurship-performance relationship: A longitudinal analysis. *Journal of Business Venturing*, 10(1), 43–58. DOI: 10.1016/0883-9026(94)00004-E

Zhang, J., Xu, Y., & Li, J. (2023). Smart sensors in supply chain management: Applications and benefits. *Sensors and Actuators. A, Physical*, 341, 112–125.

Zhang, Q., & Li, J. (2022, February). Single Exposure Phase-Only Optical Image Encryption and Hiding Method via Deep Learning. *IEEE Photonics Journal*, 14(1), 1–8. DOI: 10.1109/JPHOT.2022.3146456

Zhang, Y., Zhang, H., Ren, X., Yu, Y., Li, Q., & Tang, J. (2021). Deep learning for click-through rate prediction in sponsored search: A comprehensive review. *ACM Transactions on Intelligent Systems and Technology*, 12(1), 1–36.

Zhao, L., Zhang, J., & Li, B. (2020). Time-aware predictive modeling for click-through rate in online advertising. *Information Sciences*, 516, 164–180.

Zhao, Q., Liu, S., & Wang, C. (2024). Blockchain for product authentication and traceability: A study of recent developments. *Journal of Business Research*, 148, 189–200.

Zhao, S., & Chiang, W. (2023). Privacy-preserving, low-storage, and high-quality image processing in IoT and clouds. In *2023 International Conference on Intelligent Communication and Computer Engineering (ICICCE)* (pp. 9-13). DOI: 10.1109/ICICCE61720.2023.00008

Zheng, Z.EncryptGAN: Image Steganography with Domain Transform. https://arxiv.org/abs/1905.11582

Zhou, W., Zhang, Y., Zhao, R., Yi, S., & Lan, R. (2023). Adversarial Thumbnail-Preserving Transformation for Facial Images Based on GAN. *IEEE Signal Processing Letters*, 30, 1147–1151. DOI: 10.1109/LSP.2023.3308012

Zhou, Y., & Hentschel, J. (2018). Digital Natives and Digital Immigrants in the Era of Digital Transformation: A Critical Review of Digital Media and Learning. [iJET]. *International Journal of Emerging Technologies in Learning*, 13(8), 29–37.

Zhu, Ahn, Hu, Yau, An, & Hu. (2013). Dynamic audit services for integrity verification of outsourced storages in clouds. *IEEE Transactions on Services Computing, 6*(2), 1550–1557.

Zhu, J.-Y., Park, T., Isola, P., & Efros, A. A. (2017). Unpaired Image-to-Image Translation Using Cycle-Consistent Adversarial Networks. *2017 IEEE International Conference on Computer Vision (ICCV)*. DOI: 10.1109/ICCV.2017.244

Zou, J., He, D., Zeadally, S., Kumar, N., Wang, H., & Choo, K. R. (2022). Integrated Blockchain and Cloud Computing Systems: A Systematic Survey, Solutions, and Challenges. *ACM Computing Surveys*, 54(8), 1–36. DOI: 10.1145/3456628

Zuway, El. M. A., & Farkash, H. M. (2022). Internet of Things security: Requirements, attacks on SH-IoT platform. In *2022 IEEE 21st International Conference on Sciences and Techniques of Automatic Control and Computer Engineering (STA)* (pp. 742-747). IEEE. DOI: 10.1109/STA56120.2022.10019124

About the Contributors

Vidya Gaikwad, an Assistant Professor at Vishwakarma Institute Technology in Pune, boasts over 15 years of experience in academia. Currently pursuing her PhD with Koneru Lakshmaiah Education Foundation in Vijayawada, Andhra Pradesh, she demonstrates a commitment to advancing her knowledge and contributing to Cloud-IoT Security. Her dedication to academia is evident through her active involvement in organizing numerous national and international conferences and her prolific publication record. Vidya Gaikwad's efforts have been recognized with accolades such as the "Best Poster Presentation Award" at the national level, showcasing her expertise and contribution to her research community. Moreover, she stands out as an astute academician who prioritizes the integration of teaching methodologies with the evolving demands of the industry. By guiding students towards aligning their skills and knowledge with market needs, she plays a crucial role in shaping their future success. Vidya Gaikwad's multifaceted contributions underscore her significance in both academic and professional spheres.

Anup Ingle, a distinguished academic and industry expert, has successfully completed his Ph.D. in the Computer Networks and Security Domain from SSSUTMS. He has 17 years of teaching experience and more than a year in the industry, he specializes in Computer Networks, Cyber Security, Data Networks, and Intrusion Detection Systems. His technical skills include network configuration, programming in C, C++, Java, and Python, and proficiency in network monitoring tools like Snort and Wire shark. He published over 20 papers in national and international journals. His area of interest are Cyber Security, Computer Networks and Data Science.

Narendra Jadhav is a final year student of the Computer Engineering department at Vishwakarma Institute of Information Technology, Pune. His research interests include Machine Learning, Application Development.

Pradnya Samit Mehta is working at the Vishwakarma Institute of Information Technology, Pune. She received the BE & ME degree in Computer Engineering from SPPU University, Pune, Maharashtra. She has 15 years teaching experience and 2 years of Industrial Experience. Her research interests include Artificial Intelligence, Deep Learning, high-performance Performance Computing and Machine Learning. She has published 20 papers in National and International journals and conferences, 7 Book chapters; 7 patents; and 5 patents are granted.

Arockia Rosy N. has been working as an Assistant Professor in the Department of Information Technology at R.M.D. Engineering College, Kavaraipettai. She has completed her B.Tech., in Information Technology Degree in Cape Institute of Technology and completed her Masters in Information Technology at Sathyabama University. She is currently pursuing her Ph.D in the field of Machine learning at Anna University. She has more than 14 years of teaching experience in various engineering colleges. Her areas of interest include AI, Machine and Deep Learning.

Raghu N. has ten years of experience in Academic and Research. He received the Ph.D. (2020) in Electronics Engineering from Jain University, and B.E. in Electronics and Telecommunications Engineering from VTU University, Karnataka. His research interests were in RF Communication and Image Processing. He has published his research findings in various Scopus indexed Journals and International conferences. He is a member of various professional bodies.

Abhishek Navhal is a final year student of the Computer Engineering department at Vishwakarma Institute of Information Technology, Pune. His research interests include Machine Learning.

Baby Shamini P. is presently working as Assistant Professor in the department of Computer Science and Engineering at RMK Engineering College, Chennai, India. She has 9 years of teaching experience. She completed her Bachelor's degree in Computer Science and Engineering at Bethlahem Institute of Technology, Nagercoil in the year 2012 and obtained her master's degree in Computer Science and Engineering at Java Engineering College, Chennai, in the year 2014. She has over 20 Research Articles published in reputed journal including IEEE, Springer and Scopus Indexed Journal. She is pursuing Ph.D in faculty of Information and communication in Anna University, Chennai, India. Her research interest includes Data Analytics and Deep Learning.

Jemi Gold P. is working as Assistant Professor in RMK College of Engineering College. With a total experience of 10 years.

Manas Patil is a final year student of the Computer Engineering department at Vishwakarma Institute of Information Technology, Pune. His research interests include Machine Learning.

Shivapooja Patil is a student in Vishwakarma Institute of Information Technology, Pune, Maharashtra, India.

Deepa R. is Vice President Academics at Academy of Maritime Education and Training (AMET University) Chennai.

Vettriselvan R. is an Associate Professor, AMET Business School, AMET University, specialised in HRM and Marketing. He is acting as Mentor, Saraswathi Institute of Medical Sciences, Hapur. He served as Review Board member, National Council for Higher Education, Malawi, Head of the Department, School of Commerce and Management Studies, St. Eugene University, Zambia, and Director, Research and Publication, St. John the Baptist University, Malawi. He has published 20 books and 75 articles in peer reviewed journals and edited book chapters. Under his guidance two have completed and five are pursuing their PhD.

Snehal Rathi received the Ph.D. degree in Computer Engineering from Vishwakarma University, Pune, India. She is presently working as an assistant professor in Computer Engineering department at Vishwakarma Institute of Information Technology, Pune. She has 20 years of teaching experience. She has taught multiple subjects which includes Data Structures, Data Mining and Machine Learning. Her research interest includes machine learning, deep learning, soft computing and human computer interaction.

Abhishek Raut is a final year student of the Computer Engineering department at Vishwakarma Institute of Information Technology, Pune. His research interests include Artificial Intelligence, Deep Learning.

Index

A

B

C

D

E

H

I

L

M

N

P

Q

S

U

V

www.ingramcontent.com/pod-product-compliance
Lightning Source LLC
LaVergne TN
LVHW080341011026
849161LV00009B/2145